CONSOLIDATED
B-24 LIBERATOR

CONSOLIDATED B-24 LIBERATOR

Martin W. Bowman

The Crowood Press

First published in 1998 by
The Crowood Press Ltd
Ramsbury, Marlborough
Wiltshire SN8 2HR

www.crowood.com

Paperback edition 2004

British Library Cataloguing-in-Publication Data
A catalogue record for this book is available from the British Library.

ISBN 1 86126 709 6

Photograph previous page: PB4Y-1 Liberator of the US Navy fitted with an Erco bow turret. US Navy

Dedication

This book is dedicated to the fond memory of Bob McGuire of the B-24 Liberator Club, and to all the crews who did not return.

Typefaces used: Goudy (*text*), Cheltenham (*headings*)

Typeset and designed by
D & N Publishing
Lowesden Business Park
Hungerford, Berkshire.

Printed and bound by Antony Rowe, Chippenham.

Acknowledgements

First and foremost I am most grateful to Mike Bailey, one of the finest exponents of Liberator art in the world, for his continued help and expert advice on all matters pertaining to the B-24 Liberator, and for his marvellous contribution and loan of photos. The B-24 Liberator Club of San Diego, California, has always proved immensely supportive over the years and I am grateful for their help and that of their members through their marvellous journal *Briefing*. Bob Markel, founder and president of the 484th Bomb Group Association, and his dear wife, Bea, were instrumental in making information on the 15th Air Force available and they have also allowed me to quote from their excellent 484th Bomb Group Association journal, *The Torretta Flyer*. Derek S. Hills, Trust Librarian, Linda J. Berube, American Fulbright Librarian, Lesley Fleetwood and Christine Snowdon were all most helpful during my many forays to the US 2nd Air Division Memorial Library in Norwich, and provided much willing assistance with research.

I am most grateful and indebted to all of these enthusiastic people and to the following, who have also excelled themselves on my behalf with many valuable photos, material and contacts or who have made their experiences available for inclusion in this book: Steve Adams, Dick Bagg, Dave Becker, C. Berry RAF Retd, Patrick Bunce, Stanley Burgess, Col William Cameron USAF Retd, Art Carnot, Donald V. Chase USAF Retd, City of Norwich Aviation Museum, Forrest Clark, Alfred Cohen USAF Retd, the Collings Foundation, Seb Corriere USAF Retd, P.J. Cundy RAF Retd, Douglas Aircraft Co., Jack Dupont USAF Retd, A.G. Dyer, Patricia Everson, Flt Lt Tony Fairbairn RAF, Lt Col Robert Fish USAF Retd, Ford, Norman Franks, General Dynamics, Michael L. Gibson, Edward R. Glotfelty USAF Retd, the late Russ D. Hayes, W.J. Jones, Hugh McLaren Jr, Elwood Matter USAF Retd, Ray A. Nichols, James E. O'Brien USAF Retd, John Page, Terry Parsons USAF Retd, Steve Pope, Don Prutton RAF Retd, John Reitmeier USAF Retd, Wally Robinson USAF Retd, Mike Rondot RAF Retd, the late William E. Ruck, Bestow 'Rudy' Rudolph USAF Retd, Scottish Aviation, Francis X. Sheehan USAF Retd, Tom Smith USAF Retd, Harry R. Snead USAF Retd, Joe Staelens, Paul F. Stevens USN Retd, Swiss Air Force, Harry Sykes, the late Edgar Townsend USAF, US Navy, Elmer R. Vogel USAF Retd, Herb Weinstein USAF Retd, Dan Winston, Truett J. Woodall, and Earl Zimmerman USAF Retd.

Contents

Introduction		6
1	INCEPTION AND DEVELOPMENT	7
2	EARLY DAYS IN THE ETO	27
3	'TIDAL WAVE' The Low-level Mission to Ploesti, 1 August 1943	39
4	ETO September 1943–May 1945	57
5	THE SOFT UNDER-BELLY OF EUROPE 15th Air Force Operations from Italy	75
6	THE WAR AGAINST JAPAN Alaska, CBI and Pacific Theatres	99
7	FOR KING AND COMMONWEALTH The B-24 Liberator in RAF and Dominion Service	121
8	SEARCH, FIND AND KILL US Anti-submarine Operations in the Atlantic	145
9	THE CARPETBAGGER PROJECT	161
10	WINGS OF GOLD US Navy Liberators in the Pacific	171
11	POSTSCRIPT	179
Appendix I	B-24 Production Totals by Type	185
Appendix II	B-24 Production Airframes	186
Glossary		189
Index		190

Introduction

No other American aircraft was built in greater numbers, and no other aircraft saw such widespread and decisive service, not even the much-vaunted Boeing B-17. In five years of war the B-24 achieved a remarkable record, serving in every theatre of war with the USAAF, US Navy, RAF and Commonwealth Air Forces as bomber, supply and VIP transport, gunship, photo-reconnaissance, flying classroom and tanker. In Europe it rose from obscurity to form a unique and powerful arm of the US 8th Air Force. In August 1943 Liberators attacked the Ploesti oilfields in Rumania. In the Far East they hauled supplies across the 'hump' from India into China, resupplying B-24 squadrons so they could bomb enemy targets. In the Pacific, the US Navy and the US Air Forces put them to excellent use, and they proved the scourge of Japanese shipping and land targets.

In Europe, Liberators operated primarily as bombers, although they sometimes doubled as aerial tankers, supplying fuel on 'trucking' missions to Patton's tanks or as transports during the crossing of the Rhine and at Arnhem when B-24s were even used on night missions, dropping secret service agents, or 'Joes' as they were known, into occupied territories. All this by an aircraft which was only designed in 1939, entered service in 1941 and was withdrawn almost overnight in mid-1945: truly one of the most remarkable aircraft of all time.

Martin W. Bowman
Norwich, England, 1998

CHAPTER ONE

Inception and Development

Although the Liberator enjoyed only a short operational career, much of it in the shadow of the illustrious Boeing B-17, it was in fact far more versatile and made a vital contribution towards winning the war in the Pacific. In the eyes of both the press and historians it always played a supporting role to the B-17, and only on occasions such as the famous low-level raid on Ploesti did it aspire to star billing. Even its inception was a result of the lead taken by the Fortress.

Early in 1939 the US Army Air Corps drew up a requirement for a heavy bomber of infinitely better performance than the B-17, then in production. Chiefs of staff were looking for a bomber with a greatly improved range, some 3,000 miles (4,800km), with a top speed in excess of 300mph (480km/h) and a ceiling of 35,000ft (10,670m). The Consolidated Company of San Diego, California, had already completed a series of design studies into such a bomber. Chief architect was Isaac Machlin Laddon, who had joined the company in 1927 as chief engineer. Consolidated had a long pedigree in building flying boats and a lengthy history in long-range aircraft design. It was Laddon who in 1928 was responsible for the Admiral flying boat, and later the Catalina flying boat which was to distinguish itself in World War II. It was this reputation for flying boats that earned the Liberator the nickname 'banana boat' (mainly from B-17 crews).

In May 1938 the French government had issued a specification to Consolidated for a heavy bomber. The company's early study, designated LB-30 (land-bomber), was a landplane version of their Model 29 flying boat (PB2-Y). In April 1940 France would become very interested in obtaining the new aircraft, but by the time they placed Contract A.F.7 for 175 LB-30MFs (*Mission Français*) in June 1940, the country was on the brink of defeat and the order would be taken over by Britain. Interest shown by the Army Air Corps prompted further design study designated XB-24, which incorporated David R. Davis's high aspect ratio, low-drag, wing and the twin-finned empennage used on the Model 31 flying boat (P4Y-1).

By 20 January 1939 preliminary specifications of the Model 32 were ready and construction began. The powerplant chosen was four neatly cowled Pratt and Whitney R-1830-33 Twin Wasp engines capable of 1,200hp on take-off and 1,000hp at 14,500ft (4,420m). On the strength of a wind tunnel test in February, the Consolidated designers ventured to Wright Field to discuss their design with senior Air Corps officers. Consolidated had to carry out almost thirty changes to the preliminary specifications on the recommendation of the Air Corps before a contract for a prototype was signed on 30 March 1939.

It could be said that the Model 32 was by far the most complicated aircraft yet

An army contract for the XB-24 prototype was signed on 30 March 1939 after many changes had been deemed necessary. On 26 October the Davis wing was married to the fuselage for the first time, and on 29 December the seven-place XB-24 was flown from Lindbergh Field next to the Consolidated plant in San Diego for the first time by William A. Wheatley. USAF

seen; it was certainly the most expensive. Although it was of conventional structure, among the more unusual and innovative features was the inclusion of a tricycle gear, the first to be used on a large bomber. The nose-wheel would permit faster landings and take-offs, which in turn would allow for a heavier wing-loading on the Davis airfoil. The main gears housed in the wing had to be long to exceed the tall bomb-bays, and these were retracted outwards by electric motors. Eight 1,100lb (480kg) bombs – twice that of the Fortress – could be carried vertically in the two halves of the bomb-bay, which was enclosed by roller-shutter doors, and was separated by a catwalk connecting the flight deck and the tail section. A bombardier's enclosure began the nose of the deep fuselage, which terminated behind the twin rudders with a tail position. Armament consisted of three .50 calibre guns and four .30 calibre Browning hand-operated machine guns, which were fired through openings in the fuselage sides and dorsal, ventral positions, and in a nose-socket.

Specification – B-24A

Crew:	8/10
Powerplant:	Four Pratt & Whitney R-1830-33 Twin Wasp radials; 1,200hp at sea level, 1,000hp at 14,500ft (4,420m)
Weights:	Empty 30,000lb (13,600kg); gross 53,600lb (24,300kg)
Dimensions:	Span 110ft (33.53m); length 63ft 9in (19.43m); height 18ft 8in (5.69m); wing area 1,048sq ft (97.36sq m)
Performance:	Max. speed 292mph at 15,000ft (470km/h at 4,572m) Cruising speed 228mph (367km/h) Rate of climb 5.6min to 10,000ft (3,046m) Ceiling 30,500ft (9,296m) Range with 4,000lb (1,814kg) bombload 2,200 miles (3,540km) Max. range at 190mph 4,000 miles (6,436km)
Armament:	Six .50cal and two .30cal machine guns; 4,000lb (1,814kg) bombload

On 27 April 1939 the US Army Air Corps placed its first contract for seven YB-24s for service trials in the autumn. These aircraft were similar to the XB-24 prototype, but the wing leading-edge slots were deleted and de-icing boots were fitted to the wings and tail. On 10 August 1939 an additional order was placed for thirty-six of the initial B-24A production version. However, only nine aircraft were completed to B-24A standard, which introduced .5in machine guns in the tail in place of the .30in guns of previous models. As a result of experience gained in Europe in other combat types, the XB-24 was fitted with self-sealing fuel tanks and armour plate.

On 26 October 1939 the Davis wing was married to the fuselage for the first time, and on 29 December 1939 the seven-place XB-24 made its maiden flight. William A. Wheatley was at the controls as it took off from the Lindbergh Field next to the Consolidated plant in San Diego. (Tragically, Wheatley was killed on 2 June 1941, during the final acceptance flight of the Liberator Mk. II for the RAF, when a loose bolt jammed the elevator controls and the aircraft crashed.) When the prototype's speed was measured at 273mph (439km/h) instead of the 311 mph (500km/h) estimated by the specification, the Air Corps ordered, on 26 July 1940, that turbosuperchargers (and leak-proof fuel tanks) be installed. Redesignated XB-24B, with R-1830-41 Wasps giving 1,200hp at 25,000ft (7,620m) and wing slots deleted, the reworked prototype was flown on 1 February 1941.

It is generally believed that the generic name 'Liberator' was selected by the British, as it is their custom to give names to aircraft rather than the numerical designations applied by the American forces. However, the aircraft was christened 'Liberator' as a result of a contest held at the Consolidated plant in San Diego. Dorothy Fleet, wife of the company's founder, the aviation pioneer Reuben H. Fleet, selected the name and submitted her entry anonymously. It was chosen and adopted despite an attempt in April 1942 by John W. Thompson, Consolidated's public relations officer, to change the name to 'Eagle'; somehow it does not have the same ring as 'Liberator'.

Meanwhile, in 1941, Consolidated developed the RB-24B, fitted with turbosupercharged Pratt and Whitney R-183-41 engines, replacing the mechanically supercharged 33s. The substitution was marked with the relocation of the oil coolers on each side of the radial engines instead of underneath, and this produced the characteristic elliptical cowling seen on all subsequent models. The aircraft underwent further cosmetic changes with the installation of a Martin dorsal turret and a Consolidated-built turret. A further nine more of the 1940 consignment of the thirty-six were completed in 1941 as B-24Cs.

Liberators for the RAF

On 17 January 1941 the first LB-30A for the RAF (AM258) made its maiden flight, and the first production models began flying in the Atlantic in March that year. Six YB-24s, identical to the original XB-24 except for the deletion of wing slots and the addition of de-icers, were diverted for service as LB-30A transports on the embryonic Trans-Atlantic Return Ferry Service route between Montreal, Newfoundland and Prestwick, in Scotland, a distance of 3,000 miles (4,830km). (The seventh YB-24 had armour and self-sealing fuel tanks and was accepted by the AAC in May 1941.) At first the LB-30As were flown by BOAC crews, and later by the RAF Ferry Command pilots.

The transports did sterling work, enabling increasingly large numbers of American-built aircraft to be collected and flown to Britain for combat with the RAF. In addition many important passengers and a myriad of service and civilian personnel made the Atlantic crossing in these unarmed transport Liberators, which were designated LB-30A (equivalent to Liberator I). Later examples were designated LB-30B (equivalent to Liberator II) and were used on the newly created Trans-Atlantic Return Ferry Service route mentioned above. Their mission was also to fly ferry pilots to Canada to collect and fly home American-built aircraft for the RAF, and to transport VIPs to their destinations. The first LB-30 arrived in the UK on 14 March 1941 and was used later, in July 1941, by the British Overseas

Airways Corporation (BOAC). Despite three crashes in August and September at a cost of fifty-four lives, the service was considered highly successful. The surviving aircraft eventually served in the civil markings of BOAC. The first westbound Liberator left Prestwick on 14 May 1941.

After the fall of France in June 1940, Britain took over the French LB-30 contract, specifying 165 aircraft (139 Liberator-IIs, plus six LB-30As and twenty Liberator Is) with the self-sealing fuel tanks, armour and power-operated turrets. However, turbosuperchargers, essential for boosting power at altitude, were not fitted, although they were installed on models for the AAF. By December 1941, sixty-five of the LB-30s had been delivered to Britain. Six YB-24s, and twenty very long range B-24As had also been diverted to the RAF. The B-24As, whose delivery began on 29 March 1941, went to 120 Squadron in RAF Coastal Command at Nutts Corner, Northern Ireland, as the Liberator I (LB-30B). No. 120 Squadron had previously been operating the Short Sunderland, whose range of 1,300 miles (2,090km) was not as well suited to their requirements as was the Liberator's, which at 2,400 miles (3,860km) was infinitely better. Eventually, some twenty-two squadrons would operate the Liberator in coastal Command. Losses would be made good with Liberators Mks. II, IIIA and V, which latter type would be allotted to Nos. 59 and 86 Squadrons.

Equipment installed in the United Kingdom included the centimetric ASV (Air-to-Surface-Vessel) Mk. II radar installation, which had both forward- and sideways-looking antennae. These Liberators entered service in September 1941. The ASV was tested in the US, and in August 1941 was adopted for service use as the SCR-521. An improved microwave version, ASV-10

LB-30As served the AAF as transports, and when the USA entered the war they became the first Liberators to be used in combat by the USAF. Twelve AAF LB-30s were flown to Java by the 7th Bomb Group, from where the first three AAF Liberator combat sorties were flown, on 17 January 1942. Seventeen others fitted with ASV Mk. II radar were rushed to the Canal Zone to supplement aircraft in the 6th Bomb Group, while six despatched to Hawaii and three sent to Alaska flew a handful of sorties in June 1942. Some twenty-three Army LB-30s were returned to British control in 1942, bringing the RAF LB-30 total to eighty-seven.
IWM

Liberator I AM920 was accepted in May 1941 for the RAF. Twenty Liberator I models were built for the RAF, most being used by RAF Coastal Command, although four, including AM920 (G-AGHG), were allocated to BOAC. G-AGHG crashed on 31 August 1942. IWM

Specification – B-24D	
Crew:	10
Powerplant:	Four Pratt & Whitney R-1830-43 Twin Wasp radials; 1,200hp
Weights:	Empty 32,605lb (14,790kg); gross 60,000lb (27,216kg)
Dimensions:	Span 110ft (33.53m); length 66ft 4in (20.23m); height 17ft 11in (5.46m); wing area 1,048sq ft (97.36sq m)
Performance:	Max. speed 303mph at 25,000ft (488km/h at 7,620m) Cruising speed 200mph (322km/h) Rate of climb 22min to 20,000ft (6,096m) Ceiling 32,000ft (9,754m) Range with 5,000lb (2,270kg) bombload 2,300 miles (3,700km) Max. range 3,500 miles (5,630km)
Armament:	Ten .50cal machine guns; 8,800lb (3,990kg) bombload

(SCR-517), was developed and fitted to DUMBO I, a Liberator II (AL507), and was flown to Britain in March 1942 where it was joined later by a second DUMBO (AL593) Liberator.

The Liberator II, built under the LB-30 contract, was the first model with a longer nose, and provision was made for two power-operated gun turrets. Commercial R-1830-S3C4-G engines, and Curtiss (instead of the usual Hamilton) propellers were installed, along with fourteen .303in guns which were installed in the United Kingdom. Four were contained in the Boulton Paul top turret, four in the tail turret, two in each waist position, one at the tunnel hatch, and another in the nose. The first LB-30 crashed on a test flight on 2 June 1941, but 139 more were built, and deliveries to the RAF began on 8 August 1941. Originally these were intended for bomber squadrons in the Middle East, but when the US entered the war in December 1941, seventy-five LB-30s were taken over by the AAF, the last on January 1942. Eight .50 calibre guns could be installed, including two hand-operated tail guns, single guns in the nose, waist and tunnel positions, and two in a Martin power-operated turret, when available, located amidships.

In RAF service the B-24D became the Liberator III, and 366 were supplied under direct British contracts. Nineteen B-24Ds had already been supplied to the Royal Canadian Air Force in September 1943, while twelve others went to the Royal Australian Air Force in 1944. The RCAF Liberators were similar to the RAF Mk. II, but in the RAF version the Consolidated tail turret was usually replaced by a Boulton Paul turret fitted with four .303in machine guns. The Liberator IIIA and subsequent versions were supplied under Lend-Lease and handed over to the RAF by the USAAF. A later series B-24D was designated the Liberator Mk. V, equipped with additional fuel tanks in wing bays and ASV radar either in a retractable radome in the ventral position aft of the bomb-bays or in the 'Dumbo' or chin position. The fitting of long-range tanks, however, in both Mks. II and III Liberators proved to be a slow process and this adversely affected the supply of these desperately needed aircraft. The installation of the ASV Mk. III also took time. By February 1943, a few Liberators of 224 Squadron were equipped with the American-designed ASV Mk. IV. On the Liberator I, six to eight 250lb (113kg) depth charges could be carried on sixteen-hour patrols, along with four 20mm fixed cannon in trays under the fuselage, and six .303 calibre guns (British Brownings), two of them in an opening in the rear.

Altogether, Britain received 366 B-24Ds (as the Liberator III, and GR.Mk. V for Coastal Command), while Australia got twelve, and Canada nineteen. These were followed by deliveries to the United Kingdom of eight B-24Gs and twenty-two B-24Hs (Liberator IV); and starting in November 1943, by deliveries of the B.Mk. VI and GR.Mk. VI Liberators to the RAF. These versions were Convair-built B-24J models with American turrets, except for the tail turret which on some aircraft was by Boulton Paul. Altogether the RAF received 1,157 B-24Js. The GR.Mk. VI anti-submarine aircraft later incorporated a radome containing centimetric radar in place of the ball turret. The B.Mk. VI was used by RAF squadrons overseas, and was also used by the RCAF for training while in the Atlantic and the Bay of Biscay. Australia received 145 B-24J models, and Canada acquired forty-nine 'J's.

In the Middle East the Liberator VI was used mainly against enemy shipping in the Mediterranean. Beginning in late 1944, thirty-six Mk. VIIIs (B-24Ls) were delivered to the RAF in that theatre, each equipped with centimetric radar designed for Pathfinder (PFF) operations against ground targets. In the Far East the Mk. VI was the principal bomber used in the final Burma campaign ending with the capture of Rangoon. Twenty-six RY-3s were allocated to the RAF under the designation C.IX, and the type saw service with No. 45 Group, Transport Command on routes between Canada and SEAC across the Pacific in the closing stages of the war.

Specification – B-24J/H	
Crew:	10
Powerplant:	Four Pratt & Whitney R-1830-65 Twin Wasp radials; 1,200hp
Weights:	Empty 36,500lb (16,556kg); gross 65,000lb (29,484kg)
Dimensions:	Span 110ft (33.53m); length 67ft 2in (20.47m); height 18ft (5.48m); wing area 1,048sq ft (97.36sq m)
Performance:	Max. speed 290mph at 25,000ft (467km/h at 7,620m) Cruising speed 215mph (346km/h) Rate of climb 25min to 20,000ft (6,096m) Ceiling 28,000ft (8,534m) Range with 5,000lb (2,270kg) bombload 2,100 miles (3,379km) Max. range 3,300 miles (5,310km)
Armament:	Ten .50cal machine guns; 8,800lb (3,990kg) bombload

In the summer of 1941 the Liberator I entered RAF service with Coastal Command. This is Liberator I AM910 fitted with the early ASV radar and 20mm cannon pack under the fuselage. During ground test firing the bomb-bay doors were known to cave in, although this was not repeated in flight. IWM

British Liberator Serial Number Allocations (including numbers not assigned to aircraft)

Serials	Mark	Serials	Mark
AL503–AL667	Mk. II (LB-30)	KK221–KK378	B.VI (B-24J)/GR.VI/GR.VIII
AM258–AM263	LB-30A	KL348–KL689	B.VI (B-24J)/B.VIII/GR.VIII (B-24L)
AM910–AM929	Mk. I (LB-30B)	KN702–KN836	B.VI (B-24J)/B.VIII/GR.VIII (B-24L)
BZ711–BZ999	III(B-24D)/IV(B-24H)/C.IV/ GR.V(B-24J/C.V con/VI	KP125–KP196	Mk. VIII (B-24L)
EV812–EW322	B.VI (B-24J)	LV336–LV346	Mk. IIIA (B-24D)
EW611–EW634	C.VII (C-87)	TS519–TS539	Mk. IV (B-24H)
FK214–FK245	III/IIIA (B-24D)	TT336–TT343	B.VI (B-24J)
FL906–FL995	III/IIIA (B-24D)/GR.V/ C.V cons (B-24D)	TW758–TW769	B.VI (B-24J)
FP685	II (LB-30)	VB852	
JT973–JT999	C.IX (RY-3)	VB904	
JV936–JV999	C.IX (RY-3)	VD245	Mk. IV (B-24H)
KE266–KE285		VD249	Mk. IV (B-24H)
KG821–KH420	B.VI (B-24J)/C.VI/GR.VI/ GR.VIII/B.VIII		

By the end of World War II, Britain had received 2,445 Liberators, 2,070 of them under Lend-Lease arrangements from America. Of the Lend-Lease total, 1,865 Liberators were bombers, while there were twenty-four C-87 (Mk. VII) and twenty-six RY-3 (Mk. IX) transports. A further fifty-five B-24s were transferred to the RAF and RAAF from the USAAF. All of these were in addition to the 112 LB-30As, Mk. Is and IIs received prior to the agreement.

Army Air Corps Acceptance

Nine B-24As, fitted with R-1830-33 Wasps, were accepted by the Army Air Corps from 16 June to 10 July 1941. Mounts for six .50- and two .30-calibre machine guns were provided, but these aircraft went to the newly formed Air Corps Ferrying Command, which retained only a tail gun. Ferry Command's commanding officer was Col Robert Olds, and its express function was to deliver aircraft to Montreal for ferrying to the United Kingdom. Olds also had broader powers to 'maintain such special air ferry service as may be required'. The first pilots to join the new command were among the very best America could offer; they included Lt Col Caleb V. Haynes and Maj Curtis E. LeMay, twelve other officers, and twenty-one hand-picked enlisted men. In July, Lt Col Haynes crossed the North Atlantic, and in August he and Maj LeMay pioneered the South Atlantic route.

In September 1941, two B-24As sporting conspicuous neutrality flags of the United States, took part in the Harriman mission to Moscow via Prestwick; one continued right around the world via the Middle East, India, Australia and Hawaii, and the other returned via Egypt, central Africa, the South Atlantic and Brazil. B-24A 40-2371 was one of the two which had been fitted with cameras and three guns for a secret mission to photograph Japanese mandated islands at Jaluit, Truk and possibly Ponape, in the Pacific; sadly it was lost at Hickam Field, Oahu, Hawaii on 7 December 1941, before Lt Ted S. Faulkner's crew could depart.

Twelve AAF LB-30s were flown to Java by the 7th Bomb Group, and the first three AAF Liberator combat sorties were flown from here on 17 January 1942. Seventeen others, fitted with ASV Mk. II radar, were rushed to the Canal Zone to supplement aircraft in the 6th Bomb Group, while six were despatched to Hawaii and three to Alaska; these flew a handful of sorties in June 1942. Others served the AAF as transports, but twenty-three Army LB-30s were returned to British control in 1942, bringing the RAF LB-30 total to eighty-seven.

The B-24 Enters Mass Production

American power turrets and turbosupercharged 1,200hp R-1830-41 Wasps were used on nine B-24Cs, the first of which was delivered on 20 December 1941. The remaining Liberators on early orders became B-24Ds. Ordered in 1940, the 'D' was the first significant Liberator version to be built, and the tasks that this aircraft was asked to perform were many and wide ranging. It was basically similar to the B-24C, but it had uprated R-1830-43 engines capable of 1,200hp at 23,400ft (7,132m), and the gross weight now stood at between 55,000–64,000lb (24,950–29,000kg), depending on the load. The 'C', and the first eighty-two B-24Ds delivered from Consolidated's San Diego plant in 1942, carried seven .50-calibre guns: one in the nose, two in a Martin turret forward of the wing, two in the waist, and two in a Consolidated tail turret. Some 2,900 rounds of ammunition were also carried. Eventually, three guns were fitted in the nose of the B-24D, and belly protection on 179 'D's was provided by a Bendix power turret with periscopic sights; this was replaced by a single hand-held tunnel gun. The bomb-bay accommodated up to eight 1,100lb (500kg) bombs, but the B-24D-25-CO, the B-24-10-CF, and later models, could carry eight 1,600lb (725kg) bombs. Provision was made for two 4,000lb (1,800kg) bombs to be carried on underwing racks, but these were rarely used.

The first B-24D was delivered on 23 January 1942. Contracts awarded in 1940, and subsequent orders brought the number of B-24Ds built by 1941 to 2,738. The bulk of these – some 2,425 B-24Ds – were built by Consolidated-Vultee at San Diego. In February 1941 a manufacturing pool to build B-24 Liberators was officially established. During 1942 a second Liberator production line was opened at a new Consolidated-Vultee plant at Fort Worth, Texas, and this turned out 303 B-24Ds. (In March 1943 the Consolidated and Vultee companies merged and later adopted the abbreviated trade name, Convair.) A third production line was brought into operation at Tulsa, where the Douglas Company produced ten B-24Ds before changing production to B-24Es. The B-24E was similar in appearance to the B-24D, but it had different propellers and was varied in other details. (Also similar in appearance to the B-24D series was the B-24G-NT, the first

B-24A 40-2374 was one of two Air Transport Command Liberators (the other was 40-2373) which, sporting conspicuous neutrality flags of the United States, was used to transport William Averill Harriman and his staff to Moscow via Prestwick in September 1941. (Harriman was to become the US Ambassador to Russia, 1943–46.) 40-2374 continued right around the world via the Middle East, India, Australia and Hawaii, returning to the USA via the Far East. 40-2373 returned via Egypt, central Africa, the South Atlantic and Brazil. Flown by Lt Louis T. Reicher, 40-2374 is pictured arriving at Sembowang airport, Singapore, on 30 October 1941. USAF

Liberator II AL574/0 of 108 Squadron, which was accepted in October 1941, pictured at Bangalore, India, on 20 January 1942, after initial service in Egypt, December 1941–December 1942. IWM

Early Consolidated B-24D Liberators on the production line at San Diego, California. Altogether, 1,200 Ds were built at San Diego. Consolidated

(Below) **Nose assemblies at the Douglas Tulsa plant in Oklahoma where a third production line was brought into operation in 1943 for the construction of B-24Es (after ten B-24Ds were built). The B-24E was similar in appearance to the B-24D but it had different propellers and was varied in other details. (Also similar in appearance to the B-24D series was the B-24G-NT, the first twenty-five of which were built at Douglas Tulsa, starting in March 1943.) Most B-24Es were used for replacement training in the US, and very few were sent overseas.** Douglas

twenty-five of which were built at Douglas Tulsa, starting in March 1943.) Most B-24Es were used for replacement training in the US, and very few were sent overseas.

Construction of a fourth Liberator production line by the US government for the Ford Motor Company began in 1941 at Willow Run, Michigan, 30 miles (50km) west of Detroit. This massive aircraft factory covered 3,700,000sq ft (343,730sq m), was a quarter of a mile long, with seventy assembly lines, and it was anticipated that it would employ as many as 100,000 workers once B-24 production was in full swing. It was finished at the end of 1942 at a cost of $165 million, and Henry Ford declared that the plant would produce 100 aircraft a day. At first, Ford were contracted to produce complete B-24E aircraft as well as sub-assemblies for the Fort Worth and Tulsa plants.

The first B-24 which rolled out of its doors on 1 September 1942 was a Consolidated model reassembled at Willow Run from the sub-assemblies of two aircraft shipped from San Diego. It was hoped that mass production would speed up the production of Liberators, although the rest of the American aviation industry, opposed to Ford's participation in the programme, was cynical, and in February

Ford-built B-24H-25-FO 42-95051 in flight. In 1942 the fourth Liberator production line was opened at Willow Run, Michigan. This massive aircraft factory covered 3,700,000sq ft (343,730sq m), a greater manufacturing area than Boeing, Consolidated and Douglas combined. At first the Ford Motor Company factory began producing complete B-24E aircraft as well as sub-assemblies for the Fort Worth and Tulsa plants, but despite mass-production methods, progress was slow, and only forty-six B-24s were built at Willow Run in 1942. By January 1944, however, Ford was building more B-24s than any other plant in the country. The first B-24 which rolled out of its doors on 1 September 1942 was a Consolidated model reassembled at Willow Run from the sub-assemblies of two aircraft from San Diego. Altogether, 3,100 B-24H models were built, and Ford produced 1,780 of these. Ford

1943 Harry S. Truman, then chairman of the Senate War Investigating Committee, began an investigation of Willow Run because production of B-24s was so slow. It was not until the end of 1943 that the plant – referred to caustically as 'Willit Run' because of its poor initial output – was producing, on average, 340 Liberators a month. Willow Run delivered 490 B-24E-FO Liberators, and by the end of the war the plant had produced 6,792 Liberators, second only to Consolidated at San Diego, which produced 7,500.

C-87 and Other Liberator Conversions

Because of its very long range capability and spacious fuselage, the Liberator was also adopted for a transport role with the USAAF, the US Navy and the RAF. Altogether, 276 C-87 transport variants, developed from the B-24A and based on the B-24D, were delivered from Fort Worth to the USAAC, beginning on 14 December 1942. The first transported were converted B-24Ds from the production lines at Fort Worth. Accommodation was increased to twenty-five passengers and five crew, and windows were fitted along the fuselage. All turrets were deleted, although some were armed with four .50 calibre machine guns for 'Hump' operations in China. Some twenty-four C-87 (Liberator C.VII) models were allocated to the RAF under the terms of Lend-Lease. These served with No. 46 Group of Transport Command in England and with No. 229 Group in India.

In US service the C-87 was employed early in the war in the Air Corps Ferrying Command. The designation C-87A was applied to transport Liberators equipped

In 1942 the USN finally obtained a share in Liberator production, and the first PB4Y-1 models were from the B-24D production line in San Diego. That same year a second Liberator production line was opened at a new Consolidated-Vultee plant at Fort Worth, Texas, and this turned out 303 B-24Ds. In March 1943, the Consolidated and Vultee companies merged and later adopted the abbreviated trade name, Convair. These Convair B-24D-CF Liberators nearing completion at Fort Worth in June 1943 are for the USAAF anti-submarine squadrons *(left)* and USAAF *(right)*. The nearest aircraft is 42-40823, followed by 42-40835 and 42-40686. Author

C-87 Liberator Express **44-52987 in flight. Altogether, 276 C-87 transport variants, developed from the B-24A and based on the B-24D, were delivered from Fort Worth to the USAAC, beginning 14 September 1942. The first transported were converted B-24Ds from the production line at Fort Worth. Accommodation was increased to twenty-five passengers and five crew, and windows were fitted along the fuselage.** General Dynamics

B-24D-55-CO 42-40409 Homesick Susie **of the 459th Bomb Squadron, 308th Bomb Group taking-off (note position of flaps). Lt Oglesby crashlanded** Susie **out of gas at Kunming, China, early in 1943, and she was cannibalized for parts; her crew were given B-24D-55-CO 42-40407** Susie's Sister. **The crew were subsequently forced to abandon this aircraft over Chabua, in the north-east end of the Assam Valley in India, and they returned to fly a B-24J which they called** Susie's Little Sister. USAF

Specification – C-87/RY1/VII	
Crew:	8
Powerplant:	Four Pratt & Whitney R-1830-33 Twin Wasp radials; 1,200hp
Weights:	Empty 31,935lb (14,486kg); gross 56,000lb (25,402kg)
Dimensions:	Span 110ft (33.53m); length 66ft 4in (20.22m); height 18ft (5.48m); wing area 1,048sq ft (97.36sq m)
Performance:	Max. speed 306mph (492km/h) Rate of climb 20.9min to 20,000ft (6,096m) Ceiling 31,000ft (9,449m) Range 2,900 miles (4,666km)
Armament:	One .50cal machine gun

with ten berths to be used as executive sleepers. Six were built in 1943 and had uprated Twin Wasp engines. An armed variant, the C-87B, was never proceeded with, neither was the C-87C projected transport variant of the single-finned B-24N.

Other wartime conversions made to the basic Liberator airframe included the C-109 flying tanker, the F-7 photo-reconnaissance aircraft, and the AT-22 flying classroom. All told, 200 B-24s were converted to C-109 aerial tankers to support B-29 groups based in the CBI, while in January 1943 a B-24D was converted to an XF-7 photographic aircraft with eleven cameras. Some 213 conversions of later B-24 models followed, to F-7, F-7A and F-7B reconnaissance aircraft for use in the Pacific. Five AT-22s were manufactured to train flight engineers.

Liberators for the US Navy

On 31 December 1941 the US Navy possessed 466 patrol bombers, including 423 PBY Catalina amphibians and twenty Martin PBM Mariner twin-engined flying boats. During early combat operations the Navy quickly found to its cost that as patrol bombers these were far too vulnerable when confronted by Japanese fighters like the Zero, and the need for land-based patrol planes became all-important. In February 1942 the first request for a re-allocation of the bomber programme was submitted, especially of the very long range B-24 Liberator which was already being used extensively by the British for patrol work. Despite the urgent USAAF need for heavy bombers, on 7 July 1942 Chief of Staff George C. Marshall finally agreed to a Navy share of Liberator and all Lockheed Ventura production. Four days later, PB4Y-1 Navy versions of the B-24D were scheduled at Consolidated and these began reaching operational units in August.

PB4Y-1 deliveries were slow at first, but eventually twenty Navy bomber squadrons operated Liberators in the Atlantic and Pacific theatres. In August 1943 the USAAF transferred all its B-24 equipped, anti-submarine squadrons to the US Navy. Anti-Submarine Command was disbanded and all ASV-equipped B-24Ds were handed over to the US Navy as PB4Y-1s in exchange for an equal number of unmodified B-24s already in production for the Navy. Ultimately, the US Navy was to receive a total of 1,174 Liberators, equipping thirty-two squadrons. The last models were B-24Ms, which began arriving in January 1945.

Apart from the camouflage scheme of blue and white, outwardly Navy Liberators differed little from the USAAF model, although some, equivalent to the B-24J, were fitted with Erco bow turrets. After the war a number of US Navy Liberators were modified for reconnaissance duties as PB4Y-1Ps, and these served until as late as 1951 (the last year as P4Y-1Ps).

Pacific PB4Y-2 Privateers

The US Navy had a particular requirement for an aircraft with more armament and armour for its 'masthead' bombing runs on Japanese shipping. At the same time, Convair engineers recognized the need for a new patrol aircraft capable of accommodating the considerable advances in radio navigational aids and RCM (Radio Counter Measures) apparatus. In April 1943, Convair and the US Navy decided that the PB2Y-3 Coronado flying-boat programme should end, and that production of a new patrol bomber based on the B-24's high aspect ratio wing and tricycle undercarriage should begin. The Liberator's fuselage was stretched by 7ft (2m) to 74ft (22m 73cm) to make room for the new electronics (and two electronics operators), and more powerful R-1830-94 Twin Wasp engines were installed. A new single fin replaced the twin-tailed empennage of the B-24, and this improved stability.

The introduction of a Martin dorsal turret complemented the mid-upper turret, making six turrets in all, while a second .50 calibre machine gun was installed in each of the tear-shaped Erco side blisters, making twelve .50 calibre guns in total. All this additional weight was offset to some extent by the removal of the ball turret. The new design became the PB4Y-2 Privateer. On 3 May 1945, Convair was instructed to allocate three PB4Y-1s (B-24B) for conversion to XPB4Y-2s. The wings and tricycle landing gear were those of the B-24 but more fuel, guns and radar were added. Since patrol planes operate at low altitudes, the turbosuperchargers were deleted to produce a higher sea-level speed.

The first XPB4Y-2 made its first flight on 20 September 1943, and on 15 October a production contract was placed for 660 Privateers. Deliveries began in March 1944. A further contract, for 710 PB4Y-2s, was placed on 19 December 1944, but by October 1945, when production ceased, 740 of these aircraft had been built.

Deliveries of the PB4Y-2 began in March 1944, and by the end of the war seven of the Navy's Liberator squadrons in the Pacific had been equipped with the Privateer at one time or another. Three squadrons, VPB-109, VPB-123 and 124, were equipped with PB4Y-2Bs which could each carry two 'Bat' (SWOD-9) anti-shipping glide bombs with radar homing below their wings. These missiles were a further development of the earlier, *Azon* VB-1 (vertical) bombs used by B-24s of the 458th Bomb Group of the 8th Air Force in Europe. A PB4Y-2B of VPB-118 launched the first 'Bat' in April 1945 against enemy shipping at Balikpapen harbour, Borneo.

Privateers ranged throughout the Pacific from Singapore in the south to Korea in the north, flying the longest overwater patrols of the war. They also flew fleet barrier patrols ahead of the US Navy shipping, spotting and destroying the enemy before American sea-borne movements could be reported. In March 1945 the Japanese early warning picket boats in the path of the 5th Fleet were hounded and sunk by the PB4Y-2 squadrons, and in July 1945 the US 3rd Fleet cruised unhindered off the Japanese coastline under their protection.

The US Navy also used the transport version of the PB4Y-2, called the RY-3. A total of forty-six were built to B-24N standard and delivered to the US Navy under the designation RY-3. Of the nineteen retained by the US Navy at the end of the war, four were used as VIP transports

Specification – B-24M	
Crew:	10
Powerplant:	Four Pratt & Whitney R-1830-65 Twin Wasp radials; 1,200hp
Weights:	Empty 36,000lb (16,330kg); gross 64,500lb (29,257kg)
Dimensions:	Span 110ft (33.53m); length 67ft 2in (20.47m); height 18ft (5.48m); wing area 1,048sq ft (97.36sq m)
Performance:	Max. speed 300mph at 30,000ft (483km/h at 9,144m) Cruising speed 215mph (346km/h) Rate of climb 25min to 20,000ft (6,096m) Ceiling 28,000ft (8,534m) Range 2,100 miles (3,379km)
Armament:	Ten .50cal machine guns; 8,800lb (3,992kg) bombload

In April 1943 Convair began producing the PB4Y-2 Privateer, a new patrol bomber based on the B-24's high-aspect ratio wing and tricycle undercarriage. The Liberator's fuselage was stretched by 7ft (2m) to 74ft 7in (22m 73cm) to make room for the new electronics (and two electronics operators), and more powerful R-1830-94 twin wasp engines were installed. A new single fin replaced the twin-tailed empennage of the B-24, and this improved stability. The last Privateer was delivered to the USN in October 1945, but these aircraft continued to serve in a wide variety of roles post-war. Privateers flew flare-dropping missions during the Korean War. General Dynamics

(Below) **Navy RY-3 transport in flight. The RY-3 was the transport version of the PB4Y-2, and a total of thirty-nine were built for the Lend-Lease programme for the RAF. However, only the first RY-3 off the production line found its way overseas, and the rest were used by the USN.** USN

for the then commanding general, A. A. Vandergrift and his staff.

Although the last PB4Y-2 was delivered to the US Navy in October 1945, these aircraft continued to serve post-war in a wide variety of roles, some being fitted with anti-submarine radar (PB4Y-2S). On 8 April 1950 a Privateer was shot down by Russian Aircraft over the Baltic Sea during a photo-reconnaissance mission. Privateers also flew flare-dropping missions during the Korean War.

The installation of a Convair tail turret in the nose position was a standard measure on B-24D Liberators in the Pacific until the arrival of Liberators with production nose turrets. Here, the Convair turret has been installed in the nose of B-24D The Green Hornet **of the 7th Bomb Group at Fanafuti Island, Ellice Group, in April 1943.** USAF

Nose Turrets to the Fore

Early in 1943, the fifth and final major Liberator plant was operated by North America at Dallas, Texas. Its first 430 Liberators were designated B-24G, and the first twenty-five B-24G-NTs, built in the beginning of March 1943, were very similar to the B-24D. However, experience gained in combat had revealed deficiencies in the glass-nosed B-24Ds. Like the Boeing B-17, the B-24 suffered terribly from head-on fighter attacks when enemy pilots, recognizing that this was the bombers' most vulnerable area, took advantage of this fact and switched from rear-mounted attacks to fast-closing frontal assaults. In August 1942 a Consolidated XB-41 'escort fighter', converted from a B-24D, had been approved, but it was not put into production. It had 11,135 rounds for fourteen .50 calibre guns paired in a Bendix chin turret, two top turrets, tail turret, ball turret, and at each waist opening.

Nose turrets had been ingeniously fashioned by 5th Air Force engineers in Australia (and, similarly, by the 7th Air Force) by using salvaged hydraulically operated Consolidated tail turrets and installing them in the noses of B-24Ds to improve frontal fire-power. It led, in the spring and summer of 1943, to the instigation of a regular modification programme at the Hawaiian Air Depot for the majority of the Liberators heading for the south-west Pacific air forces, and this in turn led to the installation of Emerson and Consolidated nose turrets containing two .50in machine guns in B-24s leaving the production lines.

Starting on 30 June 1943, the changes led to a re-designation to B-24H at Convair at Fort Worth, and at Douglas and Ford, although the change at North American (where all but the first twenty-five of the 430 built were fitted with Emerson nose turrets) simply brought about a block number change, and these B-24s continued to be designated B-24G. (B-24Gs served only with the 15th Air Force in Italy.) Altogether, the B-24G/H carried ten .50 calibre guns with 4,700 rounds of ammunition, paired in the nose, top, belly and tail turrets, and at hand-operated mounts in the waist. Waist windows were provided on later blocks. Ford surprised the rest of the American aircraft industry by building no less than 1,780 B-24Hs, while Fort Worth produced 738 B-24Hs and Douglas Tulsa turned out 582 B-24H models.

Ford converted B-24J-20 FO 44-48763 into a single tail XB-24N, adding a modified tail turret and installing a ball turret in the nose. Ford

Ford followed up its success on the B-24H by building 1,587 B-24Js, which were similar in appearance to the B-24H, except for an Emersons nose turret. Nose-wheel doors were also different: on the J they opened inwards, like the B-24D-CO, whereas on most B-24G/H models they opened outwards (although in the spring of 1944, both Convair plants reintroduced outward-opening nose-wheel doors). Internally, a C-1 autopilot and M-series bomb sight were added to the B-24H later. Changes were also made to the manually-controlled turbosuperchargers, which were replaced with electrically controlled power boosters activated by the pilots using a single dial. These permitted much easier and smoother operation than the old pedestal-mounted controls.

Another operational problem affecting the fuel transfer system was also rectified on late B-24J models. Since the early B-24D had been put into production, three auxiliary fuel cells had been added in each wing aft of the outer engines to provide an extra 450 US gallons (1,703ltr) of fuel in addition to the 2,343 US gallons (8,869ltr) carried, but the engines could not be fed directly from these tanks. To do so involved the flight engineer having to transfer the fuel to main tanks first, and the original fuel-transfer system was less than ideal, so a revised auxiliary fuel-tank transfer system, which reduced the risk of fire, was adopted.

Specification – Liberator Mark VI (B-24J)

Crew:	8
Powerplant:	Four Pratt & Whitney R-1830-43/65 Twin Wasp radials; 1,200hp
Weights:	Empty 37,000lb (16,783kg); gross 62,000lb (28,123kg)
Dimensions:	Span 110ft (33.53m); length 67ft 1in (20.47m); height 17ft 11in (5.46m); wing area 1,048sq ft (97.36sq m)
Performance:	Max. speed 270mph at 20,000ft (434km/h at 6,096m) Rate of climb 40min to 20,000ft (6,096m) Ceiling 32,000ft (9,754m) Range with 12,800lb bombload 900 miles (1,448km) Max. range 2,290 miles (3,685km)
Armament:	Nine .50cal machine guns; 12,800lb (5,806kg) bombload

Early armament installed in the tail position of an RAF Liberator II. Later, RAF air gunners to fly Liberators with Consolidated tail turrets had to be a maximum 5ft 10in (1m 75cm) tall and weigh not more than 160lb (72.5kg), or they could not get into the turret with an Irvin suit on. IWM

Convair built 738 B-24Js with a Briggs Ball turret. A great many of these models were fitted with hydraulically operated Consolidated nose turrets, although from spring 1944, both San Diego and Fort Worth switched to Emerson nose turrets only, while Douglas built all 582 with the electrically operated Emerson turrets. Two other types of nose turret – the Consolidated, with staggered guns, and the hydraulically operated Motor Products turret (an improved version of the Consolidated turret) – were also used in the nose and the tail. Late on in 1944, Consolidated and North America ceased using the wing and tail assembly, leading-edge electric/rubber de-icer boot system, and switched to the thermal ice-preventative system which used hot air from the engines piped to ducting inside the leading edges.

These innovations, coupled with the addition of a nose turret, exacted a price, namely an alarming increase in the gross weight of the aircraft which now weighed in at anything between 50–70,000lb (22,680–31,750kg). Fuel consumption and overall performance suffered; with little reserve power available, take-off in particular became quite critical. It would lead, in some theatres – first in the south-west Pacific, and also in England – to the removal of the ball turret from many Liberators, although not everyone went along with the order: there were some plane commanders who for superstitious reasons, or whatever, wanted to keep their original crews intact.

(Above) **Boulton Paul rear turret installation containing four .303in Browning machine guns, on an RAF Coastal Command Liberator.** IWM

Sperry ball turret installation used on a GR.VI in India. IWM

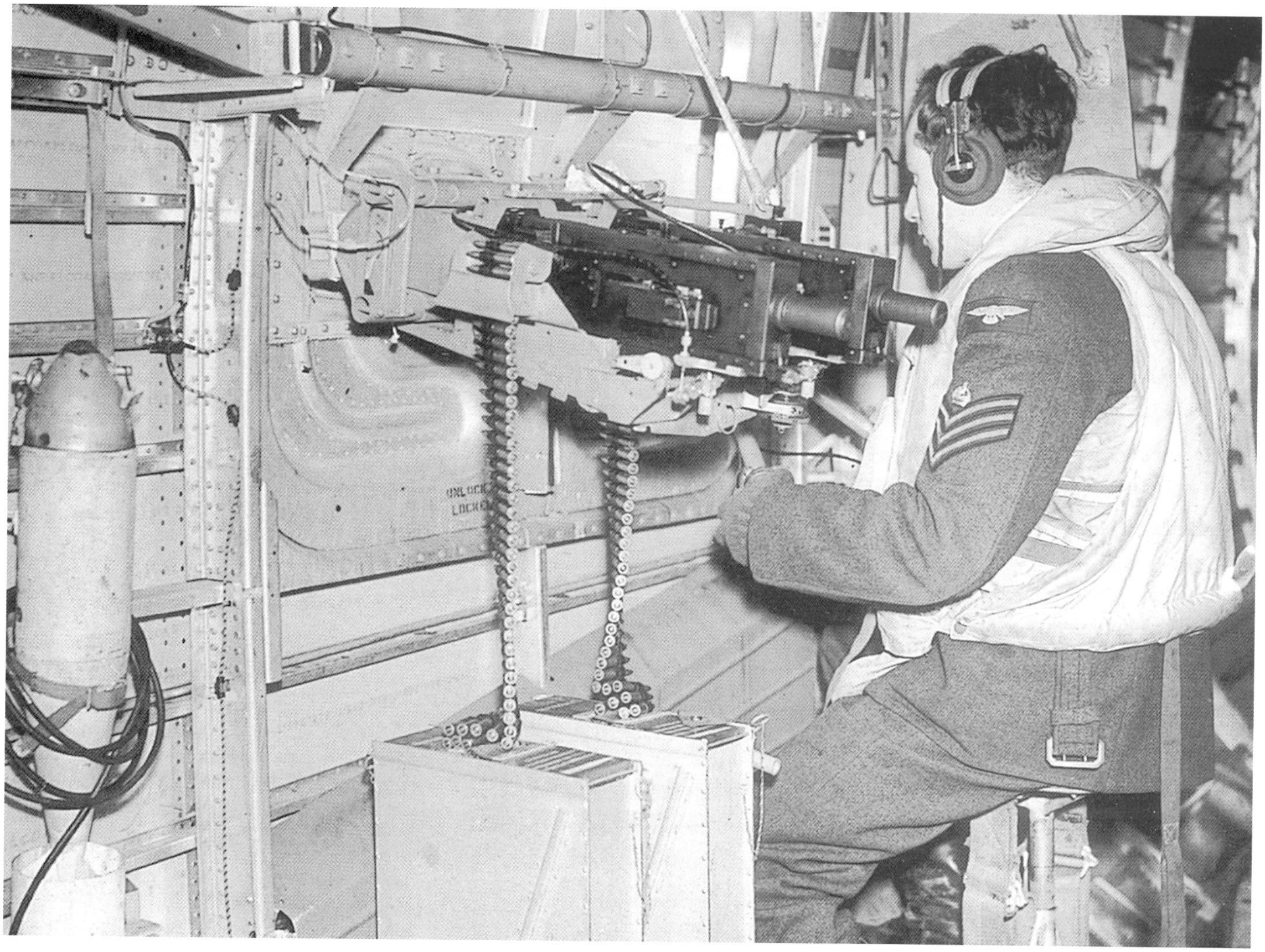

RAF gunner manning twin .303in Brownings in the right waist of an RAF Liberator in Coastal Command. IWM

Early waist gun positions aboard Liberators were cramped, as this picture shows, and staggered guns were soon installed. The ammunition belts replaced the earlier, drum-fed guns. USAF

B-24J-1-CO 42-72989 Pistol-Packin' Momma **of the 38th Bomb Squadron, 30th Bomb Group, 7th Air Force. (The 30th Bomb Group began operations from the Ellice Islands in November 1943, moving to the Gilberts in January 1944, and Kwajelin in March 1944, before ending the war at Saipan.) A total of 6,678 B-24Js, the most numerous of all the Liberator variants, was built.** USAF

(Above) **The 5,000th Liberator produced was 44-41064, a San Diego-built B-24J-195, which went on to serve with the 15th Air Force in Italy. Altogether, Consolidated built 2,792 J models.** USAF

Like model B-24s looked much the same, but this photo of the Douglas-built B-24H-20-DT 42-51093/W of the 787th Bomb Squadron, 466th Bomb Group *(foreground)*, and the Ford-built B-24H *(background)*, reveal subtle differences. Ford-built B-24s could easily be distinguished by the 'wavy' demarcation, or 'cheatline' on camouflaged models, and by the different anti-dazzle panel on all its models. 'H' models were fitted with the Sperry bombsight instead of the much-vaunted Norden, and turret installations too were often different (the Ford-built B-24H here has an Emerson front turret, while the Douglas-built model has a Motor Products' tail turret). Natural metal airframes saved valuable time, speeding up production and increasing performance by several mph. 42-51093 flew its missions in the 2nd Bomb Division, 8th Air Force, from 12 May–15 June 1944 before catching fire due to an accidental discharge of incendiary rounds from a machine gun in a nearby B-24 on 19 June 1944. USAF

All told, Consolidated built 2,792 B-24Js, Convair built 1,558, and Douglas Tulsa built 205 B-24J-DTs. When added to the Ford figures, the five plants turned out a total of 6,678 B-24Js, the greatest number of all Liberator variants produced.

The Final Models

The last combat models of note were the B-24L and the B-24M. The B-24L differed from previous models primarily in the installation of a Convair-designed tail station, which contained two hand-held .50in machine guns. Consolidated built 417 B-24Ls at San Diego, but only 186 of these received the hand-held tail mounts, the rest getting standard turrets. Beginning in August 1944, Ford meanwhile turned out 1,250 B-24Ls at Willow Run. Britain received 355 B-24L versions (Liberator VIII) and the RAF used them as heavy bombers in the Middle and Far East, while Coastal Command operated them in anti-submarine service. Australia, meanwhile, received eighty-three 'L's, and Canada sixteen.

Convair and Ford only built the B-24M, which began to appear in early 1945. Its major distinguishing feature was the installation of lightweight turrets, while late version 'M's had re-designed cockpit glazing (as in this photo), affording increased visibility, and escape panels in the roof. Some 916 'M's were manufactured by Convair, while 1,677 were built by Ford. Australia received eighty-three, while Canada got just four. In 1945, China received thirty-seven B-24Ms.

Ford-built B-24Ms coming off the production lines at Willow Run. The plant was a quarter of a mile (0.4km) long, with seventy assembly lines, and the production techniques were designed to build one Liberator an hour and meet the USAAF goal of 405 B-24s a month (later raised to 535 a month). For instance, instead of cutting out parts from metal sheets with saws and routers, Ford punched out parts with blanking dies; and rather than drilling rivet holes in stacked sheets, it pierced them during the blanking operation: a single stroke of a 500-ton press could punch 2,000 rivet holes in large sheets. Spot-welding replaced riveting in certain locations, saving some 15,000 rivets per plane, reducing weight and saving 35,000 hours of labour each month. More than 30,000 dies were finally needed to manufacture the B-24's 1,225,000 parts, which were held together by 400,000 rivets. Ford

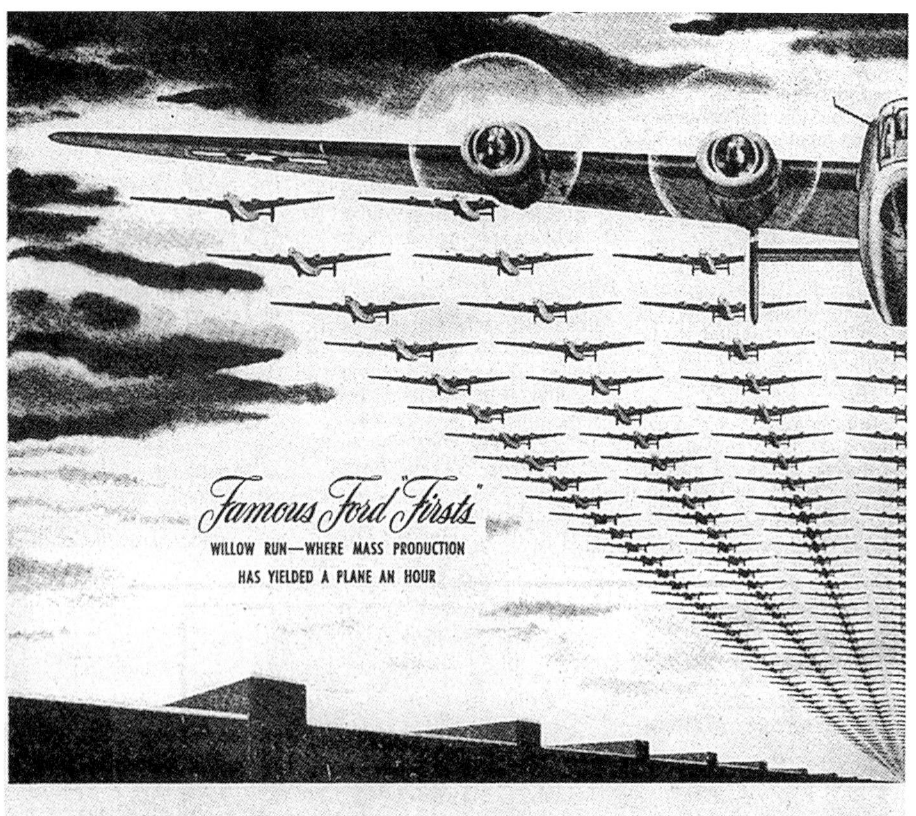

1st

to build bombers by automobile methods!

More than 8500 four-engine heavy planes have come off the twin assembly lines at the giant Willow Run plant.

Behind this achievement, unequalled in aircraft history, is an amazing story. Ford Motor Company decided to apply to plane building the precision mass-production methods it pioneered in the automobile field.

This meant erecting the largest building of its kind in the world—designing thousands of machines and fixtures—building 91 conveyor lines and 29 miles of craneways—training thousands of workers.

The plane, containing over a million parts, had to be broken down into production units which could be integrated into the assembly system. Important shortcuts were developed at every turn. In the case of the center wing section, for example, the construction time of standard aircraft methods was reduced 94%.

Raw material went in one end of the plant . . . planes came out the other, at a peak rate of one every hour, ready to fly away.

Here is another Ford "first." In the days ahead, new Ford-built cars and trucks will continue to benefit by the same skill and resourceful engineering which made Willow Run the marvel of the industrial world.

"THE FORD SHOW" Brilliant singing stars, orchestra and chorus. Every Sunday, NBC network. 2:00 P. M., E.W.T., 1:00 P. M., C.W.T., 12:00 M., M.W.T., 11:00 A. M., P.W.T.

EXPECT THE "FIRSTS" FROM FORD!

In January 1943 production at Willow Run was just thirty-one B-24s in 468 hours, in June it was 190, but by March 1944, Ford was producing 453 B-24s in this space of time.
Ford

Meanwhile in 1943, a B-24D was modified into the XB-24K by Ford at Willow Run by replacing the twin-tail empennage with a single fin and rudder. R-1830-75 engines were used, armament was revised, and a ball turret was fitted to the nose. The XB-24K first flew on 9 September 1943, and underwent testing at the Eglin Field proving ground in Florida; here it was discovered that the single-finned machine's general stability and control, although inferior to the B-17, produced greater stability and improved performance, as well as giving an improved field of fire for the rear guns. Staff at Eglin even went as far as to recommend that all future Liberators be built with single tails. Ford built an XB-24N-FO with the single tail and this was delivered in November 1944. This was followed, during May–June 1945, by seven YB-24Ns to begin production; but on 31 May 1945, 5,168 B-24Ns on order at Willow Run were cancelled, when the war in Europe ended. In July 1945 Ford modified a B-24D to create the XB-24P to test Sperry fire-control systems, and a year later a B-24L was modified to create the XB-24Q, to test the General Electric radar-controlled tail gun.

Conclusion

The peak inventory of B-24s was in September 1944, when some 6,043 Liberators were on operational strength worldwide, equipping forty-five groups. In all, nineteen 8th Air Force groups used Liberators, but five of these, in the 3rd Bomb Division, re-equipped with the B-17 in the summer of 1944. In the Mediterranean, twelve B-24 groups operated in the 15th Air Force, and eleven more B-24 groups took part in the war against Japan. More B-24s (18,482) were built than any other American aircraft of the period.

CHAPTER TWO

Early Days in the ETO

The Liberator was not well suited to the European Theatre of Operations (ETO), mainly because on missions it was expected to conform to the performance limitations imposed by the Fortress. The B-24D's operationally high wing-loading made it a difficult aircraft to maintain in formation above 21,000ft (6,400m), although its service ceiling was put at 28,000ft (8,500m), about 4,000ft (1,200m) below the optimum Fortress altitude. Also, the B-24D's operational cruising speed of 180mph (290km/h) was between 10 and 20mph (16 and 32km/h) faster than the B-17's. This caused countless problems in mission planning, and usually the Liberators were relegated to the rear of the B-17 formations where they consequently soaked up most of the punishment. The problem was that the B-17 was used in greater numbers and the B-24s had to adapt to the operational performance of the B-17, rather than the other way around.

Gen Eaker, chief VIIIth Bomber Command, had just two B-24 groups and four B-17 groups to prove conclusively that daylight precision bombing could succeed in the heavily defended sky over the continent. Not surprisingly, even the RAF remained unconvinced about the Americans' ability to survive against German opposition. The first Liberators intended for the European Theatre of Operations (ETO) were B-24Ds of the 44th – 'The Flying Eightballs' – and the 93rd Heavy Bombardment Groups.

In January 1942, six of Germany's largest U-boats arrived in North American waters, and within three weeks forty Allied ships, totalling 23,000 tons, were sunk. This effectively delayed the two B-24 groups, who began flying anti-submarine patrols over the Gulf of Mexico and along the coast of Cuba. The 44th Bomb Group was credited with the destruction of one enemy submarine, and in all, three U-boat kills were credited to the 93rd Bomb Group, commanded by Col Ted Timberlake.

Plans to introduce the B-24 into Europe were not fulfilled until September 1942, when the 2nd Bombardment Wing (which became the 2nd Bomb Division, and later the 2nd Air Division) was established in England. Seventeen Liberators of the 93rd Bomb Group decamped to Alconbury in Huntingdonshire, to remain in the shadow of Fortress operations for some time. In

B-24D-1-CO 41-23737 Eager Beaver **of the 328th Bomb Squadron, one of the first seventeen Liberators assigned to the 93rd Heavy Bombardment Group, which in September 1942 was established at Alconbury, Huntingdonshire, England.** Eager Beaver **was later transferred to the 446th Bomb Group and was renamed** Fearless Freddie. USAF

fact it was not until 9 October 1942 that the group flew its maiden mission: on this occasion, twenty-four B-24Ds made up the Liberator effort in attacks by 108 heavies on the locomotive, carriage and wagon works of the Ateliers d'Hellemmes at the Chemin de Fer du Nord at Lille, and the steel and engineering works of the Compagnie de Fives. This was the first mission flown from East Anglia in which over 100 bombers took part. Col Ted Timberlake led the group in *Teggie Ann*. One B-24 was lost over France, and *Ball of Fire Junior* made the five-hour flight only to crash-land at another airfield on its return. Altogether, four bombers were lost while only sixty-nine aircraft, including just ten Liberators, bombed their primary targets.

The 93rd remained in the shadow of Fortress operations for some time in the European Theatre of Operations (ETO), and it was not until 9 October 1942 that the group flew its maiden mission, when twenty-nine B-24Ds joined eighty-four Fortresses in attacks on targets in Lille, France. Here, maintenance men work on B-24D-1-CO 41-23729 Shoot Luke**, one of the most famous B-24Ds in the group.** USAF

On 7 November the 44th Bomb Group flew their first mission when eight B-24s flew a diversionary sweep to Cap de la Hague in Holland for B-17s attacking the U-boat pens at Brest. Two days later the Flying Eightballs flew their first combat mission when twelve B-24s, drawn from both the 44th and 93rd Bomb Groups, joined the B-17s in the bombing of St Nazaire. The Liberators bombed from between 17,500 and 18,300ft (5,300 and 5,600m), behind the Fortresses. The B-24s came through without any serious damage, although some crews reported instances of frostbite caused by the lack of protective clothing. Raids on the U-boat pens became the order of the day, but when the Allies invaded North Africa, early in November, the 93rd's 330th and 409th Squadrons were tasked to help cover the 'Torch' operation, providing long-range protection duties for the invasion fleet. Later that month both squadrons, having provided excellent service in the Bay of Biscay, returned to Alconbury.

On 27 November the 93rd's 329th Squadron transferred to Hardwick in Norfolk in order to evaluate the British *Gee* navigational device. A special force consisting of selected crews from all four squadrons, was to test the device on behalf of the USAAF, which at the time was considering various RAF operational radar equipment for bombing in overcast skies. In October 1942 the 8th had agreed to spare eight valuable Liberators to help in the work. The 329th Squadron moved to Flixton airfield, near Bungay, Suffolk, after only a week at Hardwick. Flixton was still in the throes of development when the 329th arrived. Its task was of an experimental nature, involving 'intruder' or 'moling' flights over Germany which attempted to disrupt working schedules in German factories by causing air-raid warnings to sound, thereby upsetting civilian morale and impairing industrial output. Seven 'moling' missions were made over Germany, with the last taking place on 28 March 1943. Some crews later formed the nucleus of the USAAF Pathfinder units set up to perfect blind bombing techniques.

While the 329th was engaged in 'moling' missions, Col Timberlake received orders on 5 December 1942 to lead the 328th and 409th squadrons to North Africa to participate in ten days of disruptive raids against

B-24D-5-CO 41-23816 Black Jack **in the 68th Bomb Squadron (MIA, 1 October 1943), and B-24D-5-CO 41-23817** Suzy Q **in the 67th Bomb Squadron, 44th Bomb Group, the second Liberator group to become operational in the ETO. On 7 November 1942 the 'Flying Eightballs' flew their first mission when eight B-24Ds flew a diversionary sweep to Cap de la Hague in Holland for B-17s attacking the U-boat pens at Brest. Two days later the 44th flew their first combat mission when twelve B-24s, drawn from both the 44th and 93rd Bomb Groups, joined the B-17s in the bombing of St Nazaire.** via Steve Adams

(Below) **In 1942–1943 the small force of Liberators in England were used primarily against French U-boat pens like La Pallice *(pictured)* on the Brittany coast, and as diversion feints for the Fortresses.** USAF

B-24D tunnel gunner manning his .50 calibre machine gun. Note the special headgear which incorporates R/T headphones. Early armament on the B-24D was lacking, particularly in the nose, and the tunnel gun installation was used before the introduction of the ball turret. USAF

Axis ports and shipping. One 330th Liberator crashed into a mountain south of Tafaroui and all aboard were killed. Despite almost non-existent base facilities – first at Tafaroui where bouts of heavy rain turned the short runways into a sea of mud, and then at Gambut Main, where the dry and dusty conditions played havoc with the B-24Ds – the 93rd flew over a score of missions from North Africa, serving with the 12th and later the 9th Air Forces. On 22 February 1943 the 'Travelling Circus', as they now called themselves, flew its 23rd and final mission of the first African Liberator campaign. In the three-month stint in the desert, seven B-24s were lost on missions.

During the 93rd's absence, the 44th Bomb Group carried a torch for the Liberators in the UK. On 6 December the 'Eightballs' flew its first full group mission: a diversionary raid to the airfield at Abbeville-Drucat in Picardy. Crews had flown a great many diversionary missions by now, and had painted ducks on the fuselages of their B-24s, each representing a decoy mission. On this occasion British radar tracked oncoming enemy aircraft, and nearing the French coast an abort signal was radioed to the group – but only the 66th and 67th Squadrons received the signal, leaving six B-24Ds of the 68th Squadron to continue to the target alone. The small force bombed the airfield, but was then bounced by thirty yellow-nosed Fw 190s belonging to the 'Abbeville Kids'. Lt Dubard's Liberator was shot down in flames and it crashed in the Channel, and five more Liberators all received hits. The other crews were saved by the Germans' over-estimation of the Liberators' firepower, in that they did not press home their attacks; losses were therefore not as high as they might have been.

On 20 December Eaker dispatched 101 B-24s and Fortresses to the Romilly-sur-Seine air park for the third time. Nine B-24s were forced to abort with oxygen and machine gun failures; twelve Liberators continued to the target with the Forts. A dozen squadrons of Spitfires flew cover, but they were soon low on fuel and had to return to England just before the bombers reached Rouen. The heavies were met at the coast by yellow- and black-nosed Fw 190s, and although the B-24s were spared, it was a false dawn.

On 3 January 1943 the Americans bombed St Nazaire for the sixth time: 107 bombers were dispatched, but mechanical failures accounted for many aircraft returning to base early, leaving only eight B-24s and sixty-eight Fortresses to continue to the target. The Liberators, being some 20mph (30km/h) faster than the B-17s, started out behind the Fortresses, but by the time they had reached the target the Liberators had caught them and were ready to bomb at a higher altitude. Visibility was unlimited, so an unusually long bomb-run was ordered. B-17s and B-24s were stacked upwards of 20,000 to 22,000ft (6,000 to 6,700m), but their airspeed was reduced by more than half by a 115mph (185km/h) gale during the run-in. The gale was so fierce that the bomb-run took twice as long as that briefed, and for ten minutes the bombers flew almost straight and level, taking all the flak the anti-aircraft gunners could throw at them.

Col Frank Robinson was leading the 44th and he abandoned the bomb-run, and the eight B-24s headed out to sea, jettisoning their bombs as they went. The weather over the target was clear, but their return, at a height of 200ft (60m) above the waves, was made in thick fog; crews could see only a few feet in front of them. When the Liberators neared the Brest Peninsula, however, the fog began to clear. Unfortunately the navigators' reports were ignored, and later the Scilly Isles were mistaken for Brest. Consequently, the small formation flew further and further up the Irish Sea. It was only when the very real threat of internment loomed that Col Robinson led the formation into a turn towards the Bristol Channel. Fuel in the Liberators' tanks was getting low since mission planning had only allowed for landfall at Lizard Point.

Realizing that they had missed Land's End, crews began heading for airfields in Wales. Not many were to be found in this part of Britain, however; Lt John B. Long, in *Texan*, discovered Talbenny airfield, at that time occupied by a Czech squadron, only to have his last engine fail through fuel starvation just as he made his approach. Fortunately all the crew escaped from the Liberator, which was destroyed in

The 44th Bomb Group 'Flying Eightballs' taxi out from their muddy dispersals at Shipdham. B-24D-5-CO 41-23811 *Fascinatin' Witch* **was lost at Wiener Neustadt on 1 October 1943 with Lt Richard Bridges and crew. One of the waist gunners was killed, but the rest were taken prisoner.** USAF

the crash. Others were not so lucky, such as two B-24s which crashed into stone walls obscured by hedges, killing three crewmen and injuring three. *Little Beaver* eventually landed at Talbenny also, and remained there for five days, buffeted by snowstorms. Crews in the 44th Bomb Group arrived back at Shipdham on 8 January to find that the well liked and respected Col Robinson had been replaced by Col Leon Johnson.

On 21 January the Liberators headed for France again, to Escalles-sur-Suchy. Although no B-24Ds were shot down, one which came close was *Liberty Belle*, which was piloted by 1st Lt Keith 'Buck' Cookus in the 67th Bomb Squadron, 44th Bomb Group. Cookus' following account shows graphically just how rugged and dependable the Liberator was when it came to taking punishment:

> We were out over the Pas de Calais. I was leading a section of our B-24s and I had aboard the command pilot, an experienced guy who picks secondary targets for the section and keeps the formation together. The command pilot was Maj W. N. Anderson, who stood between the second pilot and me. I also had a group bombardier, Lt Weiser, and a group gunnery officer, Capt Agar – they had come along for the ride to see how we worked. We met little opposition. We had cloud cover, anyway. We were trying to bomb through cloud and made five runs, but we could not make sure, so we turned back with our bombs.
>
> As we were crossing the French coast we found the Jerries had moved in a bunch of mobile ack-ack. They must have been tracking us quite a time. The first burst was so close I heard it, and I started evasive action. There were twelve of us in the formation, but 30 seconds after that first burst we got it at 11,000ft. It happened so fast we were thrown around completely out of control by the smack of the explosions. Jerry soon got us with seven hits in a bunch. I put the plane into a dive as soon as I got some sort of control and went down as fast as I could 3,000ft to 8,000ft, to get out of the area as quickly as possible, and we were not hit again. But I realized at once that there wasn't much of my plane left – that burst had practically blown us to pieces. One of the shells had burst right inside the bomb-bay, ripping out the catwalk, which holds the bottom of the fuselage together. It also blew Staff Sgt Trechel, the radioman, out of the machine; we never saw him again. It wounded the navigator, Chubby Campbell, and the top turret gunner, Moe Becker. There was a hole in the middle of the plane just as if a shark had taken a bite out of it.
>
> Neither my co-pilot, Tiny Holladay, nor I was touched. Maj Anderson had slumped to the floor of the cockpit and was lying in a heap. 'Take care of the major,' I said to Tiny. I couldn't get any news from the rest of the plane because nothing was working. No. 1 engine had been shot to pieces – that was the second direct hit. It was hanging in shreds, but I managed to feather the airscrew before I lost all of the pressure there. The third direct hit had blown out half of my No. 2 engine – there was nothing left to feather there. I then saw that No. 3 engine was on fire. Kowalski, the engineer, saw the hit on this engine. The flash of the explosion had set it on fire and it was blazing furiously, leaving a long lick of black smoke trailing back, streaked with red. I had to leave it to burn because I couldn't get back to the English coast without letting the motor run as long as it would. I just left it and looked the other way. But I couldn't forget it because it began to fill the plane with gas and oil smoke.
>
> 'The major's in a bad way, Buck,' Tiny yelled. 'He's been hit in the legs and through the back. He's asking for morphia.' We gave the major two shots on the way back to the English coast, but it was clear that he was in bad shape. There had been a direct hit in the base of the nose turret. Splinters sailed up all round Staff Sgt Seifreid, but by a miracle he wasn't hit, although it blew the top right off his turret. He managed to extricate himself from the wreckage and reach the cockpit. He pointed out that we had a direct hit which had gone clean through the right wing. The shell – the seventh they pumped into us – took the right main landing gear with it, and part of it is metal as thick round as your thigh. Tiny shouted at me, 'No use trying to get it down, Butch, we ain't got it with us now.' All the hydraulics were out anyway.
>
> I had to keep that blazing motor going to get us home. I couldn't ditch because we had wounded aboard. I still thought the major would live. So we strung along, going very gingerly. We weren't being attacked anyway. I couldn't give anyone orders about baling out, because the electrical system was shot away. The group bombardier and the group gunnery officer took a jump when they saw half the middle of the ship go west. We were over the coast and the wind should have taken them to land in France.
>
> Just about this time, when we were settling down to the job of getting home safe, the bombardier, Junior Cole, crawled up on the flight deck. Junior, a big guy, was covered with blood. His face looked awful, and he didn't look like Junior at all. The blast had tossed him around, but we found out that he had crawled into the bomb-bay, holding on with his hands and toes to the pieces of twisted metal and wires, anything he could find that was still rooted firmly to the rest of the plane, and he had been tossing out what he could of the mass of shattered bombs in there. The emergency release mechanism was gone. He'd cut his hands to ribbons. He'd come to say there was some he couldn't shift – then he flopped down. He couldn't see, he couldn't talk, and we couldn't get him to move: he just lay there, staring at nothing.
>
> While all this had been going on, the ball turret gunner, Staff Sgt Fong, had managed to get himself out of the ball turret. How he did it, I don't know! His turret was a jangle of twisted stuff like a train wreck, and he thought it was time to move when it began filling with blazing oil from the hydraulics. Fong joined Watbe Boyd, the tail gunner, and the waist gunner.
>
> We were going along all right, heading straight for home and not losing too much height. Then Tiny shouted in my ear: 'Coast!' And I looked, and there it was! At that moment there was a whoosh and a smack that made the plane shake like jelly; what kept her together I couldn't say. I saw that I had no power from No. 3: the engine had blown up. It was white hot, but it had got us home. A petrol pipe exploded and the fire began to look really nasty. It was still burning round the remains of the engine. I said to Tiny; 'How's Anderson?' He said, 'The landing won't hurt him, Buck. He's dead.'
>
> I had brought a plane in on one engine before, but this time the machine was more like a sieve, and practically nothing was working; so what with losing height too fast for me to care much about it, I had to pick a landing spot pretty quickly. We came down [in Kent] in a field – not too bad – but that field went up and down, and up and down again like a switchback. My stalling speed was 140 on account of all the damage she had taken. We shot across that field and its ups and downs like a piece of soap on a bathroom floor, but we were absolutely okay and slowing up in fine shape when I saw a wire fence ahead. We took it and it shook us up. We crashed through it, and when Tiny and I looked up from where we had ducked our heads, we saw a ditch and a hedge ahead. And it was in this ditch that we finished up.

The men in the rear of the Liberator – Fong, Watbe and Kowalski – were sent off to hospital. Cookus, who clambered out of a side window, and Tiny Holladay were uninjured, but Junior Cole died from suffocation in the crash. The rest of the men in the flight deck were trapped as the wrecked Liberator burned. Campbell and Becker were crushed up between the floor and the top, with the sides caved in too. Campbell's wounded legs were held in a vice between the crushed-in roof and the floor, with Anderson's body on one side and Cole's on the other; he was bent double with his head forced down in his knees, and he stayed this way for three hours. British workers – there were about sixty of them at one time – worked like beavers, but they could not put the fire out. When RAF lorries with cranes arrived they pulled the turret off and the trapped men were released and taken to hospital. Tiny, Seifreid and Cookus sat in the field, exhausted. Somehow, against all odds, *Liberty Belle* had made it back. Cookus was awarded the Distinguished Flying Cross.

On 23 January, forty-eight Fortresses and six Liberators in the 44th Bomb Group mounted raids on the U-boat pens at Lorient and Brest. Three B-17s were shot down by German fighters employing head-on attacks for the first time, and one other was lost to flak. The deputy lead ship in the 44th became the fourth bomber lost when an Fw 190 pilot attacked head-on and failed to pull out in time, colliding with the Liberator. Both aircraft crashed into the North Sea from 20,000ft (6,000m). By the end of the month casualties exceeded replacements, with only twenty-four B-17 and B-24 crews arriving to replace sixty-seven lost on missions during January. Now, while the future of VIII Bomber Command as a separate bombing force was in the balance, Eaker answered his critics by sending his heavies to bomb Germany for the first time.

On 27 January, sixty-four B-17s were assigned the U-boat construction yards at Vegasak on the Weser, while the Liberators flew a diversionary raid on Wilhelmshaven. The 44th Bomb Group failed to locate their target, so crews bombed through cloud somewhere near the Dutch–German border. Navigation went uncorrected and the 44th continued out over Friesland and encountered heavy fighter opposition. *The Spirit of 76*, flown by Lt Maxwell W. Sullivan, was shot down, and 1st Lt Nolan B. Cargyle's B-24 was destroyed in a mid-air collision when an Fw 190 careered into it after being hit by machine-gun fire from another B-24. Lt Jim O'Brien barely made it home in *The Rugged Buggy*. His bombardier, Lt Reg Grant, and his assistant radio-operator, Staff Sgt M. Deal, had both been killed and his navigator, Lt Leroy Perlowin, was severely wounded by a 20mm shell which also slightly injured one of his gunners, Sgt Guilford. Although the bombing of Vegasack was described as 'fair', the press lauded the B-17 crews while the Liberator crews received barely a mention.

Bad weather grounded the 8th for much of early February. Then on the 15th, twenty-one B-24s of the 44th Bomb Group crossed the Channel and attempted to bomb the *Togo*, a German nightfighter control ship which was holed up in Dunkirk. The *Togo* was equipped with a whole range of sophisticated early-warning radar, fighter ground-control radar, and a height-finding system for air-raid warning radars, and it was being moved up to the German Bight to fill a gap in the Ostmark area. *Betty Anne–Gallopin' Ghost*, the lead ship flown by Capt Arthur V. Cullen with Maj Donald W. MacDonald, the 67th Squadron CO, took a direct hit over the docks: for a few moments the noseless bomber flew on, only to fall away to starboard with the port inboard engine aflame and the right inboard ripped from its mounting. Finally the starboard wing fell off, and a huge explosion scattered debris among the formation. 1st Lt Rufus A. Oliphant and his crew in *Railway Express* were shot down by enemy fighters and all the crew were killed.

Capt Thomas Cramer, pilot of *Captain And His Kids*, had three engines shot out in the attack, but still managed to cross the Channel and put the Liberator down on the beach at Sandwich. Cullen and MacDonald had meanwhile baled out. Cullen, who had a broken leg, hit the tail-plane and broke his arm, and his leg a second time. MacDonald died later in a German hospital; Cullen was finally repatriated in September 1944. Despite all the 44th's efforts, the *Togo* remained afloat. The *Togo* was renamed the *Rudolf Luck* in September 1943, and would keep this name until the end of the war, when she was renamed the *Svalbard* and put back into service again as a merchant vessel. It is thought that the name '*Togo*' was shortened from Togoland, a German protectorate in Africa before World War I, but which Germany lost when the territory was confiscated by the Treaty of Versailles.

Next day, 16 February, Howard Moore assumed command of the 67th Squadron and led them to St Nazaire. Col Leon Johnson flew group lead. Shortly after leaving the English coast, Lt Fred M. Billings' B-24D, *SNAFU*, fell away to port and hit the port wing-tip of Lt John B. Long's *Texan II* and locked there. Seconds later both planes exploded, scattering debris into the Fortress formation below. Amazingly, four men were thrown clear, but Air-Sea Rescue found no trace of them in the murky sea.

On 25 February the 93rd Bomb Group returned from North Africa and landed at Hardwick, in Norfolk. Next day the B-17s and the 44th Bomb Group headed for Bremen, but heavy undercast forced the bombers to abort the primary target and seek their secondary target at Wilhelmshaven. About thirty miles from the coast they were attacked by fighters, and these were so determined in their mission that they kept up their attacks all the way into the target. *Sad Sack*, a 66th Bomb Squadron, 44th Bomb Group ship flown by 1st Lt Robert H. McPhillamey and 1st Lt Wilbur E. Wockenfuss, was attacked by fighters shortly before they reached the IP. Two engines were shot out and set on fire, and the oxygen was shot out, too, and a fire started in the bomb-bay. 2nd Lt Rexford W. Lippert, the navigator, bailed out. Sgt Alberto O. Salvo, the belly gunner, was hit in the shoulder and chest, and in several other places, but managed to bale out with the rest; but he died in hospital shortly thereafter. Wockenfuss dragged his unconscious engineer, Sgt Eugene Rudiger, to the bomb-bay by grabbing him by the collar of his fur flying jacket and dropping him out. Wockenfuss saw him later, on the ground, and commented that he looked 'like he had been through a meat grinder'; Rudiger must have regained consciousness on the way down and pulled the rip-cord. Wockenfuss, McPhillamey and three others survived from *Sad Sack*.

Maisie, flown by Capt Howard Adams, was the second ship in the 44th Bomb Group which was shot down by fighters, victim to the guns of Leutnant Heinz Knoke of I./JG1 who made a frontal attack and scored hits in the Liberator's right wing. On his second frontal attack Knoke kept firing until he had to swerve to avoid a collision. *Maisie* caught fire and sheered away from the formation in a wide sweep to the right. Twice more Knoke attacked, this time diving from above the tail. Aboard the doomed B-24, the gunners continued firing until the fire spread along the right wing which then broke off: the stricken Liberator plunged vertically, spinning into the depths. One crew member attempted to bale out, but his parachute was in flames. At 3,000ft (900m) *Maisie*

Top brass visit the 93rd Bomb Group at Hardwick, Norfolk, on 27 April 1943. To the right of the cameraman is Brig Gen James P. Hodges, Commander, 2nd Bomb Wing. On his left is Gen Frank M. Andrews, and on his left is Col Ted Timberlake, CO, 93rd Bomb Group. Behind them is a 44th Bomb Group B-24D from Shipdham. 'Ted's Travelling Circus' provided three B-24 detachments to North Africa: December 1942–February 1943, June–August 1943, and September–October 1943, while the 329th and 330th Bomb Squadrons assisted Anti-submarine Command in the Bay of Biscay from bases in south-west England from October–November 1942. via Steve Adams

exploded and disintegrated. Only two men survived from Adam's ship: Wayne Gotke, navigator, who was picked up after 'dangling between two trees about twenty feet in the air for about twenty-five minutes', afraid that if he unbuckled, he would fall; and Staff Sgt James W. Mifflin, assistant radio man. Among the dead was Harvard graduate, Robin Perkins Post, a thirty-two year old *New York Times* reporter. Five other reporters, including Andy Rooney of the *Stars and Stripes* and Walter Cronkite of *United Press*, flew with the B-17s, and all returned safely.

Night Raider, also called *Heavenly Hideaway*, a 93rd Bomb Group B-24D piloted by Capt Beattie H. 'Bud' Fleenor, was also attacked by fighters of JG1. The events that followed caught the attention of Cpl Carrol Stewart, a *Stars and Stripes* staff writer:

> At the briefing, the Liberator known as *Night Raider* was tagged for one of the hot spots, an outside position on the next-to-the-last V-formation. That was nothing new: since early the previous October *Night Raider* had been a veteran of flight over enemy territory – though never, despite its name, in a night raid. The skipper, Capt Bud Fleenor, twenty-five, of Manhattan, Kansas, was at the wheel as usual. The Kansas State College alumnus tucked his long, gangly legs into the compartment while the engines warmed; beside him sat the co-pilot, 1st Lt J. J. Leary, twenty-five, from Omaha, Nebraska. *Night Raider* went thundering down the runway and the take-off was uneventful; a few spurts of lead were fired into the thin air or into a cloud bank as the gunners warmed and tested the guns.
>
> Then things began to go wrong. As the raiders reached the Dutch coast and enemy opposition began to appear, Sgt Elmer W. Dawley, nineteen, the youngest of the crew, passed out in the high altitude: his oxygen mask was frozen. Staff Sgt T. J. Kilmer, also nineteen, waist gunner went to investigate and found icicles on the kid's eyelashes. The effort to revive Dawley, plus oxygen trouble of his own, soon had Kilmer himself unconscious, clinging desperately to wire cables that control the tail assembly. The skipper and Leary managed to stay in formation.
>
> Tech Sgt Louis Szabo, twenty-eight, the 150lb [68kg] waist gunner and engineer had an almost impossible task in trying to release Kilmer's grip, his own mask being torn from his face in the struggle. A few moments later Kilmer relaxed, and lay there blacked out, unconscious. As they approached the target, flak was puffing all around; cannon hits were heard; and shrapnel was spraying the fuselage everywhere. Enemy fighters had already made an estimated thirty passes at the *Raider*, and even when the flak was heaviest they continued to attack. Then the *Raider* began its run, its yawning bomb-bay doors wide open. Wilhelmshaven rocked under the bursts: 2nd Lt George A. Pinner, twenty-five, the bombardier, had pin-pointed his mark. But trouble mounted fast as this B-24 limped back toward England, its big belly empty. The supercharger was knocked out, ack-ack fire was intense, and German fighters were still submitting them to deadly attack – even a destroyer lying thousands of feet below in a Dutch harbour sent up a barrage of flak and hot lead.
>
> The *Night Raider* made its way doggedly into the clear, high over the Zeider Zee. The sister ships that had led the attack were now disappearing, far out on the horizon. The skipper knew the *Raider* couldn't possibly catch them up, not with the supercharger out and one engine dead, the result of enemy cannon fire. The radio, too, was dead, so it was impossible to to call for help. Staff Sgt Robert P. Jungbluth, twenty-four, the fair-headed radio operator, left his position on the flight deck to administer first aid to Kilmer, whose face was now purple. Others who saw him thought he was dead, but 'Jung' fixed an oxygen supply on him and worked hard with artificial respiration and finally Kilmer showed signs of life.
>
> By now the *Raider* was losing altitude as one of the remaining three engines began to vibrate and cough. Jung left the reviving Kilmer and worked on Dawley, the tunnel gunner who had been unconscious since first reaching the Dutch coast. Ellis left the nose to go to the rear and lend a hand. 'Big Jung saved the lives of those two fellows, all right,' The North Carolinian testified later. Then the skipper sent word for Ellis to hurry back to his gun in the nose because more trouble was brewing. Jungbluth took over one of the waist guns, and Szabo was on the other.
>
> Suddenly twenty German fighters appeared, Fw 190s, Me 109s, Me 110s and Ju 88s; they had been lurking in the sky in the hope of picking up a straggler, and this was their chance. Peeling

out of the bright sunlight, they came in a vicious running attack that was to last for forty minutes. *Night Raider* had taken care of enemy fighters before – one, two or three at a time – but this was different. Capt Fleenor eyed a large friendly cloud in the distance, perhaps a half-hour away at the speed they were travelling. It was their only hope – and a slim hope at that.

The guns of Sgt Edward M. Bates, twenty-two, the curly-haired 175lb [80kg] tail gunner, had long been silent – they had frozen up tight after he had poured only eight volleys into the Huns on the way to the target. He was bluffing now, training the sights on the Mes and Fws as they came in. 'One Ju 88 sat out there, about two hundred yards off our tail, for several minutes. I could have shut my eyes and hit him if my guns had been working,' he complained from a hospital bed, where his hands and face, frozen early in the flight, were being treated. One Jerry planted a 20mm shell inside the rear turret, barely missing him and causing the hydraulic fluid to spurt from the turret mechanism in numerous places. 1st Lt Earle E. Ellis, twenty-five, the navigator, and Pinner were pulling their triggers on everything that came into sight, and up in the top turret Staff Sgt Ronald L. Nelson, thirty-one, was shooting round 360 degrees – he didn't even have time to 'follow through on the shots'. Later he said, 'I was shooting over 2 o'clock for an Me 110 when an Me 109 came in from 11:30, putting a 20mm into one engine – if he'd been any lower he'd have sure hit Capt Fleenor and Lt Leary, and if he'd been any higher he'd have hit me!'

Dawley picked off an Me 11C. Big Jung hadn't been on Kilmer's waist gun long when he sent one Me 109 plunging in flames into the sea, and Szabo bagged another off the starboard side. Besides the three knocked down for certain, there were three 'probables': 'An Fw 190 came toward us,' Szabo recounted later. 'His wings were pure red, and I could almost see the lead coming point-blank. I froze onto the trigger. His left wing dropped off and he went hellbent into the water. But he'd fired first, and he hit Jung and me. I knew Jung was hurt worse than I was because I looked up and saw part of his arm hanging above the window – then looked around and saw his side intact. The 20mm blast had ripped his arm from his body! The shrapnel had hit us both.' Kilmer began to administer morphine and 'sulfa' to Big Jung, the Staff Sgt who'd saved his life a few minutes earlier. 'When I got to look around, I realized I was injured pretty bad,' said Jung later from his hospital bed. 'We'd been expecting the end for so long that we figured things couldn't be much worse.'

All the while there was no respite for Ellis, Pinner and Nelson, and their guns blazed steadily. Nelson, from the circular top turret, was covering the 'dead spots' where *Night Raider*'s fifties had been silenced – there wasn't even a split-second time for 'intercom' orders or questions. The skipper knew his boys in the back were 'catching hell' – but he also knew that the big cloud formation was much nearer now. Ammunition was getting low: Szabo's gun had only three shells left when he was hit. Dawley's parachute was hit and began to blaze. Then suddenly, Fleenor put the *Raider* into a dive, and they disappeared into the cloud. There was no gunfire: visibility was almost nil. 'Four Jerries followed us in,' one crewman related, 'but that was the last we saw of them.'

Night Raider was still some distance from England, however, and gaping holes as big as a fist were draining precious gasoline. Ellis, the navigator, gave the skipper a course to steer. Nelson went out on the catwalk, checked the remaining gasoline, and diverted it to the two good motors. None of the fuel gauges was working, and one engine was cut and feathered. Pinner went back and helped adjust Mae West life preservers, because a dunking in the North Sea seemed imminent. As Szabo said afterwards, 'I figured Jung and I wouldn't have a chance if we were forced down at sea.' Big Jung himself said later, 'I guess everyone took time to pray.' Bates climbed out of the tail turret to stand guard with a waist gun. 'How are you doin', Lou?' he asked. 'OK,' was the reply from Szabo. And Jung recalled, 'When Bates shouted, "There's land!" I knew our prayers had been answered!'

Both the skipper and Pinner had been in the rear helping Kilmer, who was doing a superb job of administering first aid. Dawley had taken over Szabo's gun. Ellis' uncanny navigation had steered Fleenor and Leary straight for the nearest landing field, and England's friendly coastline fields stretched out below. Emerging from the cloud at 1,500ft, the *Raider*'s two engines struggled and strained to climb to 5,000ft. 'Just as we reached the coast,' Fleenor explained later, 'our two remaining engines petered out – we were out of gas.'

The wounded didn't know that the undercarriage had been shot out, that the hydraulic system was knocked out, that the tyres were punctured and that a forced crashlanding was inevitable. The skipper sent word round that he'd 'have to crack 'er down'. Ellis and Pinner went backship again to arrange the wounded in such fashion as to lighten the shock. Dawley held Szabo in his lap to cushion his side, and Kilmer lay down with one arm around Jung's body and used his free arm as a brace. But the shock never came. Skilfully the skipper set the *Raider* down [at Ludham, Norfolk]. Said Ellis, 'It was a smoother landing than when we had wheels!'

The groundcrew chiefs handed the skipper this report on *Night Raider*'s wounds: the hydraulic and power lines in the tail turret were shot out, as were the primers, intakes, carburettors, oil coolers and oxygen regulators; the undercarriages wouldn't work; the tyres were punctured; there was a 15in hole in the right tail-flap; there were forty-seven .30 calibre holes and five 20mm holes in the rear fuselage; sixteen .30s and four cannon in the left fin; five .30s and one cannon in the stabilizers; nine .30s and four cannon in the right wing; three .30s in the right aileron; twelve .30s in the top fuselage; thirty-six .30s in the left wing; twenty-seven .30s in the bomb-bay doors; and all gun barrels were 'burned out'. One groundcrew man muttered, 'This one shouldn't have come back.' But it had, and so had the crew, and death had been cheated into taking a holiday.

(Bud Fleenor and his crew went down in the Channel on 16 April in *Missouri Sue*, though the bombardier had baled out over France.)

Altogether, the February missions cost twenty-two aircraft. On 6 March, sixty-three B-17s bombed the powerplant, bridge and port area at Lorient, while fifteen B-24s made a diversionary raid on a bridge and U-boat facilities at Brest. Two days later, thirteen Liberators bombed the marshalling yard at Rouen in a diversionary raid to aid the B-17s attacking another marshalling yard at Rennes. The American escort encountered heavy opposition and the B-24s were left to fend for themselves. 1st Lt James E. O'Brien from the 68th Bomb Squadron started out leading the Eightballs in *The Rugged Buggy* – Lt James Posey, the future 44th Bomb Group commanding officer, was also aboard – but Sgt Huseltine, one of the gunners, passed out through lack of oxygen and O'Brien was forced to return to base.

Capt Clyde E. Price of the 67th Bomb Squadron in *Miss Dianne* took over the group lead, and 1st Lt Bob W. Blaine moved up to the deputy lead. Soon after, their troubles started, when Fw 190s of JG26 attacked from head-on. Unfortunately for the bombers, the Spitfires had met heavy opposition from the Third *Gruppe* of JG26 led by Maj (later Oberst) Josef 'Pips' Priller, and the Eightballs were forced to fend for themselves. At first, crews mistook the Fw 190s of the Second *Gruppe* for Thunderbolts because of their similar radial engines, and it was all too late when they realized that they were not P-47s, but the dreaded yellow-nosed Fw

190s, otherwise known as 'The Abbeville Kids'. The fighter attack on the Flying Eightballs was led by Oblt Wilhelm-Ferdinand 'Wutz' Galland, brother of Generalmajor Adolf Galland, who led his Fw 190s of II/JG26 in a tight turn to go 'von Schnauze auf Schnauze' (snout to snout).

Miss Dianne and Lt Blaine's B-24 went down immediately. Only three gunners survived from Price's ship, which crashed in flames at Totes at 14:04 hours with the bombs still in their racks. Blaine's ship had been singled out by Uffz Peter Crump: he had fired a long burst at the B-24 from long range, and could see clearly a number of hits in the cockpit area. He dived away in split-S, then saw to his horror that he was immediately in the way of Blaine's jettisoned bombs. He managed to miss them in a tight turn, but lost sight of his target and could not say which of the falling aircraft was his kill (Blaine's B-24 crashed at Barentin at 14:05): he saw one of the doomed Liberators crash in a patch of trees north of the Seine, but without a witness he would not be awarded confirmation of his victory. Instead it went to Ofw Roth. The Spitfire escort finally showed up in time to prevent further losses. Even so, two Liberators barely made it back to Shipdham. *Peg*, a 93rd Bomb Group Liberator, was attacked by Oblt Johannes Naumann of II/JG26, but managed to limp back across the Channel; it crashed at Bredhurst, Kent. At Shipdham, the ill-fated 67th Squadron was now reduced to only three of its original crews and aircraft. (Jackson Hall had been grounded for medical reasons, leaving only the crews of *Suzy Q* and *Little Beaver*, and that of 'Bucky' Warnes, out of the original nine crews.)

On 12 and 13 March the bombers hit marshalling yards in France, and good fighter cover helped to prevent any loss to the bombers. Some 93rd Bomb Group Liberators joined the 44th Bomb Group in flying effective diversion raids for the Fortresses. With morale high, on 18 March seventy-three Fortresses and twenty-four B-24s – the highest number of heavies yet dispatched – headed for the Vulcan Shipbuilding yards at Vegasack. For almost one and three-quarter hours the Liberators came under attack, although only one B-24, belonging to the 93rd Bomb Group, was shot down. The run into the target was good and bombing was successful, but on the return leg the Luftwaffe stepped up its attacks, sometimes with as many as thirty fighters taking part.

Shoot Luke, in the 93rd Bomb Group, came in for heavy attacks, as John H. Murphy recalled later:

> The trip was uneventful until we reached our altitude, about fifty miles off the German coast, and from then on we were under constant fighter attack for an hour and forty-five minutes. Our run into the target was a good one and the bombing results 'excellent', but as we turned away from the target and headed for home the fighters by that time were really getting warmed up; at one time a mass attack developed in which about thirty enemy fighters attacked our nine ship element. One of these hit the #4 engine on Frank Lown's ship, our ex-co-pilot, and blew a large hole in the vertical stabilizer. Next, the twin-engined fighters took us on. They weren't as fast as the single-engined boys, and it was more nerve-racking because their attacks were slower and took longer to complete and break away – just as you'd think they couldn't shoot any more they'd skid their ship so that they could get in a longer burst at us. Finally these left, but then Frank's #4 engine began to smoke and vibrate very badly and he had to drop out of formation. All of us voted to go help him home. We left formation and took up a position off his wing.
>
> Suddenly, one lonely Fw 190 appeared out of nowhere. He looked us over, and came in low to attack from 9 o'clock with his four cannon and machine guns firing. There was a sudden explosion and I knew we'd been hit. I glanced over at George Black. He was OK, even if three slugs had missed his head by less than eighteen inches. The fighters had hit us with two cannon shells and about six machine-gun slugs. The cannon shells had both hit the rear part of the ship where they had exploded, one fragment going into Tech Sgt Floyd Mabee's eye and causing him several other very painful wounds. In spite of this he remained at his post, and not only continued to fire his guns, but he shot down the fighter that had hit us ... In a worse state, however, was Staff Sgt Paul B. Slankard, the tail gunner, whose left leg had been almost blown off by a cannon shell that had penetrated his left buttock and then exploded; it was only through the outstanding job of first aid performed by the bombardier, Ed Janic, that he was kept from bleeding to death.

Vegasack was officially described as 'extremely heavily damaged', and flushed with this success, on 22 March the heavies attacked Wilhelmshaven. However, flak claimed Capt 'Bucky' Warne's B-24D in the 67th Bomb Squadron, and a 506th Squadron replacement ship also went down. Lt Robert Walker was the sole survivor from the B-24s. This left *Little Beaver* and *Suzy Q* as the only remaining original Liberators in the squadron. Col Ted Timberlake, who was leading the 93rd in *Teggie Ann*, narrowly escaped death when a 20mm shell entered the cockpit and missed him by just a few inches. Four days later Col Timberlake assumed command of the 201st Provisional Combat Wing; his position was replaced, on 17 May, by Lt Col Addison T. Baker.

During April and early May of 1943 the Liberators were relegated to a supporting role for many weeks while the B-17s again took centre stage. Then on 14 May, Eaker mounted a maximum effort against Kiel, and to their chagrin the Liberator crews, despite their higher speed, had to fly behind the Fortresses to the target. The B-24D pilots zig-zagged to the target 20 miles (34km) in one direction and 40 miles (68km) in the other in order to remain behind the slower Forts while trying at the same time to maintain 180mph (290km/h) at a height of only 500ft (150m) to avoid detection by enemy radar. The Eightballs were fired on by flak batteries on the Friesian Islands, and *Victory Ship*, flown by 1st Lt Tommy Holmes, the B Flight leader of the 68th Bomb Squadron, was hit and he was forced to abort. Capt John W. 'Swede' Swanson's *Wicked Witch* was also damaged by flak in the No. 2 engine before the target, and the ship was finished off by enemy fighters making head-on attacks; Swanson and three others were the only survivors from the nine-man crew.

Altogether, five B-24Ds were shot down by enemy fighters, including three belonging to the 67th Squadron, which brought up the rear of the formation. The first to go down was Lt William Roach and his replacement crew in *Annie Oakley 'Crack Shot'*; there were only two survivors. Then *Miss Dolores*, piloted by Lt Robert I. Brown, was hit by flak over the target, knocking out all four engines; two men were killed, but the remainder managed to bale out, and were made prisoners of war.

The third 67th Squadron Liberator lost was *Little Beaver*, piloted by Capt Chester 'George' Phillips, shot down after leaving the target. Only four men from the eleven-man crew survived after three explosions rocked the ship. One was caused by a 20mm cannon shell which exploded in the nose and ignited the hydraulic fluid accumulators; the flight deck became a mass of flames and Phillips and Everett W. Wilborn Jr, the co-pilot, were killed. The aircraft went into a flat spin. Sgt Mike Denny, the engineer, put on his parachute and then tried to extinguish the flames, but his efforts were in vain. He could not get the bomb-bay doors open so he baled out through one of the waist windows. 1st Lt Tom E. Bartmess, navigator, baled out of the aircraft, and about three minutes later 1st Lt William E. 'Chubby' Hill, bombardier, followed. Bartmess landed in the water but became tangled in the shrouds of his parachute and drowned. Hill landed on dry land suffering from blows on the forehead caused by the opening of his parachute and the landing, a bruised back and shock. Hill, together with Staff Sgt Dale A. Glaubitz, assistant engineer, and Staff Sgt Charles C. Forehand, one of the waist gunners, were the only survivors.

Scrappy, piloted by Lt John Y. Reed in the 66th Squadron, became the sixth and final loss to the 44th Bomb Group. Badly damaged over the target, Reed nursed the B-24 back to Shipdham where ten of the crew baled out. *Scrappy* had to be shot down by RAF Spitfires. Of the nineteen Liberators, only thirteen returned. Maj Moore's *Suzy Q* was now the sole survivor of the original 67th Bomb Squadron. The 44th Bomb Group was awarded a DUC for its part in the Kiel raid, the first made to an 8th Air Force group.

On 17 May, the tension began again when thirty-five B-24Ds in the 44th and 93rd Bomb Groups attacked Bordeaux. Col Leon Johnson, Gen Hodges and the crew of the *Suzy Q*, which had just been fitted with four new Twin Wasps, led twenty-one B-24s, followed closely by eighteen B-24Ds in the 93rd. The Liberators flew a 700-mile (1,130km) arc over the Atlantic to minimize the chances of detection. Four were forced to abort with mechanical troubles, but those that bombed scored hits on the lock gates at Basin Number One, which collapsed and was flooded by a deluge of water from a nearby river. Direct hits were observed on the Matford aero-engine factory, and the railway yards and chemical works were also hit. The only casualties during the attack were two crewmen slightly wounded, and Tech Sgt Harry C. Hogan, left waist gunner in Capt John Diehl's B-24 *Black Jack*, who was sucked out of an open window after his parachute had accidentally opened; he was thrown against the tail-plane and pitched into the sea with his parachute in shreds. *Avenger II*, piloted by 1st Lt Ray L. Hillard in the 66th Bomb Squadron, 44th Bomb Group, was forced to seek neutral Spain after developing engine trouble shortly before the attack. Hillard landed at Alama de Aragon, north west of Saragozza, and he and his crew were repatriated via Gibraltar two weeks later.

Officers and men of the 68th Bomb Squadron, 44th Bomb Group at Shipdham early in 1943. The CO, Maj James E. O'Brien, is fifth from the left *(seated)*, second row. Maj O'Brien and his crew were shot down in B-24D-5-CO 41-23819 *The Rugged Buggy* **on 14 May 1943 when the Eightballs bombed Kiel, and he and most of his crew were made PoWs.** USAF

Bad weather throughout the latter part of May restricted deep penetration missions, and the one on 29 May to La Pallice proved to be the last of the high-level combat operations for some time for both the 44th and 93rd Bomb Groups. Despite the dissimilarities between the B-24 and the B-17, the Liberator was not giving way to the Fortress in the ETO as some might have thought; it was simply that the B-24 groups were to train for yet another role, and for one that the Fortress was totally unsuited. This is perhaps a good juncture at which to pause and pose the question, which is the better heavy, the B-17 or the B-24? Tech Sgt Donald V. Chase, a gunner, flew on both, and it was a 'Catch 22' situation, as he recalls:

> Our crew were assigned from one to the other and then back again, and we endured a frustrating two-month period in the spring of '43 as the AAF played yo-yo with our bomber allegiance. Prior to our first frustration we ten eager airmen lined up in a hangar near Lincoln, Nebraska and received our Pacific gear: shark repellent, machetes, .45s etc. We were scheduled to leave Lincoln the next morning for points west, far west: soon the infamous warriors of Japan would pay the consequences for Pearl Harbor!
>
> But the following morning found us again lined up in the hangar. Disheartened, we had to return all the gear because our pilot, Charles 'Whit' Whitlock, had received new orders: our B-24 was summarily taken and we were sent to Salinas, Kansas, for a spot of transitional B-17 training. What a blow! We cursed the US Army and reviled the stupid Pentagoners. Oh, how we bitched! Finally Harold Schwau, our bombardier, having obviously had his fill of gripers, said something to the effect that, 'If you don't like the transfer, go home to your mommies.' He stressed the word 'mommies'.
>
> The transition wasn't all that bad – we adjusted okay, and in fact, the '17s proved to be good ships. They didn't have the speed, range or bomb capacity of the '24s, but they were really manoeuvrable, reliable, airworthy craft. Their empennages at least were sturdy, a feature that some early model '24s lacked. Checked out, more or less, in our '17, we left Kansas for Prestwick, Scotland, with a refuelling stop and weather briefing at Gander, Newfoundland before we were to cross the Pond. However, reports of heavy Atlantic weather and unfavourable winds kept us grounded for about two weeks – until finally we were given the green light and headed east. About two dozen B-17s, replacement crews for various ETO groups, accompanied us, strung out in very loose formation, staying only close enough for mutual observation.

Their crossing was marked by rough air, high cloud, turbulence and embedded thunderstorms, and crews had to make a choice between wave-hopping with the other low-roaders and so fighting unpredicted headwinds, or staying on top. Whitlock's crew for one, stayed on top and reached as much as 30,150ft (9,200m) – if the altimeter was correct – largely because ahead and to the sides, flat-topped anvils crowned the cumulonimbus. They took evasive action through airy canyons between swollen thunderheads. As Don Chase recalls:

> After landing at Prestwick, we performed the half serious, half frivolous ritual of testing earth's solidity and affectionately patting the plane's fuselage, a natural follow-up to the end of a scary

Capt Chester 'George' Phillips and his crew at dispersal at Shipdham early in 1943. Phillips (KIA) and his crew were lost flying B-24D-5-CO 41-23807 Little Beaver ***(behind)*** **on 14 May 1943.** Bill Cameron Collection

B-24D-15-CF 42-63960 YO-C Dorothy **of the 564th Bomb Squadron, 389th Bomb Group, over the North Sea** en route **for the enemy coast. The 'Sky Scorpions' were the third B-24D group to arrive in England, but they did not fly their first mission until 9 July 1943, by which time they had moved to North Africa to take part in the bombing of Italy. The 389th flew their first mission from Hethel, England, on 7 September 1943.** USAF

flight. Our '17 was like a giant incarnate; a beautiful, high-soaring, life-saving sweetheart. Confidently, we knew she'd carry us safely through our combat tour. No sir, average-weighted '24s could never have topped those clouds!

Unexpectedly our exuberance was short-lived. The first depressing news we received was that only one of the five low-roader '17s had made it safely across the water: apparently the other four had run out of fuel before reaching Ireland or Scotland. A second blow was the news of our fresh orders: leave the '17 at Prestwick, proceed to Shipdham to join the 44th 'Flying Eightballs'] and prepare to re-orientate ourselves with the flight characteristics of the B-24. Shafted again!

It was bomb-aimer Harold Schwab – unflappable, wry-humoured Schwab – who arrested our mutinous stirrings: 'Navigator,' he addressed Robert Ricks, 'Which way is west?' Ricks pointed. Deadpan and wordless, Schwab picked up his B4 bag and started to walk away. 'Hey, where you going Schwab?' someone asked.

'Home,' he answered. 'I'm just not interested in this war any more.' Perhaps it was the humour, sardonic or genuine, that helped us through several unpleasant incidents both in training and, for a while, in combat.

Unbeknown to us at the time, the Ploesti low-level mission was less than two months away, and in preparation, the '24s were hedge-hopping over the English countryside. So from recently testing the ultimate height that a '17 could fly, we soon found ourselves in the company of dozens of '24s, nestled wing to wing, skimming the greenery like speedy fighter bombers. A '17 just didn't have the range to make a Lybia-Ploesti round trip; nor could it match our Lib's bomb load and low-level speed, either. And wasn't that the name of the strategic air war anyway, range and payload? Catch 17, 24!

B-24D Nana **in the 389th Bomb Group showing a pair of twin .50s in the nose and the addition of two more (field modification at Hethel).** The late Russ D. Hayes Collection

CHAPTER THREE

'Tidal Wave'

The Low-level Mission to Ploesti, 1 August 1943

By the end of June 1942 the Allied situation in the Middle East was extremely precarious and Egypt was expected to fall to the Axis. In order to help relieve the pressure, a heavy bombing raid was ordered against the oil-fields at Ploesti on the Rumanian plains, 50 miles (80km) north of Bucharest. In World War II it was the greatest single source of fuel for the German war machine in all Europe, and in 1941 refined a large portion of the 2.1 million tons of Rumanian oil supplied to the Third Reich. To bomb it and destroy it would be a great boost for the Allies' morale.

Gen Lewis Brereton was summoned from India with 'such heavy bombers as were available' – but the only ones that could be spared were twenty-three B-24Ds which were en route to join the 10th Air Force in China. This detachment, codenamed 'HALPRO', was commanded by Col Harry H. Halverson, who had been entrusted with the ambitious task of bombing Tokyo from the Chinese mainland. The detachment

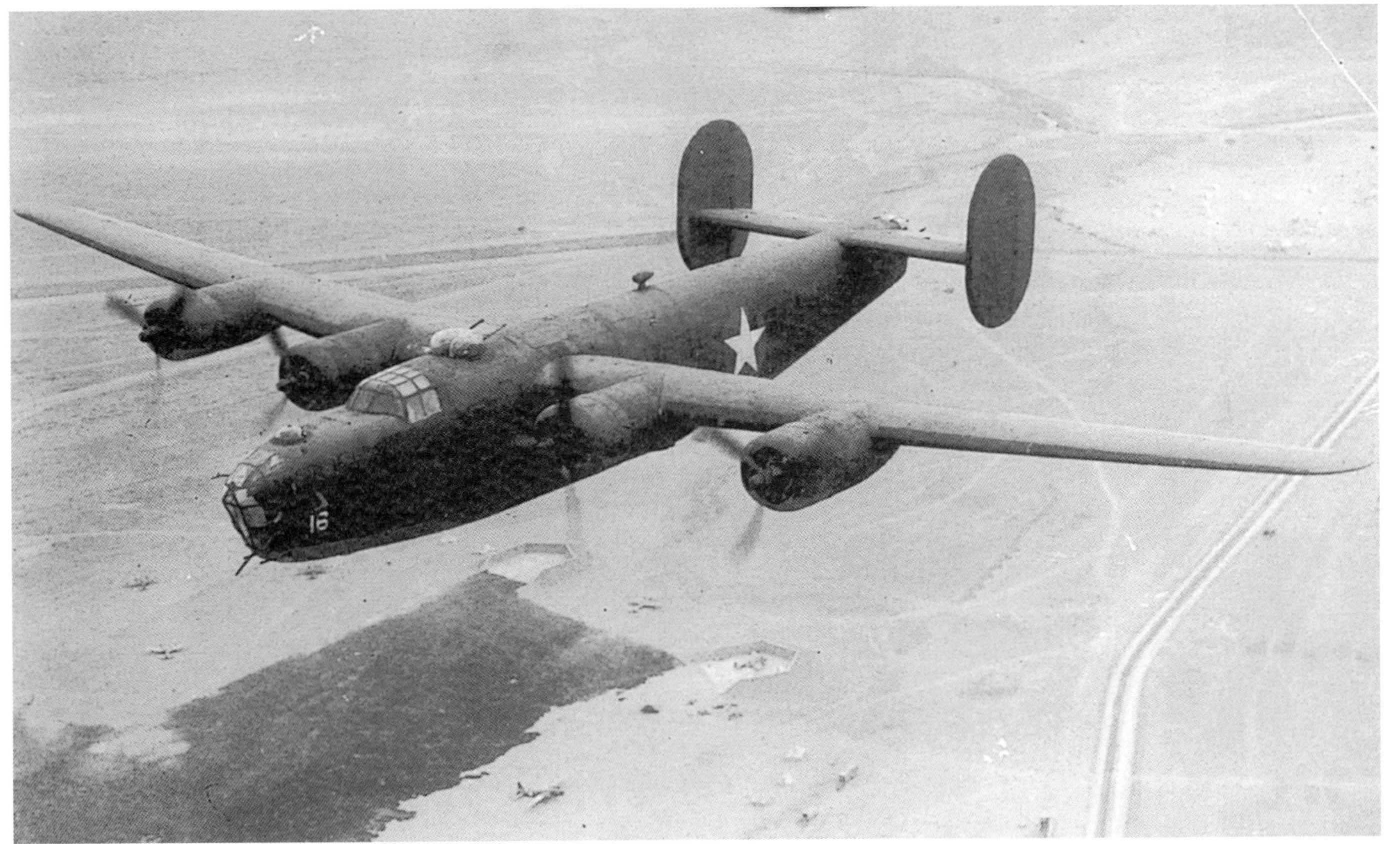

B-24D 41-11622 Edna Elizabeth **of the 'HALPRO' detachment, commanded by Col Harry H. Halverson; in June 1943 HALPRO carried out the first bombing raid on the Ploesti oilfields in Rumania from Fayid, an airport on the Great Bitter Lake near the Suez Canal. Originally, Halverson's twenty-three B-24Ds were to join the 10th Air Force in China and bomb Tokyo from the Chinese mainland. The detachment was held in Egypt to bomb Ploesti, which they did on 11 and 12 June when thirteen B-24Ds were dispatched individually to the refineries complex. Little material damage was caused, but the Ploesti had been raided and American heavy bombers had bombed a European target for the first time. No Liberators were shot down on the mission, and all, including** Edna Elizabeth **which put down near Ankara, Turkey, were able to land in neutral countries.** USAF

Early in 1943 only two B-24D Liberator groups in the 9th Air Force were based in North Africa. One was the 98th Bomb Group, otherwise known as the 'Pyramiders', and the other was the 376th Bomb Group, better known as the 'Liberandos'. Pictured here is *Fertile Myrtle* **of the 415th Bomb Squadron, 98th Bomb Group.** via Mike Bailey

was held at Fayid, an airport on the Great Bitter Lake near the Suez Canal, and their target was changed to Ploesti. Halverson's B-24Ds could just make it to the objective, but they would be operating at their absolute extreme range because from the North African coast to Ploesti is over 1,100 miles (1,770km). For this reason the plan called for the B-24Ds to proceed to airfields in Iraq after the bombing.

Late in the evening of 11 June, thirteen B-24Ds took off from Fayid and proceeded individually to the refineries complex at Ploesti. At dawn on the morning of 12 June they arrived over their target and began their bomb-runs. Ten of them bombed through solid cloud cover and hit the Astra-Romana Refinery, while one B-24 blasted the port of Constanta. Another two released their bombs on unidentified targets. Results were in proportion to the number of aircraft dispatched: one oil depot was destroyed and the port of Constanta damaged – but Ploesti had been raided and American bombers had bombed a European target for the first time.

Although none of these Liberators was shot down on the mission – indeed, there was no serious fighter opposition – they were all forced to land in neutral countries. Col Halverson and six other pilots landed in Iraq as planned, but two others, including *Babe The Big Blue Ox*, landed at Aleppo in Syria. *Blue Goose*, *Brooklyn Rambler*, *Little Eva* and *Town Hall* were interned in Turkey, although *Brooklyn Rambler* took off again some months later when its pilot, Lt Nathan J. Brown escaped!

The HALPRO detachment remained in Egypt, and on the morning of 15 June, seven of its B-24Ds joined with two Liberators of No. 160 Squadron (RAF) in a raid against Axis shipping in the Mediterranean. The HALPRO detachment moved to Lydda, near Tel Aviv, and more raids followed. However, maintenance and poor aircraft recognition (by an RAF Spitfire pilot which resulted in the loss of *Ball of Fire*) gradually reduced the force to a handful before the arrival of brand-new B-24Ds. Despite Col Halverson (now returned from Iraq) requesting permission to proceed to China, the remnants of the detachment remained in the Middle East, and in July 1942 were absorbed into the 376th Bomb Group, better known as the 'Liberandos'. Late that month they were joined by the 98th Bomb Group, commanded by Col Hugo Rush, which was established at Ramat David, 35 miles (56km) east of Haifa in Palestine. The groups B-24Ds had been painted in 'desert pink', more popularly known to crews as 'titty pink'.

On 1 August 1942 the 98th Bomb Group, otherwise known as the 'Pyramiders', attacked an enemy convoy 90 miles (145km) off Benghazi and sank one of the five tankers supplying fuel to Rommel's Afrika Korps. Further raids were made by the 98th and 376th in support of the 8th Army, and as the British moved to the offensive, the Liberators were used to disrupt communications at El Alemain. In November, Gen Louis E. Brereton was authorized to activate IX Bomber Command. On 22 November the 98th and 376th Bomb Groups attacked Tripoli, and in 1943 they moved further afield, bombing targets in Sicily and southern Italy.

In March, Field Marshal Erwin Rommel's final offensive failed and the 'Desert Fox' was recalled to Berlin. In April, US bomber chiefs in London pressed Gen Brereton to make another raid on the Ploesti refineries, which had become even more crucial to the German war machine after the failure of their Soviet adventure and the loss of the anticipated soviet oil supplies from the Baku area on the Caspian Sea. Brereton, however, was anxious to conserve his bombing force for the Tunisian and Sicilian battles that lay ahead. On 6 May 1943 Operation *Husky*, the invasion of Sicily, began. Early in June, however, Brereton was informed that the 44th, 93rd and 389th B-24D Liberator groups in the 8th

Air Force would arrive from England and join the 98th and 376th Bomb Groups for a second attack on Ploesti. This time the planners had opted for a low-level strike. B-17 Flying Fortresses were ruled out because they did not possess the required low-level range; the B-24D, on the other hand, could make the trip to the target, some 1,350 miles (2,170km), and back again.

Now, after six months of combat operations in very cold and hostile winter skies over Europe, the three 201st (Provisional) Wing Groups, which had been trained in the art of high-altitude precision bombing, were switched, without any explanation, to low-level formation practice over East Anglia. Operation *Statesman*, as the Ploesti mission was codenamed, was going ahead. Although the crews were not told, at least they now got a relief from combat, even if it was only temporary. New crews and new B-24s arrived to replace those that had been lost.

Col Leon Johnson's 44th 'Flying Eightballs', Col Addison Baker's 93rd 'Travelling Circus', and Col Jack Wood's 389th 'Sky Scorpions', which had only arrived in Norfolk in mid-June, at once began flying low-level practice missions over East Anglia at less than 150ft (46m) en route to their target range over the Wash, after a five-day orientation course. The change to low-level flying was not without incident: on 25 June, a mid-air collision between two 389th Bomb Group Liberators occurred; one B-24 made it back to Hethel, but the other crash-landed and one man was killed. Rumour and speculation increased as groundcrews sweated to remove the Norden bombsights and replace them with low-level sights. Heavier nose armament and additional fuel tanks in the bomb-bays gave the men clues as to their new role: by increasing the Liberators' fuel capacity to 3,100gal (14,093ltr) they could just make it to Ploesti from the North African desert.

In the dark morning of 30 June, 113 B-24Ds took off singly and flew, at very low altitude, to Portreath airfield, Cornwall. Next day the Liberators crossed the Bay of Biscay at low level to escape German radar, then on to the Straits of Gibraltar, and across the Mediterranean to Oran, Algeria. The forty-one Liberators of the 44th Bomb

B-24D 41-11810 of the 98th Bomb Group, 9th Air Force, in North Africa, early in 1943. Both the 98th and 376th Bomb Groups in the 9th were joined, late in June 1943, by the three 8th Air Force B-24D groups for the Italian campaign, and ultimately, the second raid on the Ploesti oilfields. via Mike Bailey

Group then proceeded to Libya, to Benina Main, 15 miles (24km) from Benghazi, while the forty-two B-24s of the 93rd, and the thirty Liberators of the 389th joined them at bases near Benghazi. For the 'Eightballs' it was an opportunity to meet the 345th Bomb Squadron of the 98th Bomb Group which had been formed from the 44th in March 1942. However, relations were often less than cordial, largely because the 98th enjoyed the choicest rations while the 44th got second best.

On 2 July the B-24Ds of the 8th Air Force flew the first of ten missions in support of the Italian campaign with a bombing mission to enemy airfields. It was not an auspicious start. Three B-24s, including two from the 44th Bomb Group, were lost. On 6 July, twenty-six Liberators in the 44th Bomb Group flew a mission to Gerbani airfield in Sicily. Two of the 'Eightballs' returned early due to mechanical troubles, but the rest of the formation bombed successfully. Tech Sgt Don Chase, radio operator in the crew of *Heaven Can Wait* who were making their combat debut, had a clear recollection of the mission:

> It was a duty of the radio operator to leave his regular position behind the co-pilot's seat, go to the belly of the B-24, straddle the narrow catwalk of the bomb-bay, and activate a push-type lever which prevented the bomb doors from creeping once they were opened preparatory to the bomb-run. Secondly, he watched the bombs fall, and to the best of his visual acuity, assessed the bombing results after the bombardier had activated the bomb-release switch in concert with the lead or first aircraft in the squadron.
>
> So there I was, on our first mission, poised in the belly of *Heaven Can Wait*, waiting for our load of twelve 500lb bombs to drop; soon I saw the bombs of our sister ships plummeting earthwards – but not ours! Could it be my fault? Were the bomb doors creeping in? I pushed the anti-creep lever as hard as I could, and no, there was no creepage. There was nothing more I could do in the bomb-bay, so I returned to the cabin area, plugged in my headset and tuned in to the intercom. 'Use the back-up release, Whit,' said bombardier Harold Schwab on intercom to pilot Charles Whitlock. Whitlock nodded to his co-pilot, William Phipps, who reached down to the console between the pilot and co-pilot seats, grabbed hold of a T-shaped handle and began pulling upwards. I looked back into the bomb-bay; the bombs were still cradled in the racks: Phipps, seated as he was and using his left hand, with his arm at an awkward angle, apparently didn't have enough pulling leverage to activate the release handle. Standing between the pilot and the co-pilot, I tapped Phipp's arm and pointed to myself and then to the handle. When he moved his hand away, I squatted, grabbed the handle with both hands, and pulled straight up with all my strength. Immediately the plane lurched upwards as 6,000lb of metal left *Heaven Can Wait*. The bombs, of course, landed far from the target and splintered hundreds of trees.

Those Liberators that did bomb the target claimed hits on the west end of the Cerbani runway and on the perimeter.

On 6 July Brereton told his five group commanders that a low-level, daylight

The Italian campaign cost the five B-24D groups in North Africa many Liberators, and the three 8th Air Force groups took more than their share of damage over the Italian harbours and marshalling yards; their losses soon approached those sustained at the height of the U-boat campaign in Western Europe.
Bill Cameron Collection

attack would be made on Ploesti to achieve maximum surprise and ensure the heaviest possible damage in the first attack. He had studied target folders for two weeks before making his decision: the attack would be made at noon to minimize losses among the slave-labour workforce. Meanwhile, Brereton must have been concerned with his own mounting losses in theatre. Most of the missions to Italian targets were flown without escort, and soon losses were assuming the proportions sustained at the height of the raids on the U-boat pens in France.

On 8 July two more Liberators – one each from the 93rd and 376th Bomb Groups – were lost. The 44th Bomb Group was one of the groups which bombed telegraph and telephone buildings at Catania, Sicily. This time *Heaven Can Wait*, which had taken a day to track down and repair the bomb-release malfunction over Cerbini, behaved well, as Donald V. Chase recalls:

> Our bombs salvoed on schedule and we returned to base without incident. Upon landing and parking at our improvised hardstand, two or three groundmen – mechanics and armourers – gave us the thumbs-up greeting and hastily removed canteens of water from the bomb-bay section. The water, still frozen from its five-mile high ride, would soon be savoured by the men in the late-afternoon desert heat. There was little variation of food at Benina: pancakes, spam, powdered milk and eggs, Vienna sausage. The worst of all was a congealed, wax-like butter substitute called 'desert butter' which even under a punishing African sun, retained the viscosity of axle grease. Our waist gunner, Edwin Stewart, a Californian, dubbed it 'a medicant for loose bowels'.

The marshalling yards at Catania were attacked on 10 July, and on the 12th with the Allied invasion troops overrunning Sicily, the Liberators made pre-invasion strikes on mainland Italy. On the mission to Foggia airfield on 15 July, twenty-nine Liberators in the 44th took part, twenty-one reaching the target at 12:38 hours. One of them was *Heaven Can Wait* In the words of Don Chase again:

> The flak, somewhat heavier on this mission, was inaccurate. Aimed flak, as it suggests, is aimed at a particular target, usually a lead group or squadron aircraft. Barrage flak, however, is not targeted on a selected plane; rather, it is a boxed pattern of anti-aircraft fire into which the enemy hopes the aircraft will fly.

None of the 'Eightballs' was lost, but the 376th Bomb Group lost three Liberators.

A raid on the Littorio marshalling yards situated next to Vatican City in Rome was briefed for 19 July. Airmen of the Catholic faith were given the choice of flying this mission or remaining at their bases. Don Chase of the 44th again:

> It was conceivable that an errant bomb could inflict damage on the home of the Pope. Stringent bomb-drop precautions were therefore invoked, though fortunately the bombing was effected as planned. And we heard that not one Catholic in our group, including our tail gunner, Bob Bonham, declined to fly on the mission – though in fact the Catholics' decision to fly the Rome mission was not unexpected. All combat flying seemed to be voluntary. Only three of our group's Libs had been downed by enemy action in some 280 individual sorties, resulting in a 44th operational loss of only 1 per cent, although several aircraft had incurred severe AA or enemy aircraft damage. The 389th Bomb Group, however, lost two Liberators.

Following the mission to Rome, the Liberator groups began training in earnest for Ploesti. Next day the five groups began twelve days' training for 'Tidal Wave' (the codename for Ploesti), with practice flights against a mock-up target in the desert. B-24s in small groups criss-crossed the Libyan desert in all directions, the formation becoming steadily larger and the manoeuvres culminating in a full dress rehearsal involving the entire force of 175 B-24Ds.

A day or two before the mission, crews were told to report to briefings and the great Ploesti attack was explained to them. The presentation was elaborate, and included movies of the models of each of several refineries that were to be attacked. It was obvious that success would depend on surprise and precise timing. Crews were told that the defences were relatively light, also that they would not have to fear

Airmen in the 44th Bomb Group in tropical kit in North Africa in the summer of 1943. Left is Capt Bill Cameron of the 67th Bomb Squadron who piloted B-24D-25-CO 41-24229 Buzzin' Bear **in the attack on Columbia Aquila at Ploesti, on 1 August 1943.** Buzzin' Bear **and 1st Lt Leighton C. Smith and crew failed to return from a raid on Foggia, Italy, on 16 August.** Bill Cameron Collection

Rumanian anti-aircraft because Sunday was a day of rest for Rumanians, even in time of war! Maj Gen Brereton was under no illusions however, and he warned that losses could reach 50 per cent. At an open-air meeting in the African sunshine the general spelt it out:

> By the use of ground troops, this job would take an entire army many months of bloody fighting. You men are going to do it from the air in a single day. This is a dangerous mission, but we feel that even if the entire force is wiped out, if the refineries are demolished it will still be worth the price.

which gunner would remain in the desert on P-Day. In Don Chase's crew, the young waist gunner, Ralph Knox, drew the 'unlucky' straw. Chase recalls:

> He complained and cursed, and feeling abandoned, withdrew from the rest of the crew, not speaking until just before take-off when woefully, he wished us luck. He was dejected by this fracture in the brotherhood of the battle. There wasn't much reason to stash aboard beer or extra water for the Ploesti run because we wouldn't fly high enough to chill it; but, even so, one of the groundmen fastened a canteen in the already crammed bomb-bay, 'Just for luck, okay', and punctuated his words with the universal thumbs-up salute.

On the day after the mission on 19 July to the Littorio marshalling yards situated in close proximity to the Vatican City in Rome, the five groups began twelve days' training for 'Tidal Wave' (the code name for Ploesti), with practice flights against a mock-up target. B-24Ds in small groups criss-crossed the Libyan desert in all directions, the formations becoming ever larger, and the whole procedure culminating in a full dress rehearsal involving the entire force of 175 B-24Ds. USAF

Orders called for a crew of nine aboard each B-24, not the usual ten. The tunnel gun position was to be unmanned because of weight restrictions for the 2,500 mile (4,022km) flight and also because of the low attack altitude and the 200mph (320km/h) target ground-speed which would cancel the effectiveness of the single, belly-fired, hand-held .50 calibre gun. Crews therefore drew straws to determine

Tech Sgt Harry R. Snead, engineer top turret gunner in *Hag Mag the Mothball Queen*, in the 68th Squadron, 44th Bomb Group, whose pilot was Lt George P. Martin, recalls:

> The CO came around to our tents and woke up those who could sleep. Then we went to breakfast, though most of us just drank coffee and juices. The food was terrible, as usual, but the cooks did the best they could with what they had, in all the dust and heat. After, we walked over to briefing, and we were all concerned and yet relieved to see what we were going to do after all the practice flights we had made in the last ten days. Then we went to our planes and got ready, though there wasn't much equipment to get ready, because of the low altitude we would be flying. We all said goodbye to Bob Pierce, our belly gunner.

It was barely daylight when the Liberators took off. Brereton had decided on seven forces from the five groups. First away at 07:00 hours was 1st Lt Brian W. Flavelle's *Wongo Wongo!* of the 376th, and the lead plane of 'Tidal Wave', which lifted off from Berka Two; on board was the mission navigator Lt R. Wilson. The other twenty-eight B-24s of the 376th Bomb Group 'Liberandos' followed; these were led by the group CO, Col Keith Compton and Brig Gen Uzal G. Ent (CO, 9th Bomber Command) in the command ship, *Teggie Ann* (Brereton had intended to go in the command aircraft but an order from Gen Hap Arnold in Washington forbade him to do so). Compton's target was 'White I', The Romana American refinery. Behind them came thirty-six B-24s of the 93rd Bomb Group, led by Col Addison Baker and Maj John 'The Jerk' Jerstad in *Hell's Wench*. Baker was assigned 'White II', Concordia Vega, while Maj Ramsey D. Potts led the balance of the 93rd (fifteen aircraft) to White III, the standard petrol block and Unirea-Spiranoza, in *The Duchess*. They were followed by forty-eight B-24s in the 98th Bomb Group formation, led by Col John R. 'Killer' Kane in *Hail Columbia*; their target was 'White IV', the Unirea-Orion and Astra Romana refineries. Nine crews from the 389th flew in the 98th formation as fill-ins.

Next came thirty-six B-24s (plus one spare) of the 44th Bomb Group, in two separate formations. Col Leon Johnson with Bill Brandon as his pilot and fourteen other B-24s, were to bomb 'White V', Columbia Aquila. Johnson's intention to lead the 'Eightballs' in *Suzy Q* had been placed in jeopardy the night before when a broken spark plug was diagnosed in No. 2 engine. However, after an anxious night of maintenance and repair the plane was pronounced well enough to fly. Behind Johnson's three-plane element came six B-24Ds trailing to the right, led by Capt Bill Cameron in *Buzzin' Bear*. Off to his left the remaining six aircraft were led by Maj Dexter L. Hodge flying with Capt Robert E. Miller in *Fascinatin' Witch*. Trailing behind was a spare aircraft, piloted by Bob Felber. Should *Suzy Q* falter for mechanical reasons en route to Ploesti, *Buzzin' Bear* would take over the lead. Johnson's deputy, Maj James Posey, flying with Capt John H. Diehl, 68th Squadron CO, in *Victory Ship*, led twelve B-24s from the 68th and 506th Squadrons which were assigned 'Blue I', Creditul Minier Brazi. Tech Sgt Harry R. Snead wrote:

> We took off at 7:50am with a heavy load: full-to-capacity wing tanks, and one extra tank mounted in the bomb-bay gave us approximately 3,100gal [14,093ltr]. In the bomb-bay we carried three 1,000lb bombs with a one-hour delay fuse and some small incendiaries (two boxes), and more than the normal supply of .50 calibre ammunition for our guns. We used the entire length of the runway, and we were off.

At an open-air meeting in the African sunshine at the 376th 'Liberandos' Bomb Group base at Benghazi, Lt Gen Lewis H. Brereton spells out the Ploesti mission to crews. Brereton was under no illusions about the high losses that could result, and warned that they could even reach as high as 50 per cent. He was of the opinion that even if the entire force was wiped out, if the refineries were demolished, it would still be worth the price. USAF

Last off were twenty-six B-24s of the 389th Bomb Group, led by Col Jack Wood in Maj Kenneth 'Fearless' Caldwell's Liberator. The 'Sky Scorpions' had been allocated Red I, Steaua Romana at Campina, the longest route of all the B-24Ds, as their Liberators were fitted with fuselage

Col Leon W. Johnson *(left)*, CO, 44th Bomb Group; Col John R. 'Killer' Kane, CO, 98th Bomb Group; and Brig Gen Uzal G. Ent, CO, 9th Bomber Command, pictured in the Libyan desert. Both Johnson and Kane would earn the Medal of Honor for their leadership on the Ploesti mission. Ent returned Stateside in October 1943, and in January 1944 took command of the 2nd Air Force at Colorado Springs, Colorado. USAF

tanks containing an additional 400gal (1,820ltr) of fuel; this adaptation meant that each B-24, which also carried a ball turret, could only carry four 500lb (227kg) bombs because of this additional weight. The bombs loaded aboard the 389th Bomb Group Liberators were fitted with ten-second delay fuses. The other six groups carried twenty-minute acid core fused bombs which would not explode until the bombs dropped by the 389th created a concussion wave in the target area. Any that did not explode in the concussion wave would eventually do so by means of the acid core fuse.

The mission began badly and would get worse. *Kickapoo*, a 389th B-24D piloted by 1st Lt Robert J. Nespor and which was flying with the 98th, lost its No. 4 engine on take-off and crashed on landing after taking evasive action to avoid two other B-24s. Only two men, badly burned, scrambled out of the wreckage. Nearing landfall at the German-occupied island of Corfu, *Wongo Wongo!* in the 376th went out of control, veered up, fell over on its back and plunged into the sea, exploding on impact. Then the deputy leader swung out of formation and turned back with two port engines out; his bomb-bay doors opened and his bombs dropped into the sea as he lightened the load on his two good engines for the long headlong dash home. As a result of this development, *Brewery Wagon*, piloted by Lt John D. Palm, took over the lead at the head of the 376th.

Nothing seemed to be going right, and so many bad breaks so early in the mission was proving very disheartening. As the 5-mile (8km) long formation headed for Corfu, inevitable malfunctions reduced the numbers; seven of Kane's 'Pyramiders' followed the leader down to look for survivors, and so the mission had effectively lost the two crews that had been specially briefed and trained to lead the entire formation to Ploesti. Gen Ent and Col Compton in *Teggie Ann*, the third and remaining aircraft of that lead element, now had the command of this vital mission unexpectedly thrust upon them.

Three more B-24s from other groups also returned early. One of them was *Heaven Can Wait* in the 44th Bomb Group, which was forced to abort 125 miles (200km) short of the target, near Craiova, Rumania. Don Chase explains why:

> Fuel transfer problems and, as proved later, oiling difficulties, caused us to shut down No. 1 engine and feather the propeller. We were tail-end Charlie, eating everyone's prop-wash, and we kept lagging further behind. Then No. 4 engine lost power and we fell even further back – we had no choice. Navigator Robert Ricks gave Whitlock a course heading to the nearest friendly landing field, Cyprus, some five flying hours distant.

After Corfu, crews veered right, to the east, and headed overland to Ploesti. At the Greek border commanders were confronted with the Pindus Range, rising to a height of at most 11,000ft (3,350m). The horizon was blotted out with cumulus clouds towering to 17,000ft (5,230m) and a decision had to be made: whether to continue as briefed and risk collision, or to climb above them. Compton decided to climb above the cloud tops to save fuel and time, and the 93rd followed him. Col Kane, whose 98th Bomb Group was following the 376th, had his mind made up for him: many of the 'Pyramiders' aircraft were not equipped with oxygen for this low-level mission, so the 98th circled and entered the cloud in threes, and after the range repeated the manoeuvre before setting course again. The 44th Bomb Group had no option but to follow the 98th, and lost valuable time searching for a route through the clouds. All of this opened up a large gap between the leading B-24s of the 93rd and the 376th who were now some distance ahead, and the groups following. Also the 44th could see no sign of the 389th behind.

The B-24s continued to Ploesti, with the 98th Bomb Group stretched out in front of the 44th and the 389th, which reappeared behind and very high. The B-24s were down to about 3,000ft (900m) as they crossed the Danube, and had a very clear view of the Rumanian countryside. Ploesti was still more than 160 miles (257km) away, and Pitesi, the first of three checkpoints before the turn on the bomb run, was less than 100 miles (160km) ahead. By now the two lead groups were some 60 miles (95km) ahead, and the planned, simultaneous attack on Ploesti by all the groups was out of the question. The leading groups had reached the first checkpoint on time, but due to a navigational error the 'Liberandos' now turned south too soon, at Targoviste, instead of at the correct IP at Floresti, and the 93rd followed. As a result they were headed for the wrong target! Nearing Ploesti, Compton and Ent prepared to take the 376th over the refineries alone. They overtook *Brewery Wagon* and nosed *Teggie Ann* into the lead slot. *Brewery Wagon*, which was on course, took the route as briefed but was shot down soon after. Palm survived the crashlanding, but his right leg below the knee 'was hanging by a shred of flesh'. The 376th's error led to the 93rd's subsequent tactical mistake in bombing the 98th's and 44th's targets, and this caused approximately twenty ineffective sorties by the 376th.

Compton and Ent decided to make the best of a worsening situation and headed for the Astro Romana, Phoenix Orion and Columbia Aquila refineries, which were the intended targets of the 98th and 44th Groups. The 'Liberandos' saw the 93rd already desperately fighting its way through to the target area, and split to attack targets of opportunity instead. But as the 376th passed Ploesti and began climbing up the foothills east of the city they saw the 'Pyramiders' coming towards them! With groups coming in from the wrong directions and bombing any target that presented itself, the plan was in ruins. The 93rd had followed Compton's force and trailed over Ploesti: some Rumanian fighters attacked them, and Staff Sgt Leycester D. Havens, the tail gunner aboard *Jersey Bounce*, flown by Lt Worthy A. Long, became the first casualty of the Ploesti battle. *Jersey Bounce* was shot down over the target and only four crew, including Long, survived.

Baker and Jerstad turned *Hell's Wench* 90 degrees left and headed for the smokestacks of Ploesti. Maj Ramsey Potts in *The Duchess* and the second formation of 93rd B-24s followed. The flak batteries enveloped the 'Flying Circus' with their fire, and at only 20ft (6m) they were sitting ducks: during the five-minute bomb-run the group was torn to shreds. *Hell's Wench* was hit and caught fire; Baker jettisoned his bombs, but he and Jerstad decided to continue to the target, where they surged up to 300ft (90m) before falling back and crashing to the ground. Both pilots were awarded posthumous Medals of Honor for their sacrifice.

Capt Walter Stewart, the deputy leader in *Utah Man*, took over the lead; despite severe damage to the B-24, he managed to land again in Lybia, fourteen hours later. 1st Lt Kenton D. McFarland, flying *Liberty Lad* on just two engines, was the last home by another two hours. Nine 93rd B-24s were lost over the target, the *Let 'Er Rip* and *Exterminator* collided in cloud. Two more were interned in Turkey. Among the survivors were *Thar She Blows*, flown by Capt Charles T. Merrill; *Ball of Fire Jr*, flown by Maj Joe Tate; *Boomerang*, piloted by 2nd Lt Luther C. Bird; and Maj Potts' *The Duchess*.

Meanwhile the 98th, led by 'Killer' Kane in *Hail Columbia*, and the 44th

B24D-53-CO 42-40364/Y Snow White and the Seven Dwarfs **in the 343rd Bomb Squadron, 98th Bomb Group, pictured in the Libyan Desert at Benina. All of the 343rd Squadron's Liberators carried 'nose art' of the characters made famous in Walt Disney's movie of the same name. Capt James E. Gunn and crew from the 389th Bomb Group borrowed 42-40364 for the Ploesti mission on 1 August 1943, and were shot down. Only Staff Sgt Stanley M. Horine Jr, tail gunner, baled out, and he survived to be made a PoW in Bulgaria.** USAF

Capt Wallace C. Taylor's crew of B-24D-20-CO 41-24198/C The Vulgar Virgin **with friends in the 98th Bomb Group, pictured in North Africa. Capt Taylor flew this aircraft on the Ploesti raid on 1 August 1943, and was the only one to survive after the Liberator was shot down.** Via Mike Bailey

crossed Ploesti from the north-west. The 'Pyramiders' suffered the highest casualties of all five groups, losing twenty-one of the thirty-eight B-24s that started out from North Africa. At least nine were destroyed by blasts from delayed-action bombs dropped by the 376th. The 'Eightballs' had arrived at Ploesti at 15:15 hours, immediately plunging into a hail of flak and ripping tracers, smoke, fire and explosives. The long gaggle of pink-coloured 98th B-24s began a wide descending turn to the right, and the 44th turned on their bomb-run to 'White V', the Columbia Aquila refinery. Col Johnson and Bill Brandon in *Suzy Q* turned their three-ship element inside the 98th, and some fifty bombers dropped rapidly to their assigned bombing altitudes, flying parallel to a railway which led directly towards their target. As they made the turn, Bill Cameron and Bill Dabney in *Buzzin' Bear* pulled their six-ship flight into position directly behind – sixteen 44th bombers in all. The last element consisted of four B-24Ds instead of three, because Bob Felber, in the spare B-24, had refused to leave the party. The remaining twelve bombers from the 44th, led by Col Jim Posey, split off at this point to attack 'Blue' target, the Brazi refinery, 5 miles (8km) to the south of Ploesti.

Harry Snead in *Hag Mag the Mothball Queen* in the 68th Squadron formation, which with the 506th headed for Blue target, recalls:

About this time all hell broke loose. A flak train was running down railroad tracks giving hell to the 98th on the left and the 44th on the right; the big guns were levelled low at us and were almost like anti-tank guns. In the fields, 20mm and .30 calibre guns were hidden in haystacks, so we were getting it from all over. It sure seemed odd shooting men off the train, out of gun towers and hidden in the fields, instead of enemy fighters which we were trained for. We saw targets to the left of us exploding, burning and planes crashing or belly-landing to try to get men out because they'd had it. Then we saw *our* target dead ahead of us, exactly the way it looked in the pictures we had seen. Raised up to about 150 or 200ft to clear stacks, gunners dropped incendiaries out the waist windows a little short of target but they set the fire in front of the plant. Then the bombardier laid the three 1,000lb bombs into the west side of the distillation plant as designated on the flight plan. Perfect navigation and bombing, just the way it was supposed to be done.

Now all we had to do was get out of there. We started to let down to tree-top level again when we were jumped from the rear by about fifteen Me 109s coming at us in pairs. They hit the plane on our left so heavy she burst into flames in the cockpit and bomb-bay. This plane was flown by Capt Rowland B. Houston. They flew straight up to try and give some altitude so the men could get out, but he stalled and winged over. Meanwhile, we scattered so he wouldn't come down on top of us. Our pilot saw a gulley in front of us and went down it. I looked out of my turret at the wing tips on both sides of it. Suddenly, some trees in front of us forced us to go up a little to clear them. At this time we saw

B-24D-85-CO 42-40664 Teggie Ann **of the 515th Bomb Squadron 376th Bomber Group; this plane carried Brig Gen Uzal G. Ent, CO, 9th Bomber Command, and Col Keith K. Compton, CO, 376th Bomb Group, to Ploesti and back. Col Compton and Gen Ent had the command of this vital mission unexpectedly thrust upon them after the loss of the original lead aircraft.** Teggie Ann, **originally named** Honey Chile, **crashlanded at Melfi, Italy, returning from a raid on Foggia on 16 August 1943.** USAF

(Below) **A B-24D of the 98th Bomb Group roars over the Astra Romana refinery, the most modern and the largest at Ploesti, amid smoke and flame. The 'Pyramiders' suffered the highest casualties of all five Liberator groups, losing twenty-one of the thirty-eight B-24Ds that started out from North Africa. At least nine were destroyed by the blasts from the delayed-action bombs dropped by the 376th Bomb Group.** USAF

A B-24D of the 44th Bomb Group comes off the blazing target amidst flame and smoke, and heads for the safety of open country at very low level. The 44th were allocated two targets: the Columbia Aquila refinery, and 'Blue' target, the Brazi refinery, 5 miles (8km) to the south of Ploesti – this was the target of twelve B-24Ds led by Col Jim Posey. 'Blue' target was completely wrecked. via Steve Adams

(Below) **The bombs dropped by Col Leon W. Johnson, CO, 44th Bomb Group, and Maj Bill Brandon, in B-24D-5-CO 41-23817** Suzy Q, **explode at 'White V', Columbia Aquila refinery. Johnson picked out the correct target, but such was the confusion in the run-in to their targets that the 376th Bomb Group attacked 'White IV', Astro Romana Phoenix Orion, and also 'White V' Columbia Aquila, which were the intended targets of the 98th and 44th Groups respectively.** USAF

a small formation of our planes so we joined them for better protection and fire power. We had been at very high RPMs and full power to get away from target, so we now throttled back to conserve fuel for our trip home. We could now look over to our right and see the target burning and exploding, and so we felt we had done what we came for.

At White V meanwhile, the rest of the 66th and 67th Squadrons saw several B-24s heading straight for them and later, it was learned that these were 93rd and 376th Bomb Group Liberators. Some had unfortunately dropped their bombs a few minutes earlier on Columbia Aquila, which the 44th were now rapidly approaching. The sky became unusually crowded with both green and pink Liberators. Miraculously there were no collisions, and the 44th formation headed for the great mass of smoke and flame which marked the Columbia Aquila refinery. *Suzy Q* disappeared into the smoke and *Buzzin' Bear* followed. The outside-air temperature gauges aboard the B-24s reached their most extreme temperature reading as they sailed through the searing heat of the great fires that seemed to engulf them. Brandon pulled up abruptly to avoid three tall smoke stacks, and then began a diving turn to the right. Down below, flak guns opened up, but Johnson and Brandon dived so low that the gunners abandoned their triggers and ducked as the B-24s roared overhead! The B-24s levelled out and began a flat turn to the right, but unable to find their pin-point targets in the smoke and flame, and the general confusion, some bomb loads were held too long. Crews could only hope that they fell in an area that contributed to the general destruction in the target complex.

Suzy Q and her two wingmen – *Bewitchin' Witch* flown by Reg Carpenter, and *Horse Fly* piloted by Ed Mitchel – turned, and were followed by *Buzzin' Bear* and her own two wingmen – *4-Q-2* flown by Charlie 'Punchy' Henderson, and *Calaban*, piloted by Jim Hill. All dropped down, hung doggedly in formation and skidded around the turn. Ahead of them *Wing Dinger*, a borrowed 376th ship flown by 1st Lt George W. Winger of the 44th, pulled straight up and then fell out of the sky; Staff Sgts Michael J. Cicon and seventeen-year-old Bernard G. Traudt popped out of the waist windows, barely 200 or 300ft above the ground – incredibly, both men survived. At the same time, upwards of fifty Fw 190s, Bf 109s, Bf 110s and Ju 88s attacked the formation. A 20mm shell exploded in the nose of *4-Q-2*, wounding the navigator, Robert S. Schminke and John R. Huddle, the bombardier. Flak exploded in the tail section, wounding Staff Sgt James M. Porter, the waist gunner.

Calaban hit a barrage balloon cable that put a tear in the wing, but otherwise Hill's crew came through intact. Both Henderson and Hill landed safely on Malta, refuelled and flew on to Benina the next day. *Buzzin' Bear* also took a hit which ripped away hydraulic lines and put the tail turret out of operation, but no one was hurt. It had now become 'every man for himself'. *Sad Sack II*, flown by Lt Henry Lasco, came under attack from repeated fighter attacks, and went down sending up a cloud of dust. Thomas M. Wood, tail gunner, was dead. Harry W. Stenborn, navigator mortally wounded by an 88mm shell in the chest, keeled over on the catwalk and held on to the open bomb-bay door; Charles Decrevel, left waist gunner, saw that his flesh was stripped away and he could see the white of his ribs. The No. 2 engine was out. Coming off the target, 88s had raked the ship and Leonard L. Raspotnik, engineer top turret gunner, and Joseph B. Spivey, radioman, were hit. Lasco just had time to shout to Joseph A. Kill, the co-pilot, 'There's a good cornfield over there,' when up to nine Bf 109s attacked. Fire severely wounded Decrevel in the back, head and knee. His back parachute pack stopped a 13mm shell. Lasco felt a 'tremendous sock on the jaw' as he was hit in both cheeks and upper palate by a 20mm shell fired from a Bf 109 while they were only fifty feet off the ground. Lasco could see nothing, but called for flaps. Kill pumped the flaps down by hand and headed for the wheatfield, left wing low. Lasco lay slumped over the control column. Kill kicked hard right rudder and picked up the wing for a crashlanding. When the plane came to rest, both his legs were broken and his right foot was out of its socket at the ankle.

B-24D-55-CO 42-40402 The Sandman **of the 345th Bomb Squadron, 98th Bomb Group, is silhouetted against the burning pyre of 'White IV' at Ploesti as 1st Lt Robert W. Sternfels, the pilot, banks in vain to avoid a balloon cable which subsequently wrapped itself around the No. 3 engine propeller. Amazingly** The Sandman **continued flying, cleared the target and made it back.** USAF

The 389th Bomb Group was the last group off from Libya, and Col Jack Wood led the twenty-six B-24s of the 'Sky Scorpions' in Maj Kenneth 'Fearless' Caldwell's Liberator to their target at 'Red I', Steaua Romana at Campina, the second-largest refinery. 'Red' target, seen burning after bombs were dropped by the Liberators, was completely destroyed. via Earl Zimmerman

Despite his terrible injuries, Lasco extricated Kill from the tangle of wires and cables and pulled him clear of the wreckage. Decrevel dragged out Al Shaffer, the right waist gunner, noticing that his leg looked like 'hamburger'; there was no morphine, so he gave Shaffer a cigarette instead. Later, Shaffer was reunited with Lasco in hospital. He said,'My name is Al Shaffer. I am on Lt Lasco's crew.' Lasco couldn't talk, so he showed Shaffer his dog-tags. Shaffer, astonished, said, 'God, Lieutenant, I didn't recognize you.'

Finally, the fighters left the 44th, although some B-24s were still attacked by fighters after they had reached the Mediterranean. Ed Mitchell put *Horse Fly* down in Turkey. *Lil' Abner'*, flown by Worden Weaver, was badly hit over the target and crashed about forty miles away. Bob Miller and Dexter Hodge put the badly damaged *Fascinatin' Witch* down on Malta; both their wingmen were lost. Meanwhile, Col Jim Posey and his twenty-one B-24Ds had made a very accurate strike on the Çreditul Minier refinery at Brazi, five miles south of Ploesti, but had lost *GI Gal*, flown by Elmer Reinhart, a short distance from the target. Reinhart was able to gain some altitude thus permitting his crew to bale out successfully, though Fg Off Charles L. Starr, the co-pilot, was killed when his parachute failed to open. Rowland Houston's B-24D was shot down by a fighter moments later, and was lost with its entire crew. Despite this, the performance of these twelve Liberators represented one of the few successes.

The greatest achievement of all, however, went to the 389th Bomb Group bringing up the rear of *Tidal Wave* and their attack on the Steaua Romana refinery at Campina, 18 miles (29km) north-west of Ploesti. The 'Sky Scorpions', led by Col Jack Wood and Maj Kenneth 'Fearless' Caldwell, had some

B-24D 42-40738 The Oklahoman, **in the 566th Bomb Squadron, 389th Bomb Group, with its bomb-log showing the horizontal bomb-mission symbol for the Ploesti low-level mission. The 'Sky Scorpions' (and the 44th and 93rd) remained in North Africa and assisted the 9th Air Force in raids in support of Operation** Juggler. **The personnel are from various crews, these having been broken up, and they are getting a ride back to England in any B-24 available after losing theirs in a trench at Benghazi (Maj Tom Conroy, 566th Squadron CO, is second from the left).** The Oklahoman **was lost on 5 December 1943 in a raid on Painsbosuf, France, when it was flown by Lt Harvey B. Mason. Only one man from the ten-man crew survived.** The late Russ D. Hayes' Collection

anxious moments when the formation turned down the wrong valley, but they pulled up and flew on for perhaps three to four minutes before starting down towards the refinery, which was marked by a great pall of smoke; as they approached they split into three sections to bomb from three different directions. 'Red' target was completely destroyed, although success was marred by the loss of four Liberators shot down.

One belonged to Lt Lloyd 'Pete' D. Hughes, flying left-wing off Lt Kenneth Fowble who led the second wave with the command pilot, Capt Philip Ardery in the co-pilot's seat. Shells ruptured Hughes' fuel tanks, but despite fuel streaming over the fuselage, he and his co-pilot, Ronald H. Helder, piloted the B-24 low over the blazing target and got their bombs away. Heat engulfed the bomber and flames licked at its fuselage as the fuel ignited. Hughes' starboard wing dipped and ploughed into the ground. Only Thomas A. Hoff, tail gunner, and Edmond H. Smith, waist gunner, survived the crash. John A. McLoughlin, bombardier, died later of his burns. Hughes was posthumously awarded the Medal of Honor for his 'unhesitatingly entering the blazing area' and 'dropping his bombs with great precision, and only then undertaking a forced landing'.

The 389th had been the last to arrive over the target area, and they paid dearly for their lack of surprise. The twenty-one survivors in the 'Sky Scorpions' formation headed for home in all directions, some landing in Cyprus and Malta. 2nd Lt James F. Gerrits, co-pilot of *Hitler's Hearse* in the 567th Squadron, piloted by Capt Robert C. Mooney, recalls:

> As we started down and saw the target, Bob Mooney was all excited. He said to me, 'There it is. Get those nose guns firing Hank!' I had a toggle switch to fire them and I flipped it a couple of times and heard them roar. We headed down in a long glide into the target. There were a lot of orange blips appearing all over from around the target area – we were looking down the barrels of the guns as they were firing at us.
>
> Everything was fine, and then suddenly there was a loud bang in the cockpit, and it quickly filled with smoke. I flinched away and turned towards my side window, and as the smoke cleared there was a horrible roar from a hole in the windscreen. I turned towards Mooney – he was leaning back, away from the control wheel, and his hands were off the wheel and just held in front of him. Blood was running all down his face. It was evident right away that he wasn't conscious any more. We were still going down on the target in a shallow dive and maybe 200ft or so off the ground.
>
> I quickly grabbed the wheel and held the run for a few seconds. Then I pulled up and to the right and we went over the refinery structures a little to the right. I could feel something down the side of my face and my left arm hurt. I looked down and I had some blood on myself, too.

Gerrits and Charles Garrett, the badly wounded engineer, managed to put the shattered B-24, low on fuel, down at Izmir without flaps and brakes. They were soon joined by Lt Harold L. James' crew. On 2 August both crews attended a funeral for Capt Mooney at a small cemetery outside Izmir.

In the 44th formation, twenty-eight B-24s remained from the thirty-seven that had left Benina that morning. *Available Jones*, flown by Fred Jones, had crashed in the Mediterranean, but the crew were rescued and taken prisoner by the Italians. *Horse Fly* and *Flossie Flirt*, flown by Charlie Hughes,were interned in Turkey. Tech Sgt Harry R. Snead in the 68th Squadron, 44th Bomb Group, sums up the mission:

> This ended up being one of the longest raids of the war up to this time. We were in the air from 7.50am to 9.12pm, a total of 13 hours 22 minutes. The next day when we went out to our plane, *Hag Mag the Mothball Queen*, the ground crew asked us 'How the heck low were we?' because they had cleared leaves out of the bomb-bay tracks and tail skid. We told them, 'Pretty

Brig Gen Leon W. Johnson *(left)* and Col Fred R. Dent, 44th Bomb Group CO *(right)* pictured in November 1943 for the award of the citation to the Eightballs for its part in the Ploesti mission. Johnson and Bill Brandon in Suzy Q **led a large part of the group in an attack on 'White V', the Columbia Aquila refinery, and put it out of production for eleven months. On 17 August Johnson, a thirty-nine-year old West Pointer, was awarded the Medal of Honor, which was presented to him at a ceremony at Shipdham on 22 November, by which time he commanded the 14th Combat Wing.** via Steve Adams

THE STARS AND STRIPES

MIDDLE EAST

PLOESTI REPRINT — AUGUST 6, 1943

9th AIR FORCE GIVES PLOESTI HELL

Just how close the U.S. Liberator bombers come to the refinery smokestacks is shown in these photographs. This congested portion of Rumania is a main nazi source of oil, and its loss would be one of the worst nightmares Hitler could experience. Only the Nazis themselves know how much the attack — one of the longest mass bombardment raids in history—had hurt them, but returning forces believed it had hurt plenty. They reported direct hits on installations, plants, fractionating columns, tank farms, and power houses. (All photos by 9th U.S. Air Force — Passed by U.S. Military Censor)

200 Liberators Write Air History in Smashing Raid

REPRINT EDITION

Because the combat crews and ground forces of the "Fighting Ninth" requested thousands of extra copies of the "Stars and Stripes" edition dealing with the Ploesti raid, the Office of War Information has decided to issue a special Ploesti reprint. This is a souvenir copy in appreciation of those who helped make the Aug. 1, 1943 raid on the Rumanian oil center.

Careful Preparation

Haystacks Spout Fire

11 Enemy Fighters Downed

(Right) Stars and Stripes **report of the Ploesti mission.** Stars and Stripes **was the GI's newspaper of World War II.**

Col Addison E. Baker, CO 93rd Bomb Group; Addison was killed at Ploesti with with Maj John L. 'The Jerk' Jerstad in B-24D-120-CO 42-40994 Hell's Wench. **Both pilots were awarded posthumous Medals of Honor for their sacrifice in the attack on 'White II', Concordia Vega. In all, five Medals of Honor, three posthumously, were awarded, and all five groups received Presidential Unit Citations. Every crew-member who had taken part received the DFC.** USAF

low', and laughed because we felt we were amongst the fortunate ones. When we walked into interrogation to relieve some tension, we found out other planes had gone to Turkey, Sicily and other points along the way. Some turned up in the next few days. After some observations and pictures we found out that our targets, 'White 5', were knocked out for nine or ten months, and that 'Blue' target was out of action for the duration! This good news did help us feel we had accomplished some of the things we started out to do on that Sunday afternoon.

Unfortunately, despite the great sacrifice, the Liberators had only destroyed 42 per cent of the plant's refining capacity and 40 per cent of its cracking capacity. Of the 177 B-24s which had set out, 167 had actually attacked their targets and had dropped 311 tons of bombs on the refineries. Some fifty-four B-24Ds were lost over the targets and three more had crashed in the sea. Six B-24D crews were interned in Turkey while nineteen had landed in Cyprus, Sicily or Malta. Overall, the 44th lost twelve Liberators, including one interned; the 93rd lost thirteen, including two interned; the 98th, twenty (including Kane's *Hail Columbia*, which landed at Cyprus); the 376th, four, including one interned; and the 389th, six, including two interned. Of the ninety-two that returned to North Africa, fifty-five had varying degrees of battle damage. Most of the refineries were repaired and within a month were operating at pre-mission capacity again. Every crew-member who

Only 42 per cent of the Ploesti oil plant's refining capacity and 40 per cent of its cracking capacity were destroyed on 1 August, for the loss of fifty-seven B-24Ds, while six were interned in Turkey, and fifty-five returned with battle damage. Most of the refineries were repaired, and within a month were operating at pre-mission capacity again, and missions to Italy and Austria by three 8th Air Force Groups and the two 9th Air Force Groups were resumed. The first major bombing mission to Italy took place on 16 August. Here, the 376th Bomb Group can be seen crossing the Alps for a raid on Wiener Neustadt, part of Operation Juggler, the joint 8th and 9th attacks on fighter plants at Regensburg and Wiener Neustadt respectively.
USAF

Crew-members from B-24D-90-CO 42-40722/B-, better known as The Little Gramper, **in the 567th Bomb Squadron, 389th Bomb Group, walk away from their B-24D in North Africa carrying their PX cigarettes. The 'Sky Scorpions' operated temporarily from Tunisia, between September–October 1943, supporting Allied operations at Salerno and bombing targets in Corsica, Italy, and Austria. They resumed operations from Hethel again in October 1943.** The late Russ D. Hayes' Collection

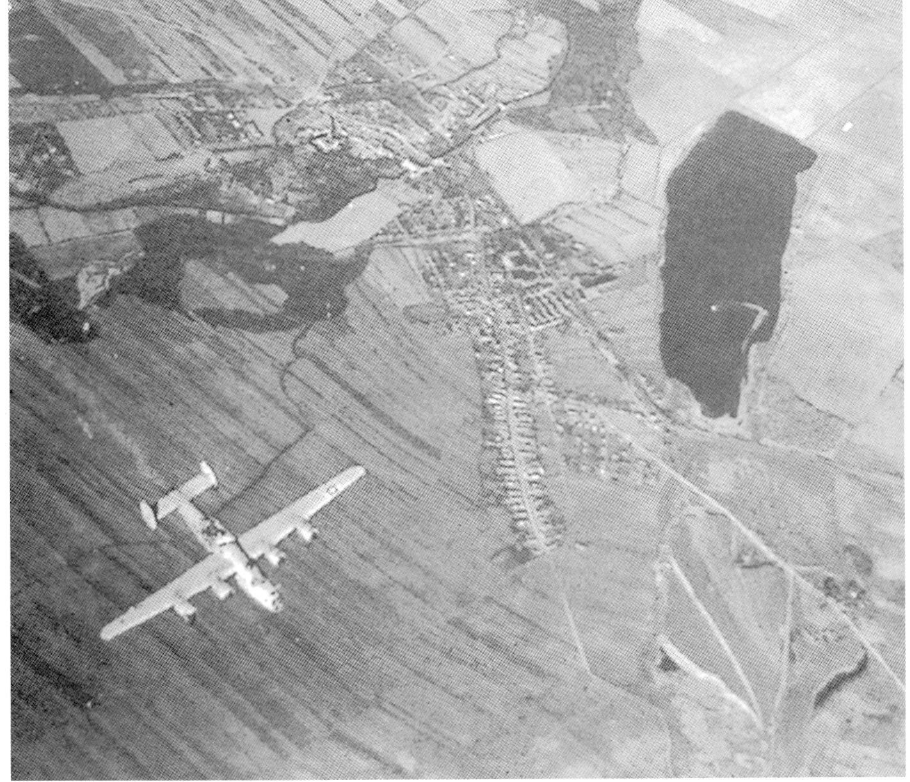

(Below) **A B-24D of the 415th Bomb Squadron, 98th Bomb Group, struggles back to North Africa with a large gaping hole in its fuselage after being hit by its own group's bombs during 'bombs away' over aircraft plants at Wiener Neustadt on 2 November 1943, part of Operation** Juggler. USAF

had taken part received the DFC; five Medals of Honor, three posthumously, were awarded, and all five groups received Presidential Unit Citations.

It took many days before all remaining thirty-six Liberators returned to their North African bases. They were badly needed because missions to Italy were resumed after the Ploesti mission. The first major bombing mission to Italy took place on 16 August, and if the losses at Ploesti had not been bad enough, this mission, to Foggia, claimed still more, as Don Chase in the 44th recalls:

> Only six of our crew of ten flew the mission: co-pilot Phipps, bombardier Schwab, engineer Holtz and I were grounded by respiratory and ear infections. We four waited for our six fellow crewmen and our four replacements to return in a ship named *Timb-a-a-ah*. It was in vain, and long after the last ships had returned and the sun had set, we two enlisted men and the two officers mournfully trekked back to our tent area. It was a night of anguish. Eight of our group's aircraft, including *Timb-a-a-ah*, failed to return. If I had been older, instead of twenty-two, perhaps I might not have searched for a symbolic reason which governs fateful events. But regardless, I picked up the kukri knife I had acquired from a Ghurka soldier in Cyprus, walked into the desert and threw the knife with the ten-inch blade across the sand into the darkness. It had brought only bad luck. More than half my crew was gone, probably dead. I cried.
>
> After losing 60 per cent of the strike planes in just two raids, Ploesti and Foggia, the 44th flew two missions without any loss at all. Late in the month 44th personnel returned to our base at Shipdham, England. Only twenty-two made the trip back, whereas forty-one, plus replacements, had come to Africa two months earlier.

B-24Ds of the 9th Air Force pass the treacherous Alps en route **to their targets, as flak bursts harmlessly high in the distance. Maj Joe M. Kilgore, who served for many months as a pilot with the 9th Bomber Command, quoted the best remark he had heard about straggling out of formation: 'When you get out of formation you have a choice of two things: either take out your .45 and blow your brains out, or sit there for a few seconds and someone will do it for you.' The 98th and 376th Bomb Groups moved to Brindisi and to San Pancrazio, Italy, respectively, on 17 and 18 November 1943, and operated with the 15th Air Force until 19 April 1945.** USAF

North African Operations

In addition to the operations carried out from U.K. bases (and on shuttle missions), B-24 aircraft and crews of the 2nd Air Division carried out operations from North African bases in three major phases: (a) Torch, 13 December 1942–20 February 1943: (b) Husky, 2–19 July 1943; Ploesti, 1 August 1943; Post Husky 1943; and (c) 5th Army Support, 21 September–1 October 1943. Eighth Air Force Groups participating in these operations (44th, 93rd, and 389th) were on D. S. from the ETO operating in conjunction with and under the operational control of Air Forces in the Mediterranean.

On the Ploesti operation, 1 August 1943, carried out from very low level in conjunction with the 9th Air Force, the oil fields were heavily hit and production substantially curtailed. Thirty B-24's of 2nd Air Division were missing in action (MIA) and seventeen enemy aircraft destroyed.

Type/Operation	*Operation dates*	*No. of days operated*	*Groups carrying out missions*	*Aircraft*		*Tons of bombs on targets*	*A/C MIA*	*E/A claims*			*Casualties*		
				Total sorties	*Effective sorties*			*DEST*	*PROB*	*DAM*	*KIA*	*WND*	*MIA*
Torch Project	13 Dec 42–20 Feb 43	23	93rd	273	224	530.2	4			(Unavailable)			
Husky, Ploesti, Post Husky	2 July–21 Aug 43	20	93, 44, 389	989	892	2,428.2	54	121	12	35	28	88	420
5th Army Support	21 Sept–1 Oct 43	4	93, 44, 389	191	172	406.6	11	50	3	6	0	4	89
TOTAL N. AFRICAN OPS		47	93, 44, 389	1,453	1,288	3,365.0	69	171	15	41	28	92	509

CHAPTER FOUR

ETO

September 1943–May 1945

On 13 September, VIII Bomber Command was officially divided into three bombardment divisions, with the nine groups in the 1st Bomb Wing forming the 1st Bomb Division, commanded by Gen Williams. The six B-17 groups in the 4th Bomb Wing were renamed the 3rd Bomb Division, under Col Curtis E. LeMay. All four 202nd Combat Bomb Wing (Provisional) Liberator groups became the 2nd Bomb Division under the command of Gen James Hodges, its headquarters located at Ketteringham Hall. Col Leon Johnson moved from the 44th to command the 14th Wing, and Lt Col James L. Posey was promoted to command the Eightballs. The 44th, 93rd and 389th Bomb Groups were ordered to North Africa again in mid-September for a short time when the Salerno landings looked in jeopardy.

On 4 October, 361 bombers were dispatched but without PFF, and cloud ruled out accurate bombing at all primary targets. Twelve B-17s were shot down, and losses would have been higher had it not been for the strong P-47 escort and a diversion mission flown over the North Sea by thirty B-24Hs in the 392nd Bomb Group, together with six Liberators from the 44th and 93rd. (These two groups, and the 389th, newly returned from North Africa, were still licking their wounds, the 44th having lost sixteen B-24s shot down or written off in crashlandings three days before on a mission to Wiener Neustadt.) They certainly flushed the fighters, because over the North Sea they were jumped by thirty Bf 109s and Fw 190s.

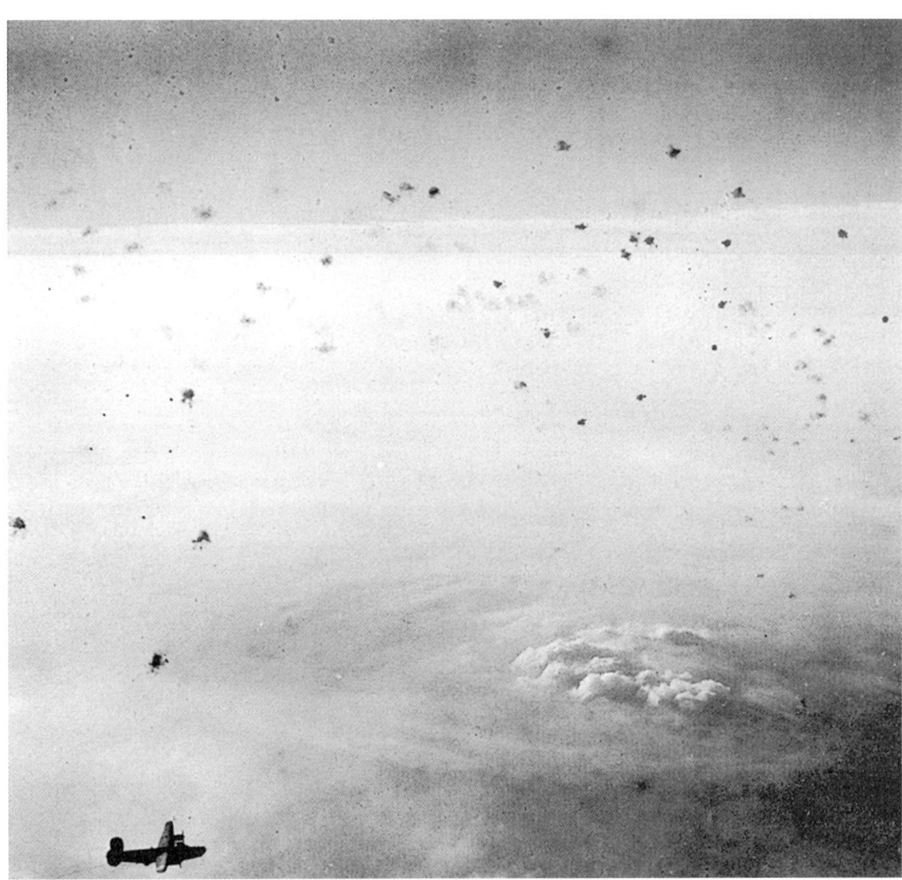

The 392nd Bomb Group was the fourth Liberator Group to join the 2nd Bomb Division in England, in August 1943; they are seen here encountering flak over France on 10 August. USAF

On 14 October, the Liberators were scheduled to participate in the double strike on Schweinfurt and Regensburg, but the third task force of sixty B-24s failed to complete assembly in the bad weather which prevailed and these took no further part in the mission which cost sixty B-17s. For the first two weeks of November, missions were cancelled because of thick fog, rain and high winds. Finally, on 16 November, the B-24 crews were dispatched to targets in Norway where visual bombing was used to advantage. Two days later the Liberators returned and bombed the Ju 88 assembly plant at Oslo-Kjeller and industrial targets in Oslo. Six Liberators were lost, three being forced to land in Sweden.

On 26 November, 633 bombers, the largest American formation ever assembled, bombed targets as far apart as Bremen and Paris. Early in December the B-24s attacked targets in France before switching to Germany again on 13 December, when the 445th Bomb Group from Tibenham flew their first mission. On the 16th, 535 heavies – including, for the first time, Liberators of the 446th Bomb Group, based at Bungay (Flixton) – bombed Bremen. The heavies were stood down on 21 December, but on the 22nd, 439 heavies bombed marshalling yards at Osnabruck and Munster. Some thirteen B-24s were lost, including two each from the 446th, 448th and 445th Bomb Groups. In the 44th formation, Lt Miller ditched in the Zuider Zee with only one man surviving, and Lt Oakley spiralled down into the clouds with only two men surviving; they became PoWs.

Regardless of enemy activity, many lives and ships could be lost to accidents, oxygen starvation, mid-air collisions or frostbite, as Tech Sgt Don Chase in the 44th Bomb Group recalls:

> At bombing altitude, temperatures of 50–55° below were not uncommon. An aircraft's enclosed forward cabin, while not heated, did protect us from wind, but aft, especially in the waist gun position, the 170mph-plus winds, coupled with Arctic-like mercury readings, caused much suffering to crewmen. Minor to severe cases of frostbite occurred. The advent of electrically-heated, snug-fitting flying suits (bunny suits) minimized the problem, although sometimes the suits shorted out (mine did once) and it was then essential to don fleece-lined jackets and pants in a hurry. Incidents occurred where a wounded crewman, unattended for just a few minutes while his fellow crewmen fought off enemy aircraft, died from exposure; others, still alive and in need of morphine, suffered extreme pain because syringe needles broke when attempting to penetrate hard, deep-frozen skin. On the other hand, freezing temperatures have saved some lives – I have heard tell that an artery severed, blood-spurting limb of a crewman was freeze-cauterized, and his life saved, simply by baring his injury to icy blasts.

On Christmas Eve the bombers were dispatched to V1 flying bomb sites in France; these sites went under the codename *Noball*. Some 670 bombers bombed twenty-three V1 sites without loss. VIII Bomber Command was stood down from Christmas Day until 30 December, when 658 heavies, escorted by fighters, bombed oil plants at Ludwigshafen near the German–Swiss border. The raid cost twenty-three heavies and twelve fighters, while twenty-three German fighters were claimed destroyed. On New Year's Eve 1943, the 8th completed its second year in England, with wide-ranging attacks on airfields in France.

Fog and rain grounded the bombers until 4 January, but then more than 500 heavies bombed the shipyards at Kiel. They returned to Kiel on 5 January, and this was the last mission under the auspices of VIII Bomber Command. The 15th Air Force had now been established in Italy, but it was decided to embrace both the 8th and the 15th in a new headquarters called US Strategic Air Forces, to be situated in Europe, at Bushey Hall, Teddington, Middlesex, previously the headquarters of the 8th Air Force. 'Tooey' Spaatz returned to England to command the new organization, while Gen Jimmy Doolittle, the famed Tokyo leader and former air racer, assumed command of the 8th Air Force, with its headquarters moving to High Wycombe. Lt Gen Ira C. Eaker was transferred to the Mediterranean theatre and replaced by Doolittle.

The first mission, under the auspices of the USAAFE, was on 7 January when 420 B-17s and B-24s caused considerable damage to chemical and substitute war material plants at Ludwigshafen and the engineering and transport industries in the twin city of Mannheim. Maj James M. Stewart, the famous Hollywood actor, CO of the 703rd Bomb Squadron, 445th Bomb Group, led forty-eight B-24s to the I G Farben Industrie plant at Ludwigshafen. As the bomb doors opened, a shell burst directly under his wing, but Stewart managed to regain control and complete the bomb-run. After the target he joined the wayward 389th Bomb Group which had strayed off course; the 389th lost eight planes, but Stewart's action probably prevented that group from total annihilation. Altogether, the 8th lost twelve bombers and seven fighters on the 7 January raids.

On 11 January a maximum effort involving over 570 B-17s and B-24s was attempted on aircraft factories at Waggum, Halberstadt and Oschersleben in the Brunswick area, a city notorious for its flak and fighter defences. However, the fighter escort soon became lost in the cloud layers over England, and many were forced to abort the mission. Two hours into the mission the order went out to the 2nd and 3rd Divisions to abandon the mission also.

Vast banks of strato-cumulus clouds covering most of Germany prevented visual bombing of targets, so attacks on targets in France throughout the remainder of January and early February became the order of the day. One exception was on 30 January, when a record 778 heavies were dispatched to the aircraft factories at Brunswick. Some 701 aircraft bombed using PFF techniques, while fifty-one dropped their bombs on targets of opportunity. Altogether, twenty aircraft were lost on the mission. Of the twenty-nine missions flown during January and February 1944, thirteen were to V1 rocket sites. On 5 February the bomber formations were swelled by the addition of B-24s in the 453rd Bomb Group, commanded by Col Joe Miller at Old Buckenham. Three days later 237 bombers attacked Frankfurt-on-Main, while 127 bombers attacked V1 sites at Watten and Siracourt, and another seventy-eight bombed targets of opportunity.

'Big Week'

Gen Doolittle had been biding his time, waiting for a period of relatively fine weather in which to mount a series of raids on the German aircraft industry. The meteorologists informed him that the week 20–25 February would be ideal for such an offensive, and it would go down in history as 'Big Week'. On 20 February the 2nd Bomb Division bombed the Bf 109 plants at Leipzig, and on 21 February the principal targets were the aircraft factories at Brunswick; on this occasion thick cloud obscured the objectives, however, and 764 bombers bombed using PFF techniques. Many groups attacked targets of opportunity, and airfields and aircraft depots were heavily bombed. Next day bad weather caused collisions during assembly, and eventually conditions became so bad that the 2nd Division received a recall while flying a scattered formation over the Low Countries. Some groups dropped their bombs on targets of opportunity, while two B-24s in the 445th Bomb Group did not receive the recall, and proceeded to their assigned target at Gotha.

On 23 February bad weather grounded the heavies, but on 24 February 867 were dispatched. Some 238 B-24s attacked the aircraft factories at Gotha, while the 458th from Horsham St Faith near Norwich flew a diversionary sweep over the North Sea. Flak was heavy and the B-24s met repeated attacks by the Luftwaffe. The 445th lost thirteen B-24s, while the 392nd Bomb Group lost seven and another thirteen returned badly damaged, and the 389th Bomb Group lost six. The 392nd Bomb Group dropped 98 per cent of its bombs within 2,000ft (610m) of the aiming point. (The average percentage of bombs dropped by the 2nd Bomb Division which fell within 2,000ft on visual missions under good to fair visibility in February 1944 was only 49 per cent.) The 44th had also achieved a highly accurate bomb-run. Intelligence

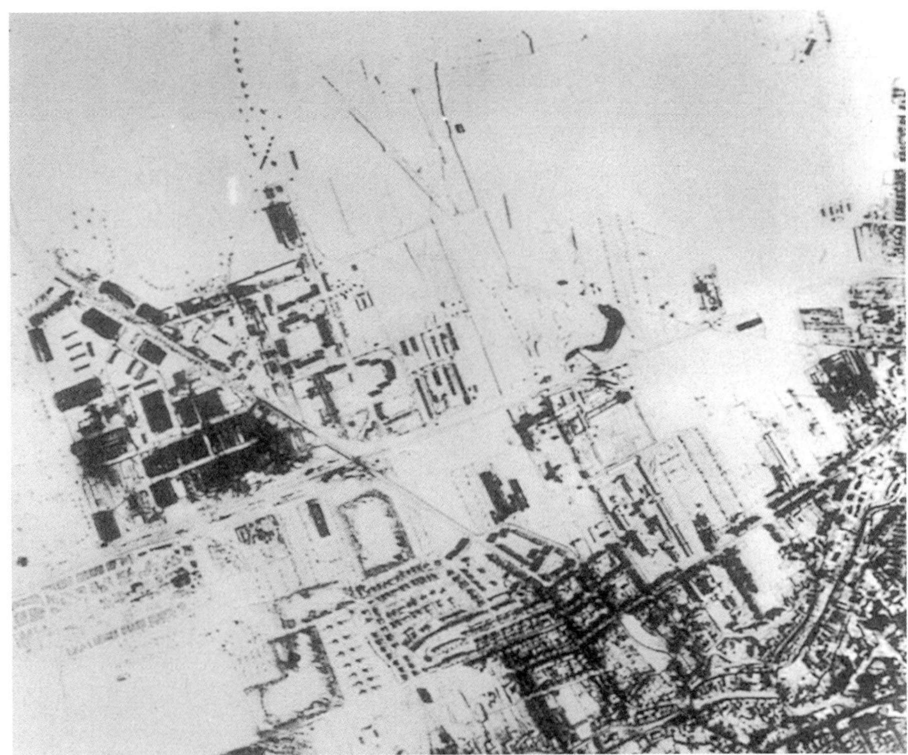

On 24 February 1944, during the height of 'Big Week', the Messerschmitt Bf 110 plant at Gotha, 'the most valuable single target in the enemy twin-engine fighter complex', was bombed by 238 B-24s from the eight bomb groups. Flak and fighters were heavy, and the 445th Bomb Group lost fifteen B-24s. The 392nd was extremely accurate, dropping 98 per cent of its bombs within 2,000ft (610m) of the aiming point. (The average percentage of bombs dropped by the 2nd Bomb Division which fell within 2,000ft on visual missions in February 1944 was only 49 per cent.) The 44th Bomb Group also achieved a highly accurate bomb-run. An estimated six to seven weeks' production of Bf 110s was lost. USAF

described Gotha as 'the most valuable single target in the enemy twin-engine fighter complex', and later estimated that six to seven week's production of BF 110s was lost. The 445th and 392nd Bomb Groups later received Presidential Unit Citations for their part in the raid.

Next day, 25 February, 'Big Week' ended when 1,154 bombers and 1,000 fighters made the deepest raid into Germany thus far, the 2nd Bomb Division attacking Furth near Nurnberg. Moreover Spaatz and Doolittle believed that, despite the loss of 226 bombers, the USSTAF, which had flown some 3,300 bomber sorties and had dropped 6,000 tons of bombs, had dealt the German aircraft industry a really heavy blow. However, while the Luftwaffe were certainly deprived of many replacement aircraft, and fighter production was halved the following month, it had cost 400 heavies and 4,000 casualties. Furthermore, machine tools, lathes and jigs had been left virtually untouched beneath the wreckage of the factories: they could be recovered and put into full production again.

The First US Raids on 'Big B'

Doolittle and his staff officers meanwhile felt confident about sending the bombers to Berlin, and after a false start on 4 March, 730 heavies, escorted by almost 800 fighters, went all the way on 6 March. Some 170 German fighters were claimed destroyed, although sixty-nine heavies were lost (the 2nd Division lost sixteen B-24s), the highest loss by the 8th in a single day. However, the Americans had at last bombed Berlin. Air Chief Marshal of the RAF, Arthur Harris, sent a message to his opposite number, Carl Spaatz, at High Wycombe: 'Heartiest congratulations on first US bombing of Berlin. It is more than a year since they were attacked in daylight, but now they have no safety there by day or night. All Germany learns the same lesson.'

The 8th was stood down on 7 March, but next day 600 bombers returned for the third raid on 'Big B' in a week. On 9 March 158 Liberators bombed targets in the Brunswick, Hannover and Nienburg areas. The 8th was stood down on 10 March, but the next day PFF techniques were used by thirty-four Liberators to attack a *Noball* site at Wizernes. V1 targets were again bombed on 12–13 March. Some 330 bombers hit Brunswick on 15 March, and the following day 679 bombers hit factory and airfield targets in Germany. The Luftwaffe was up in force, however, and twenty-three bombers were shot down. The mission to Frankfurt on 17 March was abandoned, but on the 18th, 679 bombers bombed aircraft plants and airfields in south-west Germany and Dornier works at Friedrichshafen.

The 392nd was decimated, losing fifteen Liberators. The 44th lost eight B-24s, while Col Joseph Miller, CO of the 453rd Bomb Group, who was leading the 2nd Combat Wing on only his fourth mission was also shot down. Miller survived and was taken prisoner. Col Ramsey D. Potts assumed command of the 453rd Bomb Group. Altogether forty-three bombers and thirteen fighters were lost on the 18 March raids. Next day 172 heavies carried out 'milk runs' to V1 sites in northern France.

On the 22nd, almost 800 B-17s and B-24s, including the 466th Bomb Group which would be making its bombing debut, were dispatched to Berlin. The Attlebridge group lost two B-24s in a mid-air collision (the first of six lost in collisions up until 27 March). Lt William Tinsman, co-pilot on the crew of Lt Rockford C. Griffith in the 67th Squadron, 44th Bomb Group, wrote of the Berlin mission:

> Target: Berlin, and this time we made it. It is the half-way mark for me since they raised it to thirty [the number of missions in a tour of combat: *see* quote below]. Things went beautifully

The 445th Bomb Group, seen here en route **to their target as high-flying escort fighters cross overhead, suffered another, even heavier loss on 27 September, when the Tibenham Group had twenty-five Liberators shot down in fierce fighter attacks.** USAF

until bombs away, and then persistent contrails and poor formation-flying raised hell with us. From there out it was every man for himself, just the way it shouldn't be. It was –40°, and my electric suit was out, I got kinda cold ... Flak ranged from light to heavy and accurate to inaccurate, but there was little over the target, which was located in the north-west corner of the town. We didn't see any enemy fighters as we had a beautiful escort in and out: P-38s, '47s and '51s. Five flak holes did little damage but narrowly missed several of the crew. We saw one B-24 have its tail blown off by flak, a '17 spin in ... and Pat G dropped his bombs through his bomb-bay doors, ripping the hell out of them ...

Tech Sgt Don Chase, also in the 44th formation wrote:

It was a long day. Up hours before dawn: breakfast, briefing, pre-flight; 8½ hours in flight dodging your own aircraft on the climb out through the clouds (and on return, too); sucking in your breath as shards of 88s and 110s pierce your ship's thin, olive-drab skin; checking the configuration of fighters to determine if they are bandits or Little Friends; hoping that the oil pressure of No. 4 engine doesn't drop any lower and possibly force your ship to be a straggler for enemy aircraft to prey on – all of this keeps the adrenalin surging. And it was on this mission that, as I straddled the catwalk during the bomb-run and pressed the bomb-bay anti-creep lever, a chunk of shrapnel ripped through my bunny suit, nearly making an instant soprano of me as it shorted out my suit. It was a cold flight home. The 2oz shot of 86 proof was especially welcome at the end of a difficult day.

Altogether the 8th dropped 4,800 tons of high explosive on Berlin in five raids during March 1944; then the weather closed in over the continent and shallow penetration missions to *Noball* sites in the Pas de Calais and airfields in France became the most frequent. There was also disturbing news, as Don Chase relates:

> Squadron operations passed along the news that each crewman must now fly thirty missions, not twenty-five, before his tour of combat was over. So instead of four, I now had nine missions to go. I didn't think I had enough luck to take me through nine. Operations called me in and said I'd only be required to fly a total of twenty-eight, based on the number of missions I'd already flown. Okay, fine, but that still meant three extra missions.

On 1 April, 246 B-24s of the 2nd Division headed for the chemical works at Ludwigshafen. Thick cloud over France forced all 192 B-24s of the 3rd Division to abandon the mission, however, leaving the 2nd Division to continue to the objective; but many groups failed to locate their targets, and some 162 B-24s bombed targets of opportunity at Pforzheim and Grafenhausen. On this mission Col James Thompson, CO of the 448th Bomb Group, was killed when, low on fuel, he and his crew bailed out but his parachute failed to open. (Col Jerry Mason, an ex-fighter pilot in the CBI theatre, took over at Seething two weeks later.) Further unnecessary stress was caused when some thirty-eight bombers in the 44th and 392nd Bomb Groups veered off course and bombed a Swiss town in error, an incident which led to America having to pay the Swiss thousands of dollars in reparation. Altogether the 1 April mission cost the 2nd Division ten B-24s.

It was not until 8 April that the cloudy conditions abated and allowed the 8th to assemble in force. Some thirteen combat wings, consisting of 644 bombers, were dispatched to aircraft depots throughout western Germany, including 192 bombers which attacked Brunswick. Some thirty-four heavies were shot down during the day's missions, including ten B-24s in the 466th Bomb Group.

On Easter Sunday, 9 April, 104 Liberators headed to the aircraft assembly plant at Tutow. On this occasion two B-24s, belonging to the 389th and 392nd Bomb Groups, collided at 8,000ft (2,440m) while forming up: nine men in the 392nd B-24 were killed, and seven men in the forward section of the 389th Liberator died instantly when five 500lb bombs and the full fuel load exploded. Next day, 10 April, 730 crews bombed airfield targets in France and the Low Countries; these included thirty Liberators of the 467th Bomb Group at Rackheath, making its bombing debut and led by the CO, Col Albert J. Shower.

On 13 April, overall command of the Combined Bomber Offensive and the 8th Air Force officially passed to Gen Dwight D. Eisenhower, newly appointed Supreme Allied Commander. The 2nd Bomb Division was assigned German aircraft manufacturing installations near Munich. One of the B-24s in the 453rd Bomb Group carried the 2nd Combat Wing Leader, Maj James M. Stewart, who had recently joined the Old Buckenham Group as Operations Officer.

The Hamm Debacle

On 22 April the Liberators were late taking off for a raid on the marshalling yards at Hamm, and on their return it was getting dark. Unbeknown to the B-24 crews, they were being followed by German fighters which had taken off from the bases along the coast, and over England the Luftwaffe twin-engined fighters attacked. William E. Ruck, radio operator in *Ice Cold Katie* in the 448th Bomb Group, which was piloted by James J. Bell, recalls:

> We didn't know that Me 410 night fighters had followed us back to England because it was full dark and they were apparently using clouds as cover. However, the English anti-aircraft batteries knew they were there because they showed up on radar. So a situation developed where English AA batteries were firing at the German night-fighters, who were firing at the American bombers who were firing at the German fighters. It was mass confusion on a grand scale, and no one could say who caused damage to which planes.
>
> The first plane to attempt to land at Seething was *Peggy Jo* of the 714th Bomb Squadron. Following standard procedure, it turned on its landing lights as it approached Seething, which was the signal for the tower to turn on the runway lights. Of course, with its landing lights on the plane made an excellent target, and the German fighters simply followed the runway lights and fired at a point between the two landing lights of the plane. The bomber's starboard engine was set afire, forcing the pilot [Melvin L. Alspaugh] to pull up so the crew could bail out, and the bomber crashed at Worlingham, just beyond Seething.

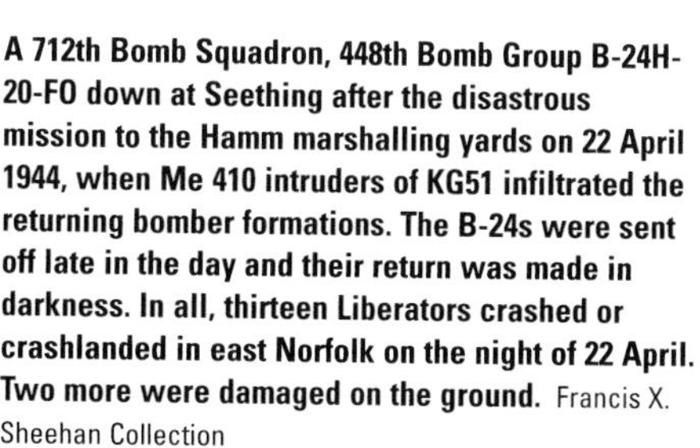

A 712th Bomb Squadron, 448th Bomb Group B-24H-20-FO down at Seething after the disastrous mission to the Hamm marshalling yards on 22 April 1944, when Me 410 intruders of KG51 infiltrated the returning bomber formations. The B-24s were sent off late in the day and their return was made in darkness. In all, thirteen Liberators crashed or crashlanded in east Norfolk on the night of 22 April. Two more were damaged on the ground. Francis X. Sheehan Collection

The second plane to come in was the *Vadie Raye* and she was on fire. Most of the crew had baled out, but the pilots, Gene Skaggs and William Blum, brought the plane down on the main runway, the swerved it off and into the field so it wouldn't block the landing of the following planes. The remainder of the crew got out and ran to safety just before the *Vadie Raye* exploded. The explosion and fire produced dense smoke which blew across the main runway and greatly reduced visibility.

The third plane to come in [*The Ruth E.K. Allah Hassid*] landed safely, but was strafed as it rolled up the runway. The crew got the plane to the end of the runway, but because of the strafing, they abandoned it there and ran for the safety of a revetment. Our plane, *Ice Cold Katie*, was the fourth plane to land, and as we came in on our final approach we could see the smoke from the *Vadie Raye* but, because of the smoke, we couldn't see the plane stopped at the end of the runway. We experienced some strafing as we rolled up the runway, and it wasn't until we passed through the smoke from *Vadie Raye* that we were able to see the plane blocking the runway ahead. The pilots were able to stop *Ice Cold Katie* just short of that plane, and because of the strafing, we left the plane and ran for the relative safety of a revetment.

The fifth plane to come in [*Tondelayo*] got down safely, but as it passed through the smoke from *Vadie Raye*, it found two planes blocking the end of the runway and wasn't able to stop before slamming into the tail of *Ice Cold Katie*, forcing it into the plane in front. When the pile-up stopped, the crew of this plane also jumped out and ran for the revetment. One of the gunners somehow caught his parachute in something as he jumped out of the waist window and the ripcord was pulled, and in the midst of the disaster and strafing we all had to laugh as we watched him run for safety with his parachute spilling out behind him!

Now there were three planes blocking the end of the main runway and one on fire beside it, so the rest of the group had to land on the short runway. The strafing continued for what seemed like a long time, but it must have been just minutes; and then the German fighters were gone from Seething.

In the night's confusion, thirteen Liberators crashed or crashlanded in east Norfolk, and two more were damaged on the ground. Thirty-eight men were killed, and another twenty-three were injured.

The B-24s were stood down, but the missions resumed on 24 April when 750 bombers were dispatched to bomb aircraft plants in the Munich area. On 25 April almost 300 bombers blasted marshalling yards at Mannheim and airfields in France. Next day, 292 heavies bombed Brunswick after thick cloud prevented bombing at primary targets, and nearly fifty more bombed targets of opportunity in the Hildesheim-Hannover areas. Furthermore for the first time, on 27 April, the 8th flew two bombing missions in one day. The following day, the heavies bombed targets chiefly in France. On 29 April, 579 bombers hit the Freidrichstrasse Bahnhof, centre of the mainline and underground railway system in Berlin, while thirty-eight other heavies attacked targets of opportunity in the area including Magdeburg. The 2nd Bomb Division, flying thirty minutes behind schedule, brought up the rear of the bomber stream, and were met in strength by the Luftwaffe. Altogether, twenty-five Liberators were lost, including a 458th Bomb Group B-24 which was forced to land in Sweden.

During the morning of 1 May, in support of the *Pointblank* directive, more than 500 heavies were dispatched to twenty-three *Noball* targets in the Pas de Calais, while in the afternoon, 328 B-17s and B-24s bombed marshalling yards and railway centres in Belgium and France. Three days later, 851 B-17s and B-24s set out to bomb Brunswick and Berlin, but bad weather forced them to abort the mission over the Low Countries. On the 5th, thirty-three B-24s bombed a *Noball* site at Sottevast, and on the 6th, seventy B-24s bombed another V1 site at Siracourt. Thick overcast cloud prevented ninety other bombers from bombing more V1 sites. On 7 May the heavies were accompanied by B-24s of the 486th and 487th Bomb Groups for the first time, when 342 heavies bombed Osnabruck, Munster and targets of opportunity. The 486th and 487th Bomb Groups, commanded by Col Glendon P. Overing and Lt Col Beirne Lay (who had been one of Eaker's original staff officers in 1942) had arrived at Sudbury (Acton) and Lavenham respectively, in April, to join the 92nd Bomb Wing. In the afternoon, twenty-eight B-24s bombed targets in Belgium.

On 8 May, Berlin was bombed in the morning by 378 B-17s, while 287 B-24s and forty-nine B-17s hit aircraft factories in the Brunswick area, and twenty-nine other heavies attacked targets of opportunity. In the afternoon, eighty-one B-17s bombed *Noball* sites, while fifty-six B-24s bombed marshalling yards at Brussels. Altogether, forty-one bombers were shot down on the two raids. Next day the Liberators attacked the railway marshalling yards at Liege, Belgium, and on the 11th, 254 B-24s bombed marshalling yards in France. Five Liberators, including one carrying Col Beirne Lay Jr, CO of the 487th Bomb Group, were shot down. (Lay evaded capture and was eventually returned to England.)

Missions were being flown almost daily, and on 12 May the target was Zeitz. For Tech Sgt Don Chase, in the 44th Bomb Group, the Zeitz mission would be his twenty-fifth of the war: survive three more and he could go home. All of the 'Eightballs' aircraft reached the target, and all returned to Shipdham safely. Off in the distance though, Don Chase saw, at about two o'clock level, a B-24 with its top turret plastic bubble completely shot away. Chase wrote: 'I kept thinking, "headless horseman … headless horseman." The crippled ship continued flying, but slowly fell behind the group formation and of course as a straggler he was a prime enemy aircraft target. Hope he makes it. Hope *we* make it!' Chase's ship did. For those that did not, there was the unhappy process of clearing a billet, as he explains : 'When a crew goes down, foot lockers are prised open and personal belongings are collected, minus any objectionable material or firearms, and shipped to their next-of-kin. Their beds are stripped and the thin mattresses folded. Soon, newly assigned young men will arrive and the beds will be made again.'

Don Chase got through his twenty-sixth mission, to Tutow, Germany, on 13 May, and to Siracourt on the 15th, when thirty-eight B-17s and ninety B-24s hit *Noball* sites in France – but bad weather meant that no further missions would be flown until 19 May. The wait was a trying time, or at least it was for a man wanting to fly his twenty-eighth and final mission. On the 13 May mission the Liberator groups' seventh mission in a row, Chase had shown his nervous frustration – probably brought on by the realization that he was almost 'home' – when, during an enemy fighter attack, he emerged from the relative safety of the armour plate that protected the co-pilot's back, and watched the action. He says, 'Oh, how I wished I could shoot back … please, don't let them strip my bed … Finally I couldn't resist any more – I just had to do something positive. As an enemy aircraft came barrelling through our formation I pulled the trigger of my Verey pistol and fired a signal flare at him. Useless? Foolish? Certainly, but I did get to fire one futile "shot" at the enemy.'

Chase now wanted to fly his final mission quickly – yet he did not want to fly it at all. What made it worse was the fact that he knew of at least one man, and had heard of others, who were killed on what was supposed to be their tour finale. Finally Chase had his chance on the 19 May, when 291 B-24s crossed into Holland and headed for Brunswick:

> This was always a tough one. Again, the marshalling yards were the centre of attention. Almost 150 enemy aircraft made attacks on the formation, but no losses were experienced by the 44th Group. We were lucky: others were not. The brunt of the enemy attacks was borne by a newly arrived group, the 492nd Bomb Group. Attracted perhaps by the non-painted silvery finish of the brand-new planes that glinted in the sun, the Me 109s and Fw 190s evaded the cordon of American fighters and pounced on the fledgling group, which was flying in tight formation off to our left and below us. I watched as enemy aircraft, lined up six or eight abreast, made a frontal attack that felled four, maybe five bombers. I saw no return fire from the B-24 gunners, who possibly held their fire thinking the oncoming fighters were friendlies. Few 'chutes were sighted as the '24s spun earthward in increasingly tight circles which caused an upward G-force that few men could overcome. Later, other B-24s fell, but I looked away, feeling nauseous, as each began its fatal spiral.

In all, the 492nd, which had been in operation for only eight days, lost eight B-24s; also Lt Wyman Bridges brought *Lucky Lass* home to North Pickenham, Norfolk, after a collision with a Bf 109, with only two engines and having lost half the starboard wing. His miraculous feat earned him the DFC. Some 273 B-24s dropped their bombs on target, but twenty-eight heavies and twenty fighters were lost. Don Chase concludes, 'So, after twenty-eight missions of varying intensity and the loss of many friends, I was through with combat. And I wished that nobody, anywhere, should ever have to go to war again.'

On 20 May, 287 heavies bombed targets in France, but 250 more scheduled to bomb Liege and Brussels, were forced to abort because of the dense cloud. Groups were stood down on 21 May, and on 22 May, ninety-four B-24s bombed a *Noball* target at Siracourt. On the 23 May, 804 B-17s and B-24s – including for the first time B-24s of the 34th Bomb Group from Mendlesham, commanded by Col Ernest J. Wackwitz – bombed several targets including Hamburg, Saarbrucken and airfields in France. Only one bomber was lost, a 458th Bomb Group B-24 which collided with a Fortress over Eye, Suffolk as planes formed up for the mission to Bourges; six crewmen were killed. Next day, 447 B-17s and B-24s bombed Berlin, while 400 B-24s bombed airfields in France. On 27 May, 923 B-17s bombed the German rail network for the loss of twenty-four of the heavies, including a 755th Squadron, 458th Bomb Group B-24 which collided with another north of Cromer during assembly. Next day the 8th dispatched a record 1,282 bombers to seven oil targets in Germany. Altogether, thirty-two bombers lost. On 29 May, 881 heavies bombed several targets, including oil plants at Politz and the Ju 88 factory at Tutow. Altogether thirty-four bombers were lost.

On the morning of 30 May, 911 heavies – including for the first time the B-24s of the 489th Bomb Group from Halesworth, Suffolk – were dispatched in six forces to attack aircraft targets in Germany, marshalling yards in Belgium and France, and *Noball* sites in the Pas de Calais. On 31 May, 371 bombers – including for the first time B-24s in the 490th Bomb Group from Eye, Suffolk, led by the CO, Col Lloyd H. Watnee – attacked targets in Germany and Belgium.

Meanwhile, four specially equipped Liberators in the 753rd Bomb Squadron in the 458th Bomb Group attempted to bomb five bridges at Beaumont-sur-Oise, Melun and Meulan in France with the revolutionary *Azon* VB-1. This was a vertical bomb, which could be released by an aircraft at a distance and then directed onto the target by a controller in a mother ship. Basically, it was a conventional 1,000lb or 2,000lb bomb fitted with radio-controlled movable tail fins: after release, a flare in the tail ignited and kept it in view of the controller in the mother ship, who steered the bomb, in the horizontal plane only, by radio. Each B-24 could carry three such bombs, but had to circle the target as many times to release them, which was an obvious disadvantage. The 30 May raid ended in failure, with none of the bombs hitting the target. Experimental raids continued into June, with at most fifteen Liberators being used on any one mission; but results did not improve, and Gen Doolittle was forced to abandon the project.

Operation *Cover*

Operation *Cover* called for raids on coastal defences, mainly in the Pas de Calais, to deceive the Germans as to the area to be invaded by the Allied armies massing in Britain. On 2 June the 8th mounted two strikes on the Pas de Calais: in the first raid, 776 B-17s and B-24s were involved; in the second, 300 bombers – including, for the first time, B-24s of the 489th and 491st Bomb Groups flying the first full 95th Wing mission – struck at airfields and railway targets in France. The two 95th Wing groups bombed Bretigny, Creil and Villeneuve airfields near Paris, for the loss of one 491st Bomb Group Liberator and four 489th B-24s. Flak also caused varying degrees of damage to fifty-nine other machines. Thirty-five 491st Liberators approached their home base at Metfield, Suffolk in gathering darkness and landed safely, but at Halesworth, three of the returning thirty-seven 489th Liberators crashed and had to be written off.

Leon Vance: Medal of Honor

For the next three days, hundreds of 8th Air Force bombers flew two missions a day to the Pas de Calais area. On 5 June, 629 heavies attacked coastal defence installations in the Cherbourg–Caen and Pas de Calais areas, together with three *Noball* sites and a railway bridge. Six Liberators were lost, including *Missouri Sue*, a 66th Bomb Squadron, 44th Bomb Group PFF ship which carried the 48th Bomb Group deputy commander Lt Col Leon R. Vance. A malfunction prevented bomb release at the target, a *Noball* site near Wimereaux, and despite protests, Vance ordered the crew to go around again. This time the bomb drop was made by hand, but two bombs hung up.

An 88mm salvo burst directly under the port wing, putting three engines out of action and instantly killing Capt. Louis A. Mazure, the pilot, and seriously wounding Earl L. Carper, the co-pilot. Vance, who was standing behind the pilot's seats, had his right foot virtually severed from his leg but despite this he managed to reach the panel and feather the three dead engines. Carper cut all four engines and turned the B-24 towards England. Vance managed to get into the cockpit and succeeded in ditching the aircraft off Broadstairs, Kent. The impact blew him clear, and he was quickly rescued by ASR who gave him immediate medical attention. He was awarded the Medal of Honor, and was the fifth and final airman in the 2nd Bomb Division to receive the award. His right foot was amputated and he was later invalided home in a C-54. But somewhere between Iceland and Newfoundland the Skymaster with its crew and patients disappeared without trace.

Lt Col Leon R. Vance Jr *(left)* pictured at Wendover Field, Utah in December 1943, with his CO, Col Ezekiel W. Napier. USAF

D-Day

On D-Day, 6 June 1944, groups flew three missions totalling 2,362 bomber sorties, comprising 1,729 B-17s and B-24s, and dropping 3,596 tons of bombs for the loss of only four aircraft. One was a B-24 from the 487th Bomb Group at Lavenham, which was shot down. (A 389th Bomb Group B-24 crashed just after take-off and all the crew were lost.) The other two came from the 493rd Bomb Group at Debach, Suffolk, which was making its combat debut, led by Col Delbert Helton, for a bombing strike on Lisieux. Ten-tenths cloud cover prevented 'Helton's Hellcats' from bombing their target. Then at 10:28 hours, at 11,000ft, *No Love – No Nothin* in the 863rd Squadron, piloted by Capt Jack Cooper, struck the tail of *Moby Dick* of the 862nd Squadron, which was being flown by by Lt Donald L. Russell. *No Love – No Nothin* was seen to disintegrate, and both Liberators disappeared into the overcast; there was only one survivor from Cooper's ship, and none from Russell's. Moreover, the death toll could have been higher, because a piece of flak went through the steel helmet worn by Sam Hale, the 861st Bomb Squadron commander, through the cloth helmet and lodged on top of his head; had he been two inches taller he would not have gone on to finish the twenty-six missions he flew.

Groundcrews worked throughout the night of 6 June and all day on the 7th so that two missions could be flown. On 8 June, 1,135 bombers hit communications targets in France. Bad weather prevented 400 heavies from bombing and next day cancelled out any bomber strikes at all; it also severely curtailed operations on 10 June. Of the 873 bombers airborne, over 200 were forced to abort because of cloud conditions. Some 589 bombers, including thirty-one PFF ships, bombed nine coastal installations in the Pas de Calais and eight airfields in France. On 11 and 12 June bad weather ruled out targets in Germany, and the 8th dispatched its bombers to France again. On 11 June, the 96th Wing – including twelve Liberators from the 753rd *Azon* Squadron, 458th Bomb Group – destroyed a vital rail bridge at Blois St Denis on the Loire, about half-way between Tours and Orleans. The 458th received a 2nd Bomb Division citation.

Tactical targets in France continued to be attacked until 15 June, when 1,225 bombers attacked an oil refinery at Misbourg. On 20 June a record 1, 402 bombers, involving two missions, were dispatched to oil and *Noball* targets. In the morning's mission 1,257 B-17s and B-24s of the 1st and 3rd Bomb Divisions made for Hamburg and the Hannover and Magdeburg areas respectively. The 2nd Division made a 9¼-hour round trip to Politz and Ostermoor. Some 760 fighters escorted the three divisions to their targets, while 130 B-24s bombed ten *Noball* targets in the Pas de Calais escorted by forty-two P-47s. Over the Baltic the Luftwaffe intercepted the 2nd Division, and Bf 110s and Me 410s wreaked havoc. The 492nd Bomb Group at North Pickenham lost fourteen B-24s, although five of the eighteen B-24s that put down at Bulltofta airfield at Malmo in Sweden, came from this group. In all, fifty heavies and seven fighters were lost this day. There was some consolation in that synthetic oil production at the Politz plant had been severely reduced.

On 21 June the 8th flew its second shuttle mission from England. The operation, codenamed *Frantic*, consisted of 1,311 B-17s. A second formation, made up of the rest of the 3rd Bomb Division, the 1st Bomb Division and the 2nd Bomb Division, bombed Berlin and returned to England. Despite the intense fighter cover near Berlin, Me 410s swooped on the rear of the 1st Division formation and made several attacks on the B-17s. Altogether, forty-four Fortresses and Liberators were shot down.

The 8th continued its bombing of *Noball* targets and airfields in France, and on 23 June two missions were flown. At midday, 211 bombers attacked twelve V1 sites escorted by four Mustang groups which, after the strikes, broke off and strafed transportation targets in the Paris area. In the late afternoon, 196 bombers attacked airfield targets in France.

Edward R. Glotfelty, a pilot in the 863rd Squadron, 493rd Bomb Group, was on the mission to St Avord, France, on 25 June, when he experienced difficulties, as he recalls:

> After we dropped our bombs we had a runaway prop on No. 2 engine. I tried to feather, but was unable to control it. The vibration was tremendous, shaking the whole plane, and the noise was deafening. We lost speed and dropped out of the formation. The shortest return route took me over Normandy beaches. My interest at the time was to hold altitude as much as possible, but we were going down because of the great drag on the plane caused by the runaway prop. I started having trouble with the No. 4 engine, the rpm surging, engine cutting out, and the plane yawing because of the loss of power on the outboard engine. We were now down to 12,000 feet [3,660m] and arriving over Normandy. I marvelled at the panorama of ships and barrage balloons. With the second engine in trouble I didn't think we could make it back to England and I saw two airfields below me, one obviously new, one runway fighter strip carved out of the countryside, and one paved mature field that was farther from the beaches. I decided to go down and chose the field closer to the coast.
>
> I circled over the field, saw fighters on the strip, guessed at the wind direction and had another engine lose power! We were out of position, no power, and dropping like a rock. I ordered wheels up and decided to land on the wide dirt strip alongside of the runway. We hit perfectly. The left wing tip hit second, after the fuselage, and seemed to help cushion the crash. The fuselage split on the right side and the crew was able to get out through the crack. No one was injured though Gene Cromer, the engineer, had some radio equipment fall on him. The force of the landing was so great that the No. 1 engine was torn off completely and the plane was totally destroyed. The last I saw of it, a large crane was trying to drag the wreck out of the way so they could continue the war!
>
> We were checked out by a Canadian doctor, loaded on a truck going to the beach, put on a British LST and by the next day were back in England. The funny thing was that the only clothes we had were electrically heated flying suits. We spent the night in London and were treated like Poles or some foreign air force.

By now tours had been raised from thirty to thirty-five missions. Headquarters also announced that deep penetration missions would rank equally with the short-haul raids in the table of missions per tour. On 7 July the 2nd Division flew an 8¼-hour round trip to the Junkers factory at Bernberg. All three divisions departed the coast of England at different points, with the 1st and 3rd Divisions converging about a hundred miles west of Berlin, leaving the B-24s to fly farther north and parallel with the Fortresses. Unfortunately for the Liberator crews, more than 200 German fighters attacked the 2nd Division, and the 492nd Bomb Group lost eleven B-24s in quick succession. Worse was to follow.

On 21 July the 8th went to Schweinfurt, and the 2nd Bomb Division lost twenty-six Liberators to enemy action and collisions. On 24 July, Operation *Cobra* was scheduled to penetrate German defences west of St Lô and secure Coutances, but bad weather prevented all but 352 of the 1,586 bombers from bombing the primary for fear of hitting their own troops. On 25 July, 1,495 heavies dropped thousands of fragmentation bombs and 100lb GP bombs on German positions in the Marigny-St Gilles region just west of St Lô, just ahead of advancing troops of the US 1st Army. Some groups bombed short when smoke markers dropped by the lead ships on bomb release were blown slowly back towards the American lines. Also bombs from the last few B-24s in the division hurtled into American forward positions, killing 102 men and wounding 380; among the dead was Gen McNair. Five bombers were shot down.

Staff Sgt Hugh R. McLaren, ball turret gunner in the 565th Bomb Squadron, 389th Bomb Group at Hethel, poses in front of the B-24J-5-FO 42-51474 which was originally just called Patches. **On 6 June 1944,** Patches **was almost cut in half by a premature explosion of a fragmentation bomb. It was repaired, and the plane's name changed to** D-Day Patches. **A total of 2,362 bomber sorties, made up of 1,729 B-17s and B-24s, was flown on D-Day, dropping 3,596 tons of bombs for the loss of only three aircraft.** Hugh McLaren Jr

James Stewart, Hollywood Star and Liberator Commander

In July 1944 James Maitland Stewart, better known as 'Jimmy', was coming to the end of a very distinguished Liberator flying career. Everywhere the Hollywood actor went he was recognized, although on duty in the air and on the ground he was treated like any other officer – almost. Born of Scottish-Irish parents on 20 May 1908 in Indiana, Pennsylvania, where his father was a hardware merchant, Stewart studied architecture at Princetown University, New Jersey, where he acted while a student. After summer stock in Falmouth, Massachusetts he made his professional debut in *Goodbye Again* and went with it to Broadway. By 1940, when he appeared on Broadway again, in *Harvey*, he had appeared in over twenty movies and won an Academy award for his role in *The Philadelphia Story*.

Then in 1941, to everyone's amazement, he gave up his £3,260 a month salary in the movie industry and tried to enlist in the Army Air Corps. Stewart owned his own aircraft, had logged over 200 hours of civilian flying and possessed a commercial pilot's licence. However, he weighed only 147lb (67kg): 10 lb (4.5kg) too light for the gangling 6ft 4in (1m 90cm) actor, and he was rejected. In less than a month he had reached the prescribed weight but before he could enlist, his draft number came up. 'First lottery I ever won,' he drawled. Stewart reported to Moffett Field, California on 21 March 1941 where he completed his basic training.

James M. Stewart. USAF

Stewart shunned the publicity and logged another 100 hours' flying at his own expense during weekend passes. All he wanted was to fly, preferably in combat. However, it was not until January 1942 that he received his commission and 'wings', and on 7 July 1942 was promoted to 1st Lieutenant. He flew AT-9 advanced trainers at Mather Field, and for six months checked out bombardiers at the Bombardier Training School, Kirkland Field, Albuquerque, New Mexico. He then completed a heavy bomber course at Hobbs Field, New Mexico, where he checked out as first pilot, or aircraft commander, before being sent to Gowen Field, Idaho for nine months as a B-17 instructor. He became Operations Officer and checked out four-engine bomber pilots in emergency procedures at 2nd Air Force Headquarters at Salt Lake City.

Finally, in August 1943, after countless requests for a transfer, Stewart was posted to the 445th Bomb Group (heavy), equipped with B-24 Liberators, at Sioux City, Iowa, as Operations Officer of the 703rd Squadron. After only three weeks, on 7 July 1943, he was promoted to captain and given command of the squadron on merit. In November 1943 the 445th left for Tibenham, Suffolk, England on the Southern Ferry Route to become part of the 8th Air Force – and Stewart went with them. On 7 January 1944 he led forty-eight B-24s of the 445th to Ludwigshafen. As the bomb doors opened, a shell burst directly under his wing, but Stewart managed to regain control and complete the bomb-run. After the target he joined the wayward 389th Bomb Group which had strayed off course, and although eight 389th B-24s were lost, his action probably prevented that group from total annihilation. On 20 January 1944 he was promoted to major, a rank he had previously refused to accept until, as he said, 'My junior officers get promoted from lieutenants.'

On 30 March 1944 Stewart joined the 453rd Bomb Group at Old Buckenham, Norfolk as Operations Officer to replace Maj Curtis Cofield who had been killed in action only three days before. Over the next few weeks Maj Stewart took his turn as Air Commander of bombing missions. On 13 April he flew 2nd Combat Wing lead against German aircraft manufacturing installations near Munich. All but one of the 453rd Bomb Group Liberators returned to Old Buckenham.

In two months the group led the 2nd Bomb Division in bombing accuracy. By now the wiry, highly strung Stewart was thirty-six years of age, and his combat career was coming to an end. Altogether he flew twenty combat missions as command pilot, including fourteen wing leads and one division lead. On 3 June he was promoted to Lt Col, and on 1 July he moved to 20th Combat Wing Headquarters at Hethel as chief of staff to Brig Gen Ted Timberlake. By July 1944 he had been awarded the DFC for 'exceptional achievement in combat while leading an attack on aircraft factories at Brunswick', and the air medal with one oak-leaf cluster.

On 29 March 1945 Stewart was promoted to full Colonel; he served at 2nd Wing Headquarters until 14 June 1945. By the end of the war he had added an oak leaf cluster to his DFC and two oak leaf clusters to his air medal, and had been awarded the distinguished service medal. In 1945 the French awarded him the Croix de Guerre with Palm. Stewart returned to Hollywood and starred in many memorable movies, including *No Highway in the Sky* (1952), *Strategic Air Command* (1955), *The Spirit of St Louis* (1957), *The Flight of the Phoenix* (1965) and *The Glenn Miller Story* (1953), which had an aviation theme. He will perhaps best be remembered, however, as the drawling, friendly-faced cowboy in westerns such as *Winchester 73, The Man from Laramie* and *The Man Who Shot Liberty Valance* (1962). Stewart remained in the Air Force Reserve, and on 23 July 1959 he was promoted to brigadier general. He died in June 1997.

Late in July the ball turrets were removed from many Liberators to improve stability and altitude performance. During the last week of July, Gen Doolittle carried out the first stage of his plan to convert the B-24 groups of the 3rd Division to B-17s. The 486th and 487th Bomb Groups in the 92nd Wing were taken off operations, and by the end of the month were ready to begin combat missions in the Fortresses. Between the end of August and mid-September, the 34th, 490th and 493rd Groups in the 93rd Wing also changed over to the B-17.

August followed the same operational pattern as July, with bombing raids on

One of the best ways an airman could express his love of home, or American womanhood in general, was to have his favourite pin-up, or his girl-friend, wife or fiancée, painted on the nose of his aircraft, quite often in nude form. Although it is not immediately apparent, B-24J-160-CO 44-40398 The Shack **in the 861st Bomb Squadron, 493rd Bomb Group at Debach is a clever pun which refers to Ann Shackleford, pilot Capt David L. 'Doc' Conger's fiancée.** The Shack **was transferred to the 458th Bomb Group at Horsham St Faith in the late summer of 1944 when the 3rd Division converted to the Fortress. Conger and his crew flew the last mission of their tour on 14 January 1945.** USAF

Bombs dropped by Liberators of the 492nd Bomb Group explode on an important rail junction at Angers, France, during a raid on 6 August 1944. Next day the North Pickenham group flew their 67th and final mission and was de-activated. The 492nd Bomb Group had lost fifty-four Liberators from May to July 1944, and four in seven missions during August, and morale had collapsed. Crews and aircraft were re-distributed among the Liberator groups. USAF

airfields in France and strategic targets in Germany. On 4 August, 1,250 heavies bombed oil refineries, aircraft factories, airfields and the experimental establishment at Peenemunde in two raids, and next day 1,062 bombers bombed eleven oil-producing centres in central Germany without loss. On 6 August, 953 bombers bombed Berlin, and oil and manufacturing centres in Germany for the loss of twenty-five bombers. On 7 August, the 492nd Bomb Group was withdrawn from combat. In the period May to July 1944, it had lost fifty-four B-24s, the heaviest loss for any group for a three-month period. The 2nd Bomb Division now totalled an unlucky thirteen groups, with the 491st Bomb Group moving from the 45th Combat Wing to take the place of the 492nd in the 14th Combat Wing. The 45th Wing, which had begun with only two groups, ceased to exist on 14 August when the 489th was transferred to the 20th Wing as a fourth group.

Changes were imminent in the 3rd Bomb Division too, but for the time being, as on 18 August, their missions continued in B-24s, to France. Tech Sgt Terry Parsons, a radio operator-gunner in the 862nd Squadron, 493rd Bomb Group, wrote:

> We went to an airfield near Amiens – Rue de Balcourt, or something like that. And was it *rough*!!! Wooee! those ack-ack gunners had really been checked out! We lost two planes and the 34th Bomb Group lost three. Their first shot blew our leader's tail off clean. He just went straight down – poor devils didn't have a chance. Washington got it too, but I guess they all got out. Hansen was really scared, for certain, but so was everybody. Our formation just split from hell to breakfast. 'A' Group didn't get much flak at all.

Trucking and *Market Garden*

On 29 August, the 93rd, 446th and 448th Bomb Groups in the 20th Wing in the 2nd Bomb Division began 'trucking' missions to the armies in France who were in urgent need of fuel and supplies. The bulk of the operation was completed using B-24s, which were ideal for the task. On 11 September the 458th, 466th and 467th Bomb Groups of the 96th Wing also started 'trucking' missions. From 19 September until 3 October the 96th Wing flew no combat missions, but established a forward base at the airfield at Clastres, near St Quentin, France, and ferried gasoline for Patton's tanks and motorized units. During

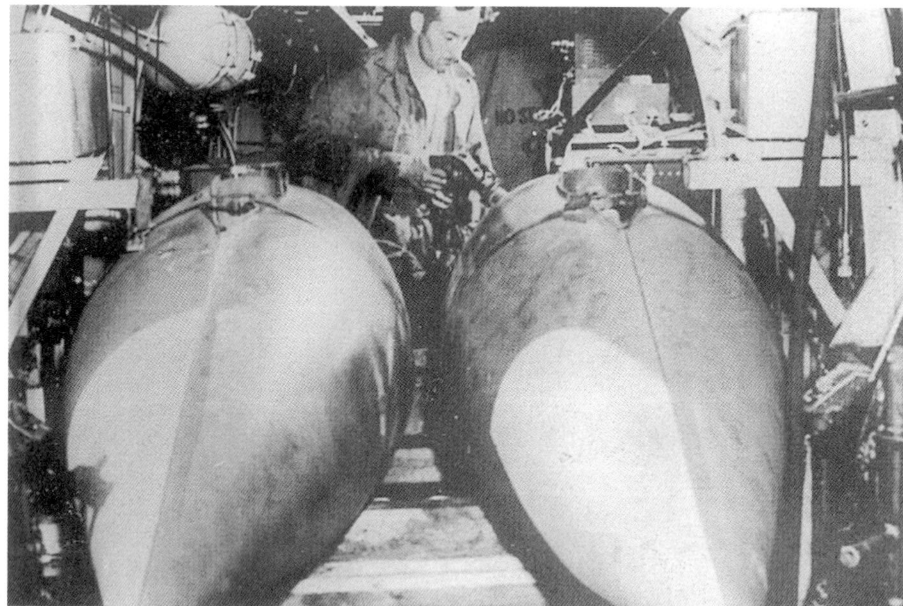

(Above) **Fighter drop tanks installed in the bomb-bay of the Liberator for 'trucking' missions to the armies in France in August 1944. During late August, early September 1944, Liberators in the 2nd Bomb Division began these missions to those who were in urgent need of fuel and supplies. During fourteen days of 'trucking' the 467th Bomb Group alone delivered 646,079gal (2,937,334ltr) of 80 octane fuel to the Allied armies, and the 458th delivered 727,160gal (3,305,960ltr) of fuel to the tank units.** USAF

Losses in the ETO could, on occasion, be heavy, but just the sight of a single B-24 going down broken and in flames could be enough to test the personal willpower and the morale of the whole squadron, group, or even the wing. Here, a 389th Bomb Group lead ship hurtles down trailing fire 200–300ft (60–90m) long after taking a direct hit in the bomb-bay on a mission to Munster. USAF

Waco gliders litter DZ.N Knapheide-Klein Amerika ('Little America'), near Groesbeek, Holland on 18 September 1944 during Market Garden **when the Liberators air-dropped supplies to the 1st Allied Airborne Army. Eighty per cent of all supplies dropped by the 20th Wing at DZ.N were recovered, but two groups of P-47s failed to suppress the almost constant small-arms fire and the 2nd Bomb Division lost sixteen Liberators and seventy more damaged, while twenty-one fighters were shot down.** USAF

its fourteen days of 'trucking', the 467th delivered 646,079gal (2,937,334ltr) of 80-octane fuel to the Allied armies, and the 458th delivered 727,160gal (3,305,960ltr) fuel to the tank units.

Meanwhile, on 9 September the Allies had launched Operation *Market Garden* using British and American airborne divisions against German-held Dutch towns on the Rhine, and on 18 September 252 supply-carrying B-24s dropped supplies at DZ.N Knapheide-Klein Amerika (Little America) near Groesbeek. The 1st Allied Airborne Army recovered 80 per cent of all supplies dropped by the 20th Wing at Groesbeek. The 14th Wing meanwhile dropped supplies to the 101st American Airborne at Best. Altogether, the 491st lost four B-24s on the mission. Two groups of P-47s to suppress the almost constant small-arms fire, and the 2nd Bomb Division lost sixteen Liberators and seventy more damaged, while twenty-one fighters were shot down.

Bloody Kassel

Bad weather throughout the rest of September severely limited missions, and only fourteen were flown that month. On the 27th, 315 B-24s visited the Henschel engine and vehicle assembly plants at Kassel in central Germany. The leading 445th Bomb Group lost twenty-five of its thirty-seven B-24s to the onslaught of German fighters: two of the remaining B-24s crash-landed in France, a third managed to cross the Channel but crashed in Kent, while a fourth crashed near Tibenham. Only seven aircraft made it back to the airfield, and they carried out one dead crewman and thirteen wounded. Losses continued to mount. On 28 September, thirty bombers were lost in the bombing of Magdeburg, Kassel and Merseburg, and on 7 October, when over 1,300 B-17s and B-24s bombed synthetic oil plants in Germany, another fifty-two heavies failed to return.

Bad weather throughout November slowed down the Allies' advance in the west, and missions were severely hampered; those that were flown were usually to oil targets. On 9 November the heavies returned to tactical missions in support of Gen George Patton's 3rd Army, halted at the fortress city of Metz. On 10 November the 489th Bomb Group at Halesworth flew its last mission in the ETO before returning to the USA to be retrained as a B-29 unit and redeployed to the Pacific. On 16 November the 8th provided support for the advancing US and British armies. The mission was very carefully planned to avoid bombing friendly troops near the targets just east of Aachen. The Allied artillery fired red smoke shells every 500yd (460m) along the front, and barrage balloons were placed along the edge of the area. The use of radio signals was especially worthwhile when eight-tenths cloud covered the front lines, and helped to ensure accurate bombing. Worsening weather conditions forced some groups to fly to the north of Britain to escape the conditions, and they were unable to return to their home bases for a few days.

On 21 November, the 8th returned to Merseburg for the first of three more raids on the refineries in a week. Merseburg had become synonymous with flak, and crews hated all missions to the city. On the 25th, well over 900 heavies attacked oil and marshalling yards targets in Germany. The 2nd Bomb Division attacked the oil refineries at Misburg. Upwards of 200 German fighters attacked the bombers, but they were protected by 245 American fighters and while these engaged the Luftwaffe, the bombers were able to continue to the target. However, their reprieve was only temporary, and shortly after the B-24s came under attack, the thirty-one Liberators in the 491st Bomb Group bore the brunt, sixteen being lost in the space of just fifteen minutes. For its action over Misburg the 491st was awarded a Divisional Unit Citation.

Highly coordinated teamwork – necessary in flying a Liberator as it was in building it – was twice a factor in *Little Joe*, a B-24H in the 448th Bomb Group on its fifty-first mission, flown by Fg Off Elliott J. Sidey in the 713th Bomb Squadron. On 21 November it returned safely to Seething after being severely damaged by flak over Germany – but this was its second reprieve: on a mission to Kiel on 5 August 1944, Sgt Louis A. Owens, the flight engineer, had demonstrated his alertness and courage in a similar situation in the same aircraft. Piloted by Fg Off Melvin Krissel, the B-24 had sustained severe flak damage, the control cables to the rudders and aileron and one elevator being severed. The Liberator had dropped out of formation immediately.

B-24J-145-CO 44-40123 She Devil **in the 852nd Bomb Squadron, 491st Bomb Group drops its bombs on target. On 25 November the group lost sixteen Liberators in the space of just fifteen minutes during the mission to the Misburg oil refineries. For its action, the 491st was awarded a Divisional Unit Citation.** Dan Winston Collection

(Below) **Bombs are dropped from B-24s of the 489th Bomb Group on enemy installations at Hamburg and Harburg, Germany, during a raid on 6 December 1944. Altogether, over 650 heavies, supported by fighters flying over 750 sorties, bombed the synthetic oil plant, and another at Merseburg/Leuna, as well as the Minden aqueduct and the marshalling yards at Bielefeld.** USAF

Owens, however, despite the unstable characteristics of the plane, had repaired the damaged cables, making it possible for the pilot to bring the aircraft safely back to base.

On the 21 November mission, *Little Joe* was riddled by flak as she left the target area after bombing. An unexploded AA shell entered her lower right side as she was in a right bank leaving the target area; it continued through the lower tail turret ammunition, which caused skin fractures inside the plane. After emerging from the ammo box, it fatally injured the left waist gunner who at that time was discharging *Chaff*, and after leaving the fuselage, finally exploded about two feet away from it. Fragments were the cause of the leg injury received by the right waist gunner, and the explosion caused perforation of an area about six feet in diameter. Tech Sgt Owens was showered with Plexiglas when a flak fragment penetrated the Martin upper turret dome and struck his gunsight. Shortly after, rudder control was lost, but as soon as Owens learned about this, he went to the waist to repair the damage. First he extinguished the fires which were consuming the wounded gunner's clothing and the *Chaff* boxes; then he undid the turnbuckle in the aft left bomb-bay in order to splice the cut cables, lengthening them and using a PU grounding wire and trim tab cable to splice the cables together, finally returning to the bomb bay to splice the turnbuckle together. Owens was successful in his work and the pilot regained control, enabling the B-24 to return to base.

On 30 November approximately 1,200 bombers pounded four synthetic oil refineries in Germany, the Liberators being given Lutzkendorf. By the end of November 1944, more than forty-three oil refineries had been destroyed – but the war was still far from won. On the 16 December, Field Marshal Karl von Rundstedt and his Panzer columns punched a hole in the American lines in the forests of Ardennes which opened up a salient or 'bulge' in the Allied front lines. December 1944 had brought the worst winter weather in England for fifty-four years, however, and the bombing force in England was grounded; on this occasion it was unable to intervene until Christmas Eve, when a record 2,034 heavies, including war-weary hacks and even assembly ships, bombed Luftwaffe airfields in the vicinity of the Ardennes. Another strike went ahead on Christmas Day, but it was a much smaller force which was dispatched from the 2nd and 3rd Division bases. Some 350 heavies bombed eighteen targets, mostly railway bridges and communication centres west of the Rhine. The raids in support of the armies in the

Beautiful top view of a 93rd Bomb Group Liberator, showing the long Davis wing to excellent advantage.
via Steve Adams

B-24 at its snow-bound dispersal, with a Fortress parked nearby, during the winter of 1944–45. USAF

bulge continued into January, until the position on the Ardennes gradually swung in the Allies' flavour and the heavies could resume deep penetration missions.

On 1 January 1945 the bomb divisions were renamed 'air divisions', and on the 16th over 550 heavies bombed oil plants and engineering centres in the Reich. The 2nd Air Division began receiving B-24Ls and B-24Ms at this time; these were the same as the earlier models, but fitted with lighter tail turrets. The B-24L sported a hand-operated turret 330lb (136kg) lighter then the conventional. The 'L' was soon replaced by the improved B-24M: this had been introduced in October, and reached the Liberator bases in early 1945.

By 3 February 1945, Marshal Zhukov's Red Army was only 35 miles (56km) from Berlin and the capital was jammed with refugees fleeing from the advancing Russians. Accompanied by 900 fighters, 1,200 B-17s and B-24s dropped 2,267 tons of bombs on the centre of Berlin, killing an estimated 25,000 inhabitants. Reconnaissance photographs revealed that an area of 1½ square miles (3.9sq km), stretching across the southern half of the 'Mitte', had been devastated. The 8th lost twenty-one bombers shot down, and another six crash-landed inside the Russian lines. Of the bombers that returned, ninety-three suffered varying forms of major flak damage. Further German disruption in the face of the Russian advance occurred on 6 February, when 1,300 heavies escorted by fifteen groups of P-51 Mustangs, bombed Chemnitz and Magdeburg.

On 11 February the Allies issued their Yalta declaration, and the policy of bombing German cities in the path of the Russian advance was put into operation. On the night of 13/14 February the old city of Dresden in eastern Germany was attacked by RAF Bomber Command. Two waves consisting of 800 heavy bombers produced fire-storms and caused horrendous casualties among the civilian population. Next day 311 bombers of the 8th Air Force attempted to stoke up the fires created by RAF Bomber Command, while 900 more bombers attacked Chemnitz, Magdeburg and other targets. On the 15th, over 1,000 heavies bombed the Magdeburg synthetic oil plant, and next day almost 1,000 B-17s and B-24s hit oil targets at Dortmund, Salzbergen and Gelsenkirchen.

On 22 February, in Operation *Clarion*, more than 6,000 aircraft from seven different commands, including 1,359 B-17s and B-24s, attempted the systematic destruction of the German communications network throughout western Germany and northern Holland. All targets were selected with the object of preventing troops being transported to the Russian front, now only a few miles from Berlin. Despite the low altitudes flown, only five bombers were lost. Next day only two bombers failed to return from the 1,193 dispatched, and on 26 February only five bombers were shot down over Berlin.

On 4 March the 466th and 392nd Bomb Groups bombed Swiss territory by mistake. The US Ambassador had only recently attended a memorial service and visited reconstruction projects of the previous bombing on 18 September 1944. Gen Marshall urged Gen Spaatz to visit Switzerland secretly, and reparation involving many millions of dollars was made to the Swiss government. A court martial was held at 2nd Division headquarters at Ketteringham Hall, with Col James M. Stewart appointed president of the court; no further action was taken, however, although at least one lead crew was restricted to base until April 1945.

On 15 March, 1,282 bombers escorted by fourteen fighter groups hit the German Army HQ at Zossen near Berlin and a marshalling yard at Orienburg. Two days later 1,260 B-17s and B-24s, again heavily supported by fighters, bombed areas in west and north-central Germany. On 18 March a record 1,327 bombers bombed Berlin again. With the Third Reich on the brink of defeat, the Luftwaffe had been virtually driven from the German skies – but even so, thirty-seven Me 262s still managed to shoot down sixteen bombers and five fighters (another sixteen bombers were forced to land inside Russian territory) for the loss of only two jets. By the end of the month a further thirty bombers were shot down by the Jagdverband.

On 22 March, 1,284 B-17s and B-24s bombed targets east of Frankfurt and ten military encampments in the Ruhr in preparation for the Allied amphibious crossing of the lower Rhine on 23/24 March. On 24 March, 1,747 8th Air Force bombers pounded German jet aircraft bases in Holland and Germany over two missions, while 240 B-24s, each loaded with 600 tons of medical supplies, food and weapons, dropped vital supplies to the armies in the field. Flying as low as 50ft (15m), the Liberators droned over the dropping zone at Wesel at 145mph (233km/h), using 10–15 degrees of flap to aid accuracy in the drop. Spasmodic and highly accurate small arms fire and 20mm cannon fire brought down six Liberators in the 20th Wing, and over one hundred B-24s returned with some degree of damage.

On 8 April, in excess of 1,150 B-17s and B-24s, escorted by fourteen groups of Mustangs, bombed targets in the Leipzig, Nurnberg and Chemnitz areas. On 14 April 1,161 heavies bombed an estimated force of 122,000 Germans holding out and

Probably the last photo ever taken of B-24J-5-FO 42-50896 Southern Comfort **of the 506th Bomb Squadron, 44th Bomb Group, pictured by Elwood Matter leaving the coast of England on the low-level supply-drop mission in support of the Rhine crossing at Wesel on 24 March 1945.** Southern Comfort **and Lt Max E. Chandler's crew failed to return. Only two men, 21-year-old Sgt Robert D. Vance, tail gunner, and Sgt Louis J. De Blasio, waist gunner, survived.** Elwood Matter via John Page

1st Lt Robert L. Main's B-24M-10-FO 44-50838 in the 714th Bomb Squadron, 448th Bomb Group, was cleaved in two by fire from an Me 262 south-east of Hamburg on the mission to Parchim airfield (Wesendorf) on 4 April 1945. The right wing burned and broke off, and the weight of the left wing threw the B-24 over on its back. Nine of the crew died, trapped inside, but Tech Sgt Charles E. Cupp Jr, the radio operator-gunner, grabbed a chest chute and baled out of the doomed Liberator between 600–800ft (180–240m) from the ground. He landed in a street in Ludwigslust where he was beaten by civilians before being apprehended and taken away to a PoW camp. Main's crew were on their twenty-eighth mission. USAF

Bombs hurtle down on positions at Royan. On 14 and 15 April 1945, an estimated force of about 122,000 Germans who were holding out and manning twenty-two gun batteries along the Gironde estuary in the Royan area thus denying the Allies the use of the port of Bordeaux, were bombed by 8th Air Force heavies, some of them carrying napalm for the first time. French forces later captured the port. The late Alan Healy

manning twenty-two gun batteries along the Gironde estuary in the Royan area; these were denying the Allies the use of the port of Bordeaux. The 467th successfully dropped all their 2,000lb bombs within 1,000ft of the MPI, half the bombs falling within 500ft, a bombing pattern unsurpassed in 8th Air Force history. The 389th Bomb Group lost two Liberators when 3rd Air Division B-17s, making a second run over the target, released their fragmentation bombs through their formation. Two more crashlanded in France, and a fifth limped back to England.

Next day nearly 850 heavies from the 2nd and 3rd Air Divisions, carrying napalm for the first time, dropped 460,000gal (2,091,344ltr) in 75–85gal (340–386ltr) liquid-fire tanks on the stubborn defenders. The 1st Air Division added 1,000 and 2,000lb GP bombs, while three fighter groups put down fire on gun emplacements. No flak was encountered, and French forces later captured the port. The end of the Reich was nigh. On 17 April, Dresden was bombed once more, and during the week 18–25 April, missions were briefed and scrubbed almost simultaneously as the ground forces overran objective after objective. Finally, on 25 April, the B-24s, escorted by four fighter groups, bombed four rail complexes surrounding Hitler's mountain retreat at Berchtesgarden. VE (Victory in Europe) Day took place on 8 May.

The bomb groups now returned Allied PoWs to England and France, and airlifted displaced persons from all over Europe. Then 'Trolley' or 'Revival' missions in bombers crammed with ground personnel were flown over bombed-out cities at heights ranging from 1,000 to 3,000ft to show them the outcome of Allied bombing over the past four years. On 13 May 1945 the 467th Bomb Group led the 'Victory Flypast' over the 8th's headquarters at High Wycombe. It was a proud day for everyone in the group, not least Col Albert Shower, the only bomb group commander in the 8th Air Force to bring his group to England and retain command of it until the end of hostilities.

The ordnance depot and marshalling yards at Landshut come under attack from the 788th Bomb Squadron, 467th Bomb Group. Left is B-24J-1-FO 42-50611/F and right is B-24J-5-FO 42-50816/S. ECM Carpet blinkers can be seen forward of the fuselage on three of the B-24s. (Nosing into the picture is B-24J-150-CO 44-40166 Monster **– formerly** Irishman's Shanty **in the 492nd Bomb Group before its disbandment – which, like 42-50816, survived the war, only to be broken up for scrap at Altus, Oklahoma, in October 1945). On 13 May 1945 the 'Rackheath Aggies' led the victory fly-past over 8th AF Headquarters at High Wycombe.** USAF

CHAPTER FIVE

The Soft Under-belly of Europe

15th Air Force Operations from Italy

The two 9th Air Force groups, the 98th and 376th, were transferred to 12th Bomber Command after Ploesti, and on 1 October 1943 they flew their first mission from Italy against the aircraft factories at Wiener Neustadt. However, the Liberators' career in the 12th Air Force was short, because that same October, Gen Henry H. Arnold proposed a plan to split the 12th Air Force in two to create a Strategic Air Force in the Mediterranean, leaving the remaining half of the 12th as a tactical organization. A Strategic Air Force based in southern Italy, which appeared to offer considerably better weather conditions than Britain, would effectively place parts of Austria, Germany and eastern Europe, previously out of range of the 8th Air Force, within easy reach. Eventually, cities in southern Germany, and even targets as far away as Budapest and Pecs in Hungary, and Czechowicka in Poland, would be within reach of the 15th Air Force.

Arnold's plan was accepted, and on 1 November 1943 the 15th Air Force was officially activated under the command of Maj Gen James Doolittle, with a strength of ninety B-24s inherited from the 12th Air Force, and 210 B-17s. Initially the 98th, the 376th and four B-17 groups formed the operational element of the 15th Air Force, based in the Foggia area. As such, the 15th Air Force flew its first mission on 2 November 1943, when 137 B-17s and B-24s bombed the Messerschmitt Bf 109 factory and surrounding industrial complex at Wiener-Neustadt again. In the first few missions, the number of Liberators which flew was small because the new B-24 groups had not yet arrived in the theatre, and the B-17s provided the bulk of planes for missions. Quite often the small force of B-24s was used against specialized targets: on 5 November, for instance, three B-24s on a low-level raid bombed the Falconara–Marittima rail and road bridge, and on the 11th, twenty-eight Liberators bombed the Annecy ball-bearing plant and viaduct at Antheor. Despite the planners' hopes of finding better conditions in Italy bad weather quite often prevented missions being flown that winter.

Italy was originally chosen for 15th Air Force operations due to its proximity to targets out of range of the 8th Air Force, and because the weather was thought to be ideal. Generally this was so, but heavy rainfall sometimes proved a big problem on the improvised airfields. USAF

On 3 January 1944, Maj Gen Nathan F. Twining succeeded Doolittle as commander of the 15th, and he would remain in command until the end of the war in Europe. Between December 1943 and May 1944, thirteen new B-24H/J Liberator groups would arrive in Italy to form four bomb wings. The first of the new groups to arrive during November 1943 through to February 1944 were the 449th at Grottaglie, and the 450th at Manduria, both of which became operational on 8 January 1944, and the 451st, which became operational at Gioia del Colle on 30 January. The 454th, which became operational on 8 February, and the 455th were based at San Giovanni, and formed the 304th Bomb Wing with the 456th at Cerignola and the 459th at Giulia. The 460th was based at Spinazzola, the 461st at Torretta, and from February to April 1944, the 464th and 465th Bomb Groups became operational at Pantanella. Finally the 484th was based at Torretta, and the 485th at Venosa.

Anzio

By 2 January 1944, the fledgling 15th Air Force was paving the way for the seaborne landings at the small west-coast fishing port of Anzio, 20 miles (32km) west of the Alban hills, by carrying out bombing raids on Axis strongpoints in Italy. The landings, which went ahead on 22 January, were intended to outflank the enemy holding the Gustav Line 70 miles (113km) to the south-east, leaving the road to Rome open to the Allies. A few days before the landings, aircraft of the 15th flew over 600 sorties in central Italy in preparation for the invasion. The landings caught the Germans completely by surprise and at first they went well, but the Allied armies failed to ram home the advantage and by 11–12 February, German attacks had forced them back to their final defence line. Next day the Allies halted their attacks on Monte Cassino. The situation worsened on 16–17 February when the German counterattack threatened to cut the Allied front in half. On the 16th the Liberators, flying unescorted, bombed marshalling yards at Pontassieve, Sienna, Poggibonsi and Prato, also a bridge at Cecina and a road near Rieto, as the Allied Air Forces tried desperately to stem the flow of German material to the front.

On the 17th, the 455th and 456th Bomb Groups became operational, giving the 15th Air Force a dozen B-24 groups. Flying unescorted again, the heavies this day hit several targets in advance of the US 5th Army's Anzio battle line. On 20 February the Liberators blasted troop concentrations in the beachhead, but the Axis effort would only finally peter out early in March. For five days, from 26 February to 1 March, bad weather prevented heavy bombing operations. On 2 March the skies cleared and the Allied air forces attacked in some strength. Nearly 300 B-24s and B-17s, swelled by the addition of the 459th Bomb Group for the first time and escorted by 180 fighters, pounded the Cisterna di Roma-La Villa area, Velletri, and troop concentrations, artillery and other targets in a battle area at several points, including the Stazione di Campoleone and Carroceto areas. The German attacks ceased the next day and deadlock set in.

Operation *Argument*

Ever since the 15th was activated, the US Strategic Air Forces (the USAAF overall command organization in Europe) had intended at the earliest possible date to

1st Lt Rex Wilkinson's crew, 456th Bomb Group, 304th Bomb Wing, 15th AF in Italy 1944. *Back row, left to right*: 1st Lt Rex Wilkinson, pilot; 1st Lt Jack L. Dupont, co-pilot; 2nd Lt Bill Jenkins, bombardier; 2nd Lt Jim McIntosh, navigator. *Front row, left to right:* Sgt Charles Miller, radioman; Sgt Alvernon Boltis, upper turret; Sgt Aaron Saloven, nose turret; Sgt Boyce Duncan, flight engineer; Sgt Fred Meisel, tail gunner; Sgt Kenneth Mayberry. Meisel was born in Minsk, Russia on 7 November 1905, to a Russian mother and a German father. In 1917 he fought in the German army on the Russian front and was awarded the Iron Cross, 1st and 2nd Class. After World War I, Fred stayed in the army, and in 1922, when he was discharged from the German army, he migrated legally to the USA. Inducted into the American army on 29 December 1941 at Fort McArthur, Meisel saw active service in the campaign to drive the Japanese out of Dutch Harbor, later seeing action on missions from Alaska in the 11th AF. via Jack Dupont

launch Operation *Argument*: this was a series of coordinated raids by the 8th and 15th Air Forces, supported by RAF night bombing, which were aimed at smashing the German aircraft industry. Bad weather and the 15th's continuing involvement in the Anzio operation caused a series of postponements, but the raids finally began on 19 February 1944, although the 15th Air Force did not participate, being limited to photo and weather reconnaissance operations only. It was the start of what has become known as 'Big Week'.

On 22 February it was intended that the 15th Air Force would strike at the Messerschmitt plant at Regensburg, while the 8th struck at other targets in the Reich, the 24th, but they resumed the offensive again on 25 February with an attack on the Fiume marshalling yards and port, and the Zell am See railway and Graz airfield. The 15th lost thirty-nine bombers.

March began with a mission on the 3rd to the Rome marshalling yards and the airfields and landing grounds at Viterbo, Canino, and Fabrico di Roma, involving about 200 B-24s and B-17s escorted by fifty-plus fighters. Four days later about 300 B-24s and B-17s attacked the Toulon Submarine base in southern France, as well as marshalling yards throughout northern Italy. The 15th returned to Toulon on 11 March when about 100 B-24s, escorted by more than thirty heavy bomb groups in theatre. Altogether, 234 B-24s and B-17s, escorted by more than a hundred fighters, bombed the airfield and town of Klagenfurt. More than 150 other B-24s bombed the Graz factory complex and marshalling yards at Metkovic and Knin. Throughout the remainder of March, the B-24s blasted targets in Italy, on the few occasions when the weather permitted.

In April 1944 the 15th Air Force embarked on a campaign against enemy oil targets, and over eighty refineries, many of which had been out of reach before the formation of the 15th, were subjected to the bombs of the B-24s and B-17s. On 2 April, the 461st Bomb Group at Torretta became

B-24H-5-CF 41-29212 of the 720th Bomb Squadron, 450th 'Cottontails' Bomb Group, in the 47th Bomb Wing, bellies in at Manduria, Italy, on 13 March 1944 after the left main gear collapsed. USAF

including the ball-bearing plants at Schweinfurt. However, the 8th had to abort because of bad weather over England. A force of 118 B-24s bombed the Obertraubling aircraft assembly plant at Regensburg, with good results, at about the same time that the Italy-based B-17s bombed the marshalling yards at Peterhausen, while more B-24s hit Sibenik and the harbour at Zara. With the 8th out of the picture, the Luftwaffe concentrated on the Italy-based force, and fourteen B-24s were shot down. Next day, the 15th Air Force Liberators bombed industrial targets at Steyr. The B-24s were stood down on fighters, bombed the harbour area; other B-24s attacked marshalling yards at Pontassieve and Prato and an airfield at Iesi. Four days later, on the 15th, Monte Cassino, a stubborn thorn of resistance in the Allied side, was bombed to rubble by more than 300 B-24s and B-17s, in support of Gen Mark Clark's US 5th Army. On the 18th, more than 350 B-24s and B-17s bombed airfields at Villa-orba, Udine, Gorizia, Lavariano and Maniago in conjunction with fighter strafing operations. Next day, the 19th March, the 460th Bomb Group became operational, giving the 15th Air Force a total of fourteen operational, making sixteen heavy bombardment groups operational in Italy; the group joined more than 500 heavies in the largest raid to date, in a mission to the ball-bearing plant at Steyr and other targets. Despite strong fighter support, however, nineteen bombers were shot down and several more went missing. On 3 April, the first major attack was carried out on the Hungarian capital, Budapest, and on the 4th it was the turn of Bucharest, capital of Rumania. On 5 April, 334 B-24s and B-17s were dispatched to transportation targets in the vicinity of the Ploesti oilfields in Rumania, a raid in which fighters and flak shot down thirteen bombers. Next day the Liberators headed for Zagreb, but numerous B-24s and B-17s were forced to abort because of bad weather. On the 7th, over 400 B-24s and B-17s escorted by almost a hundred P-38 Lightnings, attacked marshalling yards at Treviso, Mestre, Bologna and Ferrara. Despite the fighter escort and a pre-emptive strike by P-47 Thunderbolts in the Gorizia-Udine areas, twenty heavies were shot down by the enemy defences.

On 12 April, almost 450 Liberators and Fortresses, escorted by over 200 fighters, attacked the aircraft factories at Fischamend Markt and Wiener-Neustadt, and the Bad Voslau aircraft assembly plant. Next day, in the largest mission to date, 535 B-17s and B-24s were dispatched to targets in Hungary; fourteen bombers were lost. 'Incidental' damage was caused to the Ploesti refineries on 15 April when the main targets for the 448 B-24s and B-17s were Rumanian marshalling yards. The refineries were hit again on 24 April when more than 520 heavies bombed marshalling yards at Bucharest and Ploesti, among other targets. On the 29th, the 484th Bomb Group at Torretta became the eighteenth heavy bomb group to become operational, joining over 400 heavies in an attack on the Toulon naval base. Next day the 464th Bomb Group, initially at Pantanella, became operational, making thirteen B-24 groups in theatre. During May the last two bomb groups – the 465th, also at Pantanella, and the 485th at Venosa – joined the 15th Air Force, becoming operational on 5 May and 10 May respectively.

It was on 10 May that Staff Sgt Wally Robinson, tail gunner in William 'Jug' Wright's crew in the 767th Squadron, 461st Bomb Group, flew his tenth mission, to the Messerschmitt factory at Wiener-Neustadt. Robinson wrote:

> Our group hit the north airfield with frags. About thirty enemy fighters were concentrating on our group as we approached the target, attacking from the front and rolling away to the rear. By the time I saw them from the tail turret they were practically out of range, the combined speed of the fighter and the bomber going well over 500mph.

15th Air Force Liberators bombing Nice, France, on 26 May 1944. Almost 700 15th Air Force heavies attacked marshalling yards in southern France on this day. USAF

When we got to the target the fighters left, and the flak took over – the sky over the target was full of it, and it didn't seem possible that we could fly through it. We started taking hits all over the plane. Shrapnel came through the bottom of my turret and rattled around me, but I wasn't hit. However, the track carrying the ammo to the turret was cut off, though I didn't realize this until we got out of the flak area and the fighters came at us again. I started shooting, and after firing a few bursts, the guns quit – but I kept the guns and turret moving anyway to make the fighters think I was still in business.

The B-24 on our right dropped back and started down – I counted ten 'chutes. Another was spinning and burning, but there were no 'chutes from this one. Our P-51s were coming in now and there were dogfights all around us, and a lot of the fighters were going down too. A few P-38s were out there as well, and I saw one turn into a ball of fire. The Me 109s had left us by now, thanks to our escort. A Liberator from another group slid in behind us with an engine out. We were having engine trouble, too, and were dropping behind the formation, so we 'escorted' the other B-24 back to Italy and luckily weren't spotted by any of the Luftwaffe. Jug made a remark back at the base that I'll never forget: he said that when the 109s were coming in, their guns looked as big as GI cans. We got thirty-three new holes on this mission.

Life in Italy

Bud Markel was the engineer for Ben Guisband's 827th Bomb Squadron, 484th Bomb Group crew out of Torretta in 1944–45, and he has clear recollections of this period in his life:

The B-24 Liberator bomber was a cantankerous, lumbering, draughty, unforgiving son-of-a-bitch, heavy in the controls, overgrossed and difficult to fly in formation, with an ancient boiler gauge style fuel quantity system that was almost useless. The heaters never worked when you needed them, and were removed by many combat groups as being too dangerous to operate because of the fuel lines on the flight deck necessary to feed them. Nose steering, such as power steering in an automobile, was non-existent, and headway was maintained by throttles and brakes. The famously weak nose-gear had a mind of its own, often collapsing of its own volition, so the flight engineer would have to sit astride the mechanism, waiting with a heavy foot to kick the stubborn thing down to lock.

The Liberator was a plane often ridiculed by the B-17 boys who delighted in finding hundreds of new derogatory names to call it. Even today, the B-24 versus the B-17 controversy continues, because every throttle jock and gunner knows that sooner or later you learn to accept and then eventually to love the equipment assigned to you – it's not romance, but survival that triggers the match. Familiarity breeds self-confidence, at least in this case, and you soon learned not to take off with the cowl flaps open as this caused too much drag; you learned to keep the generators parallel, and to plot cruise control charts to calculate fuel consumption, or how to transfer fuel without starving the engines or pumping it overboard. Many would call this becoming professional, but we called it accommodation, a deal struck with the airplane, like a stand-off between two boxers who respect each other's strengths. With this out of the way, the war could be attended to.

The Army Air Force perfected precision daylight bombing, much to the chagrin of RAF Bomber Command, who preferred carpet bombing, often of huge cities, which could be found in the dark. But this effort, while calamitous to the civilian population, often did not have strategic significance. And did it materially shorten the war? Perhaps. In a way, like wearing down a giant with thousands of tiny clubs. But Americans thought differently: in their view, take away the giant's water and food and he became weak to the point that he could no longer defend himself. This was the role handed to the Army Air Forces of World War II: deny the enemy transportation, industry and fuel, and he would surrender.

Airmen based in southern Italy with the 15th Air Force were fed watery C rations and *spam*, a canned meat product that many today still cannot bring themselves to eat because there was so much of it, and so little of anything else. Many will remember the mud and washboard runways, and the two ounces of hootch offered to airmen returning from a mission; the smart ones saved their ration in metal canteens to accumulate enough for an important occasion, like finishing your missions in one piece, or being sent off to rest on the Isle of Capri. But most important of all, they remember the war on oil, the bombing of refineries and oil storage tanks – for the American airman of 1944 and 1945, the subject of oil did not have the same significance as it does today. They also remember the petroleum industry targets as being the most heavily defended by seemingly endless batteries of flak guns: names like Ploesti, Wiener-Neustadt, and Moosbierbaum bring a chill to the blood of any 15th veteran.

Some will say that Germany was overwhelmed by superior forces, but the boys would like to think that Hitler just plain ran out of oil – then in their hearts and minds, the loss of crews and buddies would be justified, and they could sit back and say, 'We were part of history, we were in the greatest aerial armada that ever took to the skies, or ever will again.' Their names are in the archives in Washington DC and at Maxwell field, Alabama; they are in history, and that in itself is worth remembering.

Sometimes it takes a calamity like war to transform a boy into a man – a maturity suddenly thrust upon unprepared shoulders, a maturity of need, the interdependence of each crewman upon the other: each member of the crew had a specific job to do, and all of the other lives on that airplane depended upon each other's skill. The bombardier, too, had to have skills beyond his function of dropping 'eggs' on the target. Of particular interest was the ball gunner cramped into a tiny compartment: he could not scratch his nose or go to the bathroom, and when an attack was under way, the empty shell cases and cartridge links filled what empty space was left. Because of the cramped quarters and the inevitable cold from flying at high altitude in an unpressurized aircraft, gunners often suffered from frostbite.

The airplanes were cold, and systems grew sluggish and bomb shackles would freeze, especially the lower ones nearest the draughty bomb-bay doors. Some bombs would release and fall free from the arming wires causing the propeller to spin off, so that the slightest jar might cause the bomb to explode: so there you were, the bomb-bay a confusion of wires, cables and hydraulic lines being distorted and swollen by 500lb of instant destruction. The catwalks were narrow, so that you couldn't move about with a parachute pack – one slip or a fraction of a second's lack of concentration and you 'bought the farm'. On some ships the bombardier freed the bomb shackles with a skilful foot or the deft use of a screwdriver, thus letting the bombs fall from the airplane.

When a man is exposed to the sudden danger of aerial combat, when he can look down the barrel of an 88mm flak gun and be close enough to see the bright red muzzle flash ... when the concussion and noise of exploding anti-aircraft shells shake his plane violently and tear big holes in it as though it was made of butter, he has a chance to put his life in perspective, to make promises to himself, to decide to do something with his life if he can just survive this one mission. Of course, some men weaken too and lose control, but these individuals did not represent the majority. If you were to ask a B-24 airman about his wartime experiences, many would answer: 'In a way I was glad to experience the dangers of combat, but don't ask me to do it again.'

B-24s of the 727th Bomb Squadron, 451st Bomb Group, coming off the bomb-run against the Concordia Vega oil refinery at Ploesti on 31 May 1944. Top left is B-24G-5-NT 42-78145 Con Job, **and right is B-24H-5-CF 41-29233** The Sod Buster. Con Job **and Lt Dick Turnbull's crew failed to return from a raid on Vienna on 22 August 1944, while** The Sod Buster **completed sixty-nine missions before being salvaged on 20 September 1944.** USAF

Medal of Honor Award

During the oil campaign, Lt Donald D. Puckett, a pilot in the 98th Bomb Group 'Pyramiders', brought B-24J-35-CO 42-73346 home from Ploesti on 9 July 1944 against incredible odds. Just after 'bombs away', flak tore into the B-24, killing one crew member and severely wounding six others. Puckett handed over control to his co-pilot while he inspected the aircraft, calmed the crew, and cared for the wounded. Two engines had been put out of action, the control cables had been cut, the oxygen system set on fire and the bomb-bay was awash with fuel and hydraulic fluid. Puckett managed to hand-crank open the doors and drain the fuel out, and threw out the guns and equipment – but even so the B-24 seemed doomed. Puckett therefore ordered the crew to bale out – but three refused to do so and he would not leave them. He fought hard to pull the Liberator out of its fatal descent, but it crashed into a mountainside and exploded. Puckett was posthumously awarded the Medal of Honor for giving his life 'unhesitatingly and with supreme sacrifice, in his courageous attempt to save the lives of three others'. It was the last of seven Medals of Honor awarded for raids on Ploesti.

B-24H-15-FO 42-52347/R Belle Ringer **in the 763rd Bomb Squadron, 460th Bomb Group, which put down at Dubendorf, Switzerland, at 10:51 hours on 13 June 1944. On this day over 560 B-24s and B-17s attacked the airfield at Oberpfaffenhofen, aircraft plants at Munich, Germany, and marshalling yards at Innsbruck, Austria.** Swiss AF

Operation *Anvil*

Two days earlier, on 7 July, Wally Robinson in William 'Jug' Wright's crew in the 461st Bomb Group, went to Blechhammer, Germany: the crew had a lucky escape, as he recalls:

> We developed a rough engine on the way, but we were deep into enemy territory by this time and didn't want to turn back by ourselves. We were jumped by the Luftwaffe over Hungary, and they stayed with us all the way to the target. We were doing a lot of shooting, and there were tracers all over the sky. Most of the time the Germans came in two or more abreast from the front, but one loner came in and knocked out the plane on our left. Joe [Jonas Palmer] was letting off a long burst as the fighter went by, and he put six holes in our left rudder. He and Smitty [William Smith] were throwing out the *Window* to confuse the flak guns, between fighter attacks. This probably saved Joe's life: he was bent over getting an

armful of foil when a shell (or flak) entered the bomb-bay, through the bulkhead to the waist and out the top, making a large hole where Joe's head would have been if he had been standing up. We had to shut down the bad engine over the target, right after releasing the bombs.

We were able to stay in formation – again, due to the fact that it was letting down. The fighters hit us again, but didn't stay with us long. About an hour later 'Jug' called us on the interphone to tell us we probably wouldn't make it to base because we were too low on gas, and for us to start tossing out the excess weight again.

I wonder what the people down below think when all that equipment is seen raining down? Pretty soon 'Jug' called us again and said we had better maintain ditching procedures. B-24s don't ditch well – every one I saw had broken apart, though I only ever saw two actually try it. We made it to the Italian coast, however, and put down at Amendola, about ten miles inland. The 2nd and 97th Bomb Groups are located there, both the B-17 outfits. We took a terrible ribbing about our 'banana boats' and 'flying coffins'. Some of their people fixed our engine and put some gas in, and we took off for home. So that was quite a tour: Italy, Yugoslavia, Hungary, Czechoslovakia, Poland and Germany – and return; and all in nine hours.

There were other targets, too, for the 15th Air Force to consider, not least the invasion of southern France in the early morning of 15 August 1944. Planning for Operation *Anvil*, as it was codenamed, had been set in motion as far back as 1 April 1943, and by December that year it had reached the point of decision. Missions in support of the operation can be said to have begun on 28 April 1944, when the heavies in Italy had blasted the port of Toulon. In three days, from 25–27 May, fourteen strategically located marshalling yards in the Marseilles-Toulon-Lyon area were successfully bombed by 1,393 15th Air Force B-24s and B-17s. These yards served rail traffic from Paris, the upper Rhône Valley, industrial centres of western Germany, and Toulouse and other areas of western France. This traffic passed through these yards en route to south-eastern France and

B-24H-15-CF 41-29508 of the 763rd bomb Squadron, 460th Bomb Group on fire in the mid-section during the mission to Vienna on 16 June 1944. One crew-member can be seen emerging from the escape hatch behind the cockpit as he tries to evacuate the aircraft. Above is B-24H-15-FO 42-52337 Cuddles **which was written off a few days later, on 23 June. Altogether the 15th Air Force lost fifteen aircraft to intense fighter attacks on the 16 June missions, when over 600 bombers were dispatched to oil targets at Vienna and Bratislava.** USAF

Italy, and westwards into the littoral zone of southern France.

In the three-month period 19 May–16 August, the 15th Air Force dispatched 12,451 heavies by day, and 205 Group RAF sent 320 aircraft by night, and between them, they dropped more than 18,000 tons of bombs on 113 specific targets. More than 6,000 sorties were flown and 12,500 tons of bombs fell on southern France, although the 15th was also used to cut off lines of communication as far away as Germany and Austria. On 13 June a heavy smoke-screen prevented the 484th Bomb Group from bombing marshalling yards at Munich; however, it bombed marshalling yards at Innsbruck, Austria, in spite of severe damage from flak and fighters, and later received a Distinguished Unit Citation. The 484th was awarded a second citation for its performance on 21 August, when unescorted, it fought its way through intense opposition to attack underground oil storage installations in Vienna.

In July alone the 15th Air Force lost 318 heavy bombers. On 12 July William 'Jug' Wright's crew in the 767th Bomb Squadron, 461st Bomb Group, was amongst those who bombed the marshalling yards in southern France. Wally W. Robinson, his tail gunner, wrote:

> We ran into heavy flak over the French coast and took a lot of hits. A hydraulic line in the bomb-bay was ruptured and the fluid ran back and covered the tail turret; when the enemy fighters came in I had to kick out the turret's glass in order to see out. That must have been the coldest spot in the plane, with the glass out, and there was a lot of oil whipping in.
>
> Back in Italy the weather was terrible and we couldn't find the base. It was so rough that we couldn't stay on the deck. There are no seat belts to hold you in place, and the wind kept lifting us up and then slamming us down. The bale-out alarm went off about this time and we all put on our 'chutes and opened the escape hatch – but the plane seemed to be flying OK, and so nobody volunteered to go out first! It turned out that during a particularly hard bounce the pilot had hit the alarm by mistake! We flew around trying to find a place to land, and then an engine quit. The gas was about gone, so we went down under the weather and found an emergency strip. There were horses running around us as we landed, but no other living thing was in sight. We found a road, and pretty soon a truck came along and we rode in to some sort of army base where they fed us and made arrangements for getting us home. We got back at 4.00am. When Lt Utley, the co-pilot, took off his heated suit a piece of flak fell out. We lost four of our group.

A 376th Bomb Group B-24 pictured after losing part of a wing to flak over Toulon, France. The port was hit repeatedly by heavy bombers of the 15th Air Force during the early part of 1944 and up until 20 August 1944 as part of the softening-up process for the 'Anvil' invasion. USAF

Three days later, Wright's crew went to Ploesti; the group lost one B-24, and the 461st was awarded a Presidential Unit Citation. Wally Robinson completed his thirty-seventh and final mission on 18 July when the Liberators visited a jet aircraft plant at Friedrichshafen. Wally wanted to watch the bombs fall, but he couldn't from his position in the tail. In fact he didn't miss much, because the bombs landed in Lake Constance!

During the period 19 May–16 August, by far the biggest percentage of bombs dropped was on lines of communication, ports and industry; and beginning on 10 August – D-Day minus five days – the main coastal batteries and radar stations in the assault area were hit. On 12, 13 and 14 August, 1,652 heavy bombers dropped 3,839 tons of bombs on forty gun emplacements in the Marseilles-Sete-Toulon-Savona-Genoa area, in a series of attacks coordinated with the 12th Air Force. Fighters swept the area, strafing coast-watcher and radar installations.

On 14 August, 540 B-24s and B-17s bombed gun positions in the Toulon and Genoa areas as the 'Dragoon' invasion convoy headed for the French Mediterranean coast. And on 14/15 August, the 15th Air Force accomplished the first heavy bomber mass night raid in its history, when 252 B-24s and B-17s made a pre-dawn take-off and dropped 500 tons of 100lb bombs on the beaches in the Toulon-Cannes region immediately in the advance of the 'Dragoon' forces. The first wave attacked between 07:00 and 07:39 hours, half-an-hour before the ground troops landed and secured the beach-heads. For four hours and ten minutes on D-Day the bombers caused maximum destruction to the enemy and coastal beach defences, and formations of medium and heavy bombers made attacks on the assault beaches to try and destroy the underwater obstacles and beach defences. Then on 16 August, eighty-nine B-24s, their part in the landings over, escorted by fighters, bombed the chemical works at Friedrichshafen while the B-17s made attacks on railway bridges in southern France in support of the beach-head. The B-24s returned to oil targets on the 17th, with raids by 250 Liberators on three oil refineries and targets of opportunity in the Ploesti area.

Oil!

From June 1944 the 15th Air Force bombed railway networks in south-east Europe in support of Russian military operations in Rumania. Also throughout the summer of 1944, attacks often concentrated on Austrian aircraft-manufacturing centres at Wiener-Neustadt, and at Schwechat in the Vienna area. The first strike by the 15th Air Force on Vienna was on 17 March, when more than 200 heavies were involved. A second strike by almost 600 heavies went ahead on 16 June, and then on 26 June, 677 B-24s and B-17s headed for the Vienna area to bomb the Schwechat factory, the marshalling yards and refinery at Florisdorf, and refineries at Korneuburg, Moosbierbaum, Schwechat, Winterhafen and Lobau. almost thirty heavies were lost. By the end of 1944, the 15th had attacked Vienna on no less than twenty-five occasions.

It was on a raid to the Austrian capital in 1944 that *The Libby Rayder* of the 464th Bomb Group, flown by Amos H. Ross, had a miraculous return to Italy. *Libby Rayder* was hit by flak over the target and hurtled down from 24,000ft (7,300m) to 7,000ft (2,100m) with two engines out. Ross ordered the crew to remove all equipment that was not screwed down, and throw it overboard. While they were doing this, four Bf 109s approached the lone Liberator, which was now minus most of its machine guns and ammunition! Frank L. 'Pappy' Gates, forty-three-year-old waist gunner, said later, 'All we had left was a hundred rounds of ammo and one waist gun – that and spit! As the 109s started for us, six P-38s intercepted them from on top and knocked two into flames. The others cleared outa there ... the P-38s were wonderful ships ... and great guys.' Ross and co-pilot Sidney E. Smith nursed *Libby Rayder* through mountain passes and long sloping valleys on two engines, and then the third engine burned out just before they reached the coast. Ross skilfully crashlanded the B-24 on the one remaining engine. The crew escaped without serious injury, they counted over 250 flak holes in the battered wreck.

Ray A. Nichols was flight engineer in Lt Henry Dionne's crew in the 825th Bomb Squadron, 484th Bomb Group, and his first mission on 13 August, when the Liberators attacked marshalling yards near the capital. Nichols recalls:

Combat photographer Sgt Leo S. Stoutsenberger captured the demise of the 725th Bomb Squadron, 451st Bomb Group, deputy lead ship, B-24H-30-FO 42-95379 Extra Joker **(which got its name because of a playing card found aboard on delivery to the group), on the mission to Markersdorf airfield, Vienna, on 23 August 1944. As the formation reached the IP at 22,000ft (6,700m), the group was attacked by numerous Fw 190s, and** Extra Joker **was hit by cannon fire in the main fuel tanks which spread through the flight deck and waist. The B-24 fell out of formation and slowly spiralled down some 5,000ft (1,500m) before exploding at 11:16 hours near Turnitz, Austria. Lt Kenneth A. Whiting and all his crew were lost. Lack of fighter escort was cited as the chief cause of the high losses sustained over Austria, 22–23 August. The 451st, which over the two days lost fifteen Liberators and two more so badly damaged that they had to be written off, was awarded a DUC – its third – for this mission.** USAF

> The flak was very heavy. Intelligence estimated that 450 AA guns protected the target, but we suspect there were a lot more as the flak was really thick. We came through this with flak holes scattered throughout the forward end of the plane, and spent flak bruised the bombardier and ripped through the co-pilot's flight suit near his calf – our engines, flight controls

B-24G-5-NT 42-78123 Fertile Myrtle **of the 764th Bomb Squadron, 461st Bomb Group, minus its wing de-icer boots.** USAF

(Opposite) **De-icer boot installation.**

(Below) **De-icer system.**

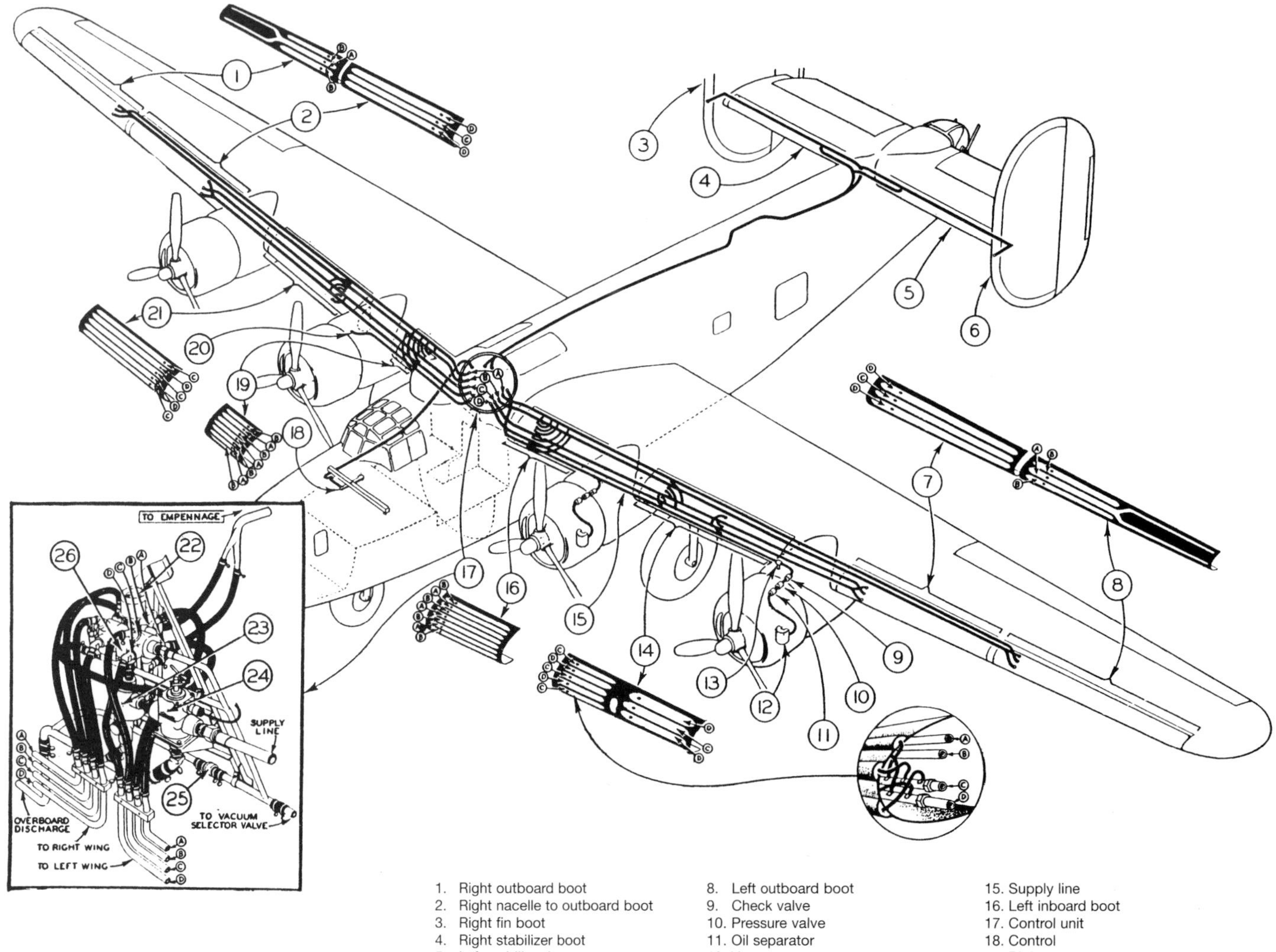

1. Right outboard boot
2. Right nacelle to outboard boot
3. Right fin boot
4. Right stabilizer boot
5. Left stabilizer boot
6. Left fin boot
7. Left nacelle to outboard boot
8. Left outboard boot
9. Check valve
10. Pressure valve
11. Oil separator
12. Vacuum pump
13. Test connection
14. Left nacelle to nacelle boot
15. Supply line
16. Left inboard boot
17. Control unit
18. Control
19. Right inboard boot
20. Overboard discharge
21. Right nacelle to nacelle boot

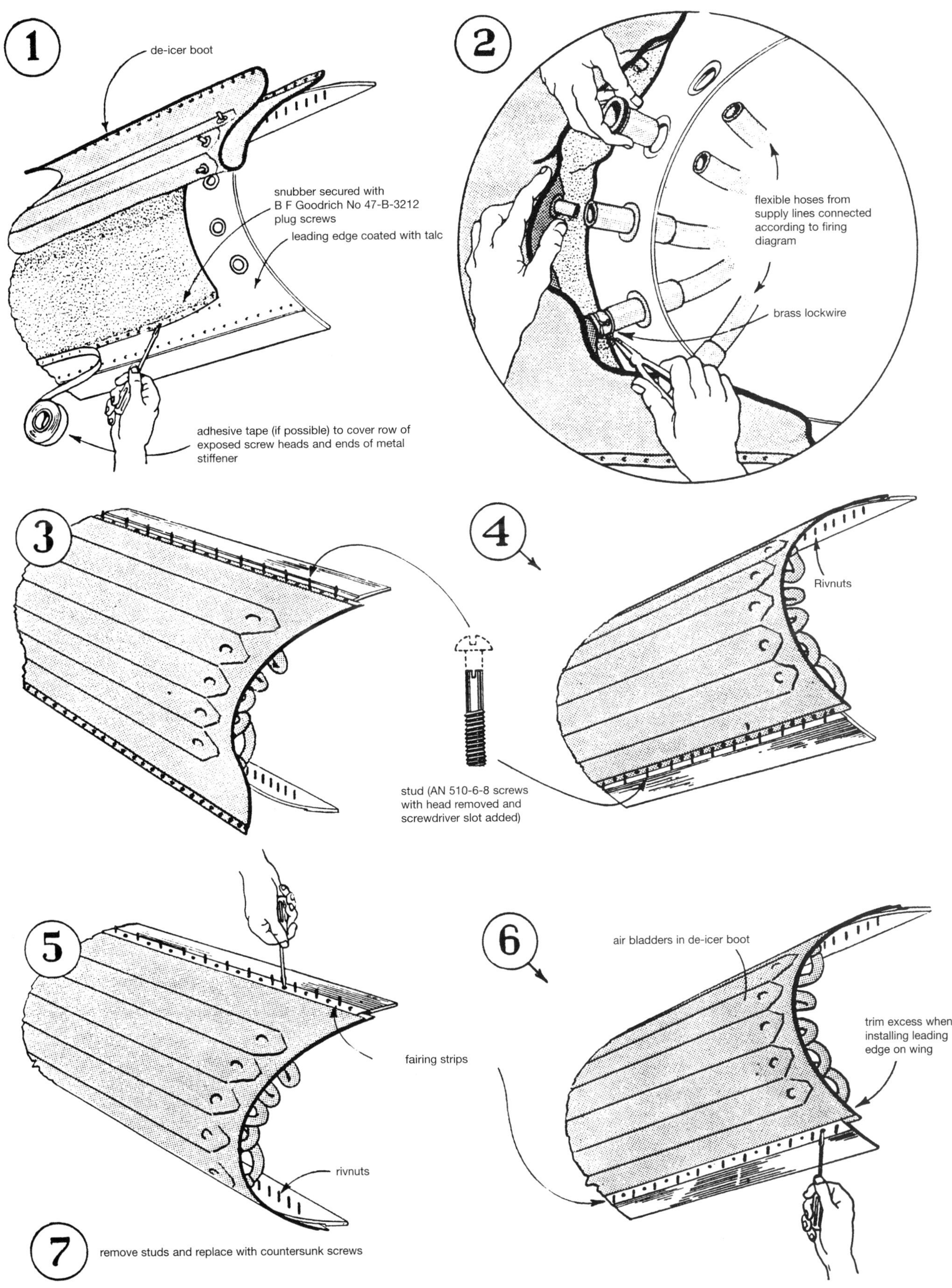
1
de-icer boot
snubber secured with B F Goodrich No 47-B-3212 plug screws
leading edge coated with talc
adhesive tape (if possible) to cover row of exposed screw heads and ends of metal stiffener
2
flexible hoses from supply lines connected according to firing diagram
brass lockwire
3
4
Rivnuts
stud (AN 510-6-8 screws with head removed and screwdriver slot added)
5
fairing strips
rivnuts
6
air bladders in de-icer boot
trim excess when installing leading edge on wing
7
remove studs and replace with countersunk screws

B-24H-25-FO 42-95282 Booby Trap, **formerly of 490th Bomb Group, 3rd Bomb Division, 8th Air Force, was assigned to the 827th Bomb Squadron, 484th Bomb Group. Modifications in England – namely the addition of armour plate on either side of the cockpit and the windshield Plexiglas, and sliding windows replaced by bullet-proof glass – greatly increased weight, and this in turn made the B-24 more difficult to manoeuvre in formation: when throttles were pulled back to maintain position, the Liberator would coast ahead.** Booby Trap **is reported to have flown back to the USA on 30 May 1945.** USAF

(Below) **B-24** Stinky **in the 764th Bomb Squadron, 461st Bomb Group, during conversion to 'squadron hack' for cargo carrying.** USAF

and flight surfaces were not damaged, and everything was normal when we peeled off for our base at Torretta Field near Cerignola, to line up for landing.

While waiting for our turn to land we saw a plane touch down hard on the runway, and one of its 500lb bombs, fully armed, fell out of the bomb-bay; it bounced, and blew-off the tail of the plane, causing it to roll over end over end. When we landed we passed the control tower and a mass of rubble in front of it – no sign of a tail, and with broken off props, hydraulic fluid and flight jackets strewn all about; it was all that remained of Mickey ship B-24H 44-50200. This was the same plane that our crew had ferried from Hamilton Field, near San Francisco, to Torretta between 26 August and 9 September.

We flew our second mission on 24 August, to a railroad bridge at Ferrara, in Italy. We lost No. 1 engine a few minutes before reaching the IP. I was in the bomb-bay trying to change a turbo amplifier when the bomb-bay doors opened on the bomb-run. We were hit by heavy flak. No. 2 engine quit immediately, and the No. 3 engine developed a large plume of oil, indicating a punctured oil tank and siphoning it empty in three or so minutes; this left the plane with one full operating engine which ran away, the bomb doors were stuck open, and one 1,000lb was stuck on one hook in the bomb-bay – I toggled out this one. There was also indication of an engine fire.

I was still in the bomb-bay and out of contact by interphone when pilot Henry Dionne gave the order to bale out. We landed in a 10-mile circle 45 miles north of Ancona in the middle of the Adriatic. Our navigator, 2nd Lt Garland A. Hall, was never seen again after we plunged into the sea; we assumed that he hit a bulkhead on bale-out and was knocked out. Ervan Hestad, tail gunner, was pulled from the sea six hours later in total darkness in a very poor condition, due to exposure. At about dusk we were picked up and taken to a British Army hospital in Ancona where we were looked after for about four days.

B-24 of the 460th Bomb Group with evidence of tail damage sustained during a raid on Munich on 22 September 1944. Some 366 B-24s and B-17s, escorted by 270 fighters, bombed the north-east industrial area of the Bavarian capital as well as the Munich-Riem jet airfield. USAF

Dionne's crew returned to mission status on 1 September and flew their third mission, again to the railway bridge at Ferrara. Two days later their fourth mission was to a rail ferry crossing on the Danube at Smederevo, Yugoslavia. Ray A. Nichols wrote:

We were flying planes delivered to us from the 8th Air Force. They were much heavier than our own planes, and flew awkwardly due to tons of armour bucket seats and flat armour around the flight deck. For instance when power was decreased, their own momentum drifted them forwards and the only control for speed was to slow down by raising the nose; of course this strategy was sometimes impossible due to the position in the formation to which a plane was assigned, because it could have rammed the plane above, which might have been fatal to both planes, and possibly others close by.

One of this type of plane flying brown-nose position was caught in a drift on the bomb-run, and being under the lead plane he couldn't slow by lifting his nose, at risk of the two planes colliding. At this moment the time came for 'bombs away' and an unarmed 500lb bomb fell on his nose just forward of the flight deck, crushing the control cables and pulleys and disabling the plane, which fell off in a tight spin into a 90 degree bank, wing tip down; this generated an overwhelming spinning force pinning anyone inside against the plane, and thus preventing their effort of escaping and baling out. Because of this the plane fell over into a tight spin and disappeared into the clouds below. We saw no parachutes and no flak, and all were presumed dead.

By late 1944, attacks on oil targets would assume top priority. Vast serial fleets of 15th Air Force B-24s and B-17s, escorted by Mustangs and Lightnings, attacked the refineries at Ploesti and bombed Budapest, Komoron, Gyor and Petfurdo in Hungary, Belgrade and other cities in Yugoslavia, and Trieste in north-eastern Italy. Bad weather curtailed operations in October and November, but on 23 October, around 500 heavies bombed the vast Skoda armament works at Pilsen, Czechoslovakia, and other targets in southern Germany and Italy, and in November several missions were flown against oil targets. One favourite of the planners – but not the crews – and which was always a high priority on the target list, was Blechhammer, one of the most heavily defended targets in Germany. This refinery was producing 20,000gal (90,900ltr) of oil monthly. On the 20th, 192 B-24s and B-17s were dispatched to the Blechhammer South refinery, while ninety-two other Liberators attacked Sarajevo marshalling yards and railway bridges at Doboj, Zenica and Fojnica.

The 55th Bomb Wing at Pantanella comprised the 460th, 464th and 465th Bomb Groups. Lt Col Clarence 'Jack' Lokker, the 781st Bomb Squadron CO, 465th Bomb Group, was designated the wing leader, and he flew the 783rd Bomb Squadron lead ship, *Blue I*, with Capt Milton Duckworth, who took the co-pilot's seat. After group and wing assembly, the 465th set course at 5,000ft (1,500m) over Spinazzola. Cloud covered the route to the target area, but the B-24s were safely joined by their P-38 Lightning escort at 11:00 hours over Lake Ballaton, and subsequently by a second escort of P-51 Mustangs at 12:10 hours in the IP area. Lt Robert Hockman, lead bombardier, exploited a gap in the clouds and after making a second run because initially they were off course, the B-24s and the following 464th Bomb Group prepared to release their salvoes of bombs on the refinery from about 23,000ft (7,000m).

On the bomb-run and just before 'bombs away', Col Lokker's B-24 took a direct hit between the No. 2 engine and the fuselage. The wing began breaking off, and immediately the B-24 burst into flames. On the flight deck Lt Joseph Whalen, Mickey operator, was killed, but Lt Joseph Kutger, wing navigator, managed to strap on a parachute and bale out. In all, six of the crew managed to save themselves, including Jack Lokker

(Above) **B-24J of the 464th Bomb Group leaving the burning Pardubice oil refinery in Czechoslovakia on 24 August 1944. Altogether, 530-plus B-24s and B-17s bombed three oil refineries at Kolin and Pardubice this day, as well as the Vinkovci marshalling yard and the Szeged and Ferrara rail bridge.** USAF

B-24H-15-FO 42-52485/F Brown Nose **of the 778th Bomb Squadron, 464th Bomb Group, which crashlanded at Dubendorf, Switzerland, at 13:40 hours on 4 October 1944. On this day, 327 15th Air Force heavies bombed the Munich marshalling yards, while 400 more raided the railway line in the Trento–Mezzaselva area covering over 50 miles (80km) of the Brenner route, and bombed other targets in Italy.** Swiss AF

B-24s of the 465th Bomb Group leaving the target – two marshalling yards at Hatvan, Hungary – on 22 September 1944. On this day, as well as the attacks on Hatvan, almost 500 B-24s and B-17s, escorted by P-38s and P-51s, bombed three rail bridges at Budapest, a marshalling yard at Gyor, also, the airfield at Malacky, and the oil district at Bratislava. USAF

B-24J-1-NT 42-78624 Miss I. Hope **in the 718th Bomb Squadron, 449th Bomb Group.** USAF

What's Up Doc? **in the 825th Bomb Squadron, 484th Bomb Group, came to grief in this crash in Italy.** USAF

B-24J-15-FO 42-52036 in the 451st Bomb Group from Castelluccio, Italy, en route **to its target at Vienna. Note the hand-held tail-guns.** USAF

and two men, namely Sgt James Bourne, waist gunner, and Sgt Lee Billings, engineer, who were blown out of the Liberator as it exploded; but five crew died or were already dead. Lokker and Capt Duckworth were captured by a German farmer near a flak gun emplacement after baling out, but they soon escaped. However, early that evening they ran into a German patrol who shot Duckworth in the leg as he and Lokker ran for it; Hockman, Kutger, Billings and Bourne were captured. The last Duckworth saw of Jack Lokker was of him running into a thick clump of underbrush with two Germans chasing him; the colonel was never seen again. Reportedly he was found dead by the Germans on 22 November and buried. However, it was not until 22 August 1949 that Colonel Lokker's remains were discovered in a civilian cemetery at Lengenlieben,

(Above) **B-24J-5-FO 42-51564 *(foreground)* and another Liberator, both from the 449th Bomb Group, pictured over the Alps** en route **to their target.** USAF

B-24H-15-FO 41-28914 of the 455th Bomb Group. USAF

Its tail knocked off by flak, a B-24 of the 451st Bomb Group dives to earth during a raid on the synthetic oil and coking plant at Odertal near Blechhammer, Germany. The 15th attacked this plant eight times, between 7 July and 26 December 1944, four of the heaviest raids taking place on 2, 17, 18 and 26 December. USAF

(Below) **Bombs fall from B-24H-15-DT 41-28853** Blue I **in the 783rd Bomb Squadron, 456th Bomb Group, as it takes a direct flak hit in the fuel tanks and explodes while on the bomb-run at about 23,000ft (7,000m) over the Blechhammer South refinery, Germany, on 20 November 1944, when 192 B-24s and B-17s hit the target. Capt Milton Duckworth, co-pilot, Lt Col Clarence 'Jack' Lokker, 781st Bomb Squadron CO, and 55th Bomb Wing leader, and four others amazingly escaped from the burning inferno, but Lokker was killed on the ground. Five crew died in the flaming inferno or were already dead.** USAF

Poland, and moved to a US cemetery near Liege, Belgium.

In December the 15th Air Force mounted twenty-five raids on the German forces in northern Italy to prevent reinforcements being sent to help Gen von Runstedt's forces in the Ardennes. Attacks also continued on oil refineries in the Reich. On the 16th the heavies bombed the Brux synthetic oil plant in Czechoslovakia. On the 17th, units of the 5th Wing bombed Blechhammer North from 26,000–29,000ft (7,900–8,800m), and the Moravska Strova oil refinery, as well as targets of opportunity. The 463rd Bomb Group could not participate because of unserviceable runways. At Blechhammer South, 105 B-24s from the 55th Bomb Wing bombed, using PFF.

Meanwhile the 49th Bomb Wing, led by the 484th Bomb Group, flew to Silesia and bombed the synthetic oil and coking plant at Odertal, which was producing 4,000 tons of aviation fuel per month. Cpl Herb Weinstein of A-2 (Intelligence), who was fluent in German, flew aboard the lead ship piloted by Col Keese to monitor German radio traffic. Weinstein wrote:

B-24s of the 15th Air Force pictured during a raid on the oil refineries at Blechhammer, Germany. USAF

> The German command headquarters for fighter command and radar interception of enemy bomber formations for the southern part of Germany, Austria, Italy and Hungary are controlled in Munich, Vienna, Udine and Budapest respectively. As we got into the range of the radar at Udine, my radio began to squawk. I listened, but the R/T, even though it mentioned our group, was of no major concern, and we were still too far away. We veered towards Vienna and the R/T was becoming serious, our flight route being continually followed and updated as we changed course. As we entered Czechoslovakian airspace, Vienna started to contact fighter squadrons *Schmetterling Anton*, *Schwalbe Anton*, *Falke Anton*, *Adler Anton*, *Nachtingall Anton* and a bunch of others; so many squadrons that they added up to more than two hundred planes. Hell, I didn't think that the Germans had that many planes left. From the position reports and the flight heading, I calculated that they would intercept us in 25 to 30 minutes, 5 miles [8km] approximately before we hit the IP.
>
> I called the colonel on the intercom and told him what I had heard and my conclusions, and suggested that he contact our fighter escort to meet us as soon as possible. I was excited. This was my first large-scale fighter intercept. A message from the flight deck informed me that our fighter escort had been contacted. I was glued to my radio, listening to changes being radioed to the German fighters. I heard the command *'Pauke! Pauke! Fahren gegen die Moebelwagen'* (Attack! Attack! Fly towards the 'furniture vans' – Luftwaffe slang for the B-24s). Someone yelled over the intercom, 'P-51s at 3 o'clock!' I yelled, 'Watch at 9 or 10 o'clock – German fighters on the way!' Sure enough, the Germans came, and our fighters engaged them. Here and there our machine guns were firing – I could hear the rat-a-tat even over the noise of our engines. Ten, fifteen minutes, all was bedlam and then we were at the IP getting ready to drop our bombs. Flak came up to meet us: it was heavy and we could see the black puffs all around us, but miraculously we were not hit. The bomb-bay doors were open, the target below us, and then came the long-awaited 'bombs away'. We made a sharp left turn as we left the target. Smoke was billowing upwards, and I hope we plastered it.

The 484th lost one B-24 to fighters, and the 451st also lost just one Liberator, but the 461st, which was attacked by a group of thirty-five to forty very aggressive and very experienced Fw 190s lost nine. At the debriefing, Col Keese attributed the 484th's low losses to the advance information Cpl Weinstein had given him, and to the fact that the fighter escort was able to engage the German fighters as they began their attack. Then he said, 'We have Sgt Weinstein here who can give you a blow by blow report.' 'At the time,' said Weinstein, 'I was only a corporal, and so I said, "Sir, may I consider this a promotion, since I am a corporal?" Everybody laughed, but it must have hit the right note because on the next promotion list I became a sergeant.'

The following day, and on the 19th, B-24s and B-17s carried out more raids on Blechhammer. On the 19 December raid, Ray A. Nichols in the 815th Bomb Squadron, 484th Bomb Group, saw several aircraft go down, including a P-38 which turned onto its wing-tip and split into two parts lengthwise at the centre of the fuselage with one side on fire: it went down during an attack by three Bf 109s. Nichols flew his seventeenth mission a few days later, on 29 December, when the 484th bombed a marshalling yard at Passau, in Germany. Nichols wrote:

> It was clouded in over most of southern Germany. After much circling looking for a hole in the clouds to attack our target, we gave up, as the winds had forced us over Switzerland; so we held our bombs and flew east to clear that country, the weather forcing us to climb up to 28,500ft [8,700m] over the Brenner Pass.
>
> On the way to Italy we stumbled into a hot nest of 88mm AA guns at Udine in the North-east corner near Yugoslavia. The Germans could see us clearly, and peppered us with their 150mm or more 88mm AA guns, which were falling into the position of the box we were leading. The pilot took our box and led us over to the opposite side of the formation, as we were taking many hits, one of which punctured our left main landing-gear tyre. The flight leader instructed all planes to take their bombs home if they had enough gas to carry them. When our pilot called me, as engineer, I replied that we would never have enough gas to carry our bombs home and land, a decision I made when I recalled what happened to the plane we ferried from San Francisco when a live bomb dropped out of the airplane, blowing off the tail. Some days you can do no wrong. My policy turned out to be a wise decision, as it saved Uncle Sam several insurance policy pay-offs that day. I still have a piece of that policy. We got back to Torretta and crash-landed without further damage to the airplane.

B-24 Liberator of the 465th Bomb Group en route **to attack a target in southern Germany.** USAF

The coming of winter with its rain and snow brought about a sharp reduction in operational flying. December 1944 saw the completion of most of the tufa stone houses and the winterization of the tents. Each tent or house had its own improvised fuel stove or fireplace, and at one base, when the smoke was pouring out of the stove pipes, one diarist noted that the area 'looked like Pittsburgh'. Christmas arrived, and trees were brought down by Special Service from the Manfredonia mountain area. Packages from home arrived in huge numbers, and the year 1944 ended in high spirits, perhaps in the belief that 1945 would see the end of European hostilities.

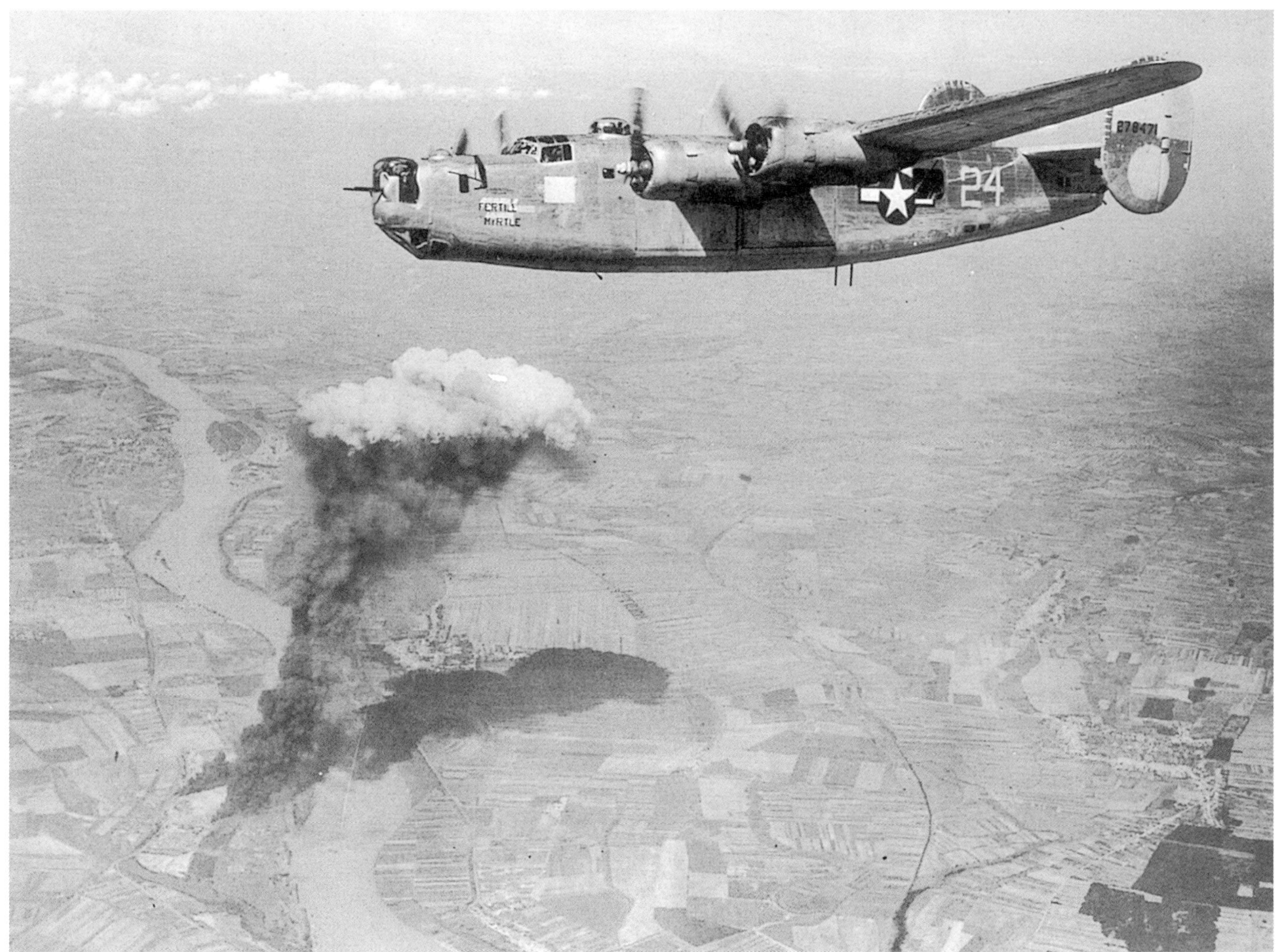

B-24G-16-NT 42-78471 Fertile Myrtle **in the 724th Bomb Squadron, 451st Bomb Group, at Castelluccio, pictured over the oil refinery at Almas-Fuzito, Hungary.** USAF

Grand Finale

Operations throughout January were greatly reduced by poor weather conditions, and few missions were flown; those that were, were led by pathfinder planes and involved raids on marshalling yards, bridges and oil refineries. Mud was a constant problem on the bases, and steady rains with occasional snow made living conditions uncomfortable. February proved little better, but at least missions reached double figures; oil targets particularly, in Germany and Austria, were attacked, and marshalling yards too were hit. The weather improved so that on the bases the mud began to dry up quickly, and from then on it was a matter of dodging the dust.

March followed much the same pattern as before, with raids on the Moosbierbaum, Florisdorf and Kagran oil refineries in Austria, and to marshalling yards in Germany and Hungary. Most were realizing that the air war in Europe was assured and that targets were becoming very limited; but there was no relaxation. In March and early April, Me 262 jet fighters were seen regularly over Europe. Fortunately their incursions were kept to a minimum by lack of fuel and a shortage of pilots to fly them. The 8th and 15th Air Forces retaliated by bombing their airfields and factories. On 21 March, the 15th Air Force dispatched 366 Liberators to the jet factory and airfield at Neuberg. The attack was carried out visually and the plant was almost completely destroyed. Three days later, 271 B-24s finished off the job, destroying twenty-five jets on the airfield in the process.

On 22 March, the B-24s of the 484th Bomb Group attacked oil refineries at Vienna again; for Ray A. Nichols and the rest of the crew, this completed their thirty-third mission and the final mission of their tour. Lt Robert E. Fritts, their original co-pilot, had taken over a first pilot after Lt Dionne had been posted to Ferrying Command after the crew's seventeenth mission. Nichols recalls:

> We took near misses from several 88mm shells over Vienna. Our No. 1 and No. 2 engines and our hydraulic system were knocked out. We flew to Hungary on the right engines, crabbing all the way. Not all of the shells were misses. I cranked down the landing gear by hand and kicked out the nose-gear, and tied my 'chute and harness to a waist gun-mount to stop the plane on the ground at the Russian airbase at Kecskemet, Hungary.

Nichols logged 255 hours' combat time during his thirty-three missions.

Two days later, on 24 March, the 15th Air Force bombed Berlin for the first time, when some 660 B-24s and B-17s attacked a tanks' works as well as airfields at Munich and Neuberg an der Donau and other targets. Next day, 650-plus heavies from Italy raided targets in Prague, and on the 26th, over 500 heavies pounded the marshalling yards at Wiener-Neustadt. A period of bad weather then curtailed operations, but by the end of March the strategic offensive was almost over.

On 2 April, nearly 600 15th Air Force heavies bombed targets in Austria. Mass raids were made again on 5, 6 and 8 April against targets in northern Italy and Germany, and on 9 and 10 April, mass saturation attacks on 'Area Apple' were made in support of the British 8th Army to enable them to move up the Po Valley. On the 10th, 648 heavies attacked 'Area Baker', and this was the largest number of 15th Air Force heavy bombers to attack targets in a single day. Another 544 B-24s and B-17s pounded communications' targets in northern Italy on 11 April, and again on the 12th; on this occasion 400-plus heavies were airborne. It was almost the same story on 14 April. Then on the 15th, the largest 15th Air Force operation of all took place when 830 B-24s and B-17s, escorted by 145 fighter escorts, were dispatched to Wowser near Bologna and the heavies attacked enemy gun emplacements, troop concentrations, tank parks, airfields and other military targets on the 5th Army Front. A second force of 312 B-17s and B-24s acted as a diversion by bombing railway bridges at Nervesa della Battaglia, Ponte di Paave, and Casarsaa della Delizia, and an ammunition factory and stores at Ghedi. In all, some 1,142 heavies bombed their targets on this day. The area was well hit and the 5th Army was able to move out the next day. A German officer, age thirty-two, said during interrogation after a mass surrender of German troops below the Po River:

> The effect on the morale of our troops was indescribable. We know now that you mean business in Italy and that we will not be able to stand up to these terrifying attacks much longer. I believe that my men were quite content to be taken prisoner after the last raid.

On 16 April Gen Carl Spaatz declared the combined bomber offensive to be over. From then on, operations were directed largely at preventing German escape along predestined routes. The end came on 25 April 1945 when Liberators of the 15th Air Force prevented German troops escaping from Italy by bombing lines of communication in Austria and the Brenner Pass.

B-24H-15-FO 42-52440 Calamity Jane **of the 725th Bomb Squadron, 451st Bomb Group, which failed to return from a raid on the Korneuburg oil refinery at Vienna, 7 February 1945. Altogether 680 heavies were dispatched this day.** USAF

B-24s of the 460th Bomb Group dropping fragmentation bombs on the airfield at Neuberg, Austria on 26 March 1945. Over 500 heavies, escorted by P-51s and P-38s, bombed marshalling yards at Wiener-Neustadt and other targets in Austria, Czechoslovakia and Hungary. USAF

(Below) **Grey pathfinder ship B-24L-10-FO 44-49710** Stevonovitch II **of the 779th Bomb Squadron, 464th Bomb Group, takes a direct hit between Nos. 1 and 2 engines from the fourth flak burst to explode near the group formation, just after 'bombs away' on Operation** Wowser, **the mission in support of group troops near Lugo, Italy, on 10 April 1945; she goes down immediately. The aircraft took its name from the son of the 779th Squadron commander, Col James Gilson, who was killed. Only Lt Edward P. Walsh, the Mickey operator, who was thrown clear, survived from the eleven-man crew. Just under three weeks later the war in Europe would be over. The final irony was that this was supposed to be a 'milk-run', so men who were about to finish their missions were sent along.** USAF

When the Germans in Italy finally surrendered, on 2 May, the 15th Air Force joined the 8th Air Force in liberating prisoners of war, and dropping food to stricken inhabitants of war-torn areas.

In its short life of less than two years, the 15th Air Force had made 151,029 heavy bomber sorties and had dropped 303,842 tons of bombs on enemy targets in twelve countries during eighteen months of operations. In doing so, almost half of all fuel production capacity in Europe was destroyed. The cost to the 15th was considerable, and of the 3,544 B-24s assigned, 1,756 were lost in combat. The 15th Air Force was inactivated in September 1945. With the organization of the Strategic Air Command the following spring, the command was reactivated at Colorado Springs as the first of three numbered air forces under SAC.

Final B-24 Group and Wing Assignments
15th Air Force, Italy, January 1944–45

15th Air Force Bari, Italy

47th Bomb Wing	49th Bomb Wing	55th Bomb Wing	304th Bomb Wing	2641st (Special) Group (Provisional)
98th BG	451st BG	460th BG	454th BG	
(343rd/344th BS)	(724th/725th BS)	(760th/761st BS)	(736th/737th BS)	885th BS (H) *
(345th/415th BS)	(726th/727th BS)	(767th/768th BS)	(738th/739th BS)	859th BS (H) **
376th BG	461st BG	464th BG	455th BG	
(512th/513th BS)	(764th/765th BS)	(776th/777th BS)	(740th/741st BS)	
(514th/515th BS)	(766th/767th BS)	(778th/779th BS)	(742nd/743rd BS)	
449th BG	484th BG	465th BG	456th BG	
(716th/717th BS)	(824th/825th BS)	(780th/781st BS)	(744th/745th BS)	
(718th/719th BS)	(826th/827th BS)	(782nd/783rd BS)	(746th/747th BS)	
450th BG		485th BG	459th BG	
(720th/721st BS)		(828th/829th BS)	(756th/757th BS)	
(722nd/723rd BS)		(830th/831st BS)	(758th/759th BS)	

*From July 1944

**From January 1945 (when 2641st (Special) Group (P) was activated

B-24L-10-FO 44-49750 Dog Patch Express **of the 756th Bomb Squadron, 459th Bomb Group, pictured during 'bombs away!'.** USAF

CHAPTER SIX

The War Against Japan

Alaska, CBI and Pacific Theatres

The Liberator was on the brink of entering operational service in the Pacific when the Japanese launched their pre-emptive attack on the US naval base at Pearl Harbor in Hawaii on 7 December 1941. Destroyed on the ground at Hickam Field was a specially modified B-24A ready for an armed reconnaissance of Japanese installations in the Marshalls and Carolines, and particularly Truk and Jaluit. Two B-24As had been prepared for this, but only one had arrived when the Japanese attacked. Immediately following the attack the USAAF repossessed fifteen Liberators, which retained their RAF serial numbers and the designation LB-30, and these were dispatched to the Pacific; however, none reached the Philippines before the Japanese occupied the islands. Four of these aircraft eventually reached the 7th Bombardment Group in Java, and on 16 January 1942 three LB-30s and two B-17s from this group carried out the first Liberator action of the war by USAAF crews with a raid on Japanese shipping and airfields from Singosari, Malang.

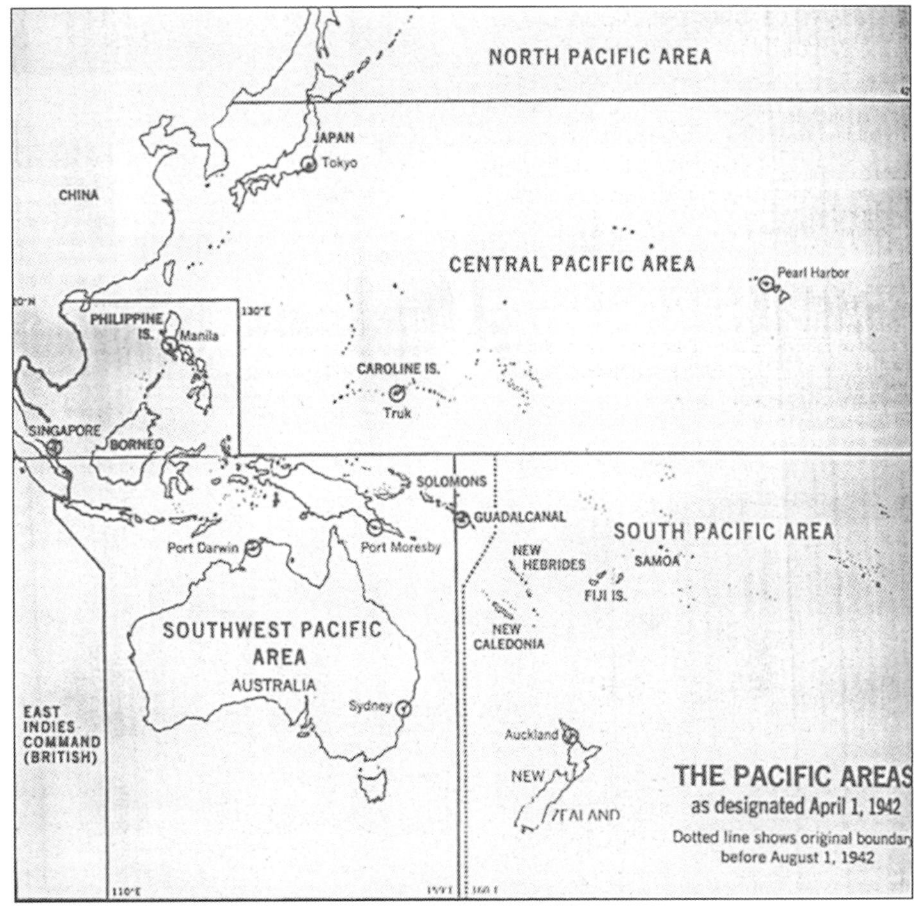

China-Burma-India

On 12 February 1942 the 10th Air Force was activated under the command of Col Harry A. Halverson for action in the China-Burma-India (CBI) theatre, using bases in India. The only combat unit available, however, was the ragged remnants of the 7th Bomb Group, which arrived at Karachi on 12 March. The 7th had been en route to the Philippines with B-17s when the Japanese attacked Pearl Harbor, and the group had then seen constant action during the enemy drive through the Philippines. Maj Gen Lewis H. Brereton had taken command of the 10th Air Force on 5 March, and although he had few resources at his disposal, he was determined to strike at the enemy without delay. On 2/3 April, Brereton led three B-24s including one of the repossessed RAF LB-30s, on a raid against shipping in the Andaman Islands. Claims for hits against a cruiser and a transport were made, and although two of the bombers were damaged by return fire and fighters, the aircraft returned safely to base.

The 10th Air Force's motley collection of B-17s and B-24s was streamlined into thirty-five Liberators late in 1942, and by the end of the year the 7th had thirty-two B-24s, at least on paper (one squadron was still in the Middle East and two others were cadres waiting for aircraft). In the first use of heavy bombers in China, the 7th Bomb Group flew its first offensive mission north of the Yangtze and Yellow Rivers on 21 October 1942 when a flight from the 436th Bomb Squadron was staged through Chengtu with the intention to flood the Lin-hsi coal mines by blasting nearby power stations and pumping facilities; but it met with little success. By January 1943 the 7th Bomb Group was up to full strength and remained on the Indian side of the Himalayas – or the 'Hump' as the range was called – while the 308th Bomb Group, which was also equipped

A 7th Bomb Group B-24 leaving the Blin rail bridge in Burma, November 1944. USAF

B-24D of the 308th Bomb Group taking off at Kunming, China, over the heads of Chinese wagons and parked C-46s and C-47s. USAF

with Liberators, was sent, in March 1943, to Kunming on the Chinese side of the mountains for operations against Japanese shipping and ground installations as distant as Hong Kong.

The 308th Bomb Group had been activated on 15 April 1942 and was originally destined for the 8th Air Force in England; but in March 1943 the group joined Maj Gen Claire L. Chennault's 14th Air Force. The 308th was unique among Liberator groups in that its B-24s doubled as transports, carrying their own supplies of fuel, oil, bombs, spare parts and any other items the group needed; loaded in this way they flew over the Hump before setting off on their first mission, on 8 May 1943, when sixteen B-24s and eleven B-25s bombed White Cloud airfield at Canton. Between 29 July 1943 and 20 August 1943, the 308th flew more supply runs over the Hump before returning to action on 21 August. The target the 308th sought was Hankow, but the fourteen B-24s and seven B-25s missed their rendezvous with eleven P-40 escort fighters, and in a battle with more than fifty Japanese fighters, two of the B-24s were shot down. The 308th was awarded a Distinguished Unit Citation for the attack. On 24 August, four B-24s were lost in a follow-up raid by seven Liberators and six B-25s on Hankow, despite an escort of twenty-two P-40s and P-38s.

For almost two more years the 308th supported Chinese ground forces, attacked airfields, coal dumps, docks, oil refineries and fuel dumps in French Indo-China, mined rivers and ports, bombed shops and docks at Rangoon, attacked Japanese shipping in the East China Sea, Formosa Strait, South China Sea and the Gulf of Tonkin. The 7th Bomb Group, meanwhile, carried out raids primarily in Burma, with attacks on Japanese airfields, fuel and supply dumps, locomotive works, railways, bridges, docks, warehouses, shipping and other targets. The Liberators also bombed oil refineries and railways in Thailand, and powerplants in China, as well as shipping in the Andaman Sea. Like the 308th Bomb Group, the 7th also ferried fuel and supplies over the Hump to China.

Eastern Air Command

In November 1943, South-East Asia Command was activated under the command of Admiral the Lord Louis Mountbatten. Maj Gen George E. Stratemeyer was

B-24J-170-CO 44-40584 Kings X **of the 375th Bomb Squadron, 308th Bomb Group, leaving Japanese supply dumps at Henyang on the Siang River in south-east China.** USAF

Fleet of C-109 'Flying tankers' operated by Air Transport Command in India, used to support B-29 operations in the CBI. All C-109s were conversions of B-24J and L models with the turrets deleted, and fitted with seven specially designed fuel tanks in the bomb-bay, and one in the nose, to give a fuel-carrying capacity of 2,900 US gallons (10,977ltr). USAF

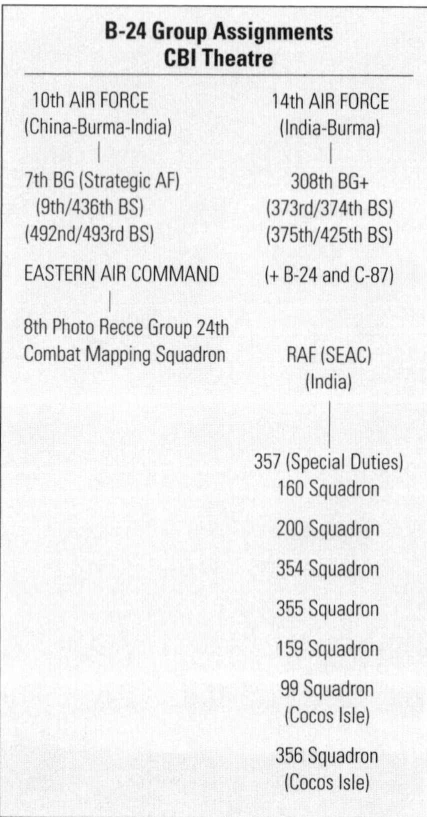

Medal of Honor

For his actions in the South China Sea on the night of 25/26 October 1944, Maj Horace C. Carswell Jr, of the 308th Bomb Group, was awarded the Medal of Honor. Carswell piloted a B-24 in a one-plane strike against a Japanese convoy of twelve ships and at least two destroyer escorts. He took them completely by surprise and made one bombing run at 600ft (183m), scoring a near miss on one warship and escaping without drawing fire. He circled and, fully realizing that the convoy was thoroughly alerted and would meet his next attack with a barrage of anti-aircraft fire, began a second low-level run which culminated in two direct hits on a large tanker. A hail of steel from Japanese guns riddled the Liberator, knocking out two engines, damaging a third, crippling the hydraulic system, puncturing one fuel tank, ripping uncounted holes in the aircraft and wounding the co-pilot. But by a magnificent display of flying skill, Carswell controlled the B-24's plunge towards the sea and he carefully forced it into a halting climb in the direction of the China Seas.

On reaching land, where it would have been possible to abandon the staggering bomber, one of the crew discovered that his parachute had been ripped by flak and was therefore useless. Maj Carswell, hoping to cross mountainous terrain and reach an airfield, continued onwards until the third engine failed. He ordered the crew to bale out while he struggled to maintain altitude, and refusing to save himself, chose to remain with his comrade and attempt a crashlanding. He died when the B-24 struck a mountainside and burned.

appointed chief of Eastern Air Command which effectively united the British and American air forces. Stratemeyer proposed using the combined strength of the 7th and 308th Bomb Groups in a mission against vital installations around Rangoon; the 308th was therefore moved, temporarily, to India and the strike went ahead on 25 November. The raid involved the B-24s, Mitchells and fighters, but unfortunately it went badly wrong: the fighters were prevented from taking off because of bad weather (which also caused the loss of two B-24s on take-off), and so the heavies proceeded to the targets alone. However, these were covered in overcast and bombing results were poor; and a third B-24 was lost over the target. Nevertheless, despite these misfortunes further raids of this nature were made, and results were more successful.

The End in China

Right up until the end of the war, the US and RAF B-24s of Eastern Air Command worked in cooperation, and in January 1944 the combined forces could call on almost eighty Liberators. The 7th Bomb Group received its second DUC for damaging the Japanese line of supply in south-east Asia with an attack against railways and bridges in Thailand on 19 March 1945; the first had been awarded during the Philippines and Netherlands East Indies campaign, in 1942. In June 1945 the 308th Bomb Group moved to India, and once more ferried fuel and supplies over the Hump to China. It had been planned to transfer the 10th and 14th Air Forces to the Pacific to coordinate with the Far East Air Forces in the Philippines, but the war ended before the transfer could be made. The group received a second DUC award for its successful attacks on Japanese shipping between 24 May 1944 and 28 April 1945.

Alaskan Operations

The Alaskan Air Force was activated at Anchorage on 15 January 1942, and was re-designated the 11th Air Force on 15 January 1942. The small Air Force had the task of defending the vast Alaskan wastes and the Aleutian island chain stretching like stepping stones into the Bering Sea; it was here, on Umnak Island, that the 11th had its advanced base, 2,400 miles (3,860km) from Anchorage. The Japanese held the other end of the Aleutians, at Attu and Kiska, as a stumbling block for

B-24Ds of the 28th Composite Group, 11th Air Force, over the Bering Sea en route **to Japanese targets on Kiska and Attu in the western Aleutian Islands.** USAF

B-24 Group Assignments (Aleutians/Alaska)

11th AIR FORCE

28th Composite Group

36th BS*

21st BS

404th BS

(* and B-17s)

any American invasion of Japan through the Aleutian chain and the Kuriles. In fact the Aleutians, with its horrendous weather and unforgiving terrain, was nothing like a suitable launching pad for any American invasion of Japan.

B-24s saw action in this command with the 28th Composite Group, from February 1941 until the end of the war. This group was composed of many types of aircraft, and included fighters as well as LB-30s during 1941–43, and B-24 Liberators and B-25s during 1944–45. At the end of 1941 the 36th Bomb Squadron had one LB-30 and several B-17s, and it received more B-24s by June 1942 with the arrival of the 21st Bomb Squadron.

On 10 June 1942, four B-24s and the single LB-30 took off from Cold Bay, Alaska and flew to Umnak to load up their bombs for an attack on enemy shipping in Kiska Harbour. The attack met with little success, and one B-24 was shot down by flak and two others were badly damaged. The 36th and the 21st were joined by the 404th Squadron, equipped with B-24s, late in 1942. This squadron was known as the 'Pink Elephants' because its B-24Ds were painted desert pink, having originally been intended for North Africa! The 404th was very successful, flying thirty-nine patrols over the Bering Sea without loss. Unfortunately this trend did not continue, and between June and October 1942 the 11th Air Force lost seventy-two aircraft. An indication of the kind of weather experienced in this theatre is that only nine of these were combat losses.

Throughout 1943 the Liberators of the 11th Air Force pounded Japanese shipping and positions in the Aleutians from its new base at Adak, only 250 miles (400km) from Kiska. Amchitka was successfully invaded on 5 January. Then on 18 July, six B-24s flew a 1,700 mile (2,735 km) round trip from Adak to Paramushiro in the Japanese Kurile islands, involving 11½ hours flying time, to bomb the Paramushiro and Katoaka naval

B-24Ds of the 28th Composite Group, 11th Air Force, landing in a snowstorm on the Aleutian Islands. USAF

B-24D-25-CO 41-24290 Hell's Belle **in the 400th Bomb Squadron, 90th Bomb Group. This Liberator finished her days with the Royal Australian Air Force as A72-8.** USAF

bases. All participants were volunteers, and the mission established a new record for distance at that time. One of the crew who became one of the very first members of the 'I Bombed Japan Club' – which was very exclusive at that time – was Fred Meisel, a 41-year-old gunner barely 5ft (1.5m) tall and weighing about 120lb (54kg), who had been born in Minsk, Russia on 7 November 1905, to a Russian mother and a German father. Meisel had fought in the German army in World War I, and was awarded the Iron cross, 1st and 2nd Class.

Meisel recalled: 'We really caught those Japs by surprise – we came in from the west and found them flatfooted.' It was one of the toughest missions he ever flew, and no man left his position on the entire 11½-hour round trip in sub-zero weather. 'And if you went down, you just gave up. They could never find you in the snow wastes of that country.' (Meisel twice turned down commissions to remain on active service. After fifty-eight missions he was sent home for reassignment. For a short time he was a gunnery instructor, but he tired of this and, 'determined to reach my one hundred mark', pressed for and got, an air combat assignment in the 15th Air Force in Italy!)

A second mission to Paramushiro Island was flown by nine B-24s from Attu on 11 August 1943, when bombs and incendiaries were dropped on several targets, including Kashiwabara airfield and Shimushu Island where the Kataoka naval base and staging area were hit. Four days later Kiska was invaded, and on 11 September a mixed force of eight B-24s and a dozen B-25s bombed Paramushiro for the third and last time that year. Six B-24s bombed the Kashiwabara staging area, and shipping was bombed and strafed while some land targets also received hits. Seven B-25s and one Liberator were lost, the latter shot down by AA fire, and two other B-24s force-landed in Russia. The badly-depleted 11th AF was reduced to training for further raids, and it would be five months before it could strike at the Kuriles again. When it did, on 5 February 1944, the six B-24s and their sixteen P-38 escort fighters were joined by some F-7 Liberators of the 2nd Photo Charting Squadron. The relatively small force flew several relays during the retirement of US light cruisers and destroyers, following the bombardment of installations in the Kurabu Cape-Musashi Bay areas. Shortly afterwards, the F-7s photographed and attacked installations at Paramushiro and Shimushu.

Unarmed photo-reconnaissance missions and 'pin-prick' raids on Shimushu and Paramushiro were mainly flown in 1944. On 19 June 1945 the 11th Air Force flew the theatre's longest mission of the war when a B-24 Liberator completed a 2,700-mile (4,340km) trip lasting 15½ hours, from Shamya to Uruppu. The crew bombed a small convoy 25 miles (40km) south-west of Shimushu Bay, sinking one vessel, heavily damaging one other, and setting two more afire. The 11th Air Force flew its last mission of the war on 13 August 1945 when six B-24s radar-bombed the Kashiwabara staging area at Paramushiro, leaving huge columns of smoke in their wake.

Pacific War

The air war over the 64 million square miles of the Pacific Ocean from Hawaii to the Philippines and Australia to the Japanese mainland was divided between three air forces: the 5th, 7th and 13th. Collectively they would become, from 15 June 1944, the Far East Air Force. The 7th Air Force was constituted as the Hawaiian Air Force on 1 November 1940 and re-designated as the 7th Air Force in February 1942. It provided air defence for the Hawaiian islands, and after mid-1943, served in the central and western Pacific. The 5th Air Force had been constituted as the Philippine Department Air Force on 16 August 1941, and activated in the Philippines on 20 September under the command of Brig Gen Henry B. Claggett. It was re-designated the Far East Air Force in October 1941, and the 5th Air Force in February 1942, when Lt Gen George C. Kenney took command. A line of longitude placed the 5th Air Force on the south-west Pacific side and the 13th Air Force, activated on 14 December 1942, on the south Pacific side, and later, south-west Pacific.

5th Air Force Operations

The 5th Air Force fought in the Philippines at the outbreak of the Pacific war, and had covered the retreat south to Java, playing a small part in the Battle of the Coral Sea; but it had really come to life late in 1942 when Lt Gen George C. Kenney took command on 3 September. All told, Kenney would have four B-24 groups at his disposal by the end of the war, or three if one does not include the 380th 'Flying Circus' which, though a member of the 5th Air Force, was attached to the RAAF until January 1945. Among its regular tasks was the training of the Australian B-24 crews for the RAAF.

The 90th Bomb Group was activated on 15 April 1942 and had moved hurriedly to Hawaii in September, where it was assigned to the 7th Air Force while it

B-24Ds of the 90th Bomb Group, 5th Air Force, taxi out from Jackson Strip at Port Moresby, New Guinea, 9 December 1942. USAF

F-7A 42-64047 Patched Up Piece **of the 20th Combat Mapping Squadron, 5th Air Force, in the south-west Pacific.** USAF

Lt Gen George C Kenney, Commander, 5th Air Force, 3 September 1942–14 June 1944, stands by while Lt Albert J. Clocksin examines the repair job done on one of the 90th Bomb Group 'Jolly Roger' Liberators with its distinctive 'skull and crossbones' insignia, 1943. (Note the tail wheel modification.) The Group took its name from their commander, Lt Col Arthur H. Rogers, who was in charge from 16–17 November 1942, and again, 11 July–December 1943. Under Rogers' command, the Group moved to the south-west Pacific in November 1942, and were assigned to the Fifth Air Force. They entered combat immediately, and from November 1942 until January 1945, operated from Australia, New Guinea and Biak, bombing Japanese airfields, troop concentrations, ground installations, and shipping in New Guinea, the Bismarck Archipelago, Palau, and the southern Philippines. The 'Jolly Rogers' were awarded a DUC for strikes, carried out through heavy Flak and fighter opposition, on enemy airfields at Wewak, New Guinea, in September 1943. The Group participated in the Battle of the Bismarck Sea in March 1943 and carried out long-range strikes on oil targets at Balikpapan, Borneo, in September and October 1943. They moved to San Jose, Mindoro, in the Philippines on 26 January 1945, and supported ground forces on Luzon as well as carrying out raids on Formosa and the Asiatic mainland, before moving to Ie Shima on 10 August 1945.
USAF

completed training. In October 1942 it transferred to the 5th Air Force in Australia, thus becoming the first complete group to reach the south-west Pacific. The group flew its first mission on 16 November 1942 to Bougainville Island. By the beginning of of 1943 the 90th were flying long-range missions to Japanese positions in the Celebes and Java. In July 1943, Lt Col Arthur H. Rogers assumed command of the 90th Bomb Group, and the 'Jolly Rogers', as they became known, operated against the enemy in New Guinea, the Bismarck Archipelago, Palau and the southern Philippines.

The 43rd Bomb Group had been activated on 15 January 1941, and was at first equipped with the B-17 Flying Fortress. Between May and September 1943 the group re-equipped with the B-24 Liberator at Port Moresby, New Guinea. On 10 December 1943 the 43rd moved to Dobodura, and again on 4 March 1944, to Nadzab, New Guinea. After moving to the Philippines in November 1944, 'Ken's Men', as they were known, made numerous attacks on Japanese shipping along the Asiatic coast, and targets in China and Formosa, and supported ground forces on Luzon. In July 1945 the group moved to Ie Shima and flew missions against airfields and railways in Japan, and against shipping in the Inland Sea and the Sea of Japan.

The fourth and final Liberator unit in the 5th Air Force was the 22nd 'Red Raiders' Bomb Group, which converted from B-26 and B-25 medium bombers to Liberators late in 1943, and was re-designated the 22nd Bomb Group (Heavy) in February 1944. The 'Red Raiders' hit the Japanese airfields, shipping and oil installations in Borneo, Ceram and Halmahera, and in September 1944, began raiding the southern Philippines to neutralize Japanese bases in preparation for the invasion of Leyte.

B-24J-160-CO 44-40428 Cocktail Hour **in the 64th Bomb Squadron, 43rd Bomb Group, 5th Air Force, in Ie Shima, 1945. The group moved to Ie Shima on 26 July 1945, and to Luzon on 10 December 1945.** USAF

(Below) **B-24J of the 11th Bomb Group, 7th Air Force, overflies swaying palms on Makin Island.** USAF

Also in September 1944, the Liberators of the 5th Air Force in the New Guinea campaign flew missions against the oil refineries at Balikpapan in Borneo. This refinery was known as the 'Ploesti of the Pacific', and was only second in production to Palembang in Sumatra. The first raid on the Balikpapan oilfields had been made at night by nine B-24s of the 380th Bomb Group on 13 August 1943 in a seventeen-hour, 1,200-mile (1,930km) round trip, from Darwin, Australia. Two further raids were made, and in September 1944 the airfield at Noemfoor in north-west New Guinea became available, reducing the flying time to fourteen hours and allowing the B-24s to carry a 2,500lb bomb load.

7th Air Force Operations

One of the strongest advocates of using the Liberator in the Pacific theatre was Maj Gen Clarence L. Tinker, who took command of the small 7th Air Force on 18 December 1941. It was Tinker who saw the great possibilities in using the long-ranging Liberator and who was determined to have it in his inventory, and he wanted to demonstrate the B-24's capabilities at the earliest opportunity. It came in June 1942 when Tinker and his staff were headquartered on Midway Island, scene of the famous sea battle between the navies of

America and Japan. With the Japanese fleet retiring westward on 5 June, Tinker wanted to bomb Wake Island, 1,250 miles (2,011km) away, using four of the five LB-30 long-range cargo planes which had landed at Midway after leaving Hawaii. Tinker's 'Southern Cross Airways', as he called them, refuelled at Midway on the evening of the 6th, and Tinker led them off again for a pre-dawn attack on Wake Island loaded with every drop of gasoline the LB-30s could hold, and six 500lb bombs apiece. Thirty minutes after take-off, AL589, Maj Gen Tinker's LB-30, with Lt Hinton at the controls, nosed forwards into some overcast and was never seen again. It was a sad end for a man whose greatest wish was that the 7th should get the long-ranging B-24s. The other three aircraft carried on but failed to find the target, and returned to Wake.

Tinker's crews did not share the general's regard for the B-24, and they were deeply concerned when the 7th began equipping with the Liberator in preference to the B-17. Tinker's successor, Maj Gen Willis H. Hale, had a difficult task in persuading his men that accepting the B-24 did not make the 7th Air Force a second-class outfit. Gradually the crews grew to accept the long-ranging bomber, and Tinker's early enthusiasm was justified on 22 December 1942 when Col William A. Matheny, commanding officer of the 307th Bomb Group, led twenty-six B-24Ds on another mission to Wake, staging through Midway Island from Hawaii. The B-24s bombed from 8,000 to 25,000ft (2,500 to 7,600m), and the only damage to the American formation was two small holes in the lead ship. In February 1943, the 'Long Rangers', as the 307th Bomb Group became known, were transferred to the 13th Air Force. Some of their B-24Ds were taken on charge by the reconstituted 11th Bomb Group; this group had previously operated B-17s in the 13th Air Force after moving to the New Hebrides in July 1942.

The 11th Bomb Group was reassigned to the 7th Air Force in spring 1943, and on 26 July 1943 flew its first B-24 mission, when ten B-24s set out to bomb Wake Island, staging from eastern Island on Midway. This, the sixth raid carried out against the island, was mounted as a diversionary mission on behalf of the US Navy, who wanted to relieve pressure in the south Pacific and to confuse the Japanese as to where the next blow would fall. *Little Hiawatha* and *Hilo Hattie* turned back with malfunctions. Going in to the target the eight remaining Liberators came under attack by upwards of thirty Zeros which continued to blaze away at the B-24s for almost an hour. *Cabin in the Sky*, flown by Lt Cason in the 42nd Squadron, crashed into the Pacific ocean after colliding with one of the Japanese fighters during the running battle, and all the crew were lost. Lt Richard S. Thompson, pilot of *Wicked Witch*, was hit in his left leg by a 20mm shell, causing him to lose the limb. The eight B-24s dropped their cargoes of 500lb GP bombs, fifty-five frag clusters and 650lb depth charges on oil storage areas,

B-24s of the 7th Air Force en route **from Marshalls to Truk.** USAF

barracks and the gun emplacement area at Peacock Point. Gunners put in claims for nine Zeros destroyed, four probables, and three damaged.

The 30th Bomb Group was based on the west coast of America from 1942–43, and had flown B-24s on maritime patrol missions; on 11 October it moved to Hawaii and was assigned to the 7th Air Force. In November, the group sailed for the Ellice Islands in the central Pacific and, despite having had only a few weeks' training, was declared ready to participate, together with three squadrons of the 11th Bomb Group, in Operation *Galvanic*, the invasion of the Japanese-held Gilbert Islands some 2,000 miles (3,200km) from Hawaii. Following the amphibious landings on Tarawa and Makin Atolls on 20 November, the 7th Air Force resumed its operations against the Marshal Islands in support of the base development phase of Operation *Galvanic*, and in preparation for *Flintlock* and *Catchpole*, the invasion of the Marshalls. From 14 November until 6 December 1943 the 7th Air Force flew twenty-nine missions to establish air superiority over Tarawa, at a cost of seven Liberators. During 6/7 December 1943, fourteen B-24s, staging through Tarawa, bombed targets on Maloelap and Wotje atolls in the opening stages of *Flintlock*, the capture and defence of Kwajalein and Majuro atolls. In January 1944 the B-24s of the 7th Air Force took part in the seventy-day pre-invasion bombardment of Kwajalein, the largest atoll in the world. altogether, *Flintlock* cost 7th Bomber Command, now established in Tarawa, eighteen Liberators.

The 7th rapidly earned a reputation for carrying out specialist, tough tasks, and the next one assigned to it were bomber support missions during Operation *Catchpole*, the invasion of Eniwetok and the Marshalls. On 14 February 1944, forty-plus B-24s from the 11th and 30th Bomb Groups, flying out of Makin and Tarawa, bombed Ponape Island in the first 7th Air Force raid on the Caroline Islands. The first heavy air strikes were made three days later, on 17 February, when B-24s from Tarawa and Abemama struck at Ponape, Kusiae Island and Jaluit. This and successive raids by Liberators of the 7th Air Force, and by US Navy PB4Ys, neutralized air bases in the Marshalls and the Carolines.

The island of Truk in the Carolines became a regular mission for 7th Air Force crews, and by late February 1944 it had been largely neutralized. At the end of March, all three army air forces (5th, 7th and 13th) had bombed Japanese airfields and positions on Ponape, Kusiae, Kapingamangari and New Guinea, and the PB4Ys of the US Navy had raided Palau, Yap and Woleai. By April the 11th and 30th Bomb Groups were based on Kwajalein, and

B-24J-5-CO of the 11th Bomb Group over Kwajalein, Marshall Islands, June 1944. The group was based on the island from 5 April 1944–24 October 1945, when they moved to Guam. USAF

Liberators of the 11th Bomb Group, 7th Air Force, taxi out in May 1944. USAF

together with the US Navy and the 5th and 13th Air Forces, they largely destroyed almost all Japanese air bases east of the Philippines. US Navy and USAAF cooperation was further extended in April 1944 when seven B-24s of the 30th Bomb Group flew a shuttle bombing mission of more than 4,000 miles (6,400km) with PB4Ys on a triangular route from Eniwetok to the Carolines and bombing Guam in the Marianas. On 15 May 1944, B-24s of 7th Bomber Command, together with other aircraft, began round-the-clock bombing of targets in the Marshalls, ending with the destruction of all targets by the end of the month.

On 14 August 1944, the 7th Air Force was reorganized as a 'mobile tactical air force', only retaining units that would function in the combat area. The 30th Bomb Group moved from Kwajalein, where it had been based since March, to Saipan, to begin attacks on shipping and airfields in the Volcano and Bonin islands; these attacks would continue until Iwo Jima was occupied early in 1945. In October 1944 they were joined by the 11th Bomb Group, which had moved to Guam. Meanwhile, in late September, the 11th and 30th Bomb Groups were joined in the 7th Air Force by the 494th Bomb Group, the last B-24 group activated (1 December 1943) in World War II. The 494th moved from Hawaii to Palau, while a new base was constructed on Angaur, in the Philippines for combat operations. The 494th Bomb Group were known as 'Kelly's Cobras' after their commander, Col Laurence B. Kelly; they landed at Angaur on 24 October 1944 and were immediately 'commandeered' by Gen Douglas MacArthur to support his ground forces in the Philippines campaign.

On 3 November, 'Kelly's Cobras' entered combat when they took off from Angaur and bombed airfields on Yap and Koror in the Carolines. Throughout the remainder of the war, 'Kelly's Cobras' served in the Philippines campaign, participating in many strikes on gun emplacements, personnel areas and storage depots on Corregidor and Caballo at the entrance to Manila Bay. They also bombed radio installations and powerplants at Japanese bases in the Philippines and enemy-held airfields, including Clark Field on Luzon. Early in 1945 they bombed airfields on Mindanao, and ammunition and supply dumps in the Davao Gulf and Illana Bay areas. After the Philippines fell on 16

B-24J-120-CO 42-109951, Madame Pelé **of the 819th Bomb Squadron, 30th Bomb Group, 7th Air Force, at Kwajalein, Marshall Islands, where the Group was based from March–August 1944. The Liberator was purchased by funds raised by Honolulu school-children.** USAF

(Below) **B-24J** Dual Sack **of the 7th Air Force just above the ocean on a shipping raid on Bonin Island.** USAF

February 1945, the 'Cobras' moved nearer Japan, and in June 1945 they moved to Okinawa. The 494th finished the war with raids in support of the guerrilla forces; they participated in strikes primarily against enemy airfields on Kyushu, Japan, until VJ-Day; and they also took part in incendiary raids, dropped propaganda leaflets over urban areas of Kyushu, and attacked airfields in China, southern Korea, and around the inland sea of Japan.

From August 1944 until 19 February 1945, the 11th, 30th and 494th Bomb Groups were engaged in strikes on Iwo Jima and surrounding islands. In March 1945 the 30th Bomb Group returned to Oahu and trained and flew patrol missions. In June and July, the 494th and 11th Bomb Groups moved to Okinawa to take part in the final phases of the air offensive against Japan.

Thirteenth Air Force Operations

The two B-24 groups attached to the 13th Air Force were the 5th, the 'Bomber Barons', and the 307th, the 'Long Rangers'. The 5th Bomb Group had left Hawaii in November 1942 and operated from bases in the south and south-west Pacific, first from Espiritu Santo in the New Hebrides, then Guadalcanal in the Solomons, with B-17s, and later B-24s during the Allied drive to the Philippines. The 307th had originally been assigned to the 7th Air Force as a B-17 outfit, but was now assigned to the 13th Air Force, and they had equipped totally with B-24s before moving, in February 1943, to Guadalcanal. The 'Canal' or 'Cactus' as it was codenamed, was a Hadean, jungle-encrusted, malaria-ridden island, 8 miles (13km) wide and 12 miles (19km) long, with black volcanic sandy beaches. Henderson Field, 1 mile (1.5km) inland, was crucial for missions to Japanese targets as distant as New Ireland in the Bismarck Archipelago, Truk in the Carolines, and Rabaul on New Britain, and 'Cactus' was 'home' to a motley collection of bombers and fighter aircraft. Conditions were very bad and were epitomized in a ditty of the day: 'There's an island they call Cactus where the sun is like a curse, and each long day is followed by another slightly worse.'

2nd Lieutenant – later Captain – Alfred B. Cohen, from Chicago, a navigator in the 5th Bomb Group's 23rd Bomb Squadron, flew fifty missions, 30 per cent of them in B-24s. Cohen was nicknamed 'The Kahili Kid', because in spite of which target was

Six of Capt Bob McKinley's crew in the 23rd Bomb Squadron, 5th Bomb Group, 13th Air Force, pictured in January/February 1944. Left to right: 'Midge', co-pilot; 2nd Lt Alfred B. Cohen, navigator; Bob McKinley, pilot and squadron CO; Capt Bob McConnell, bombardier, who had an incredible escape on a mission to Truk; radio operator; engineer. The wartime censor has scratched out the radar aerials. Alfred B. Cohen Collection

'The Army's new B-24 Liberator', or 'Flying-box car', drawn on Guadalcanal by Alfred B. Cohen. Alfred B Cohen Collection

(Below) **B-24D 42-40144** Munda Belle **in the 868th Bomb Squadron, 13th Air Force, at the 13th Air Depot Group area on New Caledonia. The 'Belle' had previously served with the 5th and 307th Bomb Groups.** USAF

scheduled, Captain Bob McKinley's crew always seemed to divert to Bougainville if he was on a mission. Cohen recalls:

The introduction of the B-24 late in 1943 for bombing operations brought targets like New Ireland, about a ten-hour round trip and previously out of range of the B-17s, within reach if we refuelled at Munda, in the New Georgia Islands. On a mission to Kavieng, New Ireland, on Christmas Eve 1943, we took off from Henderson Field on near-empty fuel tanks and landed at the short, 5,000ft [1,500m] runway on Munda. That night, in our beds, cigarettes glowed in the dark for a long time and everyone was very nervous. We were worried about the weather, and the maximum bomb load on such a short runway. However, we awoke to find the Seabees had worked all through the night to lengthen the runway by 3,000ft [900m] specially for our mission!

We set off with promises of a Christmas turkey dinner when we returned, courtesy of the Navy. There was a full moon and the coral everywhere gleamed like snow. Take-off was horrendous, because it was raining heavily and a wall of water loomed at the end of the runway. We were told that the mission would still go ahead as the weather would be OK once we reached 10,000ft [3,000m]. It was a squadron strength mission with ten to twelve aircraft. One pilot refused to take off, however, because he said he would not be responsible for the death of his crew; so Col Marion C. Unruh grounded him. Unruh was from Pretty Prairie, Kansas, and was shot down later by ground fire over New Ireland, flying *Pretty Prairie Special*, a B-24 with an enormous sunflower painted on the nose. On 'Zero Hour' that night, 'Tokyo Rose', the Nisei Propagandist, told us that he was a PoW. We were always called 'MacArthur's Bombers'. The rest of us got off and climbed with full fuel and bomb load aboard, but we didn't finally clear the clouds until 22,000ft [6,700m]. Everyone got off, but it was a terrible night and we dodged thunderstorms and the towering 'brick walls' of anvil tops all the way to the target. Pilots had their control wheels fully forwards and climbed, or fully back in their laps and dived; but still we climbed because of the vertical currents and the extreme turbulence.

We got to the target and bombed Kavieng in daylight. It was still stormy, but in the tropics the sun comes up like thunder. Then as we left the target we thought we saw Zeros – lots of them, at 12 o'clock. Luckily, just as we were

> ready to fire our guns, we realized that they were Navy SBD Dauntlesses. On the way back I heard Bing Crosby singing 'White Christmas' on the radio, and I was reminded of our promised Christmas dinner. But when we got back we discovered that the turkeys had arrived but were infested with maggots, and so all we got was a tin plate with a K-ration on it ... and a paper hat. I won't quote the language used.

B-24D-50-CO 42-40323 Frenesi **of the 370th Bomb Squadron, 307th Bomb Group (note the 'Long Rangers' on the tail), 13th Air Force, pictured in July 1944 on Los Negros, a veteran of 110 missions. The A-6 tail turret installation in the nose is a result of a field modification at the Hawaiian Air Depot.** USAF

Capt Cohen went back to the US on leave in March, having promised to telephone the mother of Capt Bob McConnell, his bombardier, who also lived in Chicago. He recalls:

> She was crying when I rang, because apparently Bob had been shot down on a mission to Truk. No one liked going to Truk, or Rabaul – they were like Berlin. But almost a month later I was in the Officers' Club at Memphis, and there at the bar was Bob McConnell! He told me the story. They had just bombed Truk when their B-24 was hit and set on fire in the bomb-bay. Bob had gone back to extinguish the fire when the pilot rang the bale-out bell. Everyone went out except Bob, who had to crawl all the way back to the nose to get his 'chute – he finally got out through the nose-wheel doors and pulled his rip-cord. His eyes haemorrhaged when the 'chute opened. One strap was loose, and he hit the water hard and it broke his ribs, puncturing a lung. Then his Mae West wouldn't inflate, but in fact his own body swelled up like a balloon because air was escaping from his punctured lung into his body cavity, and this kept him afloat. He was in the water six hours, and was in such agony that there came a point when he was ready to take a couple of mouthfuls and go under. But at the last light of the day he saw bubbles in the water nearby, and then he heard a great 'swoosh' and saw a periscope – and an American submarine surfaced! It had been submerged off Truk harbour to pick up downed B-24 crews, and Bob was rescued! The sub picked up five other survivors and they spent ten days at sea before they were put ashore at the Solomons. Mac was promoted to Major and was awarded the DFC to add to his Silver Star.
>
> The air war in the Pacific was lonely. Our search missions were from ten to eleven hours' duration, and all of them over water at about 100ft [30m]. It was easy to get lost, and everyone was frightened of going down in the sea; the B-24 didn't stay afloat as long as the B-17 did. We had a lot of water-landings – though a water-landing

Pte Elvan D. Davis, ground crewman, poses with a bomb as he prepares to load up B-24 42-72968 Ginny Lynn **of the 27th Bomb Squadron, 30th Bomb Group, based on the Gilberts, for a mission over the Marshall Islands in the spring of 1944.** USA

did earn a three-week rest in New Zealand – if you survived. Malaria was a problem until the use of DDT became widespread and oil was poured on all stagnant ponds. Bad weather, navigation errors and the sea were as dangerous as the enemy.

Snoopers

On 22 August 1943, a special unit of ten black-painted SB-24Ds, nicknamed 'Snoopers', arrived on Guadalcanal. Each Liberator was equipped with the very latest SCR-717-B search and navigation radar, an AN/APQ-5 LABS bombsight and an AN/ARN-1 radio altimeter for low-level, blind bombing sorties. At first the 'Snoopers' were attached to the 5th Bomb Group and operated by the 394th Bomb Squadron. They flew 111 missions, including ninety-four attacks against Japanese shipping between Rabaul and the Solomons at an average height of 1,500ft (460m). Only two Liberators were lost, *The Ramp Tramp* on 9 September, and *Miss Libby, the Sea-Ducer* on 14 June 1944. The strikes became known as the 'Tokyo Express', and such was their success that in January 1944 the 'Snoopers' became the 868th Squadron, reporting directly to 13th Air Force for the rest of the war.

Far East Air Forces

On 15 June 1944 the FEAF was formed, with jurisdiction over the 5th and 13th Air Forces, and Lt Gen George C. Kenney was appointed its commander; its headquarters were at Brisbane, Australia. Lt Gen Ennis C. Whitehead took over command of the 5th Air Force at Owi in the Schouten Islands. Headquarters, 13th Air Force, moved from Guadalcanal to Los Negros from which the heavies had been operating since April, and Maj Gen St Clair Streett took over as Commander General of the 13th.

The island-hopping campaign in the Pacific moved slowly but relentlessly forwards, with the ultimate goal always the Japanese home islands. The advances across the Pacific meant that targets previously out of reach of the FEAF, now came within reasonable range, especially when weight-saving devices were applied to the Liberators. Optimum range could now be achieved by such methods as moving crewmen from one part of the aircraft to another at given times, and firing all remaining ammunition soon after leaving the target.

The 5th and 307th Bomb Groups were moved to New Guinea, and on 30 September 1944, B-24s from these groups joined with the Liberators in the 90th Bomb Group, 5th Air Force, to send a combined force of seventy-two B-24s in the first of a series of raids on the Balikpapan oilfields. Three B-24s were shot down by defending Japanese fighters. On 3 October the FEAF tried again. Elmer R. Vogel, a ball gunner in Lt Paul Kimble's crew in the 372nd Squadron, 307th Bomb Group, recalls the mission, the crew's fourth:

The weather was always a problem, and this day was no exception. I lowered the ball; I had on my Mae West harness and my .45 calibre pistol in my shoulder holster. I could not wear the flak jacket in the ball. When we got in we were in some bad weather and visibility was zero. I knew we were somewhere in the Celebes area. Pretty soon we broke out of the storm after a good deal of bulleting up and down like a giant rollercoaster. Passing the Celebes group of islands I noticed the view below was anything but beautiful.

We started across Makassar Strait and approached the IP; the target was burning up ahead. Then between fifty and seventy-five Japanese fighters hit us; they seemed as thick as flies, and the flak was quite heavy – in fact their own flak knocked down some of their own. We were flying at about 9,000ft [2,750m], within range of most of their guns, and the hits on our plane were from flak as well as fighters.

Lt Paul Kimble's crew in the 372nd Bomb Squadron, 307th Bomb Group. Front row: Harvey Cauntais, co-pilot; Paul Kimble, pilot; Lt John Pfirman, bombardier. Back Row, left to right: Elmer Vogel, ball gunner; Dave McClintic, gunner; Dave Debusman, engineer-gunner; Sgt Thomas Rennaker, gunner; Peter Yanos, gunner; Bucky Walters, radio operator-gunner. Elmer Vogel

I felt the vibration of our guns being fired, and felt some of the hits on our plane – and we were hit often. I saw two or three B-24s go down; one was below me and on fire, and this must have been hard on my nervous system because I got quite sick and had to use the oxygen several times due to vomiting in the turret. It seemed that as fast as I would fire at one fighter, someone would call out 'Fighters at 3 o'clock!' or somewhere else, and I would turn the turret and try to line up the computing sight that the ball turret was famous for. But with so many fighters against us I found this most difficult to do, and in the end I relied on knowing that every fifth round was a tracer, and that I could do a better job under those conditions.

One fighter came up under me. I started giving him short bursts, but noticed he was not firing at me. Then I started with longer bursts from my twin fifties, and eventually he got so close I could actually make out his facial expression; he had on goggles and was gritting his teeth. It was then I noticed he was carrying a phosphorous bomb. He turned away, and smoke began to pour from his engine, but he

B-24 Group Assignments:
Far East Air Forces

5th AIR FORCE (SW Pacific)	7th AIR FORCE (Central Pacific)	13th AIR FORCE (China-West Pacific)
22nd BG	*11th BG*	*5th BG*
(2nd/19th BS)	(14th/26th BS)	(23rd/31st BS)
(33rd/408th BS)	(42nd/98th BS)	(72nd/394th BS)
	(431st BS)	
43rd BG	*30th BG*	*307th BG**
(63rd/64th BS)	(21st/27th BS)	(370th/371st BS)
(65th/403rd BS)	(38th/392nd BS)	(372nd/424th BS)
	(819th BS)	** From 7th AF, February 1943*
90th BG	*494th BG*	
(319th/320th BS)	(864th/865th BS)	868th Bomb Squadron
(321st/400th BS)	(866th/867th BS)	
*380th BG**	86th Combat Mapping Squadron	RAAF (Australia)
(328th/329th BS)		
(330th/331st BS)	20th AIR FORCE	
**Att to RAAF until Jan 45*	3rd Photo Recce Squadron	21 Squadron
	655th Bomb Squadron	23 Squadron
20th Combat Mapping Squadron	(55th Weather Recce Squadron)	24 Squadron
		25 Squadron

Sabu 'The Elephant Boy', who was a movie actor before service as an aerial gunner in the 424th Bomb Squadron, 307th Bomb Group where he won the DFC. His real name was Sabu Dastigir: jungle born, he was only eleven and an illiterate orphan when suddenly he was given fame. His subsequent films included The Drum, The Thief of Baghdad **and** Black Narcissus. **Sabu became an American citizen. He died at the age of thirty-nine in 1963.**

released the phosphorous bomb and it exploded off to our side. The last thing I saw of him he was spiralling towards the sea. I was credited with one probable.

I was running out of ammo, and all of this happened after bombs away. The ten 250lb bombs fell in the target area. I did not know how bad we were hit until later. Everything seemed to be happening fast, and then someone called out over the interphone that John Warne, the nose-gunner, was hit. I had no ammo left so I stowed the guns straight down and proceeded to get out of the ball turret. I did not retract the ball, as this was done later by the pilot.

The strangest feeling came over me when I heard John was hit – it was as if I knew what was going to happen: I believe God spoke to me and said 'Go help John'. I'll never believe otherwise. Also, since I was the nose-gunner only three missions before, I felt very peculiar because this would have been me if we hadn't switched turrets. As I left the turret I felt a tremendous amount of wind and thought the bomb-bay doors were open, but found it was coming from a large hole in front of the waist window. I reached for my parachute to attach my harness, and saw it had three holes in it – so I threw it out the opening as it was no longer of any use to me. I looked back and saw Staff Sgt Rennaker on his knees: he was hit in the hand and someone was helping him.

I started up to the nose, and as I passed under the command deck I noticed this red stuff dripping from above. I thought it was blood and wondered who was hit, but later I found out it was hydraulic fluid as our brakes were shot out. When I got to the nose, Lt John Pfirman, the bombardier was having a difficult time getting John Warne out of the nose turret because he was hit in the back with a piece of shrapnel. When we got John out of the turret I thought he was dead. He was hit in the right chest and his right arm was dangling. Fortunately, however, it wasn't serious. I took my pocket knife and sprinkled some morphine powder on the opening. As we were moving him from the turret, Pfirman said, 'Elmer, there is one last Jap fighter still with us. Why don't you surprise him and get in the turret when he makes the next pass?' As I tried to turn the turret I saw the fighter turning towards us, but the gun was inoperable.

We were five to six hours from home and we tied a tourniquet on John's arm. He was unconscious most of the time, but would come to and cry out for water and then pass out again. While this was going on, Lt Kimble called and said he did not know whether we could stay in the air much longer, and that we might have to ditch. We were flying at about 15,000ft.

Pfirman and I proceeded to give John some blood. This wasn't easy, as neither of us knew how to do it, but we realized it had to be done or he would die. We read the instructions on mixing the plasma with water, and we knew we couldn't have any air in the lines when we inserted the needle in his vein; but we had a difficult time getting it all done. We looked at each other as we tried unsuccessfully to insert the needle in his vein. Pfirman said, 'Elmer, let's pray. We need help.'

So we prayed aloud and cried for God's help – and truly a miracle happened, because we gave him six pints of blood and kept him alive. Our B-24 sustained many holes, including the nose turret which had received a direct hit, a large hole in the waist, many small holes throughout the fuselage, the hydraulic system shot out, two engines shot out, two large holes in the top of the fuselage in front of the pilot and co-pilot, all but one or two instruments shot out, and two large holes in the right wing outside #4 engine. The waist gunner was wounded in the right hand, Pfirman was hit in the back, Kimble had a piece of shrapnel in the right instep, and Harvey Cauntais, the co-pilot, had several wounds in each arm.

We were quite concerned whether we had enough gas left to reach Sansapar. I understand only one B-24 made it back to our base at Noemfoor. As we approached Sansapar we knew our hydraulic system was gone, so the main landing gear had to be cranked down. And we couldn't get the nose-wheel down. Knowing that we

B-24M-15-CO and B-24J-175-CO (with hand-held tail guns) of the 494th Bomb Group, pictured on 16 March 1945 en route **to their target, a Japanese bivouac area 5 miles (8km) north of Sarangana Bay, Mindanao, Philippine Islands.** USAF

would have to land without brakes and without the nose-wheel, we had to take extra emergency measures: we threw the waist guns overboard and tied the parachutes to the gun-mounts to act as brakes. As many crew-members as possible were placed in the rear of the plane to keep the nose up until the parachutes opened and slowed us down enough so that when the nose touched the runway we would not tip over. Lt Kimble did a wonderful job of bringing us in – and what a wonderful feeling it was to kiss the ground again. Several other B-24s came in behind us with various problems; one was from the 424th Squadron, and in its crew was Sabu 'The Elephant Boy' who had been a movie actor before enlisting as a gunner.

There were certainly a lot of things that happened that I can't explain, but I do know that not many airplanes could still have flown as this B-24 did with all the damage sustained. She sure took a beating, but she did get us back. With the total cooperation of all on board and with God's help, we lived to see another day. I guess it just wasn't our time to go.

Seven B-24s of the 307th Bomb Group were shot down; nineteen B-24s of the 5th Bomb Group came through completely unscathed. Further raids by a combined force of 5th and 13th Air Force groups, together with fighters, caused great damage to the plant. And in a total of five raids on the plant, twenty-two Liberators were lost.

Pacific Air Forces and the Final Assault on Japan

In September 1944 the Far East Air Forces also began attacks on the Philippines and supported the island-hopping campaign across the Pacific. The Philippines fell on 16 February 1945, and from August 1944 until 19 February 1945, the 7th AF was engaged in strikes on Iwo Jima and surrounding islands. By July 1945 all the Pacific air forces had begun moving northwards for the final assault on Japan. The 5th Air Force based at Okinawa and the 13th Air Force on Clark Field in the Philippines began attacking targets in Formosa and Indochina. The three B-24 groups in the 5th Air Force flew explosive and fire raids on Japan, but the honour of being the first B-24 group in the FEAF to bomb Japan went to the 'Cobras' of the 494th Bomb Group, 7th Air Force, when its B-24s raided Omura airfield on Kyushu, southernmost of the Japanese home islands.

The 43rd Bomb Group was based on Ie Shima and attacking targets on Kyushu. Just over one hundred B-24s of the 22nd, 90th and 380th Bomb Groups of the 5th

Line-up of B-24s and aircrew trainees at RAAF Liberator OTU at Tocumwal, New South Wales. Crews are assembling for final instructions from their CO, G Capt A.A. Barlow, and flying instructors, before taking off on training flights. Four Australian Squadrons – Nos. 21, 23, 24 and 25 were equipped with Liberators. IWM

B-24J-180-CO 44-40759 Shack Bunny **of the 867th Bomb Squadron, 494th Bomb Group, over the Gulf of Java** en route **to Japanese targets at Mintal aerodrome on Mindanao in the Philippines in March 1945.** USAF

The crew of Lil' Audrey **in the 373rd Bomb Squadron, 308th Bomb Group, celebrate the completion of forty missions in their B-24 which had completed 100 missions with various crews.** via Mike Bailey

B-24M-30-CO 44-42378 A Wing an' 10 Prayers **in the 373rd Bomb Squadron, 308th Bomb Group, on Okinawa, October 1945.** via Mike Bailey

were based at Okinawa. The 11th and 30th Bomb Groups in the 7th Air Force moved up to the Ryukus Islands, while the two 13th Air Force B-24 groups, the 5th and 307th, had moved to Clark Field in the Philippines; from there they had begun attacking targets in Formosa and Indochina. The armed forces of Japan were now being attacked from all sides. In Europe the war had finished and there was talk of sending over B-24 groups of the 8th Air Force, but the two atomic bombs dropped on Japan made the final phase of the Pacific War redundant. One by one the Liberator groups of the 5th, 7th and 13th Air Forces disbanded and began flying home. Had the war continued a little longer, the citizens of Tokyo would have witnessed thousands of Liberators flying over their capital. Thankfully the Liberators were not called upon to do so.

(Above) **B-24M-20-CO 44-42151** Bolivar Jr **of the 431st Bomb Squadron, 11th Bomb Group, Mariana Islands, June 1945.** USAF

F-7A 2-F Photo Fanny **of the 2nd Photographic Charting Squadron (which was attached to the Far East Air Forces), flown by 1st Lt Steward DeBow, pictured on Palawan, Philippine Islands, 22 July 1945 (where the unit moved, on 5 May, from Morotai). The window in the lower part of the nose is a camera port, and the mission symbols are cameras. Note the RC-108 blind landing, and SCR-729 antenna system. While on Palawan, the F-7As carried out photo-recce flights over Singapore for the USN.** USAF

CHAPTER SEVEN

For King and Commonwealth

The B-24 Liberator in RAF and Dominion Service

On 17 January 1941 the first Liberator for the RAF made its maiden flight; however the first six to come off the production lines for the United Kingdom were diverted for use as transports. These unarmed aircraft were designated LB-30A (equivalent to Liberator I), and later examples LB-30 (equivalent to Liberator II). They were used on the newly created Trans-Atlantic Return Ferry Service route between Montreal, Newfoundland and Prestwick in Scotland, a distance of 3,000 miles (4,830km). Their mission was to fly ferry pilots to Canada who would then collect and fly home American-built aircraft for the RAF and also transport VIPs to their destinations. The first LB-30 arrived in the UK on 14 March 1941 and was used later, in July 1941, by the British Overseas Airways Corporation (BOAC). The most famous of the LB-30 transports used by the RAF was AL504, a Liberator Mk. II: in 1942 it had its armament removed and became the personal transport of Winston Churchill, the British Prime Minister, who flew in it to many of his wartime conferences. It was christened *Commando* and later modified, appearing with a large single fin and rudder. Mr Churchill never flew in the modified *Commando* which disappeared during a flight over the south Atlantic in May 1945.

In August 1941, deliveries to the RAF of the 139 aircraft on the original French contract began, and by December that year sixty-five had been delivered to Britain. The RAF was closely involved in the

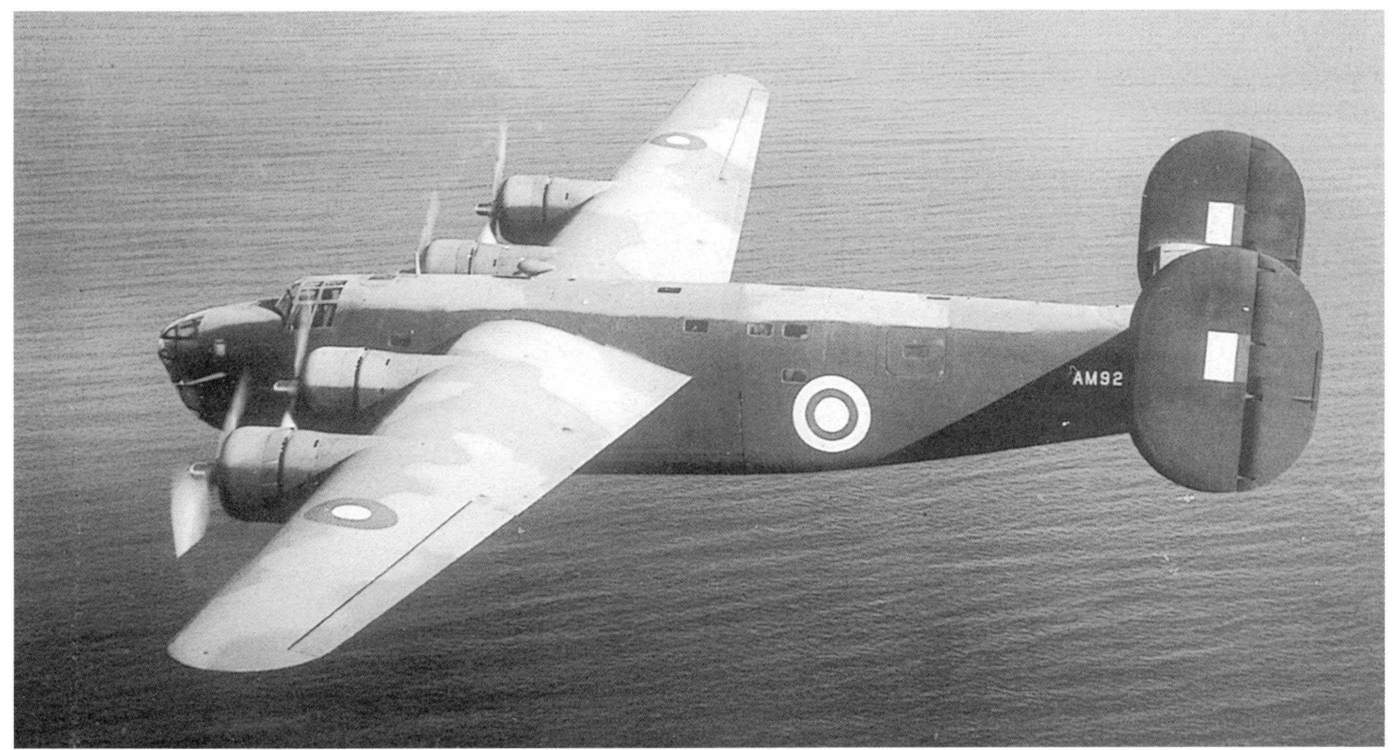

Accepted on 26 May 1941, LB-30B AM929, the last of twenty delivered to the RAF, in August 1941. After trials with the A & AEE, it was fitted with ASV and cannon by Scottish Aviation at Prestwick, and delivered to 120 Squadron at Ballykelly, Northern Ireland as H for Harry. **Sqn Ldr Terry M. Bulloch used AM929 to sink U-597 near Iceland on 12 October 1942, and on 5 November, damaged U-89. On 24 June 1943, this same plane, piloted now by Flt Lt A.W. Fraser DFC, sank U-194 near Iceland, and on 17 October 1943, flown by W/O Bryan W. Turnbull RNZAF, together with a 59 Squadron GR.V, it sank U-540 near Cape Farewell. In 1942 AM929 was withdrawn from Coastal Command service, converted to a transport and issued to 231 Squadron, 45 Group, Transport Command. It crashed in April 1945.** IWM

development of the Liberator, being able to pass on many recommendations learned the hard way in two years of war. Areas for improvement on American aircraft generally included armament, which was increased, and the fuel tanks, which were made non-inflammable. Armour plate was also added to the Liberator's vulnerable areas around the pilots' seats; this version was designated the XB-24, and twenty were supplied to the RAF as Liberator Is. This model was fitted with five manually operated .50 calibre machine guns in the nose, fuselage, tunnel and tail positions.

Into Service with Coastal Command

In September 1941, Liberator Is equipped with 'Stickleback' Air-to-Surface Vessel (ASV) radar aerials and a 20mm cannon pack under the fuselage, entered service with Coastal Command of the RAF. They were badly needed to help plug the 'Atlantic gap'. Prior to their introduction, German U-boats could operate off West Africa or in the central Atlantic, the latter being beyond the range of other Coastal Command aircraft. Liberator Is first entered service with No. 120 Squadron at Nutts Corner, Belfast, in September 1941. By January 1942 five of these had been converted into VLR aircraft whose range was 2,400 miles (3,860km). (The Sunderland had a range of only 1,300 miles/ 2,090km.) These were later supplemented by squadrons of Liberator IIIs, which were used for general maritime duties far out over the Atlantic. The Liberator V was equipped with additional fuel tanks in wing bays, and centimetric Air-to-Surface Vessel (ASV) radar either in a retractable radome in the ventral position aft of the bomb-bays, or in the 'Dumbo' or chin position.

Liberator I AM910, with early ASV 'Stickleback' radar antenna; it was accepted on 29 March 1941 and served as OH-M in 120 Squadron from 8 June 1941 to 13 April 1942, when it crashed. Note the twin .30in calibre machine guns in the waist position, a British innovation. RAF Museum

Meanwhile the shipping losses in October and November 1942 had showed a reduction over those of September, although the autumn gales and the redeployment of the U-boat packs to the Mediterranean were partly responsible. By May 1942 the U-boats were causing havoc to Allied shipping in Atlantic waters despite the addition in April that year, of a squadron of Whitleys and eight VLR Liberator Mk. Vs from RAF Bomber Command. Although 109 ships were sunk in May alone, there were important consolations. The majority of convoys plying between North America and Britain escaped virtually unscathed for a few months. In waters protected by Coastal Command, only nine merchant vessels were sunk in five months. In June 1942 there was a vast improvement in U-boat kills in the Bay of Biscay.

The U-boat Killers

Sqn Ldr Terence 'Hawkeyes' M. Bulloch, an Ulsterman from Lisburn, County Antrim, became the most highly decorated pilot in RAF Coastal Command, credited with sinking more U-boats than any other pilot. In August 1941, when he had joined 120 Squadron at Reykjavik, Iceland, from 206 Squadron, Terry Bulloch DFC had already flown the LB-30A/B since the spring of 1941, on the ferry service between Montreal and Britain. On 16 August 1942, in AM917 'F-Freddie', he seriously damaged U-89, a type VIIC submarine commanded by Kapitänleutnant Dietrich Lohmann. Two days later he attacked and damaged U-653, another type VIIC Submarine, commanded by Kapitänleutnant Gerhard Fieler. Depth-charges and cannon and machine-gun fire from the Liberator and a passing shot with two anti-submarine bombs failed to deliver the *coup de grâce*.

On 12 October, while flying close escort to Convoy ONS 136 in AM929 'H-Harry', one of Bulloch's crew sighted a U-boat 8 miles (13km) to starboard. Bulloch closed on the submarine, which was later identified as U-597, from out of the sun and lined up on its stern. He attacked along the length of the U-boat, dropping his depth-charges at 25ft (7.6m) spacing: one exploded next to the stern, two either side of the submarine's hull, and another next to its bow. With its pressure hull ruptured in several places, U-597 sank with all hands. Bulloch was awarded a bar to his DFC for this attack.

On 5 November, while operating with Convoy SC 107, Bulloch and his crew sighted a U-boat which dived before it could be attacked. They later found another U-boat, which Bulloch attacked with six depth-charges from bow to stern. The U-boat disappeared, but a few minutes later, air bubbles came to the surface. (Bulloch was credited with damaging U-89, a type VIIC submarine.) At 14:56 hours the crew found another U-boat, seen 25 miles (40km) from the convoy, and this time Bulloch attacked with two depth-charges shortly after it submerged, but with no apparent success. On 1 December, Bulloch was awarded the DSO.

On 8 December Bulloch was sent, in Liberator I AM921 to operate with Convoy HX 217, which had left Canadian waters and was being trailed by twenty-two U-boats in mid-Atlantic. On arriving

(Above) **The legendary Sqn Ldr Terry 'Hawkeyes' M. Bulloch, pictured by the side of GR.V BZ721/R (B-24D 42-40300) of 224 Squadron, which he was flying when he sank U-514 in the Bay of Biscay on 8 July 1943.** (Left) ***Crew photo:*** **Sgt R. McCall DFM, flight engineer; Flt Lt 'Brandy' Hennessay, UK; Terry Bulloch; Fg Off F.B. Lewis WOP/AG; A.G. Dyer, nose gunner; 'Ginger' Lord, 2nd pilot; Fg Off D.E.H. Durrant, observer; Flt Sgt D. Purcell WOP/AG. Note the 5in rocket rails fitted to the B-24's forward fuselage.** A.G. Dyer via Norman Franks

to lend his support, a U-boat was spotted travelling fast on the surface: it was attacked with depth-charges and disappeared from view. An hour later, two U-boats were sighted 300yd apart and and Bulloch attacked one of them with his remaining depth-charges. The other submarine submerged before he could attack it. With his depth-charges expended, Bulloch continued his patrol whilst his gunner cooked lunch of steak and potatoes on the galley stove. In Bulloch's own words:

> I was sitting in the cockpit with a plate on my knees, with 'George', the auto-pilot, in charge. I was going to enjoy that steak, but then other U-boats popped up and the plate with its steak and potatoes went spinning off my knee as I grabbed the controls and sounded the alarm. There was a clatter of plates back in the aircraft as the rest of the crew also jumped to it, forgetting how hungry they were.

Bulloch dived on the U-boat and strafed it with cannon and machine-gun fire before it dived to safety. He made another attack 23 minutes after 'lunchtime', and then another 35 minutes later, another 54 minutes after that, and a final attack after a further 24 minutes. On each occasion the U-boats were strafed with cannon fire and forced to dive to safety. In the space of five hours he made eight sightings and seven attacks. During all this, U-254 was sunk and the convoy sailed happily on with the loss of only one vessel before reaching England. Escorts sank another U-boat and other aircraft accounted for a third submarine.

Bulloch left 120 Squadron in December 1942. During his eighteen months on the squadron he had sighted no less than twenty-eight U-boats and had attacked sixteen of them. On 1 January he was awarded a bar to his DSO.

A Liberator attacks a U-boat on the surface. On 11 May 1943 the convoy SC130 sailed from Halifax, Nova Scotia, with thirty-eight ships. Four groups of U-boats were concentrated to attack them between 15–20 May, but no ships were lost – in sharp contrast to the situation in March 1943, when over half a million tons of allied shipping, mostly in convoy, had been sunk in the North Atlantic by U-boats. Almost continuous air cover during the time of the threat helped to achieve this excellent result. Thereafter there was a sudden cessation of U-boat activity, and SC130 was the last convoy to be seriously menaced. Norman Franks Collection

In July 1943 Bulloch joined 224 Squadron. On 8 July he and his crew, in BZ721 'R-Robert', took off on patrol at 08:53 hours. While on patrol off Cape Finisterre, Flt Lt Colin V.T. Campbell, and armament specialist, was looking at some Spanish fishing vessels through his binoculars when he spotted a U-boat right in among them. It was U-514, a type IXC/40 submarine, commanded by Kapitänleutnant Hans J. Affermann, which was on its fourth war cruise from Lorient bound for South Africa. Bulloch went into the attack and at 800ft (250m) loosed off two rockets, and a second salvo at 600ft (180m) and four more at 500ft (150m) from 500 yards. As the Liberator flew over, the front, rear and port-beam guns raked the U-boat along its length. However, the rockets had found their mark and had hit the U-boat below the waterline: the submarine plunged steeply beneath the waves, reappeared with its tail in the air, and finally went down at 13:20 hours. Bulloch was credited with sinking three U-boats and severely damaging two more. He finished the war flying C-87s, and later RY-3 aircraft, in RAF Transport Command.

The only man to sink two U-boats in a single sortie was Flt Lt Kenneth Owen 'Kayo' Moore, a Canadian pilot in 224 Squadron, on 8 June 1944. Moore and his crew had taken off in 'G-George' at 22:14 hours on 7 June, and at 02:11 hours on the 8th a radar contact was made dead ahead at 12 miles (19km). At 3 miles (5km) a U-boat was sighted on the surface in the moonlight. It was actually U-629, a type VIIC boat, commanded by Oberleutnant Hans-Helmuth Bugs and on its third war cruise, from Brest. Moore did not need to switch on his Leigh Light, and attacked from about fifty feet with six depth charges, which straddled the conning tower. U-629 disappeared leaving wreckage and oil on the sea. Later, another U-boat was sighted, actually U-373 commanded by Oberleutnant Detlef von Lehsten, which was on its twelfth war cruise, also out of Brest. Moore attacked with six depth-charges and sank the vessel. He took 'G-George' in again and turned on his Leigh Light to pick out three dinghies on the surface of the sea and a few survivors swimming in the oil and wreckage. Moore received an immediate DSO, while DFCs were awarded to W/O Johnston McDowell, one of the navigators, and W/O Peter Foster, the WOP/AG. Sgt John Hamer, the flight engineer, received a DFM.

Technological Advances

New depth-charges filled with Torpex – which was 30 per cent more effective than Amatol – had been introduced in 1942. The fitting of the Mk. XIIIQ pistol ensured detonation at 34ft (10m) below the surface, although this was deeper than the ideal of 25ft (7.6m). Other advances were made. For instance, very early in the war Coastal Command had realized that its anti-submarine aircraft would need something more reliable than the quickly consumed flares they were using at night to illuminate U-boats. As a result, in 1940 Sqn Ldr H. de B. Leigh was encouraged to develop the idea of an airborne searchlight. Leigh experimented with a 24inch (61cm) searchlight in the under-turret of a mine-detonating Wellington, and eventually, by substituting batteries for the generator, the Leigh Light won acceptance over the heavier Helmore Turbinlight developed originally for night fighting.

During July 1942 Coastal Command Wellingtons equipped with Leigh Lights chalked up their first U-boat kill; the following month the Air Ministry approved installations for Liberators. The Leigh Lights were carried under the wings of Liberators, mounted onto racks for easier installation than the Wellington's retractable belly-mounted light. A loaded Leigh Light Liberator GR.V, of which twenty-one were available to Coastal Command by December 1943, had a range of just under 2,000 miles (3,220km).

The Germans tried hard to counter Allied organization and ingenuity, and were particularly successful in radar countermeasures. The Germans had obtained an ASV Mk.II set from a crashed Hudson in Tunisia, and by mid-September 1942 they had developed the Metox 600, capable of receiving and recording ASV transmissions from up to 30 miles (48km), and had fitted it to large numbers of their U-boats. This enabled them to dive well before they were sighted by anti-submarine aircraft.

An attempt to flood the Bay of Biscay with ASV transmissions failed, and by January 1943 Coastal Command aircraft had almost ceased to locate U-boats by night. The answer was to replace the ASV Mk.II, which had only a 1.5m wavelength, with the long-overdue ASV Mk.III of 10cm wavelength. This apparatus was already in operation, having been tested successfully in May 1942. Within a few months USAAF Liberators on anti-submarine duties in the Western Hemisphere had been equipped with these, or similar sets; but by August 1942 it was evident that the first British models would not be available until spring 1943.

Liberator I AM923 of 120 Squadron in flight showing to good advantage the 'Stickleback' masts, underwing antenna and four cannon pack beneath the nose. Mk. Is could carry 2,500gal (11,365ltr) of petrol and were fit for an eighteen-hour patrol, or about 2,800 air miles (4,500km). via Mike Bailey Collection

(Above) **Liberator II AL547 transport, accepted September 1941, which served with 511 Squadron October 1942–June 1944, before being assigned to BOAC as G-AGKU in December 1944.** Scottish Aviation

Liberator II AL504, accepted August 1941, was built with the standard twin-finned empennage and served with 511 Squadron from October 1942–June 1944. Converted to a single-tailed aircraft with seats, berths and an electric flight kitchen, the renamed Commando **served in 231 Squadron, September 1944–January 1946 and was used by British Prime Minister Winston Churchill on several journeys to conferences overseas.** IWM

Accepted on 9 August 1941, Liberator II AL507 was fitted with SCR-517 radar and in March 1942 was allocated to 120 Squadron, and later to 224 Squadron as Z, where the 'Dumbo' was flown by Peter Cundy DSO, DFC. Cundy's crew, in FL963/J, sank U-628 on 3 July 1943. In May 1944, AL507 was allocated to BOAC as G-AHYC. P.J. Cundy Collection via Norman Franks

GR.Mk. IIIs (B-24Ds) of 120 Squadron at Aldergrove, Northern Ireland, April 1943. The nearest aircraft is FK228/M, followed by FL933/O. A Mk. IV 'Dumbo' version with ASV radar in the nose can be seen behind the latter aircraft. IMW

Closing the Atlantic Gap

Meanwhile, with U-boat packs prevented from finding any rich pickings in waters 500 miles (800km) from any Anglo-American air base, Adm Doenitz, the German U-boat chief, was forced to concentrate his forces in the 'Greenland Gap' where Allied air patrols could not penetrate. For the Allies, the only solution was to close the gaps using carrier-borne or VLR land-based aircraft. In August 1942 there were no aircraft carriers or auxiliary carriers available for trans-Atlantic convoys, while there were only five Liberator Is (from 120 Squadron) in the whole of Coastal Command (throughout the war, apart from a few PB4Y-1 squadrons in southern England, Fleet Adm Ernest King, USN, showed a tendency to keep powerful anti-submarine forces in areas close to the Americans' own Atlantic seaboard and in the approaches to the Mediterranean where they could protect their own convoys). The five Liberator Is

Colt Browning M-2 .50-calibre machine gun in the waist of a Coastal Command Liberator. IWM

had an operational range of 2,400 miles (3,860km), while the squadron's remaining Liberator Mk. IIs and IIIs could only extend 1,800 miles (2,890km) and 1,680 miles (2,700km) respectively. AVM John C. Slessor undertook a special mission to Washington to speed up the supply of Liberators.

Two Hudson squadrons, Nos. 59 and 224, began converting to the Liberator, but neither was operational until October 1942. In the meantime, 120 Squadron continued to bear the brunt of anti-submarine duties in the Atlantic. Steps were taken to help shorten the gap between American air patrols from Newfoundland and Nova Scotia and British air patrols from Iceland and Northern Ireland. In August 1942 Britain had asked the Royal Canadian Air Force if they could extend

GR.Mk. VI ZZ-K of 120 Squadron with a Leigh Light fitted below the starboard wing. The Leigh Light-fitted VIII Liberator carried an eight 250lb (113kg) bomb-load with 2,335gal (10,615ltr) of petrol, giving an endurance of thirteen hours at 138 knots (255km/h) true air-speed. The VLR Mk. Vs with the same bomb-load held 2,600gal (11,820ltr) and had an endurance of sixteen hours at 140 knots (260km/h). The LR Sunderland V carrying half the bomb-load would fly for fifteen hours at 110 knots (204km/h). IWM

their anti-submarine and convoy protection sorties to 800 miles (1,290km) to help close part of the Atlantic gap, but this was not possible as the first Canadian Liberators did not arrive until April 1943.

In September 1942, 120 Squadron provided a detachment of Liberators in Iceland. The strategic value of this remote island in the North Atlantic had been recognized as far back as 1940 when British forces forestalled a German invasion and landed at Reykjavik. Liberators from 120 Squadron operated from an airfield on the south-east edge of the capital. In October 1942, 86 Squadron began receiving

U-Boats Sunk by RAF/RCAF Liberators

Sqn	*Mk.*	*Liberator*	*Date*	*U-boat*	*Details*
120	I	AM929/H	12 Oct 42	U-597	nr Iceland. Sqn Ldr Bulloch
224	III	FL910/H	20 Oct 42	U-216	nr Ireland
224	III	FK225/G	24 Oct 42	U-599	nr Azores
120	I	AM921	8 Dec 42	U-254	
120	III	FK223/T	14 Jan 43	U-954	
120	III	FK232/S	15 Feb 43	U-225	
120	III	FK223/T	21 Feb 43	U-623	
120		FK223/N	5 Apr 43	U-635	
86	III	FL930/R	6 Apr 43	U-632	
120	III	FL923/V	23 Apr 43	U-189	nr Iceland
86	III	FL955/P	4 May 43	U-109	nr Ireland
86	III	FK229/B	14 May 43	U-266	nr Ireland
120	I	AM919/P	20 May 43	U-258	
120	I	AM919/E	28 May 43	U-304	
120	I	AM929/H	24 Jun 43	U-194	nr Iceland
224	III	FL963/J	3 Jul 43	U-628	nr Iceland
53	GR. V	BZ751/G	5 Jul 43	U-535	Bay of Biscay
224	GR. V	BZ721/R	8 Jul 43	U-514	Bay of Biscay. Sqn Ldr Bulloch
224	GR. V	BZ721/W	28 July 43	U-404	Bay of Biscay. (With a fourth anti-sub sqn USAF B-24)
200	GR. V	BZ832/D	11 Aug 43	U-468	Bathurst nr Dakar. Fg Off L. A. Trigg VC
200	GR. V		17 Aug 43	U-403	
10 RCAF		BZ586/A	19 Sep 43	U-341	Flt Lt R. F. Fisher
120	I	AM917/F	20 Sep 43	U-338	nr Iceland
120	III	FK236/X	4 Oct 43	U-279 or U-336	nr Iceland
86	GR. V	FL954/Z	8 Oct 43	U-643	nr Iceland
120	III	FK223/T	"	"	" "
86	III	FL930/R	8 Oct 43	U-419	nr Iceland
120	III	FK223/E	16 Oct 43	U-470	nr Iceland
"	"	FK223/Z	" " "	"	" "
59	GR. V	FL973/C	" " "	"	" "
59	GR. V	FL984/S	" " "	U-844	" "
86	III	FK241/Y	" " "	U-964	" "
59	GR. V	BZ712/D	17 Oct 43	U-540	nr Cape Farewell
120	I	AM929	17 Oct 43	U-540	nr Cape Farewell
224		AM929/Z	23 Oct 43	U-274	
10 RCAF		'6A' 58	26 Oct 43	U-420	Flt Lt R. M. Aldwinkle RCAF
86	III	FL931/M	16 Nov 43	U-280	
53	GR. V	BZ814/B	13 Dec 43	U-391	
59	GR. V	FL984/S	25 May 44	U-990	
59	GR. V	FL984/S	27 May 44	U-292	
224		FL984/G	8 Jun 44	U-629	Flt Lt K. O. Moore RCAF
		" "	" " "	U-373	
120		FL984/F	9 Jun 44	U-740	
206	VI	EV943/K	10 Jun 44	U-821	with Mosquitoes of 248 Sqn
224		EV943/L	29 Jun 44	U-988	
86	III	FL916/N	26 Jun 44	U-317	
311		FL916/O	26 Jun 44	U-971	
86	III	FL924/E	30 Jun 44	U-478	
224	GR. V	BZ721/R	8 Jul 44	U-514	Sqn Ldr T. M. Bulloch DSO DFC*
86	VI	EV947/E	15 Jul 44	U-319	
86	III	FK223/U	17 Jul 44	U-361	
53	VI	EV877/C	9 Aug 44	U-608	
53	VI	EW302/G	14 Aug 44	U-618	
86	III	FK223/Z	8 Oct 44	U-643	
311 Czech		FK223/Y & H	4 Nov 44	U-1060	with two Halifaxes of 502 Sqn
86	VIII	KH340/B	20 Mar 45	U-boat	possibly sunk
120	VIII	KH340/M	22 Mar 45	U-296	
224		KH340/O	29 Mar 45	U-1106	
86	VIII	KH224/V	23 Apr 45	U396	
120	VIII	KH224/Q	29 Apr 45	U-1017	
311 Czech		KH224/L	5 May 45	U-3523	Kattegat
224	VIII	KK250/T	5 May 45	U-3503	
224	VIII	KK250/T	5 May 45	U-579	
547	VI	KK250/K	5 May 45	U-1168	
86	VIII	KH347/G	5 May 45	U-534	Kattegat
224	VIII	KG959/S	5 May 45	U-2365	Kattegat
86	VIII	KH347/G	6 May 45	U-2534	Kattegat
86	VIII	KH290/K	6 May 45	U-1008	

GR.Mk. VI KG907 with radome extended. This aircraft later served with 1674 HCU. via Mike Bailey

Liberators; it acted as a training unit for 160 Squadron until February 1943 when it received its own Liberators, and in March began moving to Northern Ireland to fly anti-submarine patrols.

160 Squadron had already begun converting from Hudsons in August 1942 at Thorney Island, with Liberator IIIs from 59 Squadron. Late in March 1943, 59 Squadron returned to Thorney Island to re-equip with VLR Liberator Mk. Vs, stripped of much of their armour and armament but able to lift 2,000 gallons (9,093ltr) of fuel and still carry eight 250lb (113kg) depth-charges. Long-range tanks were fitted in the forward bomb-bays, and such was the Mk. V's range that later, on operations, one landed at Goose Bay, Labrador after an eighteen-hour patrol from Iceland.

In May 1943, 53 Squadron replaced its ageing Whitleys with Liberators, and for the following sixteen months flew patrols from Northern Ireland over the Channel and the Bay of Biscay before moving to Iceland in September 1944. During May 1943 they were joined in Northern Ireland at Aldergrove by 59 Squadron. Their Liberators carried the then top secret Mk. 24 American acoustic torpedo which revolutionized the task of killing U-boats. The Mk. 24 was popularly known as 'Fido' or 'Wandering Annie', although it was a criminal offence even to discuss it. It entered service in May 1943 and was found to be a most effective weapon against U-boats which had just dived. An 86 Squadron Liberator sank a U-boat with the device on 14 May 1943. By July 1943 the number of Liberator Squadrons in Coastal Command had risen to six.

Liberator Victoria Cross

On 11 August 1943, Liberator BZ832 *D-Dog* of 200 Squadron based at Bathurst (now Banjuil) in Gambia, was on anti-submarine patrol off the coast of West Africa. Its pilot, Fg Off Lloyd Allan Trigg of the Royal New Zealand Air Force, sighted U-468 about 240 miles (390km) south-west of Dakar. The submarine, commanded by Oberleutnant zur See Clemens Schamong, was returning to La Pallice after a war cruise in the Atlantic. Trigg immediately went into the attack. The U-boat was on the surface and prepared to defend herself with anti-aircraft guns: shells from two of her 20mm cannons hit the Liberator in the centre section, and the plane was on fire in several places when it arrived in a position to attack. Trigg could have broken off, but as he flew over the vessel at just 50ft (15m), he ordered a stick of six depth-charges to be released. Two exploded just 6ft (1.8m) from the U-boat's hull, and within twenty minutes U-468 was sinking beneath the waves. However, the stricken *D-Dog* perished with her, a victim of the submarine's anti-aircraft fire, and Trigg and his gallant crew died. About twenty German sailors managed to climb to safety, but several of them were killed by sharks and barracuda and soon only Schamong, his 1st Lieutenant and five others were left. They all clambered into one of the Liberator's dinghies which had floated clear after being released by the impact of the plane hitting the sea, and were picked up the following day by a Sunderland of 204 Squadron. Later, their evidence and outspoken admiration for the gallant attack was taken into account and Trigg was posthumously awarded the Victoria Cross, Britain's highest military decoration, on 2 November 1943.

Fg Off L.A. Trigg VC

New Methods in Coastal Command

In October 1943, Liberators of 59 and 547 Squadrons were fitted with rocket projectiles to carry out attacks on U-boats which stayed on the surface to fight it out. Some were fitted with sono-buoys and were modified to carry ninety anti-tank bombs converted for use against U-boats. Such was the hitting power of the Liberator that it soon became a feared and respected adversary of the U-boat crews.

Altogether, the Liberator equipped twelve squadrons of Coastal Command and did a magnificent job in protecting the vast waters of the Atlantic; had more been available during the early part of the war, the U-boat menace might have been better contained. Success might also have been greater had the Allies shown greater cooperation. Nevertheless, the Liberators' successes were many. In March 1944, the first nose-turreted GR Mk.VIs were received, and some operated as strike aircraft off Denmark in the closing stages of the war. In March 1945, Coastal Command Liberators from five squadrons succeeded in sinking seven U-boats in six days, and in that same month, the decision was taken to replace completely the Wellington in Coastal Command with the Liberator. However, the end of the war saw almost all Liberators being rapidly transferred to Transport Command for trooping duties, although the last Liberators to serve with the RAF were the GR VIIIs of Coastal Command, which were not replaced by Lancasters until 1947.

RAF Liberators Overseas

The training of RAF Liberator crews posed something of a problem because an environment free of interruption from enemy aircraft was needed; in the end, the island of New Providence in the Bahamas was chosen. III Operational Training Unit (OTU) turned out hundreds of RAF and Commonwealth Liberator crews who went on the Canada and their ultimate destinations in Europe or Air Command SE Asia.

The Liberator saw widespread service with the RAF and Commonwealth Air Forces overseas. As early as December 1941, 108 Squadron, then based in Egypt and equipped with Wellington bombers, received four Liberator Mk. IIs which had originally been intended for France. These unarmed Liberators remained in Egypt until it was decided that 108 Squadron should use them to convert fully from Wellingtons to Liberators. However, after they had been fitted with Boulton Paul turrets and cannon, the plan to convert the whole squadron was abandoned and only two were ever used for bombing operations. Some which had been used for conversion training were modified for supply-dropping duties.

The Mediterranean theatre is best known for the exploits of the American 15th Air Force which flew daylight bombing missions from Italy. Less publicized are the achievements of the Liberators of 205 Group RAF which flew both daylight and night missions. The group started as 257 Wing in the Egyptian Canal Zone, equipped with long-range bombers, mostly Wellingtons. In September 1941 it was re-designated 205 Group, and attempts were made to reinforce the Wellington squadrons with other aircraft. There were no suitable heavy night bombers that could be spared for 205 Group, so it was decided to equip them with the Liberator, despite the fact that the B-24 had many operational disadvantages for night work, the principal one being the bright flames and white-hot turbosupercharger exhausts which made the aircraft a beacon in the sky for night fighters. However, since night fighter activity was not as intense over Italy and Southern Europe as it was in the north-west, it was considered that losses from night fighters would not be high.

A further disadvantage was the .50-calibre machine guns: these had a much better range than the .303in guns, but as the gunner could not see far enough in the dark to avail himself of this, the only advantage

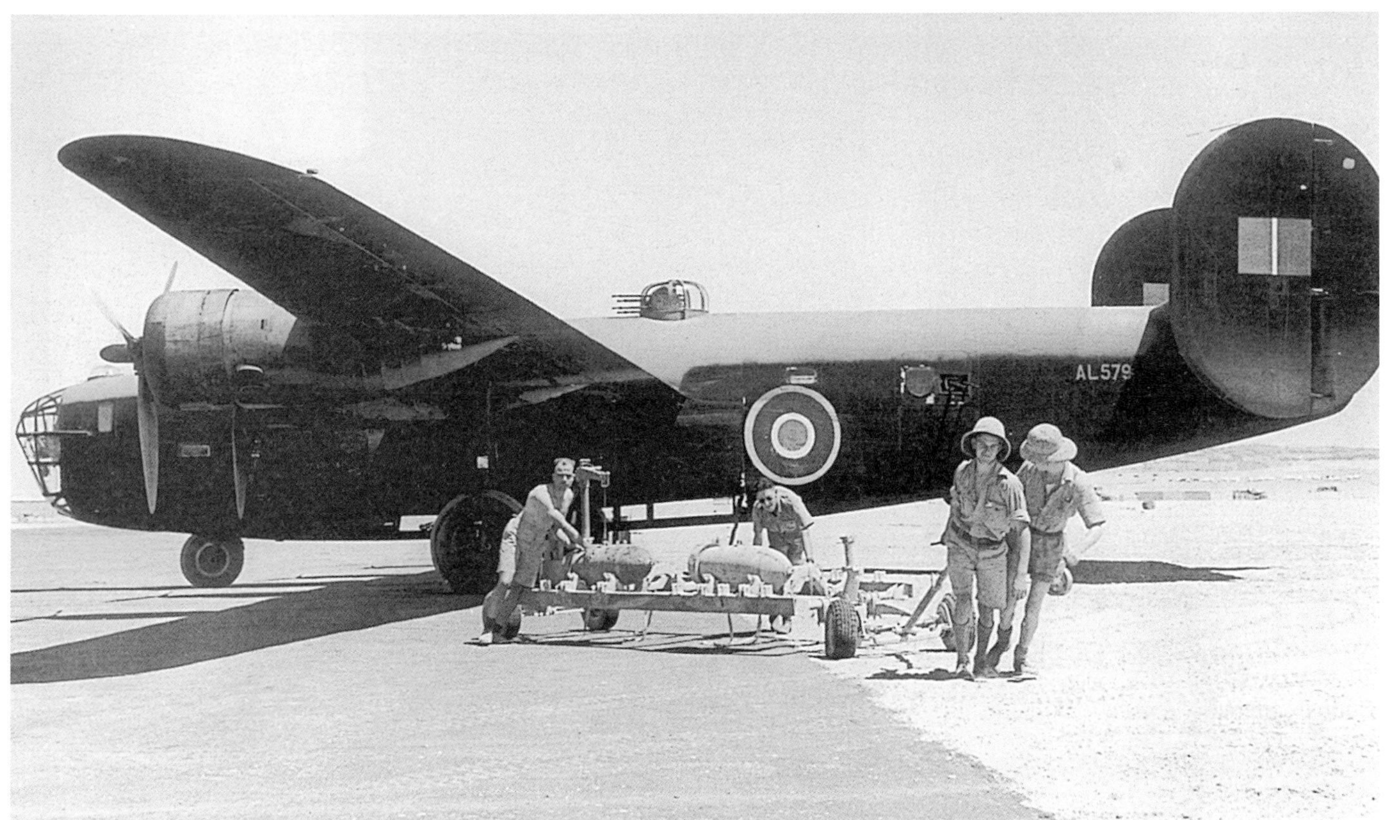

Liberator II AL579 of 159 Squadron pictured in July 1942. This aircraft, which was accepted in October 1941, served in Egypt with 159 Squadron, February 1942–June 1943, and in 160 Squadron September–October 1942. IWM

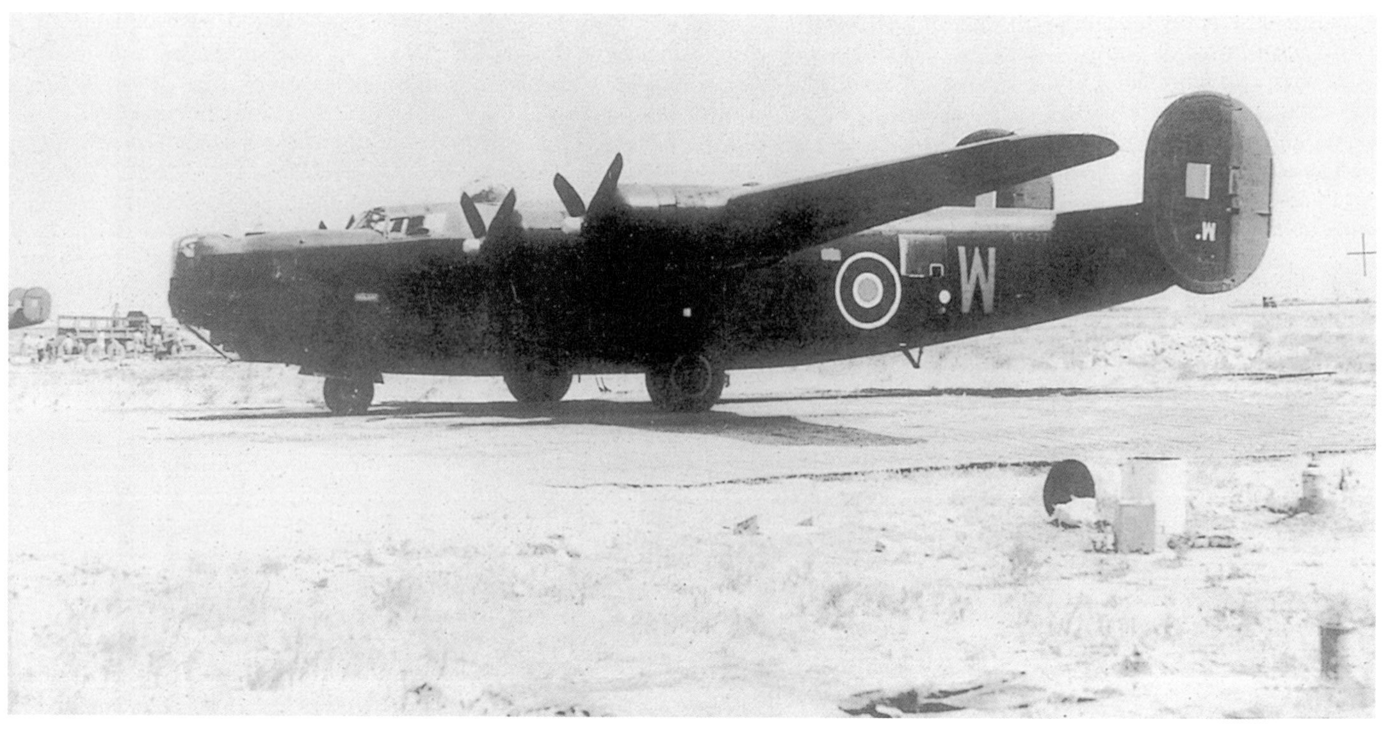

W for William **of 70 Squadron, 231 Wing, 205 Group at Foggia, Italy.** Arthur Anderson Collection

B.Mk. VI of 614 Squadron taxies in at an airstrip in Italy. F.A. Hunt

was their superior hitting power. However, it was found that as soon as the gunner fired, the flash from the guns ruined his night vision so he had little chance of aiming on a second attack. The front gun turret was also useless, as was the under gun turret, as the light from the turbosuperchargers made it impossible to see fighters at night. So the Royal Air Force removed the under gun turret and the guns from the front turret, which was then faired over with fabric. The beam guns were also taken out because it was discovered that fighter attacks always came from behind.

However, conversion to the Liberator was slow. On 15 January 1943, 178 Squadron was formed at Shandur in the Suez Canal Zone from a detachment of 160 Squadron, and began receiving Liberator Mk. IIIs. The following night three Liberators took off and bombed targets in Tripoli. It was not a full-scale beginning, and 178 remained the only full Liberator squadron in 205 Group until October 1944, although on 14 March 1943 a 'Special Liberator Flight' was formed at Gambut, Lybia. It was later re-designated 148 Squadron and began special duties, dropping arms and supplies to Resistance groups in Albania, Greece and Yugoslavia.

On Sunday 4 July 1943, a Liberator Mk. II (AL523) became involved in one of the great controversies of the war when it crashed into the sea on take-off from Gibraltar. Only the pilot, Flt Lt Edward Prchal of the Czechoslovakian Air Force, survived the crash, which killed eleven people including General Wladyslaw Sikorski, the Polish Prime Minister. Allegations of sabotage were made, but the subsequent Court of Enquiry revealed that the aircraft had been under constant guard during its stay in Gibraltar. The German propaganda machine announced that the crash was an assassination attempt to remove a man (Sikorski) who had policies which could prove troublesome to the British and Russian governments. The controversy has lasted to the present day.

In January 1944, 148 Squadron moved to Italy, and when not engaged in special operations, its Wellingtons and Liberators joined other squadrons in heavy bombing raids on northern Italy and southern Europe. Besides bombing and supply-dropping operations, 205 Group laid mines in the River Danube to prevent German river traffic linking the Fatherland with the grainlands of Hungary and the oilfields of Rumania.

In the Middle East, the Liberator Mk. VI was used mainly against enemy shipping in the Mediterranean. Beginning in July 1944, thirty-six Mk. VIIIs were delivered to the RAF in that theatre, each equipped with centimetric radar designed for Pathfinder (PFF) operations against ground targets.

Liberator Mk. VI of the SAAF, pictured in Italy in 1944. Dave Becker Collection

'Warsaw Concerto'

In August 1944, the Liberators of 178 Squadron and of 31 and 34 Squadrons of 2 (South African Air Force) Wing in Italy took part in the 'Warsaw Concerto' supply-dropping missions to the beleaguered Polish Army in Warsaw. The courageous

Poles under General Bor had received Russian encouragement to rise against the German occupation forces, but the Red Army halted its advance a short distance from the capital. Appeals for help were ignored by the Russians, so on 3 August the Polish government-in-exile in London sought help from the British government by airlifting in supplies. Britain would have sent aircraft from bases in England if, after dropping supplies in Warsaw, they could have continued on to Russian territory to refuel. However, the Russians delayed in agreeing to the plan, and the only alternative was to use Liberators of the 205 Group in Italy, which would involve a round trip to Poland and back of some eleven hours.

The first aircraft to make the 1,750-mile (2,816km) round trip were seven Liberators of 1586 (Polish) Special Duties Flight, which made successful supply-dropping missions on 8 and 9 August. All returned safely. However, as the situation deteriorated, more aircraft were needed if the partisans were to survive and so on the night of 12 August, eleven aircraft from the Polish Flight and No. 148 Squadron flew to Warsaw. Three aircraft failed to drop their supplies, but the remaining eight were successful; again all returned safely.

On 13/14 August, the first full-scale operation with Liberators of 31 and 34 SAAF Squadrons and 178 Squadron took place. Altogether, twenty-eight Liberators flew from Foggia to Warsaw with canisters of supplies. One of them was *K-King* of 31 Squadron. The outward flight was uneventful to within 60 miles (97km) of the drop zone, at which point the first of many difficulties was encountered. The hydraulics to the rear turret failed, and constant manual operation had to be employed in the gunner's search tactics, because German night fighters were shadowing the Liberators. The previous flights to the Polish capital had alerted the Nachtjagd, and crews could also expect increased flak and searchlight defences over Warsaw.

At 00:45 hours the Vistula was pinpointed just south of Warsaw: the river flowed to the capital, and there was slight flak opposition on the starboard side. The activity of the ground defences increased on approaching the city area, and at 00:49 hours *K-King* was bracketed by very accurate and intense flak. Immediately, the captain of the aircraft ordered the supplies to be jettisoned, although they were still one mile short of their briefed drop zone. Searchlights coned the Liberator, and AA guns knocked out the port outer engine. Another battery of about a dozen searchlights picked up *K-King* at a height of 4,000ft (1,220m), and AA guns subjected the B-24 to intense fire. The aircraft started a power dive to starboard – and then without warning, the captain put on his parachute, opened the bomb-bay doors, and baled out!

2nd Lt Burgess, the second pilot, took over and finally regained control at 1,000ft (300m). He and the navigator, Lt Sleed, decided to fly on to Soviet territory. Burgess managed to get the ailing B-24 up to 4,000ft, (1,220m) and then gave the crew the choice of either baling out or remaining in the Liberator; they all chose the latter. During the flight eastwards, Sleed coolly walked along the oily catwalk to the rear of the B-24 and transferred fuel from the auxiliary to the main tanks. They flew on for three hours, finally reaching 8,000ft (2,450m), before tumbling to 5,000ft (1,525m) at 270mph (430km/h) before Burgess regained control again. He successfully landed *K-King* at 05:35 hours at Emilchino, about 100 miles (160km) west of Kiev. The crew were subsequently handed over to the British Mission. Burgess was awarded an immediate DSO, and Sleed an immediate DFC. Fourteen Liberators dropped successfully that night, but eleven failed to find their drop zones, while two failed to return.

The following night, 14/15 August, twenty-six Liberators were dispatched, but only twelve succeeded in dropping in the right areas, and eight failed to return. One of these was *A-Able* of 31 Squadron, which was hit repeatedly by flak at 00:50 hours while flying at 1,500ft (460m) 3 miles (5km) south of Warsaw. Three engines were set on fire and would not extinguish. At 600ft (180m) the captain had no option but to jettison the supplies, but he managed to re-start the No.3 engine and climb to 1,000ft (300m) on a south-easterly heading. The Liberator's starboard wing was breaking up, however, and he gave the order to abandon the aircraft. One by one the crew evacuated the doomed B-24. Three men were killed, including one who pulled the rip-cord too late; the other two must have been too seriously wounded to survive the jump, or were hit by flak on the way down. *A-Able* crashed and burned out after hitting the ground near a village of Alexandrov, 15 miles (24km) south-east of Warsaw.

The drops went on every night from 12 to 27 August, and when most of Warsaw was in flames they continued in woods outside the capital. Warsaw was ablaze, and pilots had no difficulty picking out the city from 100 miles (160km) away. As the Liberators dropped their supplies they were easy targets, illuminated by the flames and multiple searchlights. Flak guns and machine gunners on roofs picked off many of the four-engined bombers. Some dropped to as low as 100ft (30m), literally following the streets to the City Hall, which was one of the dropping zones, or in search of signals which indicated an area in urgent need of supplies. Not surprisingly the casualty rate was high – something over 15 per cent, or three times higher than Bomber Command was normally prepared to accept. The AOC No. 205 Group, Brig J.T. Durrant, SAAF, drew the attention of the Air Commander-in-Chief to these losses, but the operation continued unabated.

Only a trickle of supplies actually reached Gen Bor's army, and despite the capture by the Red Army of the suburb of Praga on 15 September, the rising was doomed to failure. The last attempt to supply the partisans was made from Italy on

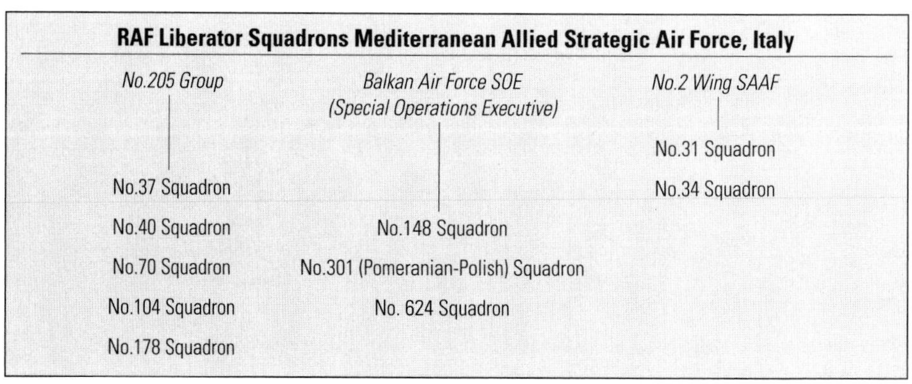

the night of 21/22 September, when twelve Liberators were dispatched. Only five B-24s succeeded in dropping their supplies, but all returned safely to Italy. Before any further sortie could be flown the Wehrmacht had crushed the uprising, and by the time the Soviet Army relieved Warsaw, all partisan resistance had ended.

Altogether, 186 Liberators were dispatched to Warsaw in twenty-two nights of operations, 8 August–21 September. Of these, ninety-two succeeded in dropping their supplies in the target areas, sixty-three were unable to find their targets, and thirty-one did not return. The South Africans of 31 Squadron lost eight Liberators in four nights. In six weeks 31 and 34 Squadrons lost twenty-four of their thirty-three aircraft. No.1586 (Polish) Flight suffered almost 100 per cent casualties. Four of its nine Liberators failed to return on two nights, and there were further losses; but then bad weather prevented any further missions.

North African Operations

Altogether, the Liberator equipped thirteen squadrons of the RAF in Italy and the Middle East: two of these were Nos.159 and 160. The former had flown from England in June 1942 bound for India, but once it reached the Middle East it was used for long-range bombing raids from Palestine and Egypt. These raids continued until September 1942. Meanwhile, 160 Squadron had flown to Northern Ireland in May 1942 for a short period of anti-submarine patrols with Coastal Command before flying on to the Middle East in June. Its passage to India was halted when five Liberators provided air cover for convoys desperately needed for the relief of Malta. This was followed by bombing raids on Tobruk and other targets in the Mediterranean area. On 15 January 1943, 160 Squadron was reorganized in Ceylon as Liberator general reconnaissance unit. For the rest of the war it operated under the auspices of Headquarters No.222 Group, and later Area Headquarters Ceylon. In addition to patrols and shipping escort duties, 160 Squadron flew long-range photographic reconnaissance missions over Sumatra and the Nicobar Islands.

Far East Service

During the first two weeks of October 1942, the first 159 Squadron Liberator IIs flew to India, touching down at Salbani. Operations over the first few months were all made at night and rarely extended to more than five aircraft, and sometimes took only two. RAF Liberators sought targets at Akyab Island, Maungdaw, Buthidaung, Schwebo and the Mandalay and Rangoon areas; later operations extended as far as Bangkok, involving air time of twelve or more hours. Losses generally were not high when compared to Europe: this was because the Japanese normally held their aircraft back from the forward airfields in Burma unless they were mounting a specific offensive. Also, a high proportion of the Liberator's flying time on operations was spent over the waters of the Bay of Bengal and thus were safe from groundfire. On the other hand, the chances of getting home or surviving from a crashed aircraft were slim as far as operations over Burma were concerned.

Crews numbered about seven men for night operations, including a first and second pilot. Later, flight engineers were posted to the squadrons, supposedly in place of the second pilot. However, both the second pilot and flight engineer were carried in the Liberators, and this proved very unpopular with the crews, especially in view of the long distances flown.

Wg Cdr J. Blackburn, the commanding officer of 159 Squadron at Digri in Bengal from July to December 1944, was responsible for greatly increasing the Liberator's range and bomb load. Blackburn was a very experienced Liberator pilot from the Middle East, and his arrival coincided with the re-equipping of the squadron with Mk. VI aircraft in place of the earlier marks. One of the disappointments had been that the

B.Mk. VI BZ825/L pictured at Chakeri, Cawnpore, India, in May 1947. This aircraft had served in 160 Squadron, June 1943–October 1945. Tilley Collection

Liberator II AL581, accepted in November 1941, was first issued to 1653 Conversion Unit at Polebrook, and later served with 159 Squadron in India, before going MIA, 22 February 1943. IWM

B-24 Liberators of 99 (Madras Presidency) Squadron pictured in India. IWM

(Above) **Liberator II AL578 was accepted in October 1941 and assigned to 231 Squadron, 45 Group RAF, as a transport where it took the name** Marco Polo. **Among the VIPs carried was Admiral of the Fleet, Earl Mountbatten of Burma, who was flown over the 'Hump' from Chabua, India, to Kunming, China, in August 1943.** IWM

B.Mk. VI KH354/F of 356 Squadron. 356 had been formed at Salbani, India, on 15 January 1944 and flew its first bombing operation of the war on 27 July 1944, when seven B-24s attacked Yeu. RAF Museum

configuration of the B-24 was such that only moderate bomb-loads could be carried over the vast distances flown. A mission to Bangkok, for instance, meant that only 4,000lb (1,800kg) of bombs could be carried; and on operations involving distances of between 1,000 and 1,100 miles (1,609 and 1770km), the maximum bomb-load was considered to be only 3,000lb (1,360kg).

Blackburn ordered the removal of the mid-position gun turrets, all armour plating and the heat exchangers in the turbo-blower system, and restricted ammunition for the remaining machine guns. Trials were carried out with the object of increasing all-up weight, until finally the Liberators were operating at 65,000lb (29,480kg) and bomb-loads were doubled, to 8,000lb (3,630kg) to Bangkok, and up to 12,000lb (5,440kg) for a trip to Rangoon. These amazing improvements staggered American Liberator squadrons in the Far East: they could not understand how their British compatriots could take off with such heavy loads of fuel and bombs. Other units

RAF Liberator Squadrons Air Command South-east Asia 1 July 1944

No. 222 Group	
No. 160 Squadron	Liberator B.Mk. VI
No. 225 Group	
No. 200 Squadron	Liberator
No. 354 Squadron	Liberator
No. 231 Group	
No. 175 Wing	
No. 99 Squadron	Wellington (converting to Liberator)
No. 184 Wing	
No. 355 Squadron	Liberator
No. 356 Squadron	Liberator
No. 185 Wing	
No. 159 Squadron	Liberator
No. 357 (Special Duties) Squadron	Hudson/Liberator

throughout South-east Asia soon followed suit, and eventually, round trips to targets as distant as the Kra Isthmus (2,300 miles/3,700km) and the Malay Peninsula (2,800 miles/4,500km) were made carrying vastly increased bomb loads. It was calculated that with a 3,000yd (2,740m) runway, a Liberator could, even with a full fuel load (including the bomb-bay overload tank) operate at an all-up weight of 68,000lb (30,845kg) – all that was needed was that crucial 3,000yd runway. One was duly found at an American airfield nearby, and in October 1944, sixteen Liberators of 159 Squadron, each carrying four 1,100lb (500kg) US mines, and led by Blackburn, made a round trip of 3,000 miles (4,830km) to attack the Japanese fleet in the approaches to Penang Harbour. The operation took twenty hours and was completely successful; and not one Liberator was lost!

The contribution made by the Liberators of Air Command, South-east Asia, was immense. From January 1944 until the final campaign in Burma, ending with the fall of Rangoon, the Liberator Mk. VI was the principal type of heavy bomber used by the RAF. Liberator Mks. VI and VIII operated with 184 (Salbani) Wing of the North Burma Air Task Force and with 175 Wing of 231 Group. Altogether, fourteen squadrons of Liberators served with the RAF in the Far East on such diverse missions as bombing operations, supply drops, anti-submarine patrols (from Ceylon) and transport duties.

Nicolson VC

In May 1945 the crash of an RAF Liberator into the sea off Bengal would not normally have attracted too much attention in England: this one, however, contained the body of Wing Commander James Nicolson. He had become famous as the only Battle of Britain VC, for his actions on 17 August 1940 when he was piloting a Hawker Hurricane of 249 Squadron. During a combat with a Messerschmitt 110 his Hurricane was hit by four cannon shells: one pierced his cockpit, injuring one of his eyes; another hit his foot; and the remaining two damaged the engine and set fire to the gravity tank. Petrol spewed out and seeped into the cockpit, and flames started to spread. However, just as Nicolson was about to struggle out of the cockpit, he saw another Bf 110. He slid back into the cockpit, up to his waist in flames, and fired at the enemy aircraft, destroying it. Somehow he managed to bale out of the blazing Hurricane; he survived his terrible burns, and returned to active service.

Still in his mid-twenties, in 1942 he was posted as Station Commander to Alipore, Calcutta; since then he was in charge of 27 (Fighter) Squadron. Subsequently in command of training at HQ, South-east Asia Air Force, he spent some time with the Liberators of 355 Squadron, studying the results of aircrew training operationally. On 1 May 1945, Nicolson boarded one of eight Liberators (KH210 *R-Robert*) involved in a night raid on Rangoon. For two hours the flight proceeded normally, until shortly before 02:45. Then the starboard outer engine caught fire, and almost immediately the starboard inner engine also began malfunctioning. Sqn Ldr G.A. de Souza, the pilot, ordered the crew to ditching stations after they had tossed out all excess equipment and the bomb-load had been jettisoned. The B-24 hit the surface of the sea and broke up. Nicolson was never found.

Early B.Mk. VIs of 215 Squadron – Ice Cold Katie, **centre, with Boulton Paul tail turret, and braced pitot tubes – being bombed up at an airfield in India. On New Year's Day 1945 a 215 Squadron Liberator piloted by Squadron Leader C.V. Beadon flew 1,000 miles (1,609km) back to base after being seriously damaged by flak and set on fire during a daylight raid on the Siam-Burma railway. The feat earned a command mention.** IWM

B.Mk. VIII KP136/P, which served in 355 Squadron from August 1945 to May 1946, pictured over the Indian Ocean. The word 'snake', introduced on 1 May 1943, indicated to units, especially in the Mediterranean, that delivery must not be diverted to other squadrons while *en route* **to India.** via Mike Bailey

ELINT and Radio-Countermeasures (RCM)

In World War II it was bombing missions which usually captured the headlines, but in fact radio counter-measures (RCM) and ELINT (Electronic Intelligence) operations in Europe and the Far East could often prove just as crucial. These innovations were used in most theatres except the Mediterranean, where the US 15th Air Force was well equipped with RCM before the end of hostilities. In the Far East it was felt that there was no need to fit RCM equipment to RAF bombers as the Japanese were equipped with only primitive radar equipment. However, a special flight was formed to monitor enemy R/T and W/T transmissions and to plot Japanese radar stations. A special ELINT flight was formed under the auspices of 159 Squadron, and this began operation in September 1944. ELINT operations were carried out until early January 1945, when the Special Flight began dropping leaflets.

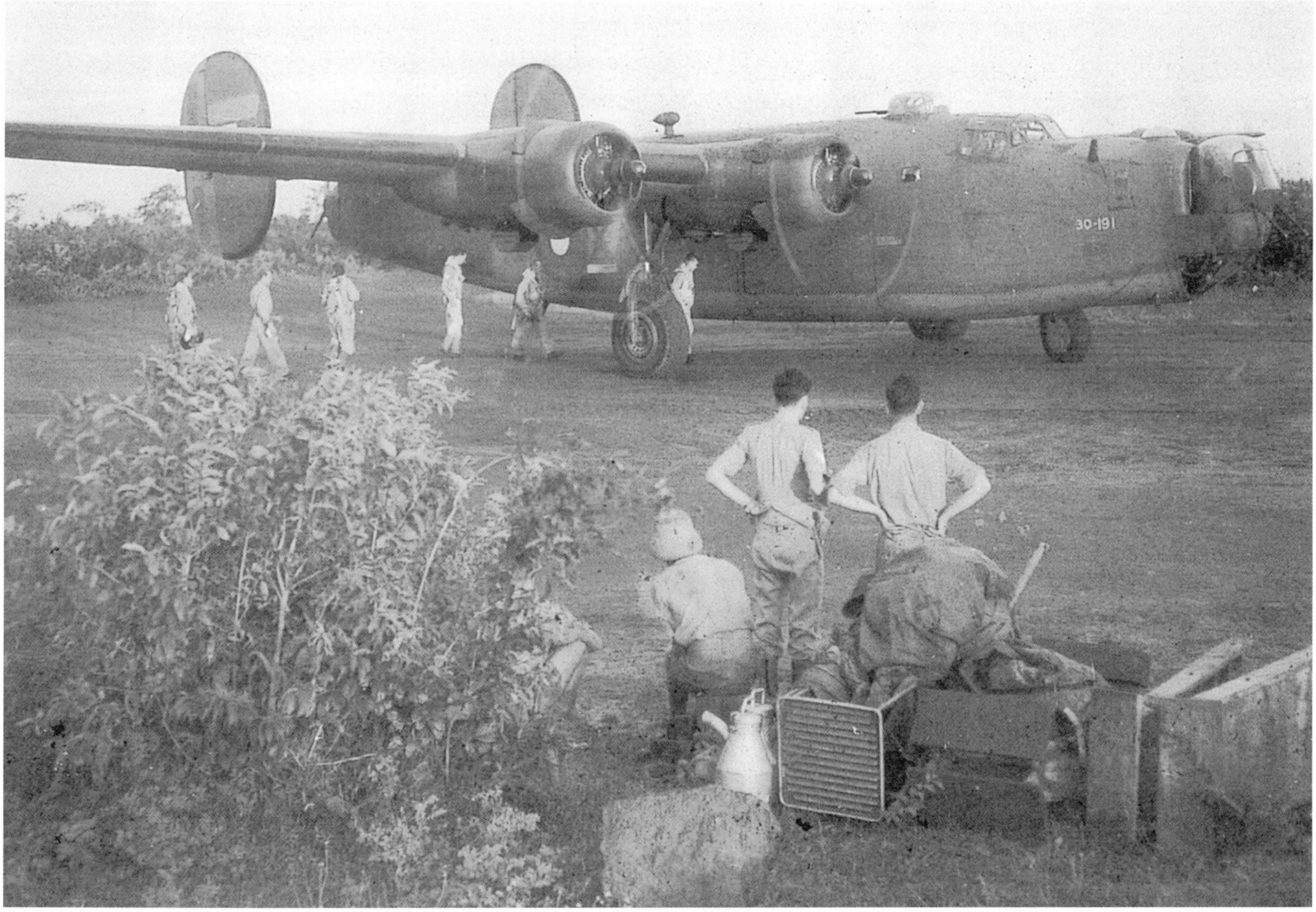

An ELINT Liberator fitted with exhaust flame dampers below the engine nacelles, prepares to take off from its base in India. IWM

In England, 100 Group RAF was formed in November 1943 principally to bring together under one command all the support units involved in RCM and Electronic Intelligence. These units received no mention because of the secret nature of the work, but they drastically reduced the losses of RAF Bomber Command. Remarkably, all of this was achieved by a few four-engined bombers, each carrying bundles of *Window* or *Chaff*, and electronic 'jamming' devices, who, night after night made 'spoof raids' against the enemy. *Window* showed up on German radar as a 'mass' bomber formation, and *Jostle* and *Mandrel* equipment effectively jammed the Nachtjagd's high fighter frequencies and VHF, and German ground and airborne radar.

Initially the RAF were assisted by a small American RCM detachment under the command of Capt G.E. Paris, which arrived at RAF Sculthorpe, Norfolk, in January 1944 to train No. 214 Squadron, which was equipped with Fortresses fitted with *Jostle* and *Airborne Cigar*. 'ABC' as it was known, was a device consisting of six scanning receivers and three transmitters designed to cover the VHF frequency band of standard German R/T sets, jamming 30–33 M/cs (*Ottokar*) and later 38–42 M/cs (*Benito*, R/T and Beam); 214 Squadron moved to Oulton, Norfolk, on 16 May and were soon joined by the US 803rd Bomb Squadron (later re-designated 36th Bomb Squadron). The 36th Squadron's eleven B-24H/J Liberators and two B-17s left Oulton for Harrington on 14 August 1944 and were replaced, on the 23rd, by 223 Squadron, which was formed initially with a handful of B-24H and J models from the 8th Air Force as the second *Jostle* unit.

223 Squadron's Liberators were capable of carrying up to as many as thirty jamming sets, and this, plus the B-24's long-range capability, made the aircraft ideal for jamming operations. However, some of the Liberators had accumulated as many as 350 flying hours in 8th AF service, and were past their best. Each B-24 carried two special operators who implemented the radar jamming devices, but security was so good that even the rest of the crew did not have the slightest idea of what they were up to.

In mid-July 1944, 223 Squadron was used to try to counter the threat posed by the V-2, and *Jostle* equipment was subsequently modified to the *Big Ben* configuration, which was thought, mistakenly, to be able to jam the rocket guidance system. On 19 September, Flt Lt A.J. Carrington DFC carried out the first *Big Ben* patrol for 223 Squadron. Crews patrolled in daylight for up to four hours' duration off the Dutch coast at about 20,000ft (6,000m), hoping to spot a V-2 on its way up from its launching pad. All of this was in vain, however, and the V-2 could not be jammed. In November 1944 *Big Ben* was deleted and replaced with *Carpet* and *Dina* jamming devices.

Liberator KH166 served with 357 Squadron from September 1944 to November 1945. The American serial number, 44-10731, is visible on the rudder. IWM

By early September, 223 Squadron was up to nearly full strength. Training was begun, and two American Liberator pilots helped to check out the captains. Five Liberators were allotted for this, and other training; extensive modifications were made to the B-24s and the crew was reduced by one as the front gunner was unnecessary. A large floor space in the rear bomb cell was provided for *Window* storage, and the whole of the navigator's position was enlarged and improved. Additional jammers were installed, and the squadron was ready to begin *Window* patrols.

W-William **and crew, and** M-Mother, **both of 223 Squadron, 100 Group, at Oulton in Norfolk in 1944. Note the sealed Emerson nose-turret painted over black, and the** Window **chute protruding from the bomb-bay below the flame damper under the engine nacelle.** Don Prutton *(above)* via City of Norwich 100 Group Museum *(right)*

Daylight patrols by 223 Squadron came to an end on 25 October, and crews began night operations with Bomber Command. These operations were of two distinct types: in the first, two or three jammers would accompany the main bomber stream and circle above the target; then the special operators would use their transmitters, in particular *Jostle*, to jam the German radar defences while the RAF bombers released their bombs; and finally everyone headed for home. The majority of operations were of the second type, however, the *Window* spoofs, the object of these raids being to confuse the enemy as to the intended target. There was a radar screen created by other aircraft patrolling in a line roughly north to south over the North Sea and France. A group of perhaps eight aircraft would emerge though this screen scattering *Window*, to give the impression to the German radar operators that a large bomber force was heading for, say, Hamburg. Then, when the Germans were concentrating their night fighters in that area, the real bomber force would appear through the screen and bomb a totally different target, perhaps Düsseldorf. After several nights, when the enemy had become used to regarding the first group of aircraft as a dummy raid, the procedure was reversed; this policy was intended to cause maximum confusion to the enemy, also dissipation of his resources and reduction in RAF bomber losses.

Throughout 1944 *Jostling* took place in every major bombing raid. By December the *Jostle* aircraft were fully equipped with the addition of *Carpet* (anti-Würzburg)

B.Mk. VI of 355 Squadron showing its three black and two white vertical stripes on the rudders. 355 flew its first operation from Salbani, India, on 19/20 November 1943, when three B.Mk. IIIs attacked the central railway at Mandalay. Its last operation was on 7 August 1945 when the Siam-Burma railway near Bangkok was bombed. IWM

and *Piperack* (anti-SN-2) equipment. At the target area they jammed, with *Piperack*, the enemy AI (Airborne Intercept), and they remained there until well after the attack, thus covering the withdrawal of stragglers. It was also the intention to increase and prolong the AI jamming in the target areas to which the enemy fighters would ultimately gravitate. The *Mandrel* screen and *Window* forces also kept up the good work of confusion and diversion during December. The Ruhr was still the favourite target, and *Window* flooding methods continued to be used with success.

Just how effective all this became is perhaps best illustrated on 4/5 December 1944, when 892 heavies set out for Karlsruhe, Heilbron, Hagen and Hamm in the north and south of the Ruhr. The *Window* force went straight into 'Happy Valley' between them, supported by PFF marking, and held between at least ninety and a hundred fighters in the area until much too late for their deployment against the heavies. Losses to the main force were kept to fifteen aircraft, or 1.5 per cent of the force.

During March 1945, 223 Squadron began changing over to the B-17, although some B-24s remained on strength right up until the last days of the war. The last operation of 223 Squadron as a heavy bomber support squadron operating with the main force of Bomber Command in Europe took place on 2/3 May 1945 when a *Window* spoof over Kiel was flown on what was the

RAF Liberators followed up their land attack raids with sorties against Japanese shipping far out into the Bay of Bengal and the Indian Ocean. This enemy vessel was bombed and set on fire by Flt Lt Borthwick of 159 Squadron on 15 June 1945. W.J. Jones

Liberator of 356 Squadron lands at Cocus Island, which was used by RAF Liberators near the end of hostilities with Japan; after the surrender it remained a staging post for flying supplies to Malaya and Sumatra and for ferrying troops to Ceylon. IWM

A 356 Squadron Liberator prepares to taxi out in June 1945. The squadron flew its last operation of the war, 13 August 1945, when three Liberators dropped supplies to clandestine forces operating in Malaya. C. Berry Collection

final Bomber Command raid of the war. Five Liberators (and four B-17s) of 223 Squadron were among the *Mandrel-* and *Window*-equipped aircraft of 100 Group that provided support for the night's operations. During 25 June–7 July 1945, Exercise *Post Mortem*, which was carried out to evaluate the effectiveness of RAF 'jamming' and 'spoof' operations on the German early warning radar system, proved conclusively that the countermeasures had been a great success.

RAF Finale

At the end of 1945 and in early 1946, Liberators of 159 and 355 Squadrons participated in Operation *Hunger*, the ferrying or dropping of rice to the starving population of south Burma. The last bombing operations of the war were carried out on 7 August 1945 by eight Liberators of No. 99 Squadron and three of No. 356 Squadron from the Cocos Islands, about 2,000 miles (3,200km) from Ceylon and 1,000 miles (1,600km) from Perth, Australia. Two months before, an 8 Squadron Liberator had established a world endurance record of 24 hours 10 minutes. Thus, as with many other American aircraft in World War II, the RAF ingeniously squeezed every last ounce of performance out of the Liberator, no matter where it served. By the end of the war, almost 2,500 Liberators of one type or another had been delivered to the RAF and Commonwealth Air Forces, of which 1,694 were supplied by Consolidated alone.

(Above) **A Liberator of 356 Squadron flown by Fg Off Schmoyer drops supplies to a PoW camp somewhere in Burma on 6 September 1945. The day after drops, two-man liaison teams were always parachuted in to assist with recovery.**
Stanley Burgess

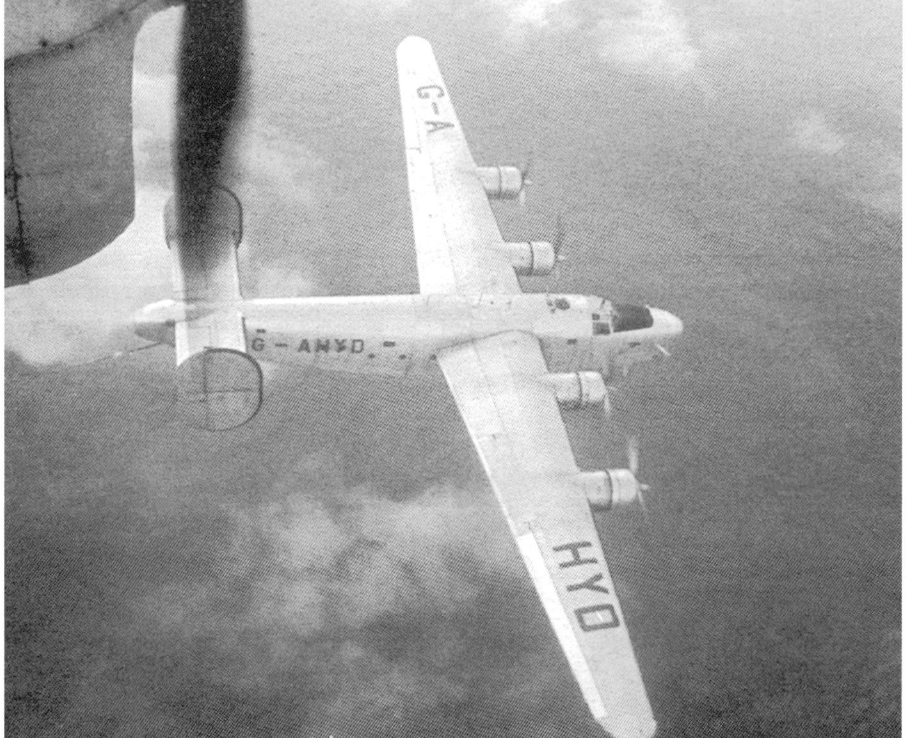

Post-war BOAC Liberators were used in trials with Avro Lancastrian tankers of Flight Refuelling Ltd in the North Atlantic. This photo was taken by the famous British photographer Charles E. Brown from a Lancastrian while G-AHYD, a BOAC Liberator was being refuelled 10,000ft (3,000m) over the Atlantic: 900gal (4,092ltr) of fuel weighing nearly three tons were transferred in 8½ minutes. A series of test flights was made to try out flight refuelling under the severe conditions of winter in the North Atlantic. For this reason the tanker based at Shannon flew to a point 500 miles (800km) westward where interception was made by radar. The 'receiver' aircraft continued uninterrupted on its non-stop flight from London Airport to Montreal, all manoeuvring being done by the tanker. Other tankers were stationed at Gander, Newfoundland, and Goose Bay, Labrador. The system permitted the Liberator's payload between England and Canada to be trebled.
Charles E. Brown

CHAPTER EIGHT

Search, Find and Kill

US Anti-submarine Operations in the Atlantic

A sharp increase in shipping losses in 1942 resulted in the activation, on 15 October 1942, in New York, of the US Anti-Submarine Command under the command of Maj Gen Westside T. Larson. Anti-submarine operations had already been in existence in the USA from 7 December 1941, the day after Pearl Harbor, and these would continue until 2 September 1945.

On occasion, heavy bomb groups en route to England did a stint tracking down U-boats from the east coast of the USA. Two Liberator squadrons in the 93rd Bomb Group already in England, at Alconbury, were also pressed into action in the Bay of Biscay. On 25 October 1942 the 330th Bomb Squadron was transferred to Holmsley South, Hampshire, for anti-submarine duties with RAF Coastal Command. Similarly, the 409th Squadron operated from St Eval in Cornwall, and both squadrons provided long-range convoy protection duties for the Operation *Torch* invasion fleet, scouring the Bay for up to twelve hours at a time looking for elusive U-boats. Despite a handful of sightings, no attacks were made, but two Luftwaffe incursions were countered in November. On the 21st, Maj Ramsey D. Potts of the 330th was faced with an onslaught of five Ju 88s; but the Liberator gunners dispatched two and damaged a third. On another occasion the 409th participated in a fruitless search for a Fortress which had disappeared with Brig Gen Asa Duncan aboard, the first 8th Air Force commanding general.

U-boat operations in the Atlantic threatened Britain's very existence, and in the spring of 1943 only seventy long-range aircraft were available in No. 19 Group, Coastal Command, to counter this threat. The British Admiralty was of the opinion that some 260 aircraft were needed, and a demand was made to RAF Bomber Command for 190 Lancasters. This was rejected, and so AVM Sir John Slessor, C-in-C Coastal Command, asked America that six additional long-range squadrons, seventy-two planes in all, should be transferred from the US to the United Kingdom where they could assist in the Battle of the Bay. (Twenty Liberators from the British allocation were also earmarked for 10 Squadron RCAF, which began operating Liberators in May 1943.) The most the RAF ever received were three squadrons (thirty-six aircraft) by January 1944, and two of these, the 1st and 2nd Arons (Anti-submarine Squadrons), both of whom were equipped with ten centimetric SCR517 radar-equipped B-24Ds, replaced the 4th and 19th Squadrons which transferred to Morocco.

Anti-Submarine Command, together with RAF Coastal Command, would, for some ten months, be responsible for hunting the U-boat wolf packs in the shipping lanes of the North and Middle Atlantic from Newfoundland to Trinidad, and the Bay of Biscay and the approaches to North Africa. The European-African-Middle East theatre was also covered by anti-submarine aircraft until 2 September 1945. The main US task of patrolling the Atlantic rested upon the 25th and 26th Anti-submarine Wings, and three groups, namely the 1st Sea-Search Attack Group, and the 479th and 480th Anti-Submarine Groups. The 13th Aron had also been activated on 18 October 1942 and assigned to Anti-Submarine Command, and for a time flew anti-submarine patrols off the New England coast until September 1943, when it was re-designated the 863rd Bomb Squadron and assigned to 2nd Air Force. In January 1944 the 863rd became one of the founding squadrons in the 493rd Bomb Group, 3rd Bomb Division, 8th Air Force.

Meanwhile the 25th SAW was activated at New York on 29 November 1942 under the command of Col Howard Moore, and totalled five squadrons: the 1st, 2nd, 4th, 14th and 19th Arons. All five squadrons were initially equipped with B-17s and B-18s at Langley Field, Virginia, and it was not until 1943 that they began receiving mainly B-24Ds. Prior to June 1943 the 4th and 19th Arons saw service overseas, in Jamaica (4th Aron), and Newfoundland (both); then on 13 July, both squadrons began operations from Devon. The 2nd Aron deployed to St Eval on 2 December 1942, and the 1st Aron joined them there on 13 January 1943. Two months later, on 11 March, the 2nd Aron moved to Port Lyautey, French Morocco.

A month earlier, on 10 February, while attached to Fleet Air Wing 15, a 2nd Aron crew captained by 1st Lt W.L. Sandford flying B-24D *Tidewater Tillie* from Port Lyautey, had had a success against a German submarine. It was a rainy and hazy day when the crew picked up a radar contact about four miles distant. They homed in, and Lt H.C. Jackson, co-pilot, sighted a heavy wake at 5 miles (8km) off the starboard beam: it was a U-boat on the surface, and there were three men in the conning tower – one was observed trying to man an 'automatic cannon'. It was U-519, a type IXC submarine commanded by Kapitänleutnant Gunter Eppen, which was on its second war cruise. Sandford attacked as U-519 was going under, and Capt R.E. Jones Jr, bombardier, released four depth-charge bombs, allowing about 1,000ft (300m) range on the water. The bombs overshot, but Staff Sgt K. Hosack, *Tidewater Tillie's* rear gunner, observed an explosion just aft of the conning tower. The explosion enveloped the after-portion of the U-boat, and it started to settle at the stern; the entire bow section from the conning tower forward was sticking up into the air, and almost immediately the submarine sank stern first. The time interval from the time of the attack to the time the bow went under the water was estimated at just 55 seconds.

Meanwhile the 26th SAW was activated at Miami, Florida on 20 November 1942 under the command of Col Harry A.

Halverson, who later led the HALPRO detachment in North Africa. The 15th Aron was the only squadron in the wing equipped with B-24s, and these were first assigned in 1943. The 15th Aron took part in anti-submarine patrols in the Gulf of Mexico until the parent organization disbanded on 15 October 1943. The 1st Search Attack Group (Medium) was activated on 18 June 1942 and was composed of three squadrons: the 2nd, 3rd and 4th SAS. Mostly, the group was tasked with testing equipment and developing techniques and tactics, and in late 1943 when Liberators were received, was responsible for the radar training of combat crews.

The 480th Anti-Submarine Group was activated at Port Lyautey, French Morocco on 21 June 1943 under the command of Col Jack Roberts, while on 8 July the 479th Anti-Submarine Group was activated at St Eval, England, under the command of Col Howard Moore. Using B-24s, the 480th Group's 1st and 2nd Arons had the primary mission of carrying out anti-submarine patrols in an area of the Atlantic extending north and west from Morocco, while the 479th Group's 4th, 6th, 19th and 22nd Arons were responsible for anti-submarine patrols in the Bay of Biscay.

The 479th ASG began operations on 13 July. Missions now reached a peak of activity as the German wolf packs scoured the sea lanes off Portugal for shipping bound for the Mediterranean. The period 18 July to 2 August resulted in five sinkings of U-boats, or sinkings in conjunction with others and credited to the group. Between 7–12 July, three U-boats were officially declared sunk by the 479th ASG, and during the period 20 July–2 August when the group was working with other Allied aircraft, it contributed to the sinking of three more.

In the Bay of Biscay on 20 July, Lt Charles F. Gallmeier and his crew in the 19th Aron got a contact, and fifteen minutes later spotted two U-boats six miles ahead of them (both were in fact returning to Brest from the Azores). They caught the submarines by surprise and went after one of them, actually U-558, a type VIIC submarine commanded by Kapitänleutnant Günther Krech. At 12:18 hours, Lt Yarousco, bombardier, using his B-1 intervelometer,

U-boats Sunk By USAAF Liberators

Squadron/Group	*Date*	*U-boat*	*Details*
99th BS/6th AF	2 Oct 42	U-512	Off French Guiana
2nd Aron/480th ASG	10 Feb 43	U-519	NW of Spain
1st Aron/480th ASG	22 Mar 43	U-524	North of Canary I.
1st Aron/480th ASG	7 Jul 43	U-951	Agadir, Canary I.
1st Aron/480th ASG	8 Jul 43	U-232	Off Portugal
1st Aron/480th ASG	12 Jul 43	U-506	Near Portugal
19th Aron/479th ASG	20 Jul 43	U-558	Bay of Biscay*
4th Aron/479th ASG	28 Jul 43	U-404	Bay of Biscay#
4th Aron/479th ASG	2 Aug 43	U-706	Eastern Atlantic°

** With an RAF Halifax of 58 Squadron*
 # With 224 Sqn RAF
° With a 415 RCAF Squadron Hampden

Capt Benjamin Meade's crew in the 22nd Anti-Submarine Squadron, at Bluenthal Field, Wilmington, North Carolina. Back row, left to right: 1st Lt John A. Reitmeier, navigator; 1st Lt John Lucy, co-pilot; Ben Meade, pilot; 1st Lt John Mead, bombardier. Front row, third from right is Staff Sgt Phillip Latta, radio operator, and far right is Sgt Graham Hasty, tail gunner. This crew later transferred to the Carpetbaggers; they were shot down on the night of 5/6 May 1944, though some members evaded. John Reitmeier Collection

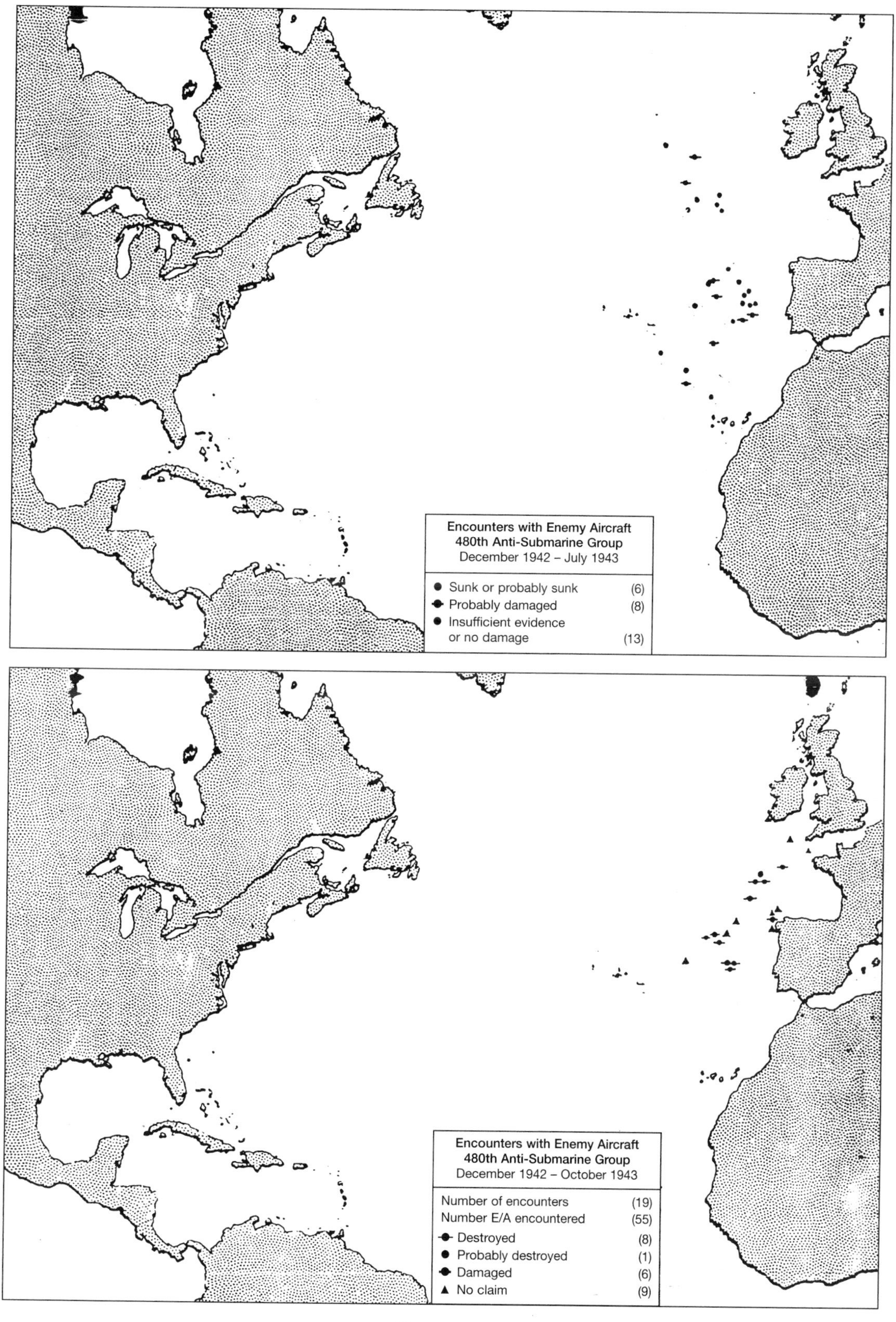

dropped a stick of seven Torpex Mk.XI depth-charges fitted with Mk.XVI pistols, set for 25ft (7.6m) at 600ft (183m) altitude, as the Liberator powered in at 180mph (290km/h) in a slight dive, giving a true spacing of 50ft (15m) to 100ft (30m). The D/Cs exploded close by the side of U-558, and Lt Rosoff, navigator, opened fire with the front gun as they closed in. Then the top and waist gunners began firing. Finally, U-558 returned fire and hit Gallmeier's Liberator, wounding

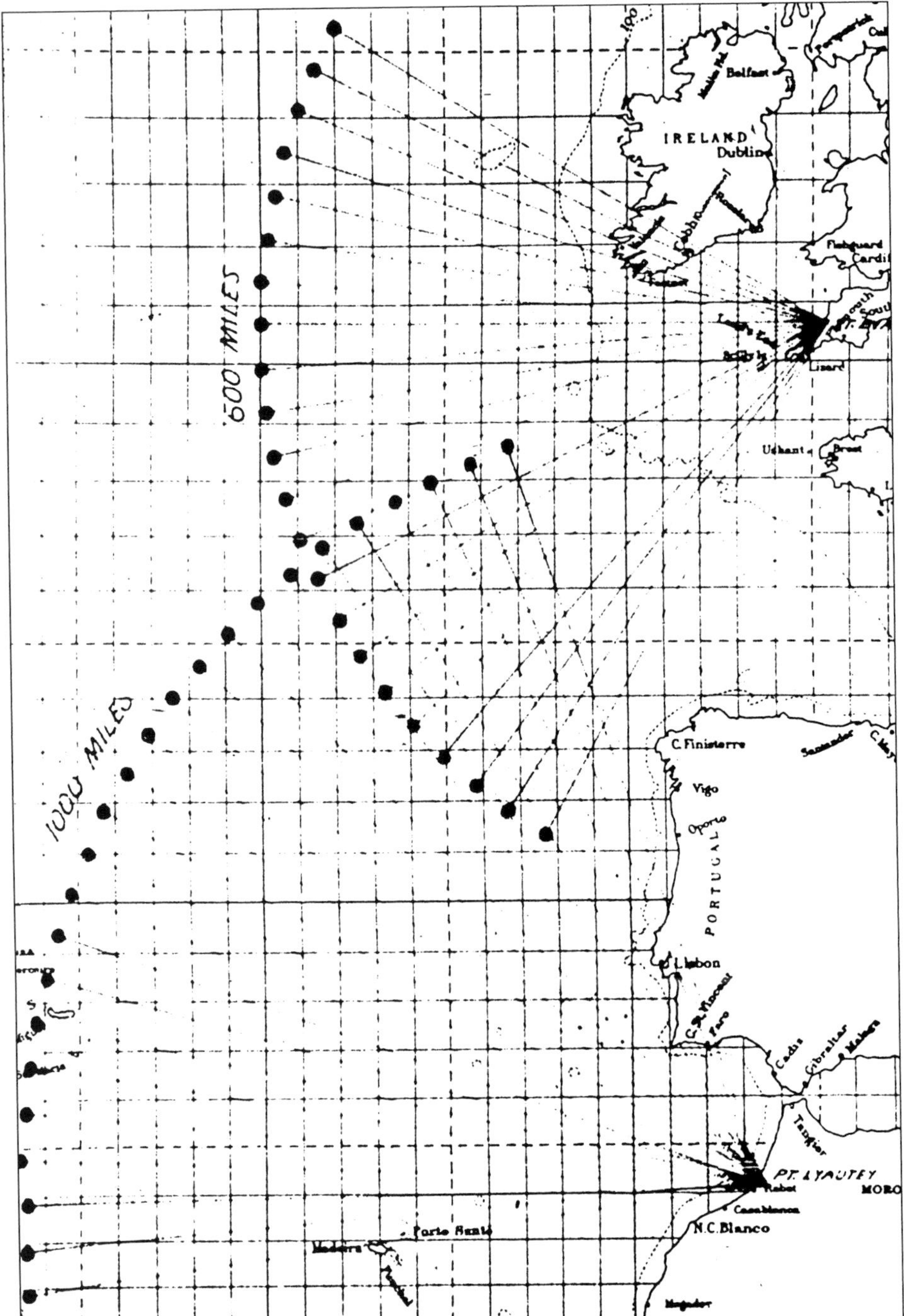

Extreme patrol range and maximum strength in aeroplanes of 480th Group, November 1942–September 1943. Each black spot represents one plane. (500 miles = 800km; 1,000 miles = 1,600km.)

one of his waist gunners in both legs. More flak came up, and Gallmeier was about to carry out a second attack when his port inner engine cut out. At this moment a Halifax of 58 Squadron RAF, flown by Flt Lt Geoffrey Sawtell, came on the scene and finished off the U-boat with a salvo of eight D/Cs.

Eight days later, on 28 July, Lt Arthur J. Hammer and crew in the 4th Aron shared in the destruction of U-404, another type VIIC submarine, commanded by Oblt Adolf Schoenberg, which was en route from St Nazaire for the North Atlantic. U-404 had already sunk seventeen ships and a destroyer on earlier war cruises. Major McElroy of the 4th Aron attacked first, but the attempt failed when his depth-charges refused to budge; a faulty intervelometer was thought to be responsible. On the second attack, McElroy's bombardier toggled out eight Torpex Mk. XI depth-charges fitted with Mk. XVI pistols, which were set for 25ft (7.6m). Then Hammer's crew picked up the signal. From 4,000ft (1,220m) they sighted visually U-404 five miles in the distance, and Hammer closed for the attack at 190mph (306km/h). Using the intervelometer, and at 110ft (33.5m) altitude, his bombardier dropped eight Torpex Mk. XI depth-charges fitted with Mk. XVI pistols, set for 25ft, and spaced at 60ft (18m). The rear gunner said that the D/Cs straddled the U-boat across the conning tower. Hammer then came in for a second attack. The top turret guns jammed and the front gunner did not have time to reload, but two submariners fell overboard as the other American gunners opened fire. This time the bombardier, using the intervelometer, released four D/Cs from less than 50ft (15m) at a speed of 190mph (306km/h) and spread 100ft (30m). The Liberator was hit in the port outer engine and also in the tail and fuselage by return fire from the enemy submarine. The rear gunner reported that the D/Cs had straddled the U-boat one third of the way between the conning tower and the bow, three to starboard and one very close on the port side of the U-boat. Hammer circled away to port and another Liberator arrived to make his attack.

The plumes caused by the Hammer's D/Cs had alerted the crew of Fg Off R.V. Sweeny's Liberator in 224 Squadron RAF, which was also on patrol in the area, and he attacked just as Hammer broke off his attack with his damaged B-24. In fact Bob Sweeny finished off the sub with seven D/Cs from 150ft (45m) – although U-404 did not go down without a fight: flak from the boat set the Liberator's No. 4 engine on fire before U-404 sank beneath the waves. There were no survivors. Hammer and Sweeny got their Liberators safely back to England, although the former had to land at Predannack because St Eval was socked in.

On 2 August the 479th ASG shared in the sinking of a third type-VIIC submarine: U-706, commanded by Kapitänleutnant Alexander von Zitzewitz, was on her fifth patrol from La Pallice, when it was attacked in the east Atlantic by a Hampden of 415 Squadron RCAF flown by Sqn Ldr C.G. Rutton RCAF. The Canadian dropped six D/Cs on the sub, and although results could not be determined, U-706 was damaged. At this point, Lt J. L. Hamilton and his crew in 'T', a 4th Aron Liberator, arrived on the scene, having picked up a radar contact at twenty miles. Then Lt Schmidt, co-pilot, sighted with the naked eye U-706's large wake about ten miles ahead. Hamilton attacked out of the sun, and the U-boat opened fire with light flak when the B-24 was about one mile away. One hit was scored on the left wheel of the Liberator, but Hamilton carried on and his bombardier dropped a dozen D/Cs set for 25ft (7.6m), from 50ft (15m) altitude. The explosions lifted the enemy U-boat out of the water, it then settled quickly by the stern; it appeared to sink ten seconds after the attack was delivered and an oil slick appeared, finally covering an area one mile (1.6km) long and ¾ mile (1.2km) wide. Several submariners could be seen floating among wreckage in the oil-stained sea. The B-24 crew flew back over the spot and dropped a dinghy, and some of the survivors were seen to climb into it. Later, a Catalina and a Sunderland flew over and helped direct rescue operations with a Royal Navy vessel. This was one of the last sightings, because after early August, the German submarines avoided surfacing during daylight and adopted a policy of evasion; but the Liberators continued their patrols, often engaging Luftwaffe aircraft in combat.

One of the crews assigned to the 18th Aron, 479th Anti-Submarine Group in 1943 was captained by 1st Lt James O. 'Augie' Bolin, from Pine Bluff, Arkansas. 2nd Lt Art Grimes, of Carlsbad, California, who was to become the navigator on Augie's crew, recalls their first meeting:

> When I arrived at McGuire Army Air Force Field, the squadron was in the midst of retraining from B-25 aircraft to B-24 aircraft. Most of the pilots were attending B-24 transition training in Virginia. I flew a few patrols in B-25s, and then our B-24 aircraft slowly began to arrive. At this point I met Augie Bolin who had just arrived from B-24 transition. He told me that he had asked for me to be assigned to his B-24, which was just being assembled. We had the newest B-24, equipped with radar, and we were moved around the various coastal areas of the Atlantic and Gulf coasts as submarine activity was reported. Towards the end of July our crew was alerted for immediate transfer to England to

A B-24D and her crew in the 479th Anti-Submarine Group at St Eval. The front fuselage has had an Oklahoma City nose modification. via Mike Bailey

B-24D-115-CO 42-40921 White Savage **of the 479th Anti-Submarine Group, with Consair A-6 nose turret, droop chin, and ASV antenna in place of the ball turret. The camouflage scheme consists of white under surfaces and olive drab upper surfaces. With the deactivation of USAAF anti-submarine squadrons late in 1943,** White Savage **was reassigned to the 482nd Bomb Group on 31 October 1943.** Mike Bailey

B-24D-115-CO 42-40938 Donna Mia **of the 479th Anti-Submarine Group pictured at the 458th Bomb Group, 2nd Bomb Division base at Horsham St Faith, Norwich.** via Steve Adams

replace a crew that had been lost in combat. We were sent to Langley Field, Virginia, to pick up a new B-24 with the latest radar and long-range bomb-bay tanks for twelve-hour patrols. We flew the plane to Dunkeswell, near Exeter in Devon.

Bolin's crew flew the long anti-submarine patrols in B-24D Liberators over the Atlantic, always on the lookout for enemy submarines and aircraft. Usually they saw the latter, as was the case on 25 August 1943 when they had a lucky escape: Bolin's crew had just investigated two Tunnyman yawls and they were flying on track at 3,000ft (900m) below 10/10ths stratus cumulus, visibility unlimited, when the right waist gunner sighted a Ju 88 about 600yd off to the left and rapidly overhauling the Liberator. The Ju 88, painted all-white, flew above them on the port side, then circled around and came in from the starboard bow at an angle of 45 degrees right; it opened fire with tracer from about 600yd, then as it came closer it opened up with cannon fire – the B-24 crew could see quite clearly the puffs of black smoke as the guns were fired. The Ju 88 crew scored hits on both the Liberator's port engines, and the port inner caught fire.

The Ju 88 broke away beneath the Liberator, circled left-handed, and began a second approach from between the starboard beam and quarter. As it approached, Bolin turned sharply to starboard, and fire from the Ju 88 was seen bursting in black puffs about 100ft astern and slightly to starboard of the Liberator. The Liberator top turret gunner opened fire, and he estimated that he scored between ten and fifteen strikes on the Junkers. The right waist gunner also fired a few rounds. The enemy aircraft then broke away, and was thought to have been hit during its departure, too.

Meanwhile Bolin climbed towards the thick cloud, and about one minute later, at 5,000ft (1,500m), they spotted the Ju 88 in the distance again, and he was approaching from astern. Bolin immediately feathered the port outer, which was giving trouble, and during the remainder of the flight he had to feather the port inner and outer several times. He successfully nursed the B-24 back to base, and none of the crew was the worse for the engagement.

B-24D Biscay Belle **of the 479th Anti-Submarine Group based at Dunkeswell, Cornwall.** via Steve Adams

U-boats under attack from USAAF Aron Squadron B-24Ds in the Atlantic. IWM

A few days later, on 7 September, Bolin's crew had a clear sight of a submarine wash, the vessel itself being in the act of diving. It was travelling at 10 knots at a bearing of 10 degrees port, and 15 miles (24km) from the Liberator, which was at 2,000ft (610m). Two minutes later, Bolin's crew sighted three RAF Beaufighters which were about to attack the U-boat. Bolin's attack was just seventy-five seconds after the submarine submerged.

Following the attack Bolin remained in the area, and a short while later he was joined by an RAF Sunderland flying boat. Half an hour later, still circling, they sighted what appeared to be a periscope wake ten miles due north and moving at slow speed. At the time of the sighting Bolin's Liberator was at 1,500ft (457m). He dived into the attack and was down to just 75ft (23m) when he bombed the wake, 20 degrees on the port bow, with five 250lb depth-charges armed with Torpex BK.XI. They were spaced 60ft (18m) apart and at a depth setting of 25ft (7.6m). The third or fourth depth-charges straddled the wake and the B-24 gunners were convinced they had hit the U-boat; however, as the depth-charges were released, Bolin and other members of the crew strongly suspected that the supposed wake was in fact a smoke float dropped by some other aircraft. This was later confirmed by a study of photographs taken during the attack by the B-24. Art Grimes Concludes:

We flew twelve-hour anti-submarine missions every other day; one of our last patrols was in early September. The US Navy was being assigned all anti-submarine patrol activities world-wide, so on 1 October, crews that had in excess of 400 hours of Bay of Biscay patrol time were returned to the States for strategic bombing training and assignment to the Pacific. A few of the newer crews, like us, who did not meet the time criterion, were assigned to the 8th Air Force. Our bombardier, J.E. Ehrenzweig,

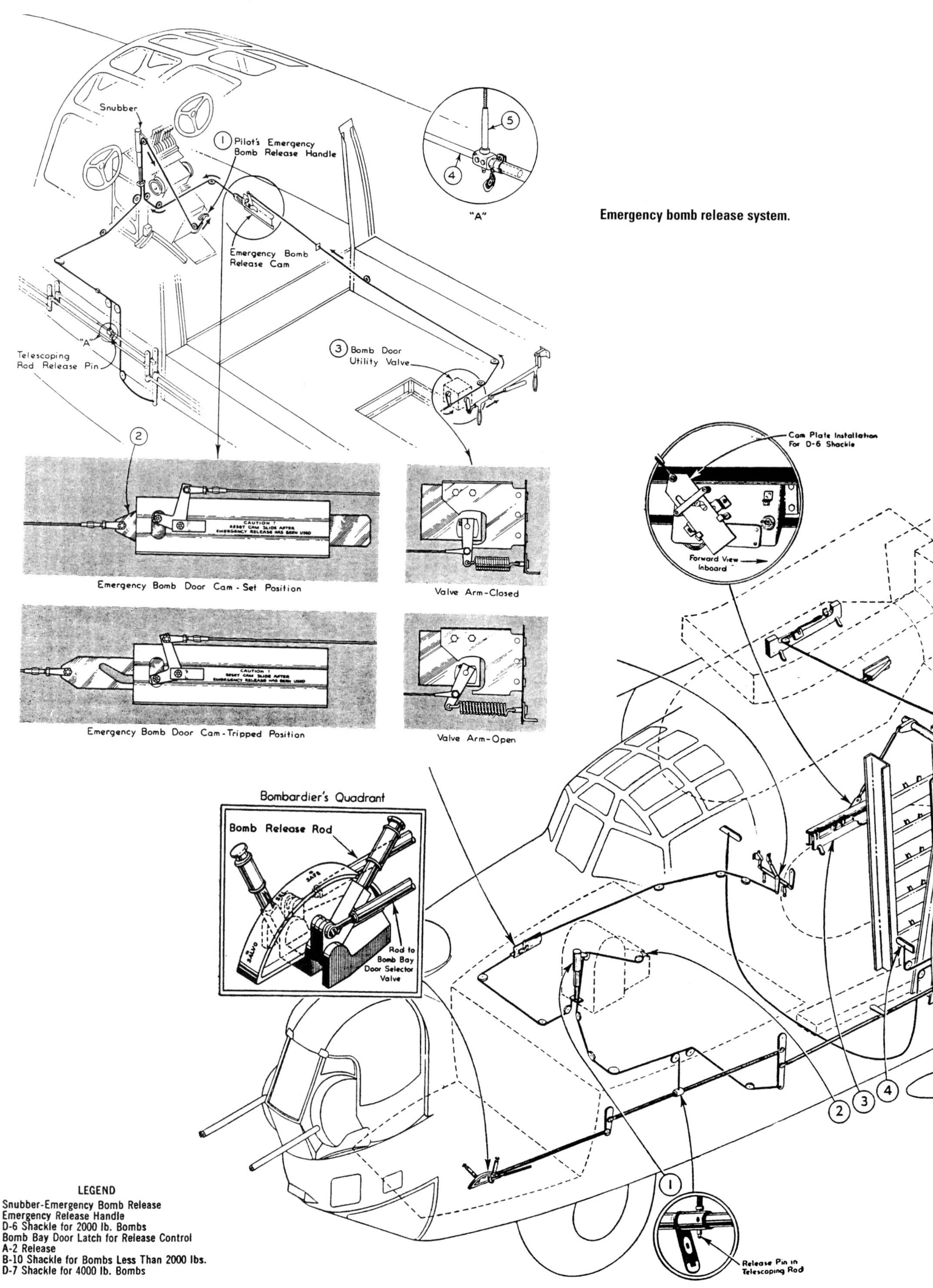

Emergency bomb release system.

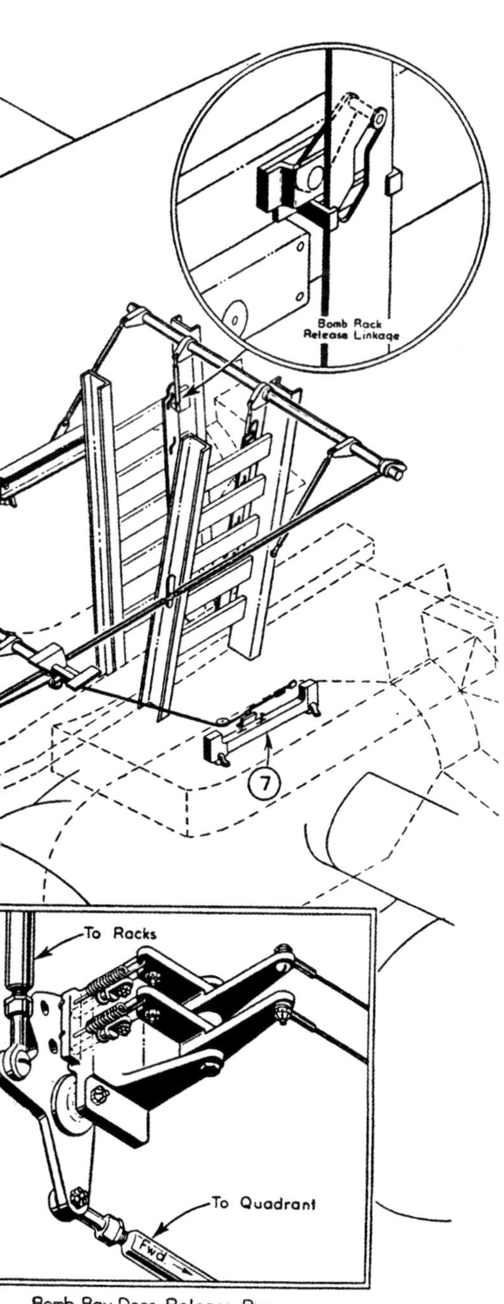

Bomb Bay Door Release Pins

Norden Bombsight

Norden bombsight in a B-24J showing the intervalometer, a mechanism by means of which bombs may be released singly or in groups, and with the groups so spaced that they will strike in a definite distance interval. This mechanism was used by bombardiers to drop depth-charges on U-boats. Mike Bailey

Instructions from Liberator instruction manual

A. Single Bomb Release:

1. Turn on battery power.
2. Open bomb doors.
3. Set quadrant lever (22) at 'SEL'.
4. Cock all A-2 Units.
5. Set selector switches (12) at 'B-7' or 'D-5' as installed.
6. Turn bomb rack switches (14) 'ON'.
7. Set switch (3) (Unit 4) at 'SEL'.
8. Operate firing keys (Unit 5) Figure 1.
9. Check sequence of A-2 Units; order of release on ships to 41-23640 should be: bottom to top of Rack 1, followed by racks 2, 3, and 4. Sequence on ships from 41-23640 should be: bottom station of Racks 1, 2, 3, and 4 and then No. 2 Station of Racks 1, 2, 3, and 4 etc.

B. Multiple Bomb Release – Using Intervalometer:

1. Repeat items 2 to 4 above.
2. Set switch (3) (Unit 4) at 'Train.'
3. Set bomb number control (2) (Unit 4) at '5' bombs.
4. Set ground interval control (1) (Unit 4) to a wide spacing at low speed, to slow down release interval for accurate check of release sequence.
5. Set rack selector switches (14) for No. 1 Rack.
6. Close and open bomb doors. (This is done after cocking A-2 Units to reset RS-2 Relays.) Or throw switch (12) to D-5 and then to D-7 to re-set RS-2 Relays.
7. Press firing key. Bombs should release in order 1, 2, 3, 4, and 5 of Rack No. 1. Check by following lights (5).
8. Recock A-2 Units of No. 1 Rack.
9. Set bomb number control (2) (Unit 4) at '20' bombs.
10. Turn all rack selector switches (14) 'ON'.
11. Close and open bomb doors, or throw switch (12) to D-5 and back to B-7 to reset RS-2 Relays.
12. Press firing key.

requested a transfer to the 15th Air Force in Italy and got it. The rest of us were assigned to the 66th Squadron, 44th Bomb Group.

On 11 November the 479th Group disbanded at Podington, Northamptonshire. Sadly there was no happy ending for Augie Bolin: on 2 February 1944, Capt Bolin and his crew were killed when *Ruthless*, their B-24 Liberator, crashed at Eastbourne returning from a mission to France. Grimes was not aboard, but he was flying with another crew that day.

Losses sustained during the period of anti-submarine operations were high; the 480th ASG alone lost 101 crewmen. In September, part of the group had moved temporarily to Tunisia, and they operated in conjunction with the assault on Italy. For its contribution towards winning the Battle of the Atlantic – the 10 November 1942 to the 28 October 1943 – the 480th ASG was awarded the Distinguished Unit Citation. In mid-November 1943, the 480th Group moved to Langley Field, Virginia; the following year, on 29 January 1944, it was disbanded at Clovis in New Mexico.

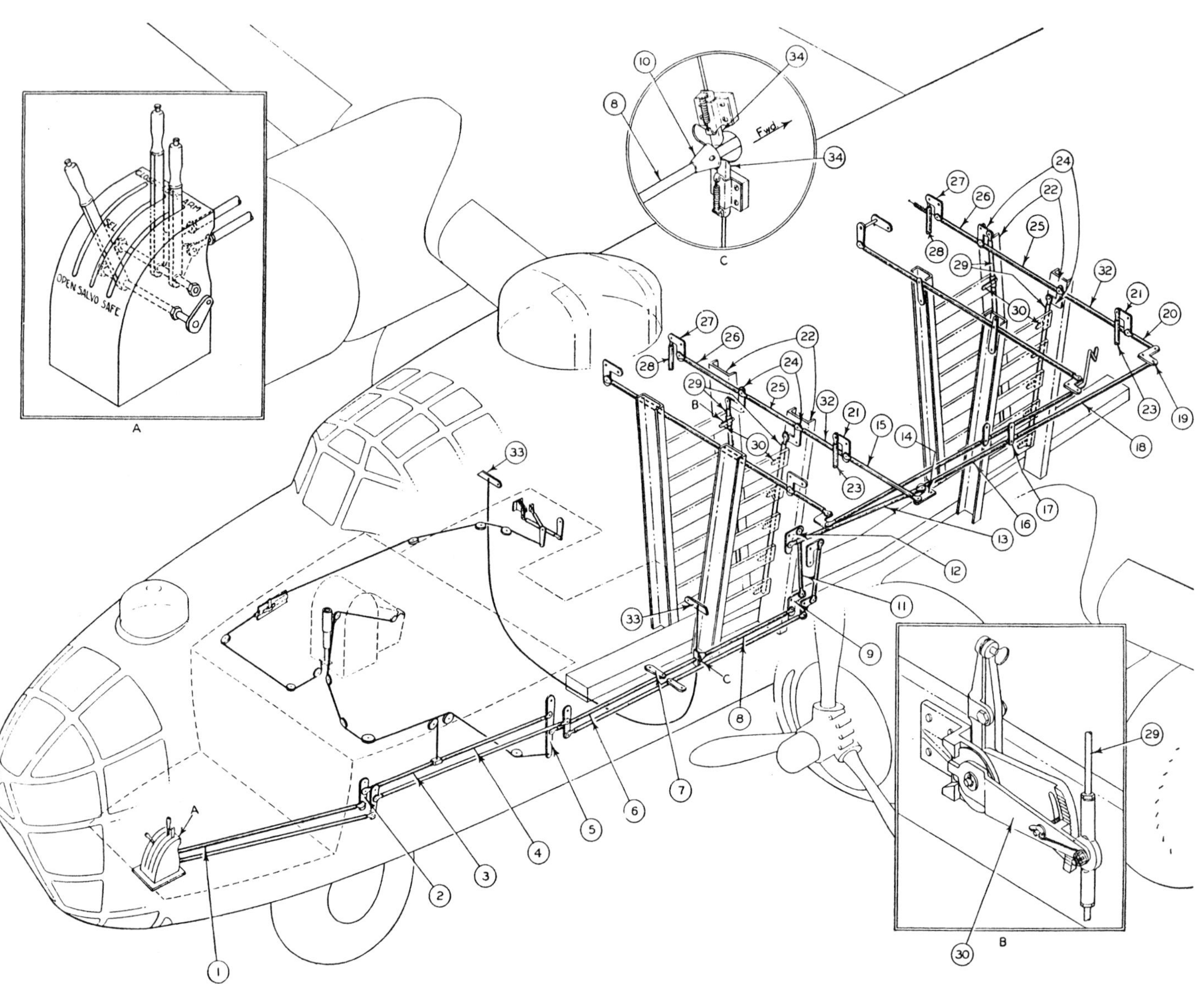

Main bomb rack release system. The numbers 1 to 34 refer to the linkages and bell cranks connecting the bomb release handles (box A) with the bomb racks and bomb shackles. In box B, the linkage (29) is connected through adjustable pawls (30) to each bomb station.

Bomb fusing, bomb warning and bomb release.

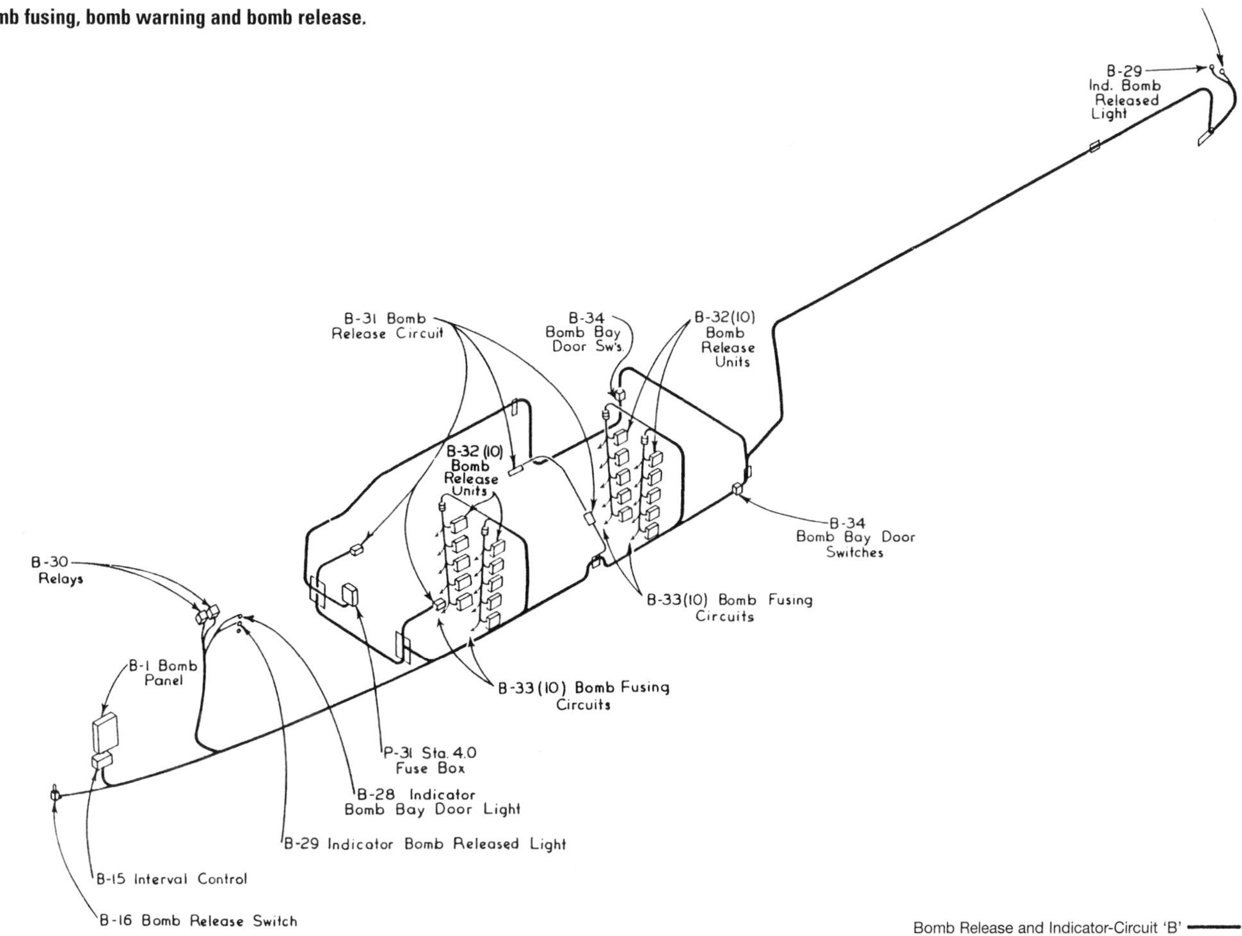

US Navy Operations in the Atlantic

On 24 August 1943 the USAAF disbanded Anti-Submarine Command, and from thenceforth all anti-submarine duties were carried out by the US Navy. At first, many of Anti-Submarine Command's B-24s were transferred to the Navy, and new B-24s were taken on charge by USAAF groups. The Navy PB4Y-1 Liberators were B-24D models equipped with ASV radar and an all-glass nose. Ultimately, some of these Liberators were fitted with Erco bow turrets in the nose, while later models (B-24J, L and M) were fitted with Consair A-6A/-B or the Emerson A-15 turret in the nose. The PB4Y was without doubt the finest patrol bomber of the war, and by January 1945 the Navy would have accepted some 977 Liberators, and twenty-four units would be so equipped. In Navy service the PB4Y-1 bombing squadrons were prefixed with 'VP' for heavier-than-air bomber, and later were re-designated 'VPB' when they combined the patrol identification. Equally incongruously (and unfortunately) for the reconnaissance squadrons, they were at first identified by the code 'VD', while the US Marine Corps Photo-recce units were known as 'VBD's.

The first PB4Y-1 squadron to see service in the Atlantic was VB-103, commissioned on 15 March 1943 at San Diego, California under the command of Lt Cdr W.T. Easton. Its transition from commission to anti-submarine patrols in the Atlantic took only seven weeks, and it was based for the following three months at Argentia, Newfoundland. During this period Bombing Squadron 103 flew 268 missions and amassed over 2,000 hours of flying time.

On 24 June, BuNo 32046 was the first loss. U-boat sightings were rare, as the German submarines had all but left the area by this time; only one attack, on 12 August, by Lt (jg) Stanley Thueson, was made and it lasted just twenty minutes. The U-boat was later declared 'probably slightly damaged'. Three days later thirteen Liberators of VP-103 began moving to St Eval on the south-west coast of England where, upon arrival, Lt Cdr G.W. von Bracht took command. At the end of September, VP-103 began operations from Dunkeswell in Devon, and for the next twenty-one months worked in conjunction with RAF Coastal Command, mainly in the Bay of Biscay.

On occasion, VP-103 B-24s came up against superior Luftwaffe forces, as on 2 September when Lt K.W. Wickstrom's Liberator failed to return. Ju 88s were dispatched in strong formations over the Bay of Biscay to give returning U-boats protection when they were at their most vulnerable from Allied attack. On 4 September, Lt Jim Alexander tussled with no less than six Ju-88s in the Bay of Biscay. Alexander's gunners claimed to have shot down one of their attackers and to have damaged two others before the Ju 88 set the Liberator on fire. Alexander was forced to ditch; they all took to their life-raft, however, and luckily reached land after thirty-six hours in the open sea. Two weeks later, on 18 September, Lt (jg) W.B. Krause and crew were attacked by eight Ju 88s, but the American gunners fended them off for fifteen minutes and escaped unscathed after damaging three of them.

The US Navy PB4Y-1 Liberator squadrons which operated in Atlantic waters were as follows:

US Navy Squadrons (Atlantic)

Unit	*Operational*	*Type*
VP-103	March 1943	PB4Y-1
VP-105	May 1943	PB4Y-1
VP-107	June 1943	PB4Y-1
VP-110	October 1943	PB4Y-1/-2
VP-111	October 1943	PB4Y-1
VP-112	October 1943	PB4Y-1
VP-113	October 1943	PB4Y-1
VP-114	November 1943	PB4Y-1
VPB-125	Feb–Mar 1944	PB4Y-1
VPB-163	Dec–43-Jan 44	PB4Y-1

During World War II, a total of thirteen U-boats were sunk by US Navy Liberators in the Atlantic. VP-107, which was based at Parnarmarin Field, Natal, was credited with sinking six U-boats using B-24D Liberators and B-24J versions of the PB4Y-1 with the Erco bow turret. On 12 July 1943, Lt Tobin carried out a night attack on a U-boat, although no confirmation of a sinking could be awarded. Tobin's B-24 was hit by return fire, and returned to Natal on three engines and a windmilling prop. Bombing Squadron 107's first confirmed U-boat sinking occurred a few days later on 23 July, when two Liberators, one piloted by Lt (jg) Waugh USNR and the other by Lt W.R. Ford, both attacked and sank U-598 near Ascension Island. However, immediately after the attack, Waugh's B-24 plunged into the sea and all hands were lost.

On 11 August, Lt Cdr B.J. 'Bert' Prueher, the CO, took off from Natal in *Spirit of 83* with an unprecedented fuel load of 3,400gal (15,458ltr), with the intention of remaining on patrol for fifteen hours to sweep the estimated position of three U-boats which had been located by D/F bearing. U-185, captained by Kapitänleutnant August Maus, and U-604 had both been badly hit by Mk. 47 bombs dropped in attacks by Prueher eight days earlier; they had then been chased for several days by surface ships, and U-604 had been further damaged during two depth-charge attacks. Now they were due to rendezvous about 500 miles (800km) north-west of Ascension Island to transfer oil and provisions. Prueher reported to base after two-and-a-half hours, but that was the last communication received from *Spirit of 83*.

Some time in the afternoon, Prueher roared out of the overcast and came upon the U-boats; these had been joined by U-172 whose commander, Kapitänleutnant Carl Emmermann, had orders to take over part of U-604's crew after they had scuppered their boat. Prueher emerged just as the transfer of men and materials was almost complete, and began strafing and bombing. U-172 immediately submerged, but the other two submarines opened fire on the PB4Y-1. *Spirit of 83* made two runs, but Prueher's Mk. 47 bombs missed their targets; as he was banking at about 1,200ft (365m) to make a third run, fire from U-185 shot the Liberator down. All hands were lost. The fate of Prueher and his crew only came to light a month later, from the survivors of the U-boat that was sunk. U-604 was scuttled east of Pernambuco.

In October, VP-107, now commanded by Lt Cdr Renfro Turner arrived at Wideawake Field on Ascension Island to extend the bombing range of aircraft on the outcrop in Mid-Atlantic. On 5 November, two PB4Y-1s took off from Wideawake, and at about 290 miles (470km) west, made an attack on U-848. Lt C.A. Baldwin carried out the first attack and straddled the submarine's port beam with D/Cs dropped from 75ft (23m). Thirty minutes later Lt W.R. Ford made the next attack on the sub and inflicted further damage – but the U-boat remained afloat, and when Lt W.E. Hill and his crew arrived on station they were met with heavy bursts of flak. Hill broke off and returned to Ascension with his No. 2 engine out. Late that afternoon, two AAF B-25s tried to drop 500lb bombs from 4,000ft (1,220m) onto the U-boat, but they missed their mark. Then Lt Samuel K. Taylor arrived on the scene in his PB4Y-1, and together with Baldwin, succeeded in sinking U-848.

On 5 November 1943, PB4Y-1s VP-107 from Wideawake, Ascension Island, made repeated attacks on U-848, until it was finally sunk late in the afternoon by Lt Samuel K. Taylor and Lt C.A. Baldwin. USN

VP-107 scored their final kill of 1943 on Thanksgiving Day, 25 November, when Lt (jg) Marion Dawkins sighted U-849 from 5,200ft (1,585m) and then sank it with a salvo of six depth-charges from just 25ft (7.6m). One D/C bounced and damaged the PB4Y-1's fin and rudder, but Dawkins managed to keep the seriously damaged Liberator airborne and returned safely to Ascension Island. That was it for 1943, but in 1944 the squadron was on the rampage again. On 1 January 1944 Lt M.G. Taylor, on barrier patrol, investigated a suspicious vessel which then failed to identify itself before opening fire on the Liberator. Taylor's plane was hit in the No. 3 engine and in the fuselage and he returned to base with a wounded ordnance man. Next day Lt Robert T. Johnson made contact with the ship at 16:20 hours. Again the vessel opened fire and this time caused a minor fuel leak in the Liberator's starboard wing tank. Johnson remained on station until relieved at 18:20 hours, but he was forced to ditch *en route* for home after three engines failed. None of the crew survived.

VP/VPB-103 was credited with five U-boat sinkings in the period November 1943 to April 1945. The first occurred on 10 November 1943 in the Bay of Biscay, and also involved other Liberators from VPB-110 and 311 Czech Squadron RAF, and an RAF Wellington of 612 Squadron. Their victim was U-966, a type VIIC submarine commanded by Oblt Ekkehard Wolf, which was making its way home to the French Atlantic coast when it was damaged in the attack by the Wellington. Lt (jg) K.L. Wright of VPB-103 received a signal giving the U-boat's position, and after avoiding a pair of Ju 88s, he attacked and straddled U-966 with four depth-charges (a fifth hung up). The enemy submarine returned fire, but this did not deter Wright, who made a second attack on the U-boat and dropped a 600lb D/C. His gunners meanwhile strafed the submarine until it settled by the stern and trailed oil. One submariner was seen hanging over the side of the conning tower.

Lt J.A. Parrish and his crew in a VPB-110 Squadron Liberator then took up the attack on U-966, which despite its wounds, still had plenty of fight left. Parrish drew fire as he circled and reduced height to make his attack out of the sun, his forward guns blazing. He dropped six depth-charges, and their combined explosions rolled the U-boat over onto its port side, but it straightened up before making a complete circle. U-966 was by now about 12 miles (19km) off the coast of Spain, and Wolf began heading for the shore. The German U-boat captain had covered 9 miles (14km) when he was attacked again, this time by a Liberator of 311 Czechoslovak Squadron, RAF, flown by Flt Sgt Zanta. The Czech pilot attacked with rocket projectiles, firing the first pair at 1,000ft (300m), and then a second pair; but both salvoes failed. Zanta fired the final four RPs at 600ft (180m) and they entered the water level with the U-boat's bows, 10ft (3m) from the hull. The U-boat must have been hit but it did not appear to slow down, and Wolf eventually beached the submarine near De Santafata Bay, where she was blown up by the crew.

On the night of 12 November, Lt (jg) Ralph B. Brownell of VPB-103 carried out an attack on U-508, a type IX/40 submarine commanded by Kapitänleutnant Georg Staats which was on its sixth war cruise, sailing from St Nazaire on 9 November, for a patrol in the North Atlantic. However, no more was heard from the Liberator after the crew gave a flash report. Next day a search revealed two oil-slicks, one large, one smaller, 5 miles (8km) apart, which suggested that Brownell had attacked and sunk the submarine just as he and his crew were shot down. Posthumous awards were made to the crew: Brownell was awarded the Navy Cross, Ensign Daniel A. Schneider, second pilot, and Capt (AA) Ridgeway K. Poole, navigator received DFCs, and the rest of the ten-man crew received the Air Medal.

During the last week in December 1943, an all-out effort against the enemy surface ships was made by PB4Y-1s of VB-103, VB-105 and VB-110 and RAF Coastal Command. By attacking and shadowing, the air forces continued to harass the enemy ships, directing surface forces to the attack. As a result of combined operations, one valuable enemy blockade runner and three destroyers were claimed destroyed on 27/28 December.

On 20 January 1944, Lt C.A. Enloe of VPB-103 attacked a surfaced U-boat, dropping six D/Cs which straddled the submarine. It settled by the stern and disappeared from sight a few minutes later, and Enloe and his crew were credited with a U-boat 'probably destroyed'. A few days later, however, while on anti-submarine patrol on 28 January, Enloe and his crew achieved recognized success: flying PB4Y-1 'E', they came upon U-271, a type VIIC submarine, commanded by Kapitänleutnant Kurt Barleben, travelling west of Blacksod Bay, west of Ireland, a little after 11:40 hours. U-271 was on its third war cruise, having left Brest on 12 January.

Enloe made his attack from out of the sun, and obviously achieved almost total surprise because few shots were fired at the oncoming Liberator. The front and top turrets opened up on the submarine, hitting the deck and conning tower, as six Mk.IX D/Cs hurtled down from 100ft (30m). They

US Navy U-boat Sinkings (Atlantic)

VB-107	23 Jul 43	U-598	Nr Ascension Island
VB-107/VB-129	11 Aug 43	U-604	East of Pernambuco+
VB-107	5 Nov 43	U-848	Nr Ascension Island
VB-103	10 Nov 43	U-966	Bay of Biscay*
VB-103	12 Nov 43	U-508	Bay of Biscay
VB-107	25 Nov 43	U-849	Bay of Biscay
VP-103	28 Jan 44	U-271	West of Ireland
VB-107	6 Feb 44	U-177	Off Ascension Island
VB-107	29 Sep 44	U-863	Brazil
VPB-112	27 Feb 45	U-327	Off Land's End
VPB-103	11 Mar 45	U-681	Off Land's End
VPB-103	25 Apr 45	U-1107	Bay of Biscay
VPB-63	30 Apr 45	U-1055	West of Brest

+ Scuttled by the crew

** With Wellington of 612 Squadron RAF, a PB4Y-1 of VPB-110, and Liberator 'D' of 311 Czech Squadron RAF.*

US Navy PB4Y-1 32032/C of VB-103 from Dunkeswell over Colebrook village, Devon, during an anti-submarine patrol. 32032 was shot down on 12 November 1943 while attacking U-508, which was sunk. US Navy

straddled U-271 just aft of the conning tower and the crew watched them explode as Enloe banked the PB4Y-1 around for another run with a 600lb (270kg) bomb. However, they could clearly see that despite the fact that the submarine was still on the surface, there were air bubbles all around it. U-271 soon sank beneath the waves with all fifty-one hands, leaving nothing but patches of oil and more bubbles on the surface.

Next day, Lt. H.H. Budd and crew in VP-110, flying PB4Y-1 'N', came upon another type VIIC submarine during a 'Percussion' patrol. Budd's second pilot was actually in the left-hand seat when they sighted U-592, on its fourth patrol, having sailed from St Nazaire on 10 January, and it was he who carried out the first attack on the enemy submarine. As the front and top gunners peppered the sub with machine-gun fire, he made a curve on the final run and released six Mk. II D/Cs from 100ft (30m). They fell short, however, because he had involuntarily hit the release button as he was about to press it and the drop had been made too soon. As they flew over, 'N' was hit by a shell in the waist compartment; but the gunners maintained their rate of fire and the return fire seemed to be reduced. The second pilot circled the PB4Y-1 out of range and Budd took command of the plane; but before he could attack, the U-boat submerged. Budd's crew would doubtless have been delighted to learn that they had damaged U-592, and that this effectively ended the submarine's fourth patrol. Two days later, on the return to St Nazaire, U-592 was sunk south-west of Cape Clear by three ships of the Royal Navy's 2nd Escort Group.

February 1944 saw the return, in the Bay of Biscay, of Ju 88s. On the 14th, Lt (jg) K.L. Wright and his crew, who had been instrumental in sinking a U-boat on 12 November, were patrolling above the cloud base when they were suddenly attacked by two German aircraft. The American gunners opened fire and damaged the leader's aircraft, but the PB4Y-1 received repeated hits, and one of the engines was put out of action. Wright escaped into cloud cover and set course for home, but he was forced to ditch the Liberator when a second engine cut out. Everyone except the two radiomen managed to scramble out of the aircraft as it sank, and they hauled themselves into two dinghies. A third crewman died shortly afterwards as a result of internal injuries. The eight survivors were picked up the next day by an RAF ASR launch.

D-Day saw a marked change in anti-submarine operations. Patrols were flown to bottle up the eastern approaches to the English Channel and prevent U-boats from intercepting the invasion fleet heading for the Normandy coast. Liberators patrolled the area at regular thirty-minute intervals, and the number of sorties was increased to seven a day. No enemy activity was reported until 8 June, when Lt Philip

R. Anderson encountered a Focke Wulf 200. In a brief encounter, his gunners scored hits on the Condor before it veered away. With the threat in the west having receded and the U-boat lairs on the Brittany coastline having been largely overrun, the Liberators were now switched to convoy escort duty.

Even so, the U-boat menace remained, and during October through to December 1944, VPB-103 alone made drops on sixteen disappearing radar contacts. Then New Year's Day 1945 opened with a bang when Lt Dwight D. Nott of VPB-103 sighted a small, compact quantity of bluish-white smoke above the surface of the sea. The sonobuoy pattern which Nott laid gave positive results, and four frigates were directed to the area. They confirmed the presence of a submarine and made two attacks; these unfortunately were not successful, but the incident proved that the U-boat threat was still a very real one.

On 23 February, Lt Ostoski of VPB-103 made an attack after investigating a surface disturbance. The sonobuoy log indicated that explosions were heard, but because there was no sonobuoy recorder in the aircraft, the effectiveness of the attack was doubted and the Admiralty decided when assessing the attack that there was: 'Insufficient evidence of the presence of a U-boat'.

As can be seen, claims for victories against U-boats had to be conclusive – but four days later the success of Lt O.B. Denison of VPB-112 in PB4Y-1 'H' was irrefutable when he and his crew were instrumental in helping to sink U-327 off Land's End. The type VIIC/41 submarine, commanded by Kapitänleutnant Hans Lemke, had left Kristiansund in Norway on 30 January for a patrol in the English Channel. Denison picked up the U-boat's periscope briefly before it disappeared again. Circling the area, the Liberator crew sighted an oil-slick, and they commenced baiting tactics before directing in escort vessels from a convoy nearby. The ships took over the search and sank U-327.

Victories by aircraft were harder to confirm, and this was the case on 1 March, when Lt Gaines of VPB-103 made an attack after investigating a suspicious oil-slick in the surface of the sea. Again the lack of a sonobuoy recorder left the Admiralty unconvinced. Lt Bozarth suffered from the same scepticism on the part of the Admiralty in regard to an attack on 8 March.

Just when VPB-103 thought that they would never again be in on a kill, Lt Russell N. Field on PB4Y 'N' was credited with sinking U-681, a type VIIC submarine, south of the Scilly Isles on 11 March. Field sighted the enemy submarine fully surfaced two miles in the distance: he immediately made a sharp turn to port and rapidly lost height in order to make his attack. Aboard the submarine Oberleutnant Werner Gebauer gave the order to 'dive!', but they were too late: Field's bombing run was fast, precise and deadly, and he straddled the submarine with eight depth-charges from 100ft (30m) while the decks and conning tower were still visible. As he turned back for a second run, the crew could see that U-681's bows were out of the water, and it then began to submerge. Shortly afterwards forty survivors were picked up from among oil and debris by ships of the Royal Navy. HMS *Lochfadda* signalled the American Liberator: 'Congratulations on a first-class knockout punch. Delighted to have been able to bring back the relics.' This time the Admiralty handed down an 'A' assessment.

VPB-103's final kill came on 25 April 1945 when Lt Dwight D. Nott, in PB4Y-1 'K', finally achieved the victory that had eluded him. He attacked a schnorkeling submarine, which turned out to be U-1107, a type VIIC/41 submarine commanded by Oberleutnant Fritz Parduhn, travelling south-west of the Brest Peninsula. U-1107 had left Kristiansund, Norway, for the Channel approaches on 31 March. Nott attacked, and the schnorkel was seen to 'jump out of the water' after the explosion, and a large oil-slick appeared; later a corpse was seen floating in the sea. Excellent photographic coverage won from the Admiralty a 'probably sunk' assessment. Nott was awarded the DFC, while the rest of his ten-man crew each received the Air Medal.

For Navy personnel, a tour of duty on a combat zone did not earn rotation to duty in the USA, and there was no quota of missions. Thus a crew could spend eight months to a year flying missions almost daily, many of them as long as ten or even sixteen hours at a stretch, and on return to the US they might be assigned to a new aircraft and have to return to combat to complete another tour. Not everyone returned.

USN PB4Y-1s at Dunkeswell, Devon. Between August 1943 and 30 May 1945 the US Navy flew 6,464 operational sorties, totalling 62,247 hours, and covering approximately 10,581,990 miles (17,026,422km). USN

Joe Kennedy Jr USN

Those who lived in the vicinity of Saxmundham in Suffolk in August 1944 could not have known that Joseph P. Kennedy Jr, son of the former United States' Ambassador to Britain, had in fact just given his life in a secret mission called Project *Anvil*, because it was not until 24 October 1945 that the full story was released to the press and radio.

Joe Kennedy Jr had, by the summer of 1944, completed a tour of duty with VPB-110 at Dunkeswell in Devon, without gaining the combat medal he so badly desired. He reasoned that D-Day would be in either June or July and he did not intend missing out on the action, so he volunteered for another tour of duty. But D-Day came and went and Lt Kennedy had still not claimed an enemy craft. He became less cautious and even more determined in his pursuit of a submarine or E-boat. On 1 July 1944 Kennedy was promoted, and offered the post of Assistant Naval Attaché at the US embassy in London; but he refused because he was as determined as ever to emulate his brother John (later to become President of the United States) who was also serving in the Navy, as a commander of an MTB in the Pacific.

Joe's chance came when Commander Smith, his CO at Dunkeswell, asked for volunteers to fly radio-controlled PB4Y-1s packed with high explosive, against German targets. The US Navy operation in England was called *Anvil*, and the Army Air Force was already carrying out a similar programme at Fersfield in Suffolk called Project *Aphrodite*. Joe had no hesitation in putting his name forward for *Anvil* and got his wish, despite attempts to talk him out of it. Early in June 1944 the first *Anvil* Liberator was modified as a 'drone' at the Naval Air Materiel Center in Philadelphia, a control system and an arming panel being installed; meanwhile two Lockheed PV-1 Venturas were modified as 'mother' aircraft to the Liberator. The idea was that the Liberator would be packed with twelve crates of Torpex – twelve times the load of a V1 – and to start with would be flown by a two-man crew; these, however, would bale out over England, and the rest of the flight would be taken over by the 'mother' aircraft whose operators would guide the drone to its target by remote control. The method chosen included a television camera installed in the nose of the drone and a receiver set in the controlling aircraft. This enabled the controllers to view the approach of the target as if they were in the nose of the drone itself. Controlling the drone and arming the explosives once the two-man crew had bailed out were effected by means of radio signals from the 'mother' aircraft.

Joe Kennedy and his co-pilot, 'Bud' Willy, were scheduled to fly the first *Anvil* mission on 11 August, but it was postponed until the following day because of the fog. The target was a secret weapon site at Mimoyecques in France, and Kennedy took off accompanied by the two Venturas, two photo-reconnaissance Mosquitos and an escort of sixteen Mustangs of the 8th Air Force. The formation left Fersfield and continued at 2,000ft (610m) to Framlingham where they were to change course for Beccles. Altogether, the PB4Y-1 was crammed with 21,170lb (9,603kg) of Torpex in 374 crates stowed throughout the aircraft. Kennedy would arm the bomb-load before he and Willey left through the nosewheel doors. The drone would be remotely armed for detonation on impact only after it had left the English coast. At 18:15 hours, just before Framlingham was reached, Kennedy radioed that he was ready for the first radio control check. This was carried out successfully, and the second stage of the mission was proceeding satisfactorily, when suddenly the drone was ripped apart by two explosions over Saxmundham at 1,500ft (460m). An enquiry subsequently eliminated sabotage, and no blame was attached to the Torpex. It would seem that there was overheating in the electrical circuitry of the arming panel aboard the Liberator, and later tests indicated weaknesses in the hastily assembled and installed remote arming and fusing arrangements.

Kennedy and Willy were both decorated, and Joe's father, Joseph S. Kennedy Sr, received the Navy Cross (a Medal of Honor was requested but not approved for Joe Jr) on his son's behalf. A month later, on 3 September 1944, Navy Lt Richard Spaulding took off without a co-pilot in a similar Torpex-loaded PB4Y. After Spaulding baled out, the drone Liberator was guided into a coalyard in Heligoland. Spaulding was awarded the Navy Cross. Unfortunately, while returning to the States, his aircraft flew into a mountain on take-off at Marrakesh and he was killed with his crew.

Joe P. Kennedy Jr. USN via Flt Lt Tony Fairbairn

CHAPTER NINE

The Carpetbagger Project

In the summer of 1943 the major USAAF effort to supply the Resistance movements and secret armies in Europe on behalf of SOE (Special Operations Executive) and OSS (Office of Strategic Services) began under the codename 'Carpetbagger'. Initially its personnel were drawn from the 4th and 22nd Squadrons of the 479th Anti-Submarine Group, disbanded in August 1943. They were selected because of their experience in long navigational patrols at night: for almost three months, operating from Dunkeswell in Devon, these two squadrons, flying B-24Ds, had carried out anti-submarine sweeps over the Bay of Biscay, flying lone patrols of up to twelve hours' duration looking for German U-boats. In October the air and ground echelons of both the 4th and 22nd Arons left for Alconbury in Huntingdonshire, where they shared the base with the 482nd (Pathfinder) Group.

The two anti-submarine squadrons were not going to be pathfinders, though: instead, their B-24Ds were painted black, and on 24 October the CO, Lt Col Clifford J. Heflin, learned why. Their job now was to supply the resistance groups operating in occupied Europe with vast supplies of small arms, light automatic weapons, munitions, explosives, and demolition and incendiary equipment. Also, they were to drop secret agents, or 'Joes', and 'Jedburgh' teams: these consisting of three members, usually an Englishman, a Frenchman and an American, and they were to be dropped into France just prior to and after the Allied invasion of Normandy in order to provide a general staff for the local resistance wherever they landed. They also organized sabotage missions and the disruption of enemy supplies, and harried the retreat of enemy troops. 'Jedburgh' teams usually remained in the field until they were overrun by the advancing Allied forces.

At first, operations were on a limited scale because British experience had shown that considerable time would be needed to train crews for clandestine operations. Each crew-member had to fly two combat missions with the RAF squadrons at Tempsford. The first to arrive was a party led by Lt Col Robert W. Fish, and they spent two months at the top secret Bedfordshire airfield. The American officers and crews found the training routine very demanding. Converting to special duty operations at night after flying long-range bomber sorties in daylight was hard. In order to make accurate drops, pilots had to

Col C.J. Heflin *(right)*, CO of the Carpetbaggers, with Lt Col Robert Fish, deputy CO.

get down to within 400–600ft (120–180m) of the ground, and reduce their flying speed to 130mph (209km/h) or less. The low speed reduced the chances of damage to parachutes, as the shock is much less at a slower speed. The pilots, navigators and bombardiers each made two operational flights with RAF crews in the Halifax.

Meanwhile, aboard the Liberators, ball turrets had to be removed and replaced with cargo hatches, nicknamed 'Joe-holes' because the secret agents or 'Joes' would be dropped through these. A static line was installed for them, and to facilitate the bale-outs, the hole had a metal shroud inside the opening. If the Liberator did not have a ball turret, a hole was made there. Plywood was used to cover the floors, and black-out curtains graced the waist windows and navigator's compartment, while blister side windows had to be installed to give the pilots a better all-round view. Later models had their nose turrets removed, and a 'greenhouse' fashioned instead to allow the bombardier a good view of the drop zone and to enable him to carry out pilotage for the navigator. Suppressors or flame dampers were fitted to the engine exhausts to stifle the tell-tale blue exhaust flames. Machine guns located on both sides of the waist were removed, leaving only the top and rear turrets for protection. In flight the entire aircraft would be blacked out except for a small light in the navigator's compartment. Oxygen equipment was not needed at low level, and so was removed.

A variety of special navigational equipment and radar aids were installed to increase the accuracy of a drop. During the non-moon period, flights at night would be made with the use of an absolute radio altimeter, and with 'Rebecca', a British radar directional, air-to-ground device which was originally fitted to aircraft in the RAF Special Duties squadrons. 'Rebecca' recorded impulses or 'blips' on a grid and directed the navigator to the ground operator. By varying the intensity or frequency of the blip, the ground operator (whose set was known as 'Eureka O'), could transmit a signal letter to the aircraft. These signals could be activated from up to 70 miles (113km) away to enable the aircraft crew to pinpoint its drop zone.

The air echelon of the 22nd Aron and the ground echelon of the 4th Aron were used to form two new squadrons, the 36th and 406th Bomb Squadrons, which would not be officially activated until 4 December. They were assigned to the 1st Bomb Division, which was equipped with B-17s! While the Liberators were made ready for night operations it was decided that for the next operational moon period (December), the squadrons would again operate from Tempsford but would use their own aircraft.

On 14 December, Lt Col Heflin relinquished command of the 406th to Capt Robert Boone, and was assigned to the parent 482nd Group as air executive, Special Project. Maj Fish became operations officer, and command of the 36th Squadron passed to Capt Rodman St Clair, who since 5 December had been in charge of the latest group of American trainees seconded to Tempsford. At Alconbury the flight was becoming overcrowded with Carpetbagger aircraft trying to operate alongside the Pathfinder aircraft of the 482nd, and vice-versa. Meanwhile, a new base at Harrington, just west of Kettering and only 35 miles (56km) from the packing and storage depot at Holme in Huntingdonshire, was prepared

Personnel of the 814th Bomb Squadron, 482nd PFF Group, at Alconbury, England, where the former anti-submarine squadrons which formed the Carpetbaggers were based until the move to Harrington. The 482nd Group groundcrews originally came from the 479th Anti-Submarine Group. The late Edgar Townsend

for the Carpetbaggers. Until then the 406th Squadron would have to operate from RAF Watton in Norfolk, while seven crews and six Liberators were left behind to continue operations with the 36th Squadron. Skeleton ground sections and some combat crew also remained behind at Alconbury. However, no billets could be found for the Carpetbaggers contingent so they had to live mainly in tents, and the grass runways with pierced steel planking (PSP) proved totally unsuitable. On 27 February the Carpetbaggers were assigned to Headquarters, 328th Service Group.

The first two missions in March 1944 resulted in the loss of three crews in the 36th Squadron. First, on the night of 2/3 March 1944, Lt Frank C. McDonald and crew failed to return: their Liberator was hit at low altitude by flak guns mounted on railway wagons, and crashed at Fienvillers. They were too low to bale out, so McDonald decided to ride the aircraft down. One man was killed, but the rest survived; Lt Fred C. Kelly, the co-pilot, was taken in by the French Resistance, and eventually crossed France to Spain, finally returning to England on 1 June. Then on 3/4 March, Capt Gerald S. Wagstad's Liberator is believed to have gone down in the Channel off the coast of France; and Lt Wade A. Carpenter crashed at Humbercourt after being hit by flak at low altitude. All nine crew survived, but Lt William D. Rees, bombardier, was trapped under the wreckage and later had to have both legs amputated, and he died from shock. At the end of March the Carpetbaggers left Alconbury for Harrington, where they were joined by the remaining sections and crews from Watton.

The *Sonnie* Project

Also during March a handful of Carpetbagger Liberators were detached to Leuchars, Scotland, to begin *Sonnie* operations to Bromma Airport in Stockholm, to bring back thousands of Norwegians to Britain. Since early 1944 about 2,000 Norwegians – by 1945 the figure would reach 15,500 – were undergoing military training in Sweden, partly under the direction of Swedish officers. The Norwegian government-in-exile wanted to airlift this 'pocket army' to England and thence to Canada for further training. Norwegian-born Col Bernt Balchen, the famous polar pilot was put in charge of the project, codenamed *Sonnie*. To maintain Sweden's neutrality, all flights were put on a civilian footing and the *Sonnie* project began with

Modified Carpetbagger Liberator with guns fitted with flame dampers highly visible. Joe Staelens Coll

Norwegian-born Col Bernt Balchen was the leader chosen for the task – codenamed the Sonnie **project – of airlifting the Norwegian 'pocket army' to England and thence to the Norwegian base near Toronto, Canada, for further training. Balchen had piloted Admiral Richard E. Byrd over the South Pole in 1929 and had made several flights over the North Pole and Antarctica during the early 1930s. In 1931 Balchen became a naturalized American subject. Besides his experience gained on polar flights, Balchen knew almost every inch of the mountainous Norwegian terrain, having been a pre-war operations manager and President of Norwegian Airlines.** (DNL) Nat. Geo.

(Below) **Carpetbagger Liberator dropping a supply canister.** Seb Corrière

five Liberators, two crews from Air Transport Command, one from the 93rd Bomb Group, and two from the 389th. Gradually the force was enlarged to include five C-87s and eleven flight crews. All the Liberators were unarmed and carried no military markings. The Swedish Air Ministry cooperated and informed Americans of any German fighter activity along its borders. As an additional precaution, any German shipping movements out of Norwegian ports were radioed by the Norwegian Resistance to Stockholm.

Col Balchen flew the first three *Sonnie* missions himself, including the first on 31 March. Allied intelligence estimated that about 250 Luftwaffe night fighters were based in southern Norway, but the B-24 crews made long detours northwards before crossing Norwegian territory into Sweden. Then in April 1944, flights really got going. First passengers were the Norwegian trainees, sixty to seventy of whom were crammed into the Liberators on each trip. The Luftwaffe was alerted to Balchen's flights, and sent up numerous patrols in an effort to shoot down the Liberators. However, during the period from March to December 1944, 110 round trips were made and not one Liberator was lost to enemy action. The *Sonnie* Project was so successful that ultimately 3,016 passengers were evacuated, including 1,847 Norwegian trainees and 965 American internees. The remainder included French, Soviet and Dutch government officials, and on one occasion, the entire personnel of the Norwegian government-in-exile were flown to Sweden.

Operations from Harrington

On 4 April, HQ 8th Air Force Composite Command officially assigned the 36th and 406th Squadrons to the 801st Bomb Group (H). The first mission flown from Harrington took place on the night of 5/6 April, when the 801st dispatched seventeen Liberators to occupied Europe. Lt William W. Nicoll and his seven-man crew in the 406th Squadron, who were flying their first mission, failed to return from a sortie to drop a 'Joe' when they were shot down by flak just after crossing the coast of France. a burst shot away the B-24s tail, killing Ralph Kittrell, the rear gunner; then almost immediately the nose took a direct hit and killed William G. Harris, navigator. By now the Liberator was enveloped in a fiery inferno,

Relaxed scene at Harrington. Maj Bestow 'Rudy' Rudolph is at centre front *(kneeling)*; Lt Col Boone, 406th Squadron CO, is far right, middle row. Rudolph and Boon were just two of the ex-anti-submarine group pilots in the Carpetbaggers. Bestow Rudolph

and down to only 300ft (90m); altogether, five of the crew were killed outright but Joe Porter, the waist gunner and dispatcher, and the co-pilot both escaped and they were eventually returned to England. The 'Joe' was tortured and killed by the Gestapo three days later. Had they been captured alive, the American Liberator crews would have been treated as prisoners of war. Agents, however, were not covered by the Geneva Convention.

The next Carpetbagger mission took place on 10/11 April, when twenty-three Liberators were dispatched. Then on 11/12 April, twelve B-24s flew sorties over Europe. Both missions were flown without loss. On 23 April Lt Col Heflin, with Lt Col Gable of OSS, flew in a B-24 to Algiers; their purpose was to show the Algiers Squadron, then being set up for Carpetbagger missions in southern Europe, a modified B-24, and also to discuss ways of coordinating operations from OSS London and Algiers. During Heflin's absence, the Carpetbaggers dispatched twenty-three Liberator sorties without loss. Then on the night of 27/28 April, twenty-one B-24s were dispatched from Harrington.

1st Lt George W. Ambrose and his crew in the 36th Bomb Squadron in *The Worry Bird* failed to return from a sortie to the drop zone at 'Lackey 3a' near the French village of St Cyr de Valorges near Lyon, after they hit a hillside during the Liberator's third descending circle. The French reception committee, which was already gathering up the load dropped by another Liberator, saw the aircraft crash just 500 metres away from them. Five of the crew, including, Ambrose, were killed, but Sgt George Henderson, tail gunner, and Staff Sgt James J. Heddleston, radio operator, survived because they were catapulted out of the aircraft on impact; and a few minutes before, the dispatcher had fallen out of the 'Joe' hole while pushing out supplies. Henderson and Heddleston successfully evaded, and late in July they returned to the Carpetbaggers after being picked up by a Hudson of 161 Squadron RAF from Tempsford.

On the night of 5/6 May, twenty-one B-24s were dispatched. Lt Murray I. Simon's Liberator in the 406th Squadron failed to return from a mission to France, a victim of flak fired from guns mounted on a troop train, 12½ miles (20km) north of Cheney le Châtel. The black bomber was blasted with 20mm and 40mm flak which knocked out the rudder control, interphone and electrical systems. The main fuel tank was hit, and a flak shell exploded in the nose section between the navigator's and the bombardier's stations, knocking out all the bomb levers. Flak also punctured the port and starboard wing auxiliary tanks, and fires began to engulf the entire wing. Simon smelled petrol fumes in the cockpit, and ordered the crew to bale out. Eight of them, including Simon himself, Lt John A. Reitmeier, navigator, and Lt John Mead, bombardier, evaded; Mead stayed on to fight alongside the Resistance. The rest of the crew were captured. On 5 September, Mead and Reitmeier presented themselves at the advance headquarters of the 12th Air Force, twenty miles to the east of Lyon.

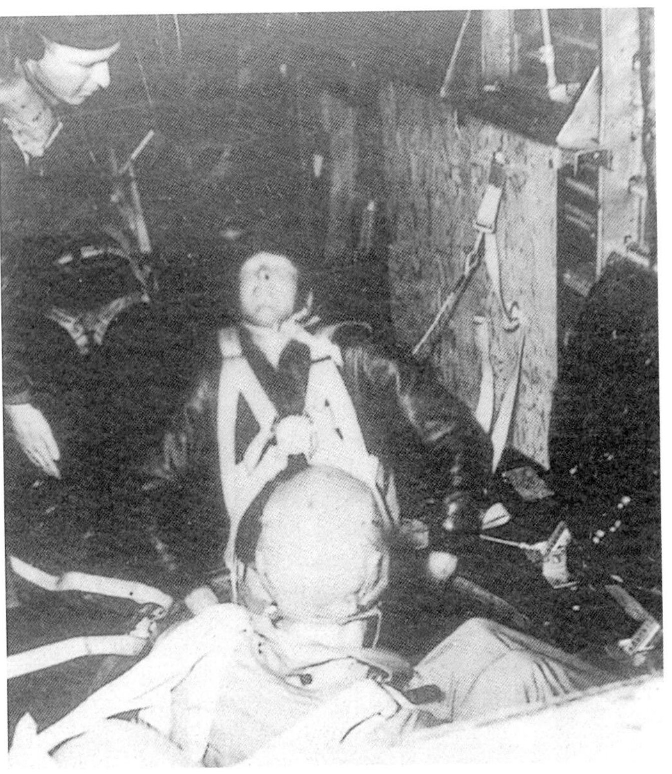

A secret agent exits from a Carpetbagger Liberator via the 'Joe-hole'.
Michael L. Gibson

On the night of 6 May, Lt George Pipkin in the 406th Bomb Squadron failed to return from a mission to Denmark: about forty-five minutes after leaving the target, a single anti-aircraft gun fired five shell bursts and put their No. 3 engine on fire; the flames spread rapidly to the fuel tanks, then No. 4 engine caught fire. Two men, namely Floyd N. Holmes, bombardier, and Jack C. Wengert, radio operator, made it back to England.

Crews who fell to the German guns were normally protected by the Geneva Convention, but agents who parachuted into occupied Europe were only too aware of the fate that awaited them if they fell into the clutches of the Gestapo. For instance, on 8 May the Carpetbaggers dropped a Frenchman, OSS agent M. Jean Remy, into his homeland, south of the city of Troyes. After several months of espionage activities he was captured, tortured unmercifully, and dragged in front of a firing squad. At the last minute the German officer stopped the execution and threw Remy back into jail. The Frenchman tried suicide, unsuccessfully, very proud of the fact that he had not given his captors any information. Remy finally managed to escape in time to help welcome Patton on 1 September 1944 when he liberated Nancy.

On the night of 28/29 May, Lt Henry W. Wolcott III and his eight-man crew in *Charlie* in the 858th Squadron, failed to return from a mission to 'Osric 53' in Belgium when they were shot down by a Bf 110 night-fighter near Enghien. By 11 September 1944, all members of the crew were back at Harrington, with the exception of Sgt Richard G. Hawkins, the tail gunner, who was found dead on the ground at Aaigem, his parachute unopened. The night following, 29/30 May, Lt Ernest B. Fitzpatrick and crew in the 406th Squadron failed to return from a mission to 'Osric 14', also in Belgium. 'Osric 14' had been the subject of a successful visit by the Carpetbaggers the previous night, and as a result, the Germans had occupied the ground and all adjacent areas; mobile flak units had been positioned in the vicinity, and night-fighters alerted.

Unfortunately for Fitzpatrick and his crew, the Belgian Underground had not been able to transmit this information to London, and so all unknowingly, they were flying into a German ambush. An hour after midnight Lt James S. Sherwood, navigator, identified the target below. There were no lights to indicate the presence of a reception committee: as the Liberator circled, all hell was suddenly let loose from a flak battery on the ground, and the aircraft was hit. As it veered away, a Ju 88, waiting in the wings, came in for the kill, raking the bomber with 20mm cannon fire. The Liberator was doomed. Everyone cleared the aircraft before it crashed, 25 miles (40km) from Landen. Fitzpatrick and five of his crew evaded, though one was captured later during a Gestapo raid on Belgian White Army safe houses.

In the run-up to D-Day more personnel had to be dropped, and so the Carpetbaggers received another two squadrons. The 850th Bomb Squadron, equipped with B-24H Liberators and commanded by Maj Jack M. Dickerson, flew in direct from the States, although it had been earmarked to join the 490th Bomb Group in the 3rd Bomb Division. The 788th Squadron arrived by courtesy of the 467th Bomb Group, 2nd Bomb Division. Maj Leonard M. 'Nate' McManus was named the 788th Squadron commanding officer. By the end of May 1944, approximately forty Liberators were available for Carpetbagger Missions.

In June 1944, the 'S' phone and the 'Homing S-Phone' were first introduced on Carpetbagger aircraft. The latter device, which had been developed by the US Navy, used a radio compass in the aircraft and permitted the navigator to direct the aircraft towards the ground operator, as on a radio beam. All Carpetbagger aircraft were fitted with a 'Gee' box, a British-developed radar navigational aid which picked up signals from ground stations in England. A 'Master' station and two 'slave' stations sent out combinations of signals which were picked up and recorded on a grid, and this indicated the aircraft's position. The Germans had some success in jamming 'Gee' signals once crews reached the continental coast.

On the night of 1/2 June, twenty-two B-24s were dispatched; the following night, eighteen were sent out; and on the night of 3/4 June, twenty-three, resulting in seventeen successful sorties, the largest number of successes so far achieved in one night. No losses were incurred during these three nights of operations. Next, on the night of 5/6 June, British and American missions were mounted in support of the Allied landings in Normandy, and groups of SAS troops were dropped near Dijon and south of Châteauroux.

On the night of 12 June, Col Fish took off for a mission to 'Hugh 1' in France. In addition to the cargo of twelve containers and eight packages, he had aboard a 'Jedburgh' team of two officers and a sergeant, all of them paratroopers, who were to be dropped near the Château Rouge for the purpose of organizing harassing units. Fish brought the Liberator in quite low over the target, and the containers, packages and 'Joes' were dropped, in that order. Unfortunately the sergeant was killed when his parachute failed to open, and one of his officers broke both his legs. Lt Burton OIC of the harassing unit, landed safely but discovered he was three hundred yards from where he should nave landed. Despite the inauspicious start to the mission, the rest went well, and in six months of hard fighting the team blew up bridges and railway tracks and generally disrupted enemy transportation and communications

On the night of 18/19 June, Lt John R. McNeil of the 850th Squadron flew too low over the target at 'Historian 14' and hit a tree before dropping the containers he was carrying. All eight crew were killed. This was the squadron's first operational loss. A few nights later, on 27/28 June, another Liberator piloted by Lt William E. Heunekens, on a training flight, was lost east of Bedford when it was shot down by a German night-fighter. Robert L. Sanders, bombardier, and Robert Callahan, navigator, survived when they came down together using one parachute. The only other crew-member to escape from the burning aircraft was the badly burned radio operator, Randall G. Sadler. Callahan was later awarded the Silver Star for his bravery.

The month of June 1944 saw the 801st breaking all records, flying 424 sorties, of which 347 were successful. Seven of these were to Belgium, but the remainder were all flown to France. It was a far cry from January when, during the Carpetbaggers' first month of operations, only eighteen sorties were flown. During July 1944 the Carpetbaggers flew a total of 397 sorties, dropping thousands of containers, packages and bundles of leaflets, and sixty-two 'Joes'.

On the night of 4/5 July, thirty-six Liberators were dispatched to France: three aircraft failed to return, while a fourth ship crashed on landing, the highest losses sustained by a group in a single night. One B-24, piloted by Lt John C. Broten and shot down near Orleans by a German night-fighter after a successful drop in the area, belonged to the 36th Squadron, while the other two piloted by Lts John J. Meade and Charles R. Kline, came from the 850th Squadron.

A fourth Liberator, piloted by Lt Oliver C. Carscaddon, also from the 850th Squadron, was attacked by three Ju 88s, 15 miles (24km) inside the French coast while flying at 8,000ft (2,500m). The co-pilot, Otis W. Murphy, baled out and was hit in his leg from a 20mm shell, as the Ju 88 continued to fire at him on the ground. Murphy managed to drag himself to safety, and was picked up by the French Underground with whom he waited in hiding until liberation. The German fighters had knocked out the Liberator's No. 2 engine and it caught fire. The crew fended off constant fighter attacks, and Carscaddon took the Liberator down to tree-top height and headed for the French coast amid machine-gun fire and the occasional burst of flak. He nursed the B-24 across the Channel and crossed the coast at Shoreham before putting down at RAF Ford, where he landed without brakes and the bomb-doors open: the Liberator hurtled down the runway, hit a ditch and finally came to rest in a field with a smashed nose and damaged right undercarriage. Another B-24 was lost that month, on 18/19 July when Lt David A. Michelson failed to return from a sortie to target 'Dick 89' in France.

The 'Ball Project'

On 17 July 1944, Carpetbagger Balchen began the 'Ball Project' (so named because of the removal of the ball turret from the B-24), with the first of many supply drops in daylight to the Norwegian Underground, which was on the point of collapse. Into the bomb-bays went twelve 350lb (160kg) containers packed full of Sten guns, ammunition, explosives and sundry supplies. Packages of food and clothing were stowed in the waist section. Balchen and his crew flew across the North Sea at minimum altitude and crossed the Norwegian coastline at approximately 6,000ft (1,830m). They had to make their final run in at

1,000ft (305m) and drop the supplies within an area of 100yd of fires lit by the Norwegians.

Eventually, six Liberators and seven veteran crews were detached for Norwegian operations. During the final phase of the 'Ball Project', Lt Keith Allen and Lt Schreiner dropped two Allied secret agents equipped with radio transmitters close to Altenfjord in Norway so that they could radio back badly needed information about the German battleship *Tirpitz* which was anchored there. The Liberator had to be specially modified to permit installation of additional fuel tanks in the bomb-bay for the 2,600-mile (4,180km) round trip. The flight from Britain to the drop zone and back again took some 16½ hours, and was probably the longest combat mission ever flown in Europe. The two agents were dropped safely, and within twenty-four hours had made contact with England. (Allen was killed on 21 September 1944 on another spy-dropping mission to Norway, when his Liberator crashed in Russia.)

In September 1944 when the 'Ball Project' was finally terminated, the task of supplying the Norwegian Underground reverted to the 8th Air Force and later the RAF. The six Liberators of the 'Ball Project' dropped a total of 120 tons of cargo and OSS personnel, mostly in southern and central Norway during their sixty-seven missions. Forty-one of these were successful, but the Luftwaffe made an appearance on fifteen of them, and although the fighters caused no immediate damage, bad weather and other operational hazards resulted in the loss of two Liberators (including Allen's) and twelve men killed. Late in November 1944, Balchen's American Air Transport Service moved to the former Liberator bomber base at Metfield in Suffolk.

The 492nd Bomb Group is Re-activated

On 5 August, the 801st Bomb Group were re-designated the 492nd Bomb Group, taking this appellation from the 2nd Bomb Division Group of the same name. The original 492nd had been withdrawn from combat after losing a staggering fifty-one B-24s missing in action in just sixty-four missions in less than four months. The Carpetbagger also took the former group's squadron numbers, and so the 36th became the 856th, the 850th became the 857th, the 406th was now the 858th, and the 788th became the 859th. August proved a very busy month for the Carpetbaggers, which flew a record total of 442 missions, some 342 of these being successfully completed. The Carpetbaggers dropped over 700 tons of supplies to Resistance groups, and 227 agents were ferried across the Channel at a cost of two Liberators.

On the night of 6/7 August, thirty-six Liberators were dispatched from Harrington. Unfortunately Lt Robert C. McLaughlin and his crew, who were flying their thirty-third mission, failed to return from a sortie to Belgium; in fact McLaughlin and six crew evaded, and were finally liberated by units of the FFI and White Army; two were later arrested by the Germans. On 8 August, a B-24 flown by Capt William L. Bales returned to Harrington after a sortie to Belgium with over 1,000 flak holes in the fuselage, most of which were caused by anti-aircraft guns while flying at 7,500ft (2,285m), and by several Ju 88 night-fighters. In mid-August the Carpetbaggers delivered a group of nineteen men known as 'Lindsey' to France; initially these men were to seize and hold a hydro-electric plant at La Truyère. However, only one Liberator got over the target on 16/17 August, and just five men were dropped. The next night was better, and three Liberators reached the target, and fifteen men were dropped at 02:10 hours on the morning of 18 August at Sauvat. 'Lindsey' destroyed the hydro-electric plant, and after many clashes with the Germans, returned to Harrington in a Dakota on 21 September.

From 19 to 24 August bad weather prevented missions from being flown. The news on 23 August was that Paris had been liberated by the French Forces of the Interior, and this success owed much to the support missions flown by the Carpetbaggers and other clandestine units over the preceding eight months. Then on 25 August, Harrington bade farewell to Col Clifford J. Heflin, who left for a new appointment at the B-29 training facility at Wendover Field, Utah. His new role would involve training the aircrews and the support personnel who would ultimately drop the atomic bombs on Japan. His popular deputy, Lt Col Robert W. Fish, assumed command of the Carpetbaggers.

Carpetbagger operations in September got off to a bad start, when on the night of 1/2 September, forty-four Liberators were dispatched, but thirteen were forced to abort. Results were better on the night of 3/4 September when ten Liberators transported the fifty-seven members of Operation Group 'Christopher', Jedburgh team 'Desmond', and all supplies to Yonne, in France, so that 'Christopher' could slow down and harass enemy columns moving from the south-west and the Bordeaux area towards Poitiers and Châteauroux. Space had to be found for the group's twenty-four M-1 rifles, four Bren guns, fifty-six rucksacks, light machine gun, spares and twenty chests of ammunition for the gun, 500 prepared charges, 170 grenades, fifty-six gas masks, eleven boxes of ammunition, a box of Gammon grenades, four radios, twenty cans of gas, two Very pistols and fourteen TSMG pouches, filled. Of the 120 containers dropped, only six were damaged, and all four W/T sets were recovered in working condition.

On 4/5 September, forty Liberators and four C-47s were dispatched, and a record thirty-nine successful sorties resulted. The following night, 5/6 September, forty-six B-24s were dispatched, and on the night of 7/8 September forty sorties were flown. although one Liberator was lost. On 14 September, the Carpetbagger outfit dispatched its Liberators in the hours of daylight to France. They dropped their loads successfully and returned to base at 14:30 hours. On the night of the 16/17th, thirty-two Liberators and a C-47 were dispatched to France. One B-24 in the 858th Squadron, flown by Lt James M. McLaughlin and crew, who were on their thirty-fifth and final mission, failed to return from their sortie when they were brought down by an American anti-aircraft battalion which had moved into the area that very morning. Four men perished in the crash, but McLaughlin baled out and was picked up by the US 79th Infantry Division.

With most of France overrun, the Allied chiefs of staff thought that relatively few Carpetbagger missions would be needed, and so the aircraft were used to fly fuel and supplies to the troops in France. Droppable tanks were installed in and over the bomb-bays and back where the 'Joe-holes' were, and these were filled full of avi-octane gasoline; even the Liberators' wing tanks were used. The fumes were very explosive, and crews believed it was more hazardous than flying Carpetbagger missions over the continent. However, no Carpetbagger Liberators were lost on trucking missions, which finished on 30 September. Next day the Carpetbaggers were formerly relieved from

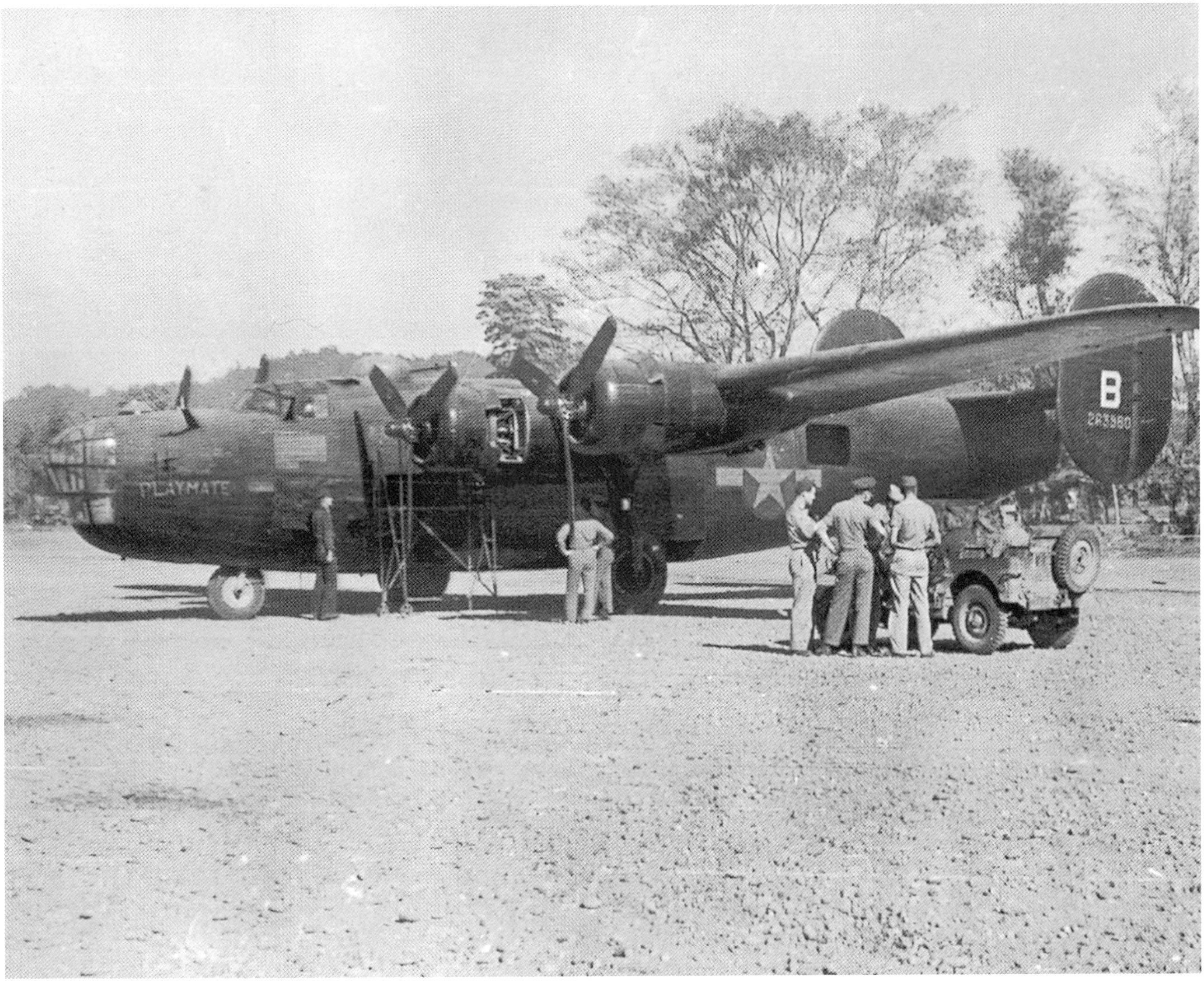

On 29 November 1944, Major Bestow 'Rudy' Rudolph of the 858th Bomb Squadron flew B-24 Liberator *Playmate* **to New Delhi, India, and to China with 856th Squadron crew and OSS personnel whose brief it was to investigate the possibilities, and discuss with local OSS officials the feasibility of conducting Carpetbagger operations in the CBI (China-Burma-India) theatre.** *Playmate* **was selected for the operation because it was one of the oldest Liberators in the group, having flown eighty-nine Carpetbagger missions, and could therefore demonstrate the modifications and general appearance of a typical Carpetbagger aircraft. This** *Playmate* **was actually the second to bear the name, the first having been shot up and having crashlanded at Land's End following an anti-submarine patrol by another crew in 1943;** *Playmate* **no. 2 is seen here being repaired at Myitkyina, Burma.** Bestow Rudolph

NORSO Group commandos prepare to board a Carpetbagger Liberator to be parachuted into occupied Europe. via Seb Corriere

the 8th Air Force Fighter Command. At Harrington, only the 856th Squadron was officially retained for Carpetbagger operations. So it seemed that the Carpetbaggers' clandestine war was largely at end.

On 17 December Col Hudson H. Upham took command of the Carpetbaggers; he had spent some years at the military academy at West Point and therefore had no prior combat experience. Two days earlier, the 859th Squadron was ordered to Brindisi, Italy, to form the second of two squadrons in the 2641 Special Group which carried out Carpetbagger-type operations in support of OSS over northern Italy, Greece and Yugoslavia. Meanwhile the 857th and 858th Squadrons were also detached, to fly high-altitude, night bombing missions with 100 Group RAF Bomber Command. This transition was difficult, because the Liberators were unsuitable for night bombing, having been extensively modified for Carpetbagger work. Enough H_2X radar-equipped aircraft were needed to equip one squadron, so in the end, B-24s had been acquired from bomb groups such as the 486th Bomb Group at Sudbury, Suffolk, which had been re-equipped with B-17s in July 1944. Missions began on 24 December 1944, when eighteen black B-24s were dispatched, in daylight, to coastal defences around Bordeaux. They returned to the area on the night of 28/29 December when seven B-24s from a force of sixteen dispatched, successfully bombed De La Colibre using H_2X. Another notable success was achieved on the night of 4/5 January 1945 when ten B-24s, dispatched by the 492nd Bomb Group, and again using H_2X, successfully bombed the Coubre coastal battery near Bordeaux.

On 20 February 1945, following a period of training with 100 Group, RAF Bomber Command, night bombing missions were resumed with a raid on Neustadt. The RAF issued the orders for each raid, because they were flown as a diversion for the actual raids undertaken by the main force in Bomber Command. Of six missions flown that month, two Liberators were left on the Continent and two battle-damaged B-24s force-landed in England. American night bombing had become a resounding failure. On average, only about a dozen H_2X-equipped B-24s were dispatched at night from Harrington. In March 1945, when one B-24 was lost, only seven missions were flown before the American's participation came to an abrupt end on the 15th: this was because of an order to resume Carpetbagger operations.

On 6 March 1945, Gen Jimmy Doolittle instructed that the 857th Bomb Squadron would be required for operation of the scouting-force, and the weather and bomber relay flight of the 1st Air Division. The squadron was disbanded and most of its crews were dispersed to the 856th Squadron, now all that remained of the Carpetbaggers. Four C-47s were detached for use during the evacuation of Allied PoWs and escaped internees from Switzerland from a central assembly point near Annecy. Meanwhile, the handful of Carpetbagger missions continued to Norway, Denmark and Holland. Col Upham was assigned to the 306th Bomb Group at Thurleigh shortly thereafter, and Col Jack Dickerson assumed command of the new operations.

On 19 March the 492nd flew the first of fifty-four successful operations from Dijon into Germany on behalf of OSS. For the most part, missions involved dropping intelligence agents equipped with wireless transmitters into key locations in Germany from where they could transmit vital information to the Allies. Each aircraft that arrived from Harrington to carry out missions from Dijon brought its own crew chief.

When the final Carpetbagger mission was flown on 16 April 1945, a total of eighty-two agents had been parachuted into Germany by aircraft of the Dijon Mission, principally Liberators. It brought to an end an illustrious career by the Carpetbaggers. Twenty-six aircraft had been destroyed and 208 men had lost their lives in missions of mercy to aid Belgians, Danes and Dutch men and women, French and Norwegians, and to help free their countries from Nazi domination. By June 1945 the last of the Carpetbaggers had departed the shores of England.

Carpetbagger Liberators temporarily suspend clandestine missions for a bombing mission to Duisberg, in March 1945. Art Carnot

CHAPTER TEN

Wings of Gold

US Navy Liberators in the Pacific

Early in the war the US Navy had recognized the need for a very long-range patrol aircraft and the Liberator was the answer, because its 3,000-mile (4,830km) range was just what the Navy needed to extend *its* range beyond that of the amphibious aircraft then in service. However, the Army Air Corps had no intention of letting the Navy muscle in on their land-based bomber offensive, and aircraft for anti-submarine operations were operated by the USAAF. Nevertheless, early in 1942 the Navy and Army chiefs reached a compromise: the AAF wanted a fourth production facility to turn out more B-29s, so the Navy agreed to give up production of the PBB-1 Sea Ranger seaplane at the Boeing Navy plant at Renton so that Superfortresses could be built there. In return the Army ensured that, starting on 7 July, some B-24s, and B-25s and Venturas, could now go to the Navy.

The first B-24 squadron in the Navy was VB-101, and it evolved from VP-51, the Navy patrol squadron flying PBY Catalinas from Ford Island, Pearl Harbor in January 1942. This squadron, commanded by Lt Cdr William A. Moffett, moved to Barber's Point Naval Air Station on Oahu, Hawaii in October 1942 and there received fourteen PB4Y1-D Liberators. Training was cut short because of high losses in the south Pacific, and in January 1943, VB-101 was ordered to Guadalcanal via Palmayra, Canton, Nandi and Espirito Santo. At about the same time, VP-102 and a marine photo squadron also flew out to the forward area in the Pacific. (In the spring of 1943 they were joined by Navy Photo Squadron VD-1.) On 12 February, off the coast of Bouganville, nine Liberators from VB-101, escorted by P-38s, F6-Fs and F4U Corsairs, bombed and sank a large Japanese transport and destroyer from 22,000ft (6,700m). Later referred to as the 'St Valentine's Day Massacre', two

Medal of Honor

In July 1943, thirty-five-year-old Lt Cdr Bruce Avery van Voorhis was in charge of VP-102 during the Battle of the Solomon Islands. On 6 July, he and his crew took off in darkness for the Japanese-held Greenwich Islands to help prevent a surprise enemy attack on American forces. Despite treacherous and varying winds, limited visibility and difficult terrain, the crew reached their target, a seaplane tender off Kapingamarangi (a small atoll north-west of the Solomons). Van Voorhis was forced lower and lower by overwhelming aerial opposition. Despite this, the gallant crew executed six low-level attacks, destroying the Japanese radio station, anti-aircraft guns and other installations with bombs and machine-gun fire. Voorhis's gunners destroyed one Japanese fighter in the air and another three on the ground; but caught in his own bomb blast, van Voorhis and his crew perished. For his sacrifice and lone fight against insuperable odds, Lt Cdr van Voorhis was posthumously awarded the Medal of Honor.

Liberators and four escorting fighters were shot down when the formation was attacked by around sixty enemy fighters. VB-101 would continue to make patrol and bombing missions for seven-and-a-half months, at which time the squadron was relieved by VP-104.

VP-104 had been commissioned at Naval Air Station, Kaneohe Bay, Hawaii, on 10 April 1943, with Lt Cdr Harry E. Sears as commanding officer. Formation of the squadron resulted from splitting VP-21 in two, thereby immediately creating a unit experienced in flying PBY-5 aircraft. By mid-July all the air crews were proficient in all operational procedures, and a month later the squadron was dispatched to Carney Field, Guadalcanal to form the first Navy long-range search group with VP-102. In March 1944 VPB-116 began flying ECM missions from Eniwetok Atoll against Japanese radars on Truk.

On Patrol in the Pacific

Meanwhile VP-104 and VP-102, now under the command of Lt Cdr Gordon Fowler, continued operations against the enemy in the Pacific. In addition to their primary role of daily search and tracing of enemy task force units, a large number of formation strikes were made against the land targets, and one strike against a Japanese destroyer fleet. Individual strikes were made when the opportunity arose. Burton Albrecht and his crew made a lone strike on a convoy of nine armed cargo ships, sinking three and fending off fourteen fighters. He claimed three kills. He also avenged van Voorhis's death with an attack on Kapingamarangi, sinking six Zero floatplanes from among the dozen or so high and dry on the beach.

On 6 February 1944, VPB-104 moved to Munda Field, New Georgia where it continued operations until the end of March 1944 when it was relieved by VPB-115. VPB-104 had flown well over a thousand sorties, destroying or damaging thirty aircraft and fifty-one enemy surface vessels for the loss of only seven Liberators. VPB-104 returned Stateside for leave and reformation and was subsequently awarded a Presidential Unit Citation. On 15 May 1944, VPB-104 was reformed at Naval Air Station, Kearney, Mesa, California. Training was carried out until late June 1944, with Lt Henry S. Noon as acting commanding officer. In the summer of 1944 the 'Buccaneers of Screaming 104' came under the command of Lt Cdr Whitney Wright.

On 30 October 1944, after months of intensive training and familiarization flights, VPB-104 began its move to the Pacific war zone, at Morotai in the Netherlands East Indies, arriving there on 3 November after bucking bad weather fronts en route, to relieve VPB-115, which had originally relieved the Buccaneers. VPB-104 and VPB-101, also equipped

The US Navy's first Liberators were PB4Y-1 models off the B-24D production line in San Diego. B-24D-7-CO 41-23827 Bu.No.31937, seen here on an early test flight, was the second PB4Y-1 assigned to the Navy. USN

US Navy PB4Y Squadrons

Unit	*Op Liberators*	*Type*	*Details*
VD-1	January 1943	PB4Y-1	Photo-Reconnaissance
VD-3	February 1943	PB4Y-1	Photo-Reconnaissance
VD-4	August 1943	PB4Y-1	Photo-Reconnaissance
VD-5	July–Aug 1943	PB4Y-1	Photo-Reconnaissance
VB-101	October 1942	PB4Y-1	
VB-102	October 1943	PB4Y-1	Received first Libs as VP-51
VB-104	April 1943 (?)	PB4Y-1	Began ops May 1943
VB-106	June 1943	PB4Y-1	
VB-108	June 1943	PB4Y-1	
VB-109	September 1943	PB4Y-1	
VB-115	December 1943	PB4Y-1	
VB-116	January 1944	PB4Y-1	
VB-117	1944	PB4Y-1	Began ops October 1944
VPB-118	1944	PB4Y-1	Began ops January 1945
VPB-119	1944	PB4Y-2	Began ops January 1945
VPB-121	November 1944	PB4Y-2	Began ops February 1945
VPB-123	?	PB4Y-2	Bat missile squadron
VPB-124	?	PB4Y-2	Bat missile squadron
VPB-200	May 1944	PB4Y-1	1st squadron to receive PB4Y-2
"	August 1943	PB4Y-2	

with PB4Y-1s, and VPB-146, equipped with PV-1 Harpoons, now formed the Navy search group attached to the US Seventh Fleet. Morotai was anything but peaceful, and crews were 'welcomed' on the first night by a large Japanese air raid. By the end of the month this had been followed by a further forty-five attacks. Day and night artillery and mortar fire could be heard near the Japanese lines close by. Skirmishes and infiltrations made for little sound sleep, and crews kept their sidearms close by at all times. There are other diversions too, like the appearance of large, lithesome pythons around the tents and 'Long Tom' trees which were brought down on living quarters by strong winds.

But Whit Wright soon had his men organized, and preparations were made to get eighteen flight crews and fifteen PB4Ys ready for combat. On 6 November, Whitney Wright made the first flight from Morotai and successfully intercepted a 150 ton lugger. He achieved three direct hits with 250lb bombs, and the 90ft (27m) long craft sank immediately. Another lugger loaded with oil-drums was also sighted, and repeated fire from Wright's gunners soon had it alight from end to end. It burned fiercely until it sank. But on 11 November, Lt Maurice Hill was attacked by two 'Tonys' while on regular patrol and his PB4Y-1 hit the water and broke up. Only four of the eleven-man crew survived, although they were rescued by friendly natives.

After less than two months' operations from Morotai, the Buccaneers prepared to follow the advance north to Leyte, where 'Screaming 104' came under the new command of Fleet Air Wing Ten. Lt Paul Stevens was a PPC (patrol plane commander) and squadron executive who had flown PBY Catalina missions at night against the 'Tokyo Express' and against airfields in the Rabaul area 1942–43; he recalls:

> Operating the PB4Y-1 – a B-24J painted blue – for armed reconnaissance missions in the south Pacific during World War II provided the flight crews with the full range of emotions –

excitement, exhilaration, boredom, poor living conditions and on occasions, stark terror. As a matter of fact, living in tents, sleeping under a mosquito net and existing on dried rations was enough to make most of the patrol plane commanders (PPCs) downright mean.

On 9 December, fourteen crews flew to Tacloban on Leyte, which was to be their new home, and they were joined by the remaining four crews later that month. Although everyone was relieved to leave Morotai, Tacloban was not without its problems, as Paul Stevens explains:

Tacloban was the only Allied air strip in operation in the area and consisted of a single strip built of lashed steel Marston matting laid on loose sand. Aircraft were parked wing-tip to wing-tip on each side of the runway. This allowed only about thirty feet of wing-tip clearance for take-off and landing, and the dimly lit flare pots provided little line-up guidance. Take-off was critical. The B-24/PB4Y-1 Liberator was one of the all-time great combat aircraft – with outstanding performance in all areas, it could take punishment and still get the crew home. It had a high degree of reliability, due in large part to the Pratt and Whitney R-1830 engines. However, the unwary or careless could experience some nasty characteristics. We did operate the airplane well above its maximum emergency war overload to achieve the range and carry the bomb-load for our missions [The Liberator had originally been designed for a gross operating weight of 56,000lb (25,400kg) and had been cleared for an overload weight of 63,000lb (28,577kg), and further cleared for an emergency war overload to 65,000lb (29,480kg) gross weight. The crews on Tacloban were operating the PB4Y at 68,000lb (30,845kg) gross weight.]

Because of the overload condition, every take-off from Tacloban presented a challenge. To add to our giggles, immediately after lift-off we were only about ten feet above the black waters of Leyte Gulf. Nor did our fun end with the lift-off, gear-up and flaps-up, because a climb to about 8,000ft [2,450m] was then required to clear the mountains of the central Philippines. Power was set at 45in MAP and 2,500rpm, and our cylinder-head temperatures usually exceeded the maximum of 232° – temperatures of 240° to 260° were common. It was a continual play of opening cowl flap to control

Cdr Norman 'Bus' Miller, CO, VB-109, flew Thunder Mug **which was fitted with the Erco bow turret. On 14 July 1944 Miller and Joseph Jobe, the PPC of a second PB4Y-1, made the first raid by land-based aircraft on Iwo Jima, 670nm (1,240km) south of Tokyo, when they took off from a 3,700ft (1,130m) strip on Saipan and flew 625nm (1,158km) north to bomb airfields and buildings on the island. The two PB4Y-1s attacked at an altitude of 200ft (60m) from the north just after sunset, setting several buildings on fire and destroyed about forty parked aircraft. They finished by dropping 2,000lb (900kg) bombs on the anchorage area, sinking at least six vessels, before finally escaping, and with only minor damage. Seven times Miller, unescorted, flew** Thunder Mug **into Truk lagoon to bomb and strafe Japanese shipping and shore installations.** Thunder Mug **was credited with sinking twenty Japanese ships, totalling at least 35,000tons, including a 10,000-ton tanker and a destroyer. It probably sunk or damaged another forty-six enemy surface craft, including a light cruiser, destroyer and two DEs. 'Bus' Miller's crew were awarded sixty-six medals and citations, and VB-109 was the most decorated flying group in the Pacific, with 301 awards.** USN

temperatures, and avoiding spoiling lift with too great an opening.

The area of search from Leyte included two sectors extending to Cap San Jacques and Camranh Bay, French Indo-China, another sector to Balabau Strait, and down the west coast of Borneo. Other sectors covered the area from Hainan Strait up the coast of China to Foochow and eastward to include Okinawa and Daito Jima. During the first few days at their new base a number of VPB-104 crews made repeated attacks on Japanese shipping and aircraft. On 2 December, Lt Ray Ettinger sighted a convoy of six ships north of Balikpapan, Borneo. He went in about four miles off the convoy and was fired upon, first by one of the ships, and then by three Oscars; these opened fire at 600yd, making a co-ordinated attack from 3, 5 and 9 o'clock. They closed to 200yd, but the PB4Y's return fire forced them to climb 1,500ft (460m) above it. The Oscars then dropped four phosphorous bombs dead ahead of Ettinger, but they exploded 200ft (60m) distant at about 8 o'clock. For thirty minutes the Oscars made high side- and tail-runs before the PB4Y was able to lose them in cloud.

On 10 December, Lt Henry S. Noon's PB4Y-1 was attacked by eight 'Zekes' (Zeros) and two 'Tonys' which dropped a total of eight phosphorous bombs, some bursting very close to Noon's aircraft. He managed to reach safety after a running fight involving head-on attacks and passes from every position of the clock, lasting for about an hour. One 'Zeke' was definitely destroyed, bursting into flames as it hit the water, and two more limped away from the scene trailing smoke after being hit in the engines and wing-roots.

When ships could not be found, the PB4Y-1 crews sought targets inland. On 12 December, Lt Joseph D. Shea's crew bombed and strafed numerous targets in and around Brunei Town, Borneo. First he attacked an airstrip under construction, and then a motor convoy loaded with ships. Proceeding over the harbour, Shea made three bombing and strafing runs on shipping, setting a 1,500 ton 'Sugar Charlie' on fire and damaging other ships and luggers. Return fire put many holes in the PB4Y, holing a fuel line from the main wing-cell and filling the aircraft with fumes. Five crew-members were overcome by the fumes and the bomb-bay door was opened to secure some fresh air. Tragically, William E. Abbott passed out while transferring fuel by holding the connection together by hand; he became unconscious and fell through the bomb-bay door at an altitude of 1,500ft over Borneo. All the other crew-members later recovered after treatment at base. Recalls Paul Stevens:

Freely translated, armed reconnaissance missions boiled down to two things: one, it was a must that you covered your assigned search sector; and two, having accomplished that, then a PPC could do just about anything he had the guts to do. VB/VPB-104 was therefore running an impressive kill record. Utilizing mast-head bombing attacks against Japanese shipping and other targets of opportunity, scoring against enemy aircraft to an amazing degree, the squadron was to receive a second Presidential Unit Citation for this combat cruise. Morale was very high – and even occasionally, a two-bottle ration of Iron City beer became available.

An armed reconnaissance on 5 February 1945 provided emotions for this PPC and crew beyond that normally experienced. Rolling out of my cot at 02:00 and striving for an early take-off, I was delighted with my assigned search sector – virgin territory! Departing our home base at Leyte in the central Philippines, my patrol was to proceed south-westwards through the South

Liberators flying through exploding phosphorus bombs. via Mike Bailey

Lt Paul F. Stevens USN, Executive Officer, 'Screaming 104' and his crew. *Back row,* L–R: Allen Anania, radio operator/top turret gunner; David Gleason, mechanic/bow turret gunner; Lee Webber, bombardier; Lee Little, ordnance/port waist gunner; Adrian Fox, radioman/gunner; Arvid Rasmussen, mechanic/tail gunner. Front row, L–R: Marx Stephan, ordnanceman/belly gunner; ENS John McKinley, co-pilot; Lt Paul Stevens, plane commander; Lt (jg) Edwin Streit, navigator; Derral Pedigo, mechanic/gunner. Paul Stevens Collection

China Sea, then east to the coast of Borneo, and then back to Tacloban. As per usual this was a 1,000 nautical mile leg outbound, a 100 nautical mile cross-leg and on back to home base. But what a great joy – the fast carrier task force had not swept this area, nor had the USAAF bombers hit here. There was no question about it! I would make a kill, or kills, this day.

To achieve the range for the assigned patrols, careful planning and close attention to cruise control was a must. A target speed of 135 to 140 KIAs [knots indicated airspeed] was difficult to maintain initially with maximum continuous cruise. Often, the first hour or so of the patrol was flown with auto-rich and 35in MAP and 2,300rpm; the airplane was truly behind the power-required curve during this period. Also, at this time much of the wing panel could be seen from the cockpit over the engine nacelles; later, as the aircraft weight was reduced due to fuel burn, the nacelles blocked this view.

Once clear of the mountains and when daylight had arrived, I let down to about 1,500ft; this would provide defence against enemy fighters, and at the same time provide a good search pattern by our ASP-15 radar. At this stage of the war there were still plenty of 'Zekes' to create a real hazard if caught high. Though the might of the Japanese had been 'broken' by this time, a great many of the enemy fighter pilots did not know this and had plenty of fight in them. Then, too, those fighter airplanes with the stars and bars sometimes generated an even greater hazard to our single airplane patrols.

Arriving at the end of my search sector, I made the turn eastward toward the coast of Borneo. My plan was to approach the coast at Bintulu airfield. Almost immediately we gained a radar contact. Since the contact appeared to be quite small, and always conserving fuel, I just sauntered on, believing a small, wooden 'sugar dog' vessel awaited us just beyond a few scattered showers. These small ships were easy kills for us, and collectively, they transported a great deal of tonnage for the enemy.

Surprise! Just clearing a shower, a Terrisuki destroyer greeted us with bursts from his heavy AA batteries. We had learned to respect this class of destroyer: they were tough customers and could shoot very well. Fortunately, being just beyond effective gun range and combined with a diving turn, his firing was inaccurate. Had I taken the initial radar contact seriously and approached at wave height with max power, we

A smiling Lt Paul F. Stevens, with good reason. On 17 March 1945 he shot down Vice-Admiral Seigo Yamagata, who was en route **to Tokyo in a H8K2-L 'Emily' for an audience with the Emperor and to be promoted to full Admiral, and become the Under Secretary of the Imperial Japanese Navy.** Paul Stevens Collection

could have made a mast-head bombing attack and possibly scored a kill – or the Jap destroyer guncrews could have painted another American flag on their gun-mount. Whatever, add one notch to my frustration level.

About fifty miles from Bintulu we set max power and descended to 50ft altitude. This gave us a blinding 205 KIAs, and as the sea state was slick calm, we were generating a wake upon the water by our down-wash. While this approach was evading radar detection, it also limited our forward visibility. Even so, as we identified the coast line, it became apparent that we had hit our landfall of Bintulu right on. The opening of the harbour was sighted, as well as a good-sized warehouse on the dock. Our bomb-load for the day was ten 100lb GP bombs with 4–5 second delayed fuses, and the warehouse qualified for at least half of that. Immediately after release, and by laying my head in the bubble side-window, I saw that warehouse blow up with a force well beyond that generated by our bombs. Most enjoyable, and even more so due to the lack of return gunfire. This indicated that we had achieved complete surprise.

Now we were coming upon the airfield. Two 'Oscars' (the Japanese Army's 'Zero'), two trucks and a number of people were obviously servicing the fighters and were unaware of our presence. I heard sounds similar to shrapnel hitting our airplane, but seeing mud splashes upon the windshield, I realized that the forward-firing .50 guns were kicking up mud from the dirt runway and we were flying into it. My thought was to avoid the rain on the way home so as to keep the mud splashes as evidence. Previous such occurrences had been met with considerable scepticism as to my claims of very low strafing attacks. We were hitting the fighters, as the tracer bullets were flashing as they hit along the fuselages of the 'Oscars', and I saw three men fall as they were hit. But pulling up and looking back I was disappointed that neither airplane was burning. There could be no claim for a kill if the airplanes did not burn. Obvious hits did not count.

Pulling hard to come around for another firing run, I could now see the left tyre of one of the fighters burning, but no other apparent damage. Now, into the second strafing run, I pressed in even lower and closer. Yes, many tracer flashes, but again the airplanes were not burning. This was ridiculous! We had hit them repeatedly, but still there was no fire. A third run was made, with the same disappointing results – I was furious. Also, I had broken the cardinal rule when attacking well-defended targets: make one firing/bombing run and keep right on going! We were lucky, there had been no return gunfire. But I had been very foolish and over-eager. Add several more notches to my level of frustration.

Some degree of sanity had been regained. We departed Bintulu and proceeded north-westerly toward Brunei. This was a hit spot. The Japanese had been receiving oil from the Brunei oil-fields for some period of time. Their fleet had used Brunei Bay as an anchorage, and major units sortied from here for the Battle of Leyte Gulf. I flew several miles inland and at 500ft or so to avoid radar detection. We swept the South China Sea with our radar to cover our search sector. As we passed the oil-fields and were approaching Miri airfield, a 'Val' [Japanese dive bomber] was seen turning into a final run for landing. I had a dangerous mind-set: we would make this kill! But we must do it quickly, for to follow the 'Val' over the airfield would have been suicidal, since Miri served as the airfield for Brunei and was heavily defended.

We added power and closed quickly. Opening fire at a close range, both the bow and top

En route **to his rendezvous with the 'Emily', Stevens sighted and surprised the 3,000-ton AGS-2** Koshu, **a Japanese freighter. He sank it after two bombing and strafing runs at mast-head level.** Paul Stevens Collection

gun turrets were shooting very well. We must have been hitting, but I could see no results. Continuing to close I could now see tracer hits, but no fires, no evidence of real damage to the 'Val'. Very close now, I started to fly under him. We were now at about 300–400ft above the ground. Suddenly he pushed over, or stalled – he was coming down on top of us – *we were going to collide!*

I could see every detail of that 'Val' – the neat rivet rows, the bomb hanging between his landing gear: there was no question, he was coming right into our cockpit. We'd had it! There was little we could do. My life did not flash in front of me; my thought was, 'I wonder what the guys back at the squadron will think when I don't get back tonight.'

The 'Val' passed over the cockpit unbelievably close. I felt a jolt and shudder as he struck the right vertical stabilizer. The top turret gunner, who had been firing at him and had swung his guns around aft to see him hit the tail, said with amazement, 'Well, that son-of-a-bitch is still flying!' However, the collision momentarily straightened the 'Val' upright, he immediately rolled inverted and crashed, and there was a large explosion. Our airplane was descending. At 200–300ft I instinctively pulled hard, but the elevator was jammed. My co-pilot had a strong sense of survival, however, and he joined to pull, which we did with all our combined

The Koshu **burns after the PB4Y-1 attack.** Paul Stevens Collection

(Right) **H8K2-L 'Emily' patrol seaplane under attack from a PB4Y-1.** National Archives

strength. The elevator broke free, but our pull-out was much too low; the empennage was twisted and distorted, the rudder remaining jammed. But we were still flying!

We were a long way from Tacloban and would be very vulnerable should we encounter enemy fighters, so we decided to try for San José airfield on Mindoro Island, which was some newly acquired realestate. Needless to say, our course for Mindoro would be carefully planned to stay well clear of Japanese airfields.

San José was a very busy airport, and we landed and taxied without directions to a hard stand; there was no attention given us or our aircraft whatsoever. Lee Webber, our bombardier and a first-class metalsmith, climbed onto the horizontal stabilizer and began to hack away at the damaged tail. Soon the shattered metal pieces were cut away and the rudder was freed; we took on 1,400 gallons of fuel and departed for Tacloban. The one-and-a-half hour flight was relatively uneventful. The entire empennage was replaced with a salvaged USAAF model, so my PBY4-1 was now unique: it was the only blue B-24 with a bare aluminium tail dressed with the 13th Air Force black markings!

In some instances, adverse occasions may be for the best. In this case, I became convinced that I was not totally invincible. I had done it to myself, and an over-eagerness for a kill had backfired quite badly. While we continued to make kills and covered our sectors aggressively, you can believe that more sober judgements prevailed.

CHAPTER ELEVEN

Postscript

LB-30 AM927 N12905 Diamond Lil, **seen here with Jaguars from RAF Coltishall, near Norwich, Norfolk on 10 June 1992, after flying in from Fort Worth, Texas, via Canada, Iceland and Prestwick, Scotland. The visit to the UK was part of the USAAF Fiftieth Anniversary celebrations. Engine problems** en route **delayed** Diamond Lil**'s arrival in Britain, and plagued its appearances and departure, which only went ahead in July after a replacement engine was airlifted to Biggin Hill.** Mike Rondot

Only sixteen Liberators and just four Privateers exist. Eleven B-24s are displayed in museums, two are in store, and only three are airworthy examples. LB-30 AM927 (N12905) *Diamond Lil* is operated by the Confederate Air Force; No. 18 off the production lines, it is the oldest-surviving B-24 in existence. AM927 was originally intended for 'special duties' with the RAF, but it suffered an accident on its delivery flight and was subsequently rebuilt by Consolidated. Converted to C-87 configuration, it operated as a company plane throughout the war. Flying a scheduled route between San Diego, Fort Worth and New York, the LB-30 became familiar as 'Old 927', from its original British serial number. Post-war it served with the Continental Can Company for ten years, then Petroleos Mexicanos, the Mexican national oil company. The CAF acquired 'Old 927' in 1967, and it now flies in the colours and markings of the 9th Air Force.

B-24J-95-CF 44-44272/N94459, built by Consolidated at Forth Worth, was delivered to the RAF as a B.Mk.VI late in 1944. It subsequently served with No. 6 Squadron of the Indian Air Force and was acquired by David Tallichet Jr, of 'Yesterday's Air Force' at Chino, California, in 1973. N94459 was flown from Poona, India to the USA, but developed engine trouble and had to put down at RAF Mildenhall, England. It was flown to Duxford nearby for repairs, and remained there

B-24J-CO 44-44272 Delectable Doris. Dick Bagg

B-24J 44-44272 Joe **(formerly** Delectable Doris**) in its new scheme at Kermit Weeks' 'Fantasy of Flight', at Polk County, Florida in 1997.** Tom Smith

until August 1975, by which time it had been fitted with a new No. 3 engine and restored to represent *Delectable Doris* of the 389th Bomb Group, 8th Air Force, based at Hethel, Norfolk, during 1944. *Delectable Doris* was flown to Prestwick on 25 August 1975, but the nose-wheel collapsed on landing, and she only continued on her way to the USA via Iceland after repairs costing £4,000. *Doris* was later purchased by Kermit Weeks in Florida, the owner of the world's largest private aircraft collection; she was repainted as *Joe*, but retaining the 389th Bomb Group markings, and put on permanent display in his 'Fantasy of Flight' aviation theme park at Polk City.

B-24J-CF-85 44-44052 KH191 is another ex-Indian Air Force Liberator (B.VIII), *in situ* at the Indian Air Force Technical College at Jalahalli in 1982, when it was air-freighted to Great Britain for Warbirds of GB Ltd at Blackbush. In 1986, KH191 was shipped to the USA and faithfully restored to airworthy condition by Tom Reilly at his warbird restoration facility at Kissimmee, Florida for the Collings Foundation of Stowe, Massachusetts. The B-24J emerged completely rebuilt in August 1989 as the *All American*, and has become a regular attraction at air shows and a visitor to airports across the USA, much to the delight of veterans and enthusiasts alike.

In America there are six Liberators and two Privateers on static display in museums. The most famous of these is undoubtedly Consolidated-built B-24D-160-CO 42-72843 *Strawberry Bitch*, which is on display in the Air Force Museum at Wright Patterson AFB, Dayton, Ohio. In World War II it served in the 512th Squadron, 376th Bomb Group. Despite the misguided 'political correctness' which has ridiculously been used to 'clean up' other bombers, *Strawberry Bitch* has nonetheless retained the name and nose artwork made famous by Alberto Varga's *Torches at Midnight* pin-up of 1943. *Strawberry Bitch* flew fifty-nine missions with the 'Liberandos' and spent thirteen years at Davis-Monthan AFB, Arizona, before being flown to the museum in 1959 by Col Albert J. Shower, wartime CO of the 467th Bomb Group, 8th Air Force.

Consolidated-built B-24D-160-CO 42-72843 Strawberry Bitch**, which is on display in the Air Force Museum at Wright-Patterson AFB, Dayton, Ohio.** Author

B-24J-20-FO 44-48781 *Laiden Maiden* is displayed at the Eighth Air Force Museum, Baresdale AFB, Louisiana, while B-24J-90-

CF 44-44175 HE877/N7866, another ex-Indian Air Force B.VII, is on show at Pima County Air Museum, Tucson, Arizona; here it is called *The Bungay Buckaroo*, although its real name is *Red Ass* and it is of the 446th Bomb Group at Bungay (Flixton). In the early hours of 6 June 1944 the 446th Bomb Group received Field Order No. 328 over the teletype machine, informing them that the 'Bungay Buckaroos' would be leading the 8th Air Force on the momentous day. Col Jacob J. Brogger, the CO and air commander, flew the mission in B-24H-25-FO 42-95203 *Red Ass* – which, for public relations' purposes, was renamed *The Buckaroo* especially for the occasion.

At the National Aeronautical Collection at Trenton, Ontario is B-24L-20-FO 44-50154 HE773; while at Lackland AFB, San Antonio, Texas, is an EZB-24M-FO, 44-51228, the last Liberator to be used by the USAF. During 1953–54 it was used for ice-research tests. Finally Castle AFB, California, has B-24M 44-41916 in storage.

Four PB4Y-2 Privateers can be found in museums. Bu.59819/N3739G, formerly 'Tanker 30' of T & G Aviation, is owned by the Lone Star Flight Museum at Galveston, Texas. Bu.No. 66261 (composite with the cockpit of 66304) is on display at the Naval Aviation Museum, Pensacola, Florida. Bu.59876, known as 'Tanker 125' was operated by Hawkins & Powers Aviation at Greybull, Wyoming, until it crashed, on 9 August 1975, at the end of the Port Hardy runway in British Columbia, after a fire-fighting contract in Alaska. It was recovered, and after being unceremoniously cut into sections, was finally rescued by the Yankee Air Force Museum at Ypsilanti, Michigan, who restored the aircraft to display condition. A fourth PB4Y-2, Bu.59932, is currently being restored by Tom Reilly. As late as the mid-1990s, Hawkins & Powers Aviation were still operating five Privateers on fire-fighting duties.

In England only one complete B-24 currently exists, although there is a front fuselage section at the American Air Museum, Duxford. The 'Cosford Liberator' is an ex-RAF/Indian Air Force Liberator, built as a B-24L-20-FO (44-50206) and delivered to 99 Squadron (RAF) on 26 June 1945. It served on detachment on the Cocos Islands where it was flown by both the Squadron CO and the Station Commander, an SAAF officer with the honorary rank of Air Vice-Marshal in the RAF. No. 99 Squadron disbanded in November 1945 and the Liberator was finally struck off charge on 11 April 1946 at No. 322 M.U. Cawnpore. It was later refurbished by Hindustan Aeronautics for service with No. 6 Squadron, RIAF at Poona. As HE807 it remained in service until 31 December 1968, when it was placed in open storage at Bangalore. Six years later it was presented to the RAF Museum, arriving at RAF Lyneham on 7 July 1974 and was then sent to RAF Colerne. When Colerne closed as a result of defence cuts, the Liberator ignominiously had its wings cut

PB4Y-2 Privateer Bu. No. 59701/N6884C, Tanker 127 **was used post-war by Hawkins and Powers Aviation of Greybull, Wyoming, for fire-bombing.** QAP

The 'Cosford Liberator' is an ex-RAF/Indian Air Force Liberator, built as a B-24L-20-FO 44-50206 and delivered to 99 Squadron (RAF) on 26 June 1945. Author

B-24M-20-FO 44-51228 at Lackland AFB, Texas, in 1986. This aircraft has been acquired by the American Air Museum in England for display as a B-24J version. Martin Bowman

off and was transported by road to its present location at RAF Cosford, near Wolverhampton. Unfortunately the removal of its wings (since restored to the fuselage) means that the B-24 is no longer flyable. It serves, however, as a fitting reminder of all those RAF and Commonwealth personnel who gave their lives while flying the type in India and the Far East.

The Indian Air Force Museum at Palam has retained B-24J-90-CF 44-44213; while at the American Air Museum, Duxford, the IWM acquired, from the National Air and Space Museum in Washington DC, a nose assembly from a B-24D and the forward fuselage of B-24J-5-FO, 42-51457, one of 1,587 Liberators built by Ford at Dearborn in Michigan. These have been amalgamated to create a nose exhibit which has been painted to represent B-24D-90-CO, 42-40738, *Fightin' Sam* – the squadron insignia – of the 566th Bomb Squadron, 389th Bomb Group (*see* Chapter 3) when it became the ship commanded by Maj Tom Conroy, the squadron CO. Plans are well advanced to acquire a complete Ford-built Liberator for display, but for now, visitors can view the illuminated interior and gain an insight into the life and conditions of a wartime Liberator crew.

A museum without a Liberator is like an oyster without a pearl.

B-24J-85-CF 44-44052 KH191 All American, **owned and flown by the Collings Foundation.** Patrick Bunce

APPENDIX I

B-24 Production Totals by Type

MODEL	BUILT	FACTORIES	NOTES
LB-30A	6	Consolidated	
Liberator I	20	Consolidated	
Liberator II	140	Consolidated	
XB-24/XB-24B	1	Consolidated	
YB-24	6	Consolidated	
RB-24 (YB-24)	1	Consolidated	
B-24A	120	Consolidated	
RB-24A	9	Consolidated	
RB-24C	9	Consolidated	
B-24D	2,696	Consolidated (2,381)	
		Convair (305)	
		Douglas (10)	
B-24E	801	Ford (490)	R-1830-65 engines
		Convair(144)	R-1830-65 engines
		Douglas(167)	R-1830-43 engines
XB-24F	(1)		Converted from B-24D for testing thermal de-icing system
B-24G	430	North American	R-1830-43/-65 engines
B-24H	3,100	Ford (1,780)	R-1830-43/-65 engines
		Convair (738)	R-1830-43/-65 engines
		Douglas (582)	R-1830-43/-65 engines
B-24J	6,678	Consolidated (2,792)	R-1830-65 engines
		Ford (1,587)	
		Convair (1,558)	
		Douglas (205)	
		North American (536)	
XB-24K	(1)		Single-finned version modified by Ford from B-24D
B-24L	1,667	Ford (1,250)	
		Consolidated (417)	
RB.24L/TB-24L			B-24L conversion for B-29 training
B-24M	2,593	Ford (1,677)	
		Consolidated (916)	
XB-24N	(1)		B-24J converted to single tail
YB-24N	7	Ford	
B-24N			Orders for 5,168 cancelled
XB-24P	(1)		B-24L converted by Sperry for airborne fire-control research
XB-24Q	(1)		B-24L converted by General Electric for radar-controlled turret-development work
C-87	278	Consolidated	*Liberator Express* transport version of B-24D
C-87A	6	Consolidated	3 built for USN and 3 for USAAF
XC-109	(1)		Converted by Ford from B-24E to fuel tanker
C-109	(208)		B-24Js & Ls converted to C-109 tankers
AT-22/TB-24D	(5)		Converted C-87s for flight engineer training
XF-7	(1)		B-24D converted at Lowry AB, Colo to PR configuration, to include eleven cameras in nose, bomb-bay and tail
F-7	(4)		B-24Ds converted by Lockheed for PR at Northwest Mod Ctre, St. Paul, Minn.
F-7A	(89)		B-24H/J conversion. Three cameras in nose, and three vertical cameras in aft bomb-bay
F-7B	(124)		122 B-24J/2 B-24M conversions. Six cameras located in aft bomb-bay
Liberator Ferret			B-24D and 172 B-24Js converted for passive *Ferret* mission
XB-41	(1)		B-2D converted for bomber escort
PB4Y-1	977	Consolidated	USN B-24D
PB4Y-2	736	Consolidated	USN single-finned version
RY-1/2	(8)		C-87/C-87A transport conversion
RY-3	39		PB4Y-2 transport version
R2Y	2		*Liberator Liner*

APPENDIX II

B-24 Production Airframes

MODEL	SERIAL RANGE	NUMBER BUILT
LIB II (CO)	AL503/AL641	139
LB-30A (CO)	AM258/AM263	6
LIB I (CO)	AM910/AM929	20
LIB II (CO)	FP685	1
XB-24 (CO)	39-680	1
YB-24 (CO)	40-696/701	6
B-24D (CO)	40-2349/2368	20
B-24A (CO)	40-2369/2377	9
B-24C (CO)	40-2378/2386	9
B-24D (CO)	41-1087/1142	56
B-24D-CO-1	41-23640/23668	29
B-24D-CO-1	41-23671/23693	23
B-24D (CO)	41-11587	1
B-24D (CF)	41-11588/11589	2
B-24D (CO)	41-11590/11603	14
B-24D (CF)	41-11604/11605	2
B-24D (CO)	41-11606	1
B-24D (CF)	41-11607	1
C-87 (CF)	41-11608	1
B-24D (CO)	41-11609/11626	18
B-24D (CF)	41-11627/11628	2
B-24D-(CO)	41-11629/11638	10
B-24D (CF)	41-11639/11642	4
B-24D (CO)	41-11643/11654	12
B-24D (CF)	41-11655/11657	3
B-24D (CO)	41-11658/11673	16
B-24D (CF)	41-11674/11676	3
B-24D (CF)	41-11674/11676	3
B-24D (CO)	41-11677/11703	27
C-87 (CF)	41-11704	1
B-24D (CF)	41-11705	1
C-87 (CF)	41-11706/11709	4
B-24D (CO)	41-11710/11727	18
B-24D (CF)	41-11728/11733	6
B-24D (CO)	41-11734/11741	8
C-87 (CF)	41-11742/11747	6
B-24D (CO)	41-11748/11753	6
B-24D (DT)	41-11754/11756	3
B-24D (CO)	41-11757/11787	31
C-87 (CF)	41-11788/11789	2
C-87 (CF)	41-24160/24163	4
B-24D-CO-20	41-24164/24171	8
C-87 (CF)	41-24172/24173	2
C-87A (CF)	41-24174	1
B-24D-CO-20	41-24175/24219	45
B-24D-CO-25	41-24220/24311	92
B-24D-CO-25	41-24339	1
B-24E-DT-1	41-28409/28416	8
B-24E-DT-10	41-28417/28444	28
B-24E-DT-15	41-28445/28476	32
B-24E-DT-20	41-28477/28500	24
B-24E-DT-25	41-28501/28573	73
B-24H-DT-1	41-28574/28639	66
B-24H-DT-5	41-28640/28668	29

MODEL	SERIAL RANGE	NUMBER BUILT
B-24D (CO)	41-11790/11799	10
C-87 (CF)	41-11800	1
B-24D (CO)	41-11801/11836	36
C-87 (CF)	41-11837/11838	2
B-24D (CO)	41-11839/11863	25
B-24D (DT)	41-11864	1
B-24D (CO)	41-11865/11906	42
C-87 (CF)	41-11907/11908	2
B-24D (CO)	41-11909/11938	30
B-24D (CO)	41-23640/23668	29
C-87 (CF)	41-23669/23670	2
B-24D (CO)	41-23671/23693	23
C-87 (CF)	41-23694/23696	3
B-24D-CO-1	41-23697/23724	28
B-24D-DT-1	41-23725/23727	3
B-24D-CO-1	41-23728/23755	28
B-24D-DT-5	41-23756/23758	3
B-24D-CO-5	41-23759/23790	32
C-87 (CF)	41-23791/23793	3
B-24D-CO-5	41-23794/23824	31
B-24D-CO-7	41-23825/23849	25
B-24D-CO-7	41-23853/23858	6
C-87 (CF)	41-23859/23862	4
C-87A (CF)	41-23863	1
B-24D-CO-10	41-23864/23902	29
C-87 (CF)	41-23903/23905	3
B-24D-CO-10	41-23906/23919	14
B-24D-CO-13	41-23920/23958	39
C-87 (CF)	41-23959	1
B-24D-CO-13	41-23960/23969	10
B-24D-CO-15	41-23970/24003	34
C-87 (CF)	41-24004/24006	3
B-24D-CO-15	41-24007/24026	20
C-87 (CF)	41-24027/24029	3
B-24D-CO-15	41-24030/24099	70
B-24D-CO-20	41-24100/24138	39
C-87 (CF)	41-24139/24141	3
B-24D-CO-20	41-24142/24157	16
C-87 (CF)	41-24158	1
C-87A (CF)	41-24159	1
B-24D-CO-53	42-40435/40392	48
B-24D-CO-55	42-40393/40432	40
B-24D-CO-60	42-40433/40482	50
B-24D-CO-65	42-40483/40527	45
B-24D-CO-70	42-40528/40567	40
B-24D-CO-75	42-40568/40612	45
B-24D-CO-80	42-40613/40652	40
B-24D-CO-85	42-40653/40697	45
B-24D-CO-90	42-40698/40742	45
B-24D-CO-95	42-40743/40787	45
B-24D-CO-100	42-40788/40822	35
B-24D-CO-105	42-40823/40867	45
B-24D-CO-110	42-40868/40917	50
B-24D-CO-115	42-40918/40962	45

MODEL	SERIAL RANGE	NUMBER BUILT
B-24H-DT-10	41-28669/28752	84
B-24H-DT-15	41-28753/28941	189
B-24H-DT-20	41-28942/29006	65
B-24E-DT	41-29007/29008	2
B-24E-CF-10	41-29009/29023	15
B-24E-CF-15	41-29024/29042	19
B-24E-CF-20	41-29043/29061	19
B-24E-CF-25	41-29062/29115	54
B-24H-CF-1	41-29116/29187	72
B-24H-CF-5	41-29188/29258	71
B-24H-CF-20	41-29607/29608	2
B-24E-FO-1	42-6976/7005	30
B-24E-FO-5	42-7006/7065	60
B-24E-FO-10	42-7066/7122	57
B-24E-FO-15	42-7123/7171	49
B-24E-FO-20	42-7172/7229	58
B-24E-FO-25	42-7230/7464	235
B-24H-FO-1	42-7465/7717	253
B-24H-FO-5	42-7718/7769	52
B-24E-FO	42-7770	1
B-24D-CO-30	42-40058/40137	80
B-24D-CO-35	42-40138/40217	80
B-24D-CO-40	42-40218/40257	40
B-24D-CO-45	42-40258/40322	65
B-24D-CO-50	42-40323/40344	22
B-24H-FO-15	42-52303/52776	474
B-24D-CF-1	42-63752/63796	45
B-24D-CF-5	42-63797/63836	40
B-24D-CF-10	42-63837/63896	60
B-24D-CF-15	42-63897/63971	75
B-24D-CF-20	42-63972/64046	75
B-24J-CF-1	42-64047/64141	95
B-24J-CF-5	42-64142/64236	95
B-24J-CF-10	42-64237/64328	92
B-24J-CF-12	42-64329	1
B-24J-CF-10	42-64330/64346	17
B-24J-CF-15	42-64347/64394	48
B-24E-CF-25	42-64395/64431	37
B-24H-CF-10	42-64452/64501	50
B-24D-CO-155	42-72765/72814	50
B-24D-CO-160	42-72815/72864	50
B-24D-CO-165	42-72865/72914	50
B-24D-CO-155	42-72765/72814	50
B-24D-CO-160	42-72815/72864	50
B-24D-CO-165	42-72865/72914	50
B-24D-CO-170	42-72915/72963	49
B-24J-CO-1	42-72964/73014	51
B-24J-CO-5	42-73015/73064	50
B-24J-CO-10	42-73065/73114	50
B-24J-CO-15	42-73115/73164	50
B-24J-CO-20	42-73165/73214	50
B-24J-CO-25	42-73215/73264	50
B-24J-CO-30	42-73265/73314	50
B-24J-CO-35	42-73315/73364	50
B-24J-CO-40	42-73365/73414	50
B-24J-CO-45	42-73415/73464	50
B-24J-CO-50	42-73465/73514	50
B-24G-NT	42-78045/78069	25
B-24G-NT-1	42-78070/78074	5
B-24G-NT-5	42-78075/78154	80
B-24G-NT-10	42-78155/78314	160
B-24G-NT-15	42-78315/78352	38
B-24G-NT-16	42-78353/78474	122
B-24J-NT-2	42-78475	1

MODEL	SERIAL RANGE	NUMBER BUILT
B-24D-CO-120	42-40963/41002	40
B-24D-CO-125	42-41003/41047	45
B-24D-CO-130	42-41048/41092	45
B-24D-CO-135	42-41093/41137	45
B-24D-CO-140	42-41138/41172	35
B-24D-CO-145	42-41173/41217	45
B-24D-CO-150	42-41218/41257	40
B-24H-CF-20	42-50277/50354	78
B-24H-CF-25	42-50355/50410	56
B-24H-CF-30	42-50411/50451	41
B-24J-CF-401	42-50452/50508	57
B-24J-FO-1	42-50509/50759	251
B-24J-FO-5	42-50760/51076	317
B-24H-DT-20	42-51077/51103	27
B-24H-DT-25	42-51104/51181	73
B-24H-DT-30	42-51182/51225	44
B-24J-DT-1	42-51226/51292	67
B-24J-DT-5	42-51293/51395	103
B-24J-DT-10	42-51396/51430	35
B-24J-FO-5	42-51431/51610	180
B-24J-FO-10	42-51611/51825	215
B-24J-FO-15	42-51826/52075	250
B-24J-FO-20	42-52076	1
B-24H-FO-5	42-52077/52113	37
B24H-FO-10	42-52114/52302	189
B-24J-NT-1	42-78476/78794	319
B-24H-FO-15	42-94729/94794	66
B-24H-FO-20	42-94795/95022	228
B-24H-FO-25	42-95023/95288	226
B-24H-FO-30	42-95289/95503	215
B-24J-FO-1	42-95504/95628	125
B-24J-CF-15	42-99736/99805	70
B-24J-CF-20	42-99806/99871	66
B-24J-CF-25	42-99872/99935	64
B-24J-CO-55	42-99936/99985	50
B-24J-CO-60	42-99986/100035	50
B-24J-CO-65	42-100036/100085	50
B-24J-CO-70	42-100086/100135	50
B-24J-CO-75	42-100136/100185	50
B-24J-CO-80	42-100186/100235	50
B-24J-CO-85	42-100236/100285	50
B-24J-CO-90	42-100286/100335	50
B-24J-CO-95	42-100336/100385	50
B-24J-CO-100	42-100386/100435	50
C-87 (CF)	42-107249/107265	17
AT-22 (CF)	42-107266	1
C-87 (CF)	42-107267/107275	9
B-24J-CO-105	42-109789/109838	50
B-24J-CO-110	42-109839/109888	50
B-24J-CO-115	42-109889/109938	50
B-24J-CO-120	42-109939/109988	50
B-24J-CO-125	42-109989/110038	50
B-24J-CO-130	42-110039/110088	50
B-24J-CO-135	42-110089/110138	50
B-24J-CO-140	42-110139/110188	50
C-87 (CF)	43-30548	1
AT-22 (CF)	43-30549	1
C-87-(CF)	43-30550/30560	11
AT-22 (CF)	43-30561	1
C-87 (CF)	43-30562/30568	7
C-87A (CF)	43-30569/30571	3
C-87 (CF)	43-30572/30573	2
AT-22 (CF)	43-30574	1
C-87 (CF)	43-30575/30583	9

MODEL	SERIAL RANGE	NUMBER BUILT
AT-22 (CF)	43-30584	1
C-87 (CF)	43-30585/40627	43
B-24J-CF-30	44-10253/10302	50
B-24J-CF-35	44-10303/10352	50
B-24J-CF-40	44-10353/10374	22
B-24J-CF-45	44-10375/10402	28
B-24J-CF-50	44-10403/10452	50
B-24J-CF-55	44-10453/10502	50
B-24J-CF-60	44-10503/10552	50
B-24J-CF-65	44-10553/10602	50
B-24J-CF-70	44-10603/10652	50
B-24J-CF-75	44-10653/10702	50
B-24J-CF-80	44-10703/10752	50
B-24J-NT-30	44-28061/28276	216
C-87 (CF)	44-39198/39298	101
B-24J-CO-145	44-40049/40148	100
B-24J-CO-150	44-40149/40248	100
B-24J-CO-155	44-40249/40348	100
B-24J-CO-160	44-40349/40448	100
B-24J-CO-165	44-40449/40548	100
B-24J-CO-170	44-40549/40648	100
B-24J-CO-175	44-40649/40748	100
B-24J-CO-180	44-40749/40848	100
B-24J-CO-185	44-40849/40948	100
B-24J-CO-190	44-40949/41048	100
B-24J-CO-195	44-41049/41148	100
B-24J-CO-200	44-41149/41248	100
B-24J-CO-205	44-41249/41348	100
B-24J-CO-210	44-41349/41389	41
B-24L-CO-1	44-41390/41448	59
B-24L-CO-5	44-41449/41548	100
B-24L-CO-10	44-41549/41648	100
B-24L-CO-15	44-41649/41748	100
B-24L-CO-20	44-41749/41806	58
B-24M-CO-1	44-41807/41848	42
B-24M-CO-5	44-41849/41948	100
B-24M-CO-10	44-41949/42048	100
B-24M-CO-15	44-42049/42148	100
B-24M-CO-20	44-42149/42248	100
B-24M-CO-25	44-42249/42348	100
B-24M-CO-30	44-42349/42448	100
B-24M-CO-35	44-42449/42548	100
B-24M-CO-40	44-42549/42648	100
B-24M-CO-45	44-42649/42722	74
B-24J-CF-85	44-44049/44148	100
B-24J-CF-90	44-44149/44248	100
B-24J-CF-95	44-44249/44348	100
B-24J-CF-100	44-44349/44448	100
B-24J-CF-105	44-44449/44501	53
XB-24N (FO)	44-48753	1
B-24J-FO-20	44-48754/49001	248
B-24L-FO-1	44-49002/49251	250
B-24L-FO-5	44-49252/49501	250
B-24LFO-10	44-49502/49751	250
B-24L-FO-15	44-49752/50001	250
B-24L-FO-20	44-50002/50251	250
B-24M-FO-1	44-50252/50451	200
B-24M-FO-5	44-50452/50651	200
B-24M-FO-10	44-50652/50851	200
B-24M-FO-15	44-50852/51051	200
B-24M-FO-20	44-51052/51251	200
B-24M-FO-25	44-51252/51451	200
B-24M-FO-25	44-51452/51928	477
YB-24N (FO)	44-52053/52059	7
C-87 (CF)	44-52978/52987	10

Navy Cognisance Aircraft

PB4Y-2 (CO)	59350/60009	660
PB4Y-2 (CO)	66245/66324	80
RY-3 (CO)	90020/90050	31
RY-3 (CO)	90057/90059	3

Glossary

Ack ack	anti-aircraft
AI	Airborne Intercept (radar)
AM	Air Marshal (RAF)
Aron	Anti-submarine squadron
ASV	Air-to-Surface-Vessel (radar)
AVM	Air Vice-Marshal (RAF)
Capt	Captain
Col	Colonel
CBI	China-Burma-India Theatre
D/Cs	depth charges
DFC	Distinguished Flying Cross
DSO	Distinguished Service Order
Flak	*Fliegerabwehrkanonen* (German anti-aircraft fire)
Flt Lt	Flight Lieutenant (RAF)
Fg Off	Flying Officer (RAF)
Flt Sgt	Flight Sergeant (RAF)
Faehnrich (Fahnenjunker)	Flight Sergeant (German)
Feldwebel	Sergeant (German)
FTR	failed to return
Gp Capt	Group Captain (RAF)
Gee	British navigational device involving a special aircraft radio receiver working on signals pulsated by two ground stations
Generalmajor	Air Commodore (German)
Generaloberst	Air Chief Marshal (German)
hp	horse power
H_2S	British 10cm experimental radar
Hauptmann	Flight Lieutenant (German)
IP	Initial Point
Kapitänleutnant	(Kriegsmarine) US Navy equivalent, Lieutenant
Lieutenant (Lt)	Pilot Officer (German)
Lt (1st, 2nd)	Lieutenant, first and second (USAAF)
Lt (jg)	(US Navy) Lt junior grade
Lt Cdr	(US Navy) Lieutenant Commander
Lt Col	Lieutenant Colonel
LR	long range
Major	Squadron Leader (German)
MoH	Medal of Honor
MPI	Mean point of Impact
Noball	Flying bomb (V1) or rocket (V2) site
Oberfaehnrich	Warrant Officer (German)
Oberfeldwebel (Ofw)	Flight Sergeant (German)
Oberleutnant (Oblt)	Flying Officer (German)
Oberleutnant zur See	(Kriegsmarine) US Navy equivalent, Lieutenant (jg)
Oberst (Obst)	Group Captain (German)
Oberstleutnant (Obstlt)	Wing Commander (German)
OSS	Office of Strategic Services (US)
Plt Off	Pilot Officer (RAF)
PFF	Pathfinder
PPC	(US Navy) Personal Plane Commander
PR	Photo reconnaissance
R/T	Radio Telephony
SAS	Special Air Service (British)
SEAC	South-East Asia Air Command
Sgt	Sergeant
Sqn Ldr	Squadron Leader (RAF)
SOE	Special Operations Executive (British)
schnorkel	device which allows U-boat to run their diesel engines while submerged
Staff Sgt	Staff Sergeant (US)
Tech Sgt	Technical Sergeant (US)
U-boat	*Untersee Boot*, German underwater boat, or submarine
Unterfeldwebel	Sergeant (German)
Unteroffizier (Uffz)	Corporal (German)
VC	Victoria Cross
VLR	very long range
Wg Cdr	Wing Commander (RAF)
W/O	Warrant Officer (RAF)
ZOI	Zone of Interior (USA)

Index

Andrews, Brig Gen Frank M. 33
Anvil, Project 160
Anzio, Operation 76
Aphrodite, Project 160
Argument, Operation 76–7
armament 20–4
Arnold, Gen Henry H. 75

Baker, Lt Col Addison T. 35, 41, 45, 47, 53
Balchen, Col Bernt 164–5, 167–8
Ball, Project 167–8
Berlin raids 59
Big Week 58–9
Blackburn, Wg Cdr J. 135–6, 138
Blechhammer 87–8, 92–4
Brereton, Gen Louis E. 40, 42, 44–5
Brogger, Col Jacob J. 182
Bulloch, Sqn Ldr Terry M. 121–4

C-109 tanker 17, 101
Cameron, Col Bill 43, 45
Carpetbagger B-24s 161–70
Carswell MoH, Maj Horace C. Jr 102
Chase, Tech Sgt Don V. 37–8, 42–4, 46, 56, 58, 60–1, 62–3
Chennault, Gen Clair L. 100
Churchill, Winston 121, 126
Claggett, Brig Gen Henry B. 104
Clarion, Operation 72
Cohen, Capt Alfred B. 112–15
Compton, Col Keith 44, 49
Cookus, 1st Lt Keith 31–2
Cover, Operation 63

D-Day 64, 158, 167
Davis, David R. 7
Doolittle, Gen Jimmy 58, 75–6
Duncan, Gen Assa 145
Durrant, Brig J. T. 134

Eaker, Gen Ira C. 27, 30, 58
Ent, Brig Gen Uzal G. 44, 46–7, 49

Far East Air Force 104
Flavelle, 1st Lt Brian W. 44
Fleenor, Bud 33–4
Fleet, Reuben H. 8
Frantic, Operation 64–5

Gates, Frank L. 'Pappy' 83
Gerrits, 2nd Lt James F. 52
Glotfelty, Edward R. 65
Gotha raid 58–9
Grimes, Lt Art 150–1

Hale, Maj Gen Willis H. 108
HALPRO 39–40
Halverson, Col Harry H. 39, 145–6
Hamm raid 61–2
Harriman mission 12–13
Haynes, Lt Col Caleb V. 12
Heflin, Col Clifford 161–2, 168
Helton, Col Delbert 64
Hodges, Gen James P. 33
Hughes MoH, Lt Lloyd D. 52
Hunger, Operation 143

Jerstad Moh, Maj John 45, 47, 53
Johnson, Gen Leon W. 31–2, 41, 45–6, 48, 50, 53, 57
Juggler, Operation 54

Kane MoH, Col John R. 'Killer' 45–7
Kassel raid 69
Kelly, Col Laurence B. 110
Kennedy Jr, Joe 160
Kenney, Lt Gen George C. 104–6, 115

Laddon, Isaac M. 7
Larson, Maj Gen Westside T. 145
Lay, Lt Col Beirne 62
LeMay, Col Curtis E. 12
Lokker, Col Clarence 'Jack' 88, 91–2

Markel, Bud 79
Market-Garden, Operation 68–9
McLaren, Staff Sgt Hugh R. 65
Miller, Cdr Norman 'Bus' 173
Moling missions 28

Napier, Col Ezekiel W. 64
Nichols, Ray A. 83, 87, 94, 96
Nicholson VC, Wg Cdr James 138

O'Brien, Maj Jim 32, 34, 36
Olds, Col Robert 12
Overing, Col Glendon P. 62

Parsons, Tech Sgt Terry 68

PB4Y-1/2 18–19
Ploesti 39–56, 80
Politz raid 64
Posey, Col James 34, 48, 50, 53, 57
Post Mortem, Operation 143
Potts, Maj Ramsey D. 45, 47, 59, 145
Puckett MoH, Lt Donald D. 80

RAF and Commonwealth Squadrons:
- 10 Squadron RCAF 145
- 21 Squadron RAAF 116
- 23 Squadron RAAF 116
- 24 Squadron RAAF 116
- 25 Squadron RAAF 116
- 31 Squadron SAAF 133–5
- 34 Squadron SAAF 133–5
- 37 Squadron 134
- 40 Squadron 134
- 58 Squadron 149
- 59 Squadron 9, 130
- 70 Squadron 134
- 86 Squadron 9, 129
- 99 (Madras Presidency) Squadron 102, 136, 138, 143, 182
- 104 Squadron 134
- 108 Squadron 13, 131
- 110 Squadron 157
- 120 Squadron 9, 122, 124, 127–9
- 148 Squadron 133–4
- 159 Squadron 102, 131, 138–9, 142
- 160 Squadron 40, 102, 130, 133, 135, 138
- 178 Squadron 133–4
- 200 Squadron 102, 138
- 206 Squadron 122
- 214 Squadron 140
- 215 Squadron 138
- 223 Squadron 140–3
- 224 Squadron 123–4, 149
- 231 Squadron 137
- 301 Pomeranian-Polish Squadron 134
- 311 Czech Squadron 157
- 354 Squadron 102, 138
- 355 Squadron 102, 138–9, 142
- 356 Squadron 102, 137–8, 143–4
- 357 Squadron 102
- 415 Squadron RCAF 149
- 511 Squadron 126
- 547 Squadron 130

614 Squadron 132
624 Squadron 134
RAF and Commonwealth Wings:
2 Wing SAAF 134
175 Wing 138
184 (Salbani) Wing 138
185 Wing 138
231 Wing 132
257 Wing 131
RAF Groups:
19 Group 145
45 Group Transport Command 11, 137
46 Group Transport Command 16
100 Group 140, 143, 170
205 Group 131–4
222 Group 135, 138
225 Group 138
229 Group 16
231 Group 138
RAF Units, Miscellaneous:
111 Operational Training Unit 131
322 MU 182
1586 (Polish) Flight 134–5
1653 Conversion Unit 136
Roberts, Col Jack 146
Robinson, Staff Sgt Wally 78–82
Rogers, Lt Col Arthur H. 106
Rome 43
Ruck, William E. 61–2
Rush, Col Hugo 40

Sabu 116
SE Asia Command 100
Shower, Col Albert J. 61, 74, 181
Sikorski, Gen Wladyslaw 133
Slessor, AVM Sir John 145
Snead, Tech Sgt Harry R. 44–5, 48, 50, 52, 54
Snoopers 115
Sonnie, Project 165
Spaatz, Gen 'Tooey' 58, 96
Stevens, Lt Paul 172–8
Stewart, Maj James M. 58, 66, 72

Thompson, Col James 61
Timberlake, Col Ted 28, 33, 35
Tinker, Gen Clarence L. 107–8
Tinsman, Lt Williams 59–60
Torch, Operation 145
Trans-Atlantic Ferry Service 8–9
Trigg VC, Fg Off L. A. 130
Trucking missions 68–9
Twining, Maj Gen Nathan F. 76

Unruh, Col Marion C. 113
USAAF Units:
US Air Divisions:
1st BD 64
2nd BD 58–9, 64, 68, 72
3rd Bomb/Air Division 58, 61, 64–5, 74, 86
US Air Forces:
2nd AF 145
5th AF 20, 104–7, 109, 115, 118–19
7th AF 104, 107–12, 118–19
8th AF 27–38, 40–74, 86, 181
9th AF 40–56
10th AF 39, 99, 102
11th AF 76, 102–4
12th AF 75
13th AF 108–9, 112–14, 118–19
14th AF 102
15th AF 20, 24, 58, 75–98, 131, 139
20th AF 116
USAAF Groups:
1st Sea Search Attack Group 145–6
5th BG 112, 115–16, 118
6th BG 9
7th BG 9, 12, 20, 99–100, 102
11th BG 107–10, 112, 116, 119–20
22nd BG 106, 116, 118
28th Composite Group 102–3
30th BG 24, 109–12, 115–16, 119
34th BG 63, 66
43rd BG 106–7, 116, 118
44th BG 27–38, 40–8, 49–56, 58–9, 63, 73
90th BG 104–6, 115–16, 118
93rd BG 27–8, 30, 32–8, 40–56, 68, 71, 145
98th BG 40–56, 75, 80, 98
307th BG 108, 112, 115–16, 118
308th BG 17, 100–2
370th BG 114
376th BG 40–56, 75, 82, 98, 181
380th BG 107, 116, 118
389th BG 38, 40–8, 50–2, 54–6, 58, 61, 64, 68, 181, 184
392nd BG 57–9, 61, 72
445th BG 57–60, 66
446th BG 57–8, 68, 182
448th BG 58, 61–2, 68, 70, 73
449th BG 76, 89, 91, 98
450th BG 76–7, 98
451st BG 76, 80, 83, 90, 92–3, 95–6, 98
453rd BG 59, 61, 66
454th BG 76, 98
455th BG 76, 91, 98
456th BG 76, 92, 98
458th BG 18, 58, 63–4, 67–8, 150
459th BG 76, 98
460th BG 76–7, 80–1, 87–9, 97
461st BG 76–80, 82, 84, 93, 98
464th BG 76, 78, 88, 97–8
465th BG 76, 78, 88, 94, 98
466th BG 24, 59, 68, 72
467th BG 61, 68, 74, 181
479th Anti-Submarine Group 145–6, 149–51, 161
480th Anti-Submarine Group 145–6, 151
482nd BG 162
484th BG 76, 78–9, 83, 86, 90, 93–4, 96
485th BG 76, 78, 98
486th BG 62, 66, 170
487th BG 62, 64, 66
489th BG 63, 69–70
490th BG 63, 66, 86
491st BG 63, 68, 70
492nd BG 63, 67–8, 74, 168–70
493rd BG 64–8
494th BG 110, 112, 116, 118
801st BG (P) 165
2641st Special Group (Provisional) 98, 170
USAAF Squadrons:
1st Aron Squadron 145
2nd Aron Squadron 145
2nd Photo Charting Squadron 120
4th Aron Squadron 145–6, 149, 161
4th Bomb Squadron 161
6th Aron Squadron 146
13th Aron Squadron 145
14th Aron Squadron 145
15th Aron Squadron 146
18th Aron Squadron 150
19th Aron Squadron 145–6
20th Combat Mapping Squadron 105, 116
21st Bomb Squadron 103
22nd Aron Squadron 146, 161
22nd Bomb Squadron 161
23rd Bomb Squadron 112–14
27th Bomb Squadron 115
36th Bomb Squadron 103, 140, 162, 165–8
38th Bomb Squadron 24
64th Bomb Squadron 107
66th Bomb Squadron 30, 32, 36, 50
67th Bomb Squadron 30–2, 34–6, 50
68th Bomb Squadron 29–30, 36, 44–5, 48
86th Combat Mapping Squadron 116
304th Bomb Squadron 76
328th Bomb Squadron 27
329th Bomb Squadron 28
330th Bomb Squadron 30, 145
343rd Bomb Squadron 47
345th Bomb Squadron 42, 51
372nd Bomb Squadron 115–18
373rd Bomb Squadron 119
375th Bomb Squadron 101

400th Bomb Squadron 104
404th Bomb Squadron 103
406th Bomb Squadron 162–3, 165–6, 168
409th Bomb Squadron 145
415th Bomb Squadron 40
424th Bomb Squadron 116
431st Bomb Squadron 120
436th Bomb Squadron 99
459th Bomb Squadron 17
506th Bomb Squadron 45, 48–9, 73
512th Bomb Squadron 181
515th Bomb Squadron 49
564th Bomb Squadron 38
565th Bomb Squadron 65
566th Bomb Squadron 52, 184
703rd Bomb Squadron 66
713th Bomb Squadron 70
714th Bomb Squadron 73
718th Bomb Squadron 89
720th Bomb Squadron 77
724th Bomb Squadron 95
725th Bomb Squadron 83, 96
727th Bomb Squadron 80
753rd Bomb Squadron 64
756th Bomb Squadron 98
763rd Bomb Squadron 80–1
764th Bomb Squadron 84, 86
767th Bomb Squadron 78, 82
778th Bomb Squadron 88
779th Bomb Squadron 97
783rd Bomb Squadron 92
787th Bomb Squadron 24
788th Bomb Squadron 74, 167–8
803rd Bomb Squadron 140
819th Bomb Squadron 111
825th Bomb Squadron 83, 90
827th Bomb Squadron 79, 86
850th Bomb Squadron 167–8
852nd Bomb Squadron 70
856th Bomb Squadron 18, 168, 170
857th Bomb Squadron 168, 170
858th Bomb Squadron 166, 168–9, 170
859th Bomb Squadron 168, 170
861st Bomb Squadron 64, 67
862nd Bomb Squadron 64, 68
863rd Bomb Squadron 64–5, 145
867th Bomb Squadron 119
868th Bomb Squadron (Snoopers) 113, 115
USAAF Wings:
2nd Bomb Wing 27, 33
4th Bomb Wing 57
5th Wing 93
14th CBW 53, 68–9
20th CBW 66, 68
25th Anti-Submarine Wing 145
26th Anti-Submarine Wing 145
45th CBW 68
47th Bomb Wing 77, 98
49th Bomb Wing 98
55th Bomb Wing 88, 92, 93, 98
92nd Bomb Wing 62, 66
96th Bomb Wing 68
201st Provisional Combat Wing 35, 41
202nd CBW 57
304th Bomb Wing 76, 98
US Navy Units:
Fleet Air Wing Ten 172
Fleet Air Wing 15 145
VPB-101 171
VP-102 171
VB-103 155–9
VP-104 171
VB-105 157
VP-107 156–7
VPB-109 18
VPB-110 157–8, 160
VPB-112 159
VPB-115 171
VPB-118 18
VPB-123 18
VPB-124 18

van Voohris MoH, Lt Cdr Bruce A. 171
Vance, Lt Col Leon R. 63–4
Vienna 80, 83, 90, 93, 96
Vogel, Elmer R. 115–18

Wackwitz, Col Ernest J. 63
Warsaw Concerto, Operation 133–5
Watnee, Col Lloyd H. 63
Weinstein, Col Herb 93–4
Wheatley, William A. 7–8
Wiener Neustadt 30, 54, 57, 75, 78–9, 96–7
Willow Run 15–16, 25–6
Wood, Col Jack 41, 45, 51
Wowser, Operation 97
Wright, Lt Cdr Whitney 171–2